Constraining Chance

AGM STUDIES

AVANT-GARDE & MODERNISM

Constraining Chance

Georges Perec and the Oulipo

ALISON JAMES

Northwestern

University Press

Evanston

Illinois

Northwestern University Press
www.nupress.northwestern.edu

Printed in the United States of America

10 9 8 7 6 5 4 3 2 1

Library of Congress Cataloging-in-Publication Data

James, Alison Sibn, 1976–

Constraining chance : Georges Perec and the Oulipo / Alison James.

p. cm.—(Avant-garde & modernism studies)

Includes bibliographical references and index.

ISBN 978-0-8101-2531-5 (pbk. : alk. paper)—ISBN 978-0-8101-2530-8 (cloth : alk. paper)

1. Perec, Georges, 1936–1982—Criticism and interpretation. 2. Chance in literature. 3. Oulipo (Association) I. Title. II. Series: Avant-garde and modernism studies.

PQ2676.E67Z73 2009

848′.91409—dc22

2008041615

♾ The paper used in this publication meets the minimum requirements of the American National Standard for Information Sciences—Permanence of Paper for Printed Library Materials, ANSI Z39.48-1992.

Contents

Acknowledgments

Many people have helped me to write this book. First of all, I wish to thank Dominique Jullien, my doctoral thesis director, for years of mentoring, advice, and encouragement. Special thanks also go to Jacques Neefs, whose attentive readings of early drafts were crucial in helping me to conceptualize my project. Henri Mitterand and Peter Connor gave me invaluable guidance at early and later stages of my work. I am also grateful for Priscilla Ferguson's meticulous reading and her suggestions for further research. James Helgeson offered insights both on philosophical questions and on the broader cultural context, in particular the debate on chance procedures in music. Discussions with Noëlle Batt, and participation in her seminar at the Université Paris 8, provided inspiration for my efforts to formulate a theoretical account of Oulipian constraints. Anne Herschberg-Pierrot also read an early version of this work, and I greatly appreciate her feedback.

The support of the Whiting Foundation allowed me to focus entirely on research and writing from 2003 to 2004. The Association Georges Perec was an essential resource, and I am grateful to Danielle Constantin for helping me explore the collections. Bernard Magné, whose knowledge of Perec's work is unparalleled, gave me the opportunity to present part of this book at the Séminaire Perec in February 2004 and drew my attention to some specific examples of chance events in Perec's novels. Marcel Bénabou and Paulette Perec also offered encouraging remarks on this occasion.

My former teachers at Columbia University and my colleagues at the University of Chicago deserve thanks for many intellectual exchanges that have influenced this book. As I completed my final revisions, I benefited from the assistance of colleagues and friends who read and commented on specific chapters: Liesl Olson, Thomas Pavel, and Robert von Hallberg. Among those who have responded to my talks and conference presentations, I should single out Larry Norman, Jean-Jacques Thomas, and Warren Motte, whose questions and comments motivated me to rethink certain aspects of the book and to broaden the scope of my argument. I owe a special debt of gratitude to several dear friends who have provided not only opinions on my work, but also moral support at all stages of the writing process: Leigh Allen, Maria Muresan, Raina Uhden, and Priya Wadhera.

Finally, I wish to thank my family. My parents, Howard and Dianne James, have expressed unwavering faith in my work. Above all, I am immensely grateful for the patience, friendship, and love of my husband, Marc Downie, who was my most constant source of inspiration as I wrote this book. I dedicate this book to Imogen, who arrived in this world just as I completed the manuscript.

Note on the Text

In French text, bracketed ellipses indicate an omission, and suspension points indicate a pause. This system has been followed in all English translations of French text.

All translations are by the author, Alison James, unless otherwise cited.

Abbreviations

The following works by Georges Perec are cited parenthetically in the text by abbreviations.

A	*Alphabets: Cent soixante-seize onzains hétérogrammatiques.* Paris: Galilée, 1976.
"AQ"/"AW"	"Approches de quoi?" In *L'Infra-ordinaire,* 9–13. Translated by John Sturrock as "Approaches to What?" in *Species of Spaces and Other Pieces,* 205–7.
BO	*La Boutique obscure: 124 rêves.* Afterword by Roger Bastide. Paris: Denoël-Gonthier, 1973.
C/T	*Les Choses: Une histoire des années soixante.* Paris: Julliard, 1965. Reprint, Paris: Pocket, 1990. Translated by David Bellos as *Things: A Story of the Sixties* (Boston: David R. Godine, 1990).
D/V	*La Disparition.* Paris: Denoël, 1969. Reprint, collection L'Imaginaire no. 215. Paris: Gallimard, 1999. Translated by Gilbert Adair as *A Void* (London: Harvill, 1994).
EC	*Entretiens et conférences.* Edited by Dominique Bertelli and Mireille Ribière. 2 vols. Paris: Joseph K., 2003.
EE/SS	*Espèces d'espaces.* Paris: Galilée, 1974. Translated by John Sturrock as *Species of Spaces,* in *Species of Spaces and Other Pieces* (London: Penguin Books, 1997).
"53J"/"53D"	*"53 jours."* Text established by Harry Mathews and Jacques Roubaud. Paris: P.O.L., 1989. Reprint, collection Folio no. 2547. Paris: Gallimard, 1994. Translated by David Bellos as *"53 Days"* (Boston: David R. Godine, 2000).

"HL"	"Histoire du lipogramme." In Oulipo, *La Littérature potentielle (Créations, Re-créations, Récréations)*, 77–93. Paris: Gallimard, 1973.
"LC"	"La Chose." *Magazine littéraire* 316 (December 1993): 55–64.
L.G.	*L.G.: Une aventure des années soixante.* Paris: Éditions du Seuil, 1992.
"LR"/"SS"	"Les Lieux d'une ruse." In *Penser/Classer,* 59–72. Translated by John Sturrock as "The Scene of a Stratagem," in *Species of Spaces and Other Pieces,* 161–69.
"NSC"	"Notes sur ce que je cherche." In *Penser/Classer,* 9–12.
PC	*Penser/Classer.* Paris: Hachette, 1985. Reprint, Paris: Hachette/Littératures, 2000.
"PC"/"TC"	"Penser/Classer." In *Penser/Classer,* 151–77. Translated by John Sturrock as "Think/Classify," in *Species of Spaces and Other Pieces,* 184–201.
QPV/WM	*Quel petit vélo à guidon chromé au fond de la cour?* Paris: Denoël, 1966. Translated by Ian Monk as *Which Moped with Chrome-Plated Handlebars at the Back of the Yard?* in *Three by Perec* (London: Harvill, 1996).
REI/EI	*Récits d'Ellis Island: Histoires d'errance et d'espoir.* With Robert Bober. Paris: P.O.L., 1994. Translated by Harry Mathews as *Ellis Island* (New York: New Press, 1995).
TE	*Tentative d'épuisement d'un lieu parisien.* Paris: Christian Bourgois, 2000.
UHD/MA	*Un homme qui dort.* Paris: Denoël, 1967. Reprint, Folio 2197. Paris: Gallimard, 1999. Translated by Andrew Leak as *A Man Asleep* (Boston: David R. Godine, 1990).

VD/WJ — *Le Voyage d'hiver.* Paris: Éditions du Seuil, 1993. Translated by John Sturrock as *The Winter Journey* (London: Syrens, 1995). *Le Voyage d'hiver* was first published in 1983 in *Magazine littéraire.*

VME/LUM — *La Vie mode d'emploi.* Paris: Hachette/P.O.L., 1978. Paris: Le Livre de Poche, 1998. Translated by David Bellos as *Life A User's Manual* (London: Harvill, 1996).

W/WMC — *W ou le souvenir d'enfance.* Paris: Denoël, 1975. Reprint, collection L'Imaginaire no. 293. Paris: Gallimard, 1993. Translated by David Bellos as *W, or the Memory of Childhood* (London: Harvill, 1988).

Constraining Chance

Le hasard est le plus grand romancier du monde: pour être fécond, il n'y a qu'à l'étudier.

Chance is the greatest novelist in the world: to be productive, one has only to study it.

—Balzac

Introduction

Chance is a perennial concern in literature. It appears in various guises, from the ancient and medieval figure of Fortune to modern efforts to come to terms with contingency. Many thinkers have either rejected the idea altogether or attempted to formulate strict definitions of chance. Yet it is perhaps the very slipperiness of the concept that explains the fascination it continues to hold for writers. In its resistance to precise definition, it indicates a rupture or point of tension in our conceptualizations of experience, and therefore poses a challenge to representation. A token of the world's instability and of human powerlessness, chance is inevitably a crucial literary theme. It is also a problem of form. Is the artist bound to struggle against chance in order to produce a flawless, necessary work? Or does chance have a place in the artistic process or product?

The construction and ordering of the work of art are tied to particular worldviews. It is by comparing the world to a text that Cicero argues against the Epicurean idea that the world was created by the fortuitous concourse of atoms; anyone who believes such a thing, he claims, might as well believe that a random collection of letters of the alphabet, shaken out onto the ground, might form the *Annals* of Ennius.[1] While this age-old debate on the origins of the universe has not faded away,[2] it is more common in the modern era to contrast the order of art with the disorder of life. However, the idea of a randomly generated text is no longer quite so inconceivable. These developments are linked to shifting philosophical attitudes as well as to the changing formal possibilities of the work of art. Modernity has been associated both with the scientific "taming of chance" (to borrow Ian Hacking's phrase) and with the pervasive appeal of indeterminacy.[3] In Baudelaire's words, modernity is "the transitory, the fugitive, the contingent."[4] Although the literary treatment of chance in the nineteenth and twentieth centuries echoes and participates in contemporary debates on determinism, the problem of chance in modern literature in many ways exceeds such arguments. In the twentieth century, the fascination with randomness and contingency had an impact on artistic forms across different media, including music, dance, painting, and literature.

This book examines the representation and staging of chance in literature through the study of a specific case: the work of the twentieth-century French writer Georges Perec (1936–82). Perec's texts effectively exploit the possibilities of chance, both tapping into its creative potential and controlling its operation. In doing so, these works capture essential aspects of human life: its "considerable energy" (to adopt Perec's expression),[5] its boundless possibilities, but also the constraints and limitations to which it is subject. It is largely by exploring the problem of chance that Perec revitalizes the novel form. A member of the Ouvroir de littérature potentielle (Workshop for Potential Literature, known as Oulipo), Perec adopted the group's dictum that the literary work should be "anti-chance"—a product of fully conscious creative processes. Yet his texts give a twist to this notion, using Oulipian constraints both to explore the role of chance in human existence and to redefine the possibilities of literary form. The investigation of chance links his writing methods, which harness chance for creative purposes, to the thematic exploration of causality, chance, and fate in his writings.

A fascinating and elusive writer who claimed never to have written two similar books, Perec produced a body of work that is astonishing in its breadth and originality. Perec's works combine formal play and realist detail, erudite allusiveness and exuberant storytelling, bridging the gap between popular fiction and sophisticated literary experiment. His novels offer abundant rewards to scholars in search of hidden meanings and references, as well as to a general readership seeking amusement and food for thought. In investigating the place and functions of chance in Perec's texts, this study unites formal and thematic concerns and addresses both the philosophical and aesthetic implications of his works. The notion of chance offers a guiding thread that will allow me to reformulate the connections between the author's apparent formalism and his realist and autobiographical ambitions.[6] Conversely, Perec is an exemplary figure, an ideal case study for investigating the place of chance in literature.

The Notion of Chance

The English noun *chance* is derived from the late Latin *cadentia,* "falling," (from *cadere,* "to fall") and can signify "the falling out or happening of events; the way in which things fall out; fortune; case." In this sense, chance is simply what happens or the way things happen. Applied to particular events or sequences, the term refers to "a happening or occurrence of things in a particular way; a casual or fortuitous circumstance," or "a matter which falls out or happens; a fortuitous event or occurrence." A single chance can also be "an opportunity that comes in any one's way"; used in the plural, the word designates "a possibility or probability of anything happening." However, chance is also an "absence of design or assignable cause, fortuity; often itself spoken of as the cause or determiner of events, which appear to happen without the intervention of law, ordinary causation, or providence."[7] The French word *hasard* (derived from the Arabic *az-zahr,* "die") is defined in similar terms: "un hasard" is an accidental case or event, an unexpected or unexplainable set of circumstances, while "le hasard" is the fictitious (and often personified) cause of that which happens without apparent or explainable meaning.[8] The English *chance* and the French *hasard* do not have exactly the same semantic values: the first can have the positive meaning of "opportunity" or the neutral sense of "the way in which things fall out," while the second is more negative, referring to the absence of explanation or cause. (The French word *chance* has more positive connotations, close to those of the English *luck.*) However, in both of these cases the dictionary definitions point to a fundamental ambiguity: the word may refer either to an event or to that which determines this event, and to a cause or design that is in fact an absence of cause or design.

The imprecision of these definitions has its source in the conflicts and complexities of Western philosophical history. Roughly speaking, attitudes about causal order can be traced back to two main lines of thought: on the one hand, the vision of universal cosmic order directed by a divine power, as put forward by Plato in the *Timaeus;* on the other, the Epicurean vision of a world based on chance. The Stoic and the religious conceptions of divine providence, which belong to the first tendency, relegate chance to a mere appearance. Stoic thinkers saw fortune or chance as the manifestation of fate in the sublunary world, as it is experienced subjectively by the individual who is ignorant of causes.[9] Lucretius, giving an account of the Epicurean position in *De rerum natura,* presents a very different view: the world and the generation of living creatures are the result not of any design in the universe but of "the seeds of things themselves of their own accord, knocking together by chance, clashed in all sorts of ways, heedless, without aim, without intention."[10] Lucretius presents chance as an absence of design or final cause (the movement of atoms is not governed by any intention), yet it is also an absence of efficient cause—the inexplicable swerve (clinamen) of some atoms from their usual course.[11] This fundamental duality is at the heart of philosophical reflections on chance.

Indeed, as Aristotle suggests in book 2 of the *Physics,* it is this confusion of cause and design that defines the concept of chance, as we ordinarily use it. Aristotle defines chance in general (*to automaton*) as a cause "by virtue of concurrence" in the field of things that are subject to teleological determination ("things which in a general way come to be for something"); the latter category, for Aristotle, includes animals and many inanimate objects as well as people.[12] In this context, a chance outcome is an event that does not correspond to the final cause or intention of the object or person but that might otherwise have come about as a result of "thought or nature." Thus the fall of a stone that strikes a man is a chance event if the stone did *not* fall for that purpose but *might* nevertheless have fallen through someone's agency for the purpose of hitting.[13] Luck or fortune in a more restricted sense (*tuché*) is applicable only to beings capable of choice.[14] Aristotle gives the example of a man who goes to a particular place and happens to meet his debtor upon the way when this was not his intention.[15] In other words, a combination of efficient causes brings about something that might have been the outcome of a final cause but in fact does not correspond to the object's final cause or the person's intention. As Hervé Barreau puts it, Aristotle's account presents chance as a rupture between the order of efficient causes and the order of final causes.[16]

Chance, according to this definition, is not so much a special type of cause as a certain type of relationship between causes and outcomes. Yet Aristotle does nevertheless refer to chance and fortune as causes,[17] and chance was often personified as a real agent in the ancient world, in the form of the Hellenistic goddess Tuché and the Roman Fortuna.[18] This figure later enjoyed a mixed fate in Western thought, for Christian theology apparently leaves little room for the idea of chance as a force in the universe. While St. Augustine ironically suggests that Fortune ought to occupy a preeminent place among the pagan gods, since their fame is governed by caprice, he ultimately argues that events on earth are governed not by chance but by divine providence.[19] The personified figure of Fortune nevertheless reappears within a Christian context in Boethius's *De Consolatione*

Philosophiae, which attempts to reconcile Fortune with Providence on the basis of the inscrutability of God's designs.[20] The personification of Fortune in Boethius's text and in later literature testifies to the appeal of the notion of chance. Fortune appears in Alain de Lille's *Anticlaudianus* (twelfth century), in the *Roman de la Rose* (ca. 1230–80), in Guillaume de Machaut's *Remède de fortune* (ca. 1341), and in the poetry of Charles d'Orléans (fifteenth century), to cite just a few examples. In Italian literature, a Christianized version of Fortune appears in Dante's *Inferno* (canto 7, lines 67–96), while Machiavelli famously discusses the ways to withstand her power in chapter 25 of *The Prince.* Whether or not she is integrated into a religious account, Fortune represents a constraint on human aspirations, standing for the limits of our power to predict and control our own destinies.

The modern era is marked by key shifts in the Western understanding of causality. With the advent of the scientific revolution, philosophers rejected the Aristotelian distinction between efficient and final causes; according to the new account, the only real causes are efficient causes, and final causes are figments of the human imagination.[21] Newtonian mechanics provided the framework for a deterministic vision of the universe, understood as a movement from prior causes to future effects governed by the laws of physics. Enlightenment thinkers generally considered the idea of chance to be empty, indeed meaningless—a symptom of our ignorance of causes.[22] Laplace formulated the classic statement of the deterministic view in 1820: a sufficiently intelligent being who knew at any given moment all the forces of nature, along with the respective position of everything in the universe, would be able to encompass past, present, and future in a single gaze.[23] As Ian Hacking has shown in *The Taming of Chance,* the nineteenth century nevertheless saw a gradual erosion of determinism through developments in statistical research on natural and social phenomena. The discoveries of twentieth-century science—in particular, quantum mechanics and chaos theory—have made Laplace's omniscient demon an increasingly unlikely figure.[24] Although these new theories to some extent associate chance with disorder and disorganization, they also suggest that chance can be a source and generator of order. Similarly, the evolution and organization of the living being also show that order can emerge from accident, allowing apparent progression toward a goal to occur without design.[25]

The use of the term *chance* in discussion of scientific theories has nevertheless given rise to heated debate in recent years. Some scientists and philosophers of science gladly proclaim the end of Laplacian determinism and herald the "re-enchantment" of a world that now seems irreducibly random.[26] Others assert that the notion of chance itself is inherently unscientific.[27] The resulting quarrels, pitting determinism against indeterminism, tend to reach an impasse. We may move beyond this stalemate by questioning the common assumption that chance implies the absence of a cause. In fact, chance is more often associated with a plurality of causes than with their absence. Recognizing this fact, the nineteenth-century philosopher Antoine-Augustin Cournot defines chance as the intersection of two independent causal series, using the example of a roof tile falling on the head of a passing philosopher.[28] At the beginning of the twentieth century (and anticipating later developments in chaos theory), the mathematician Henri Poincaré suggests that what we call chance events occur when small, imperceptible differences in initial conditions have significant consequences for the resulting phenomena.[29] Yet causal complexity in itself does not suffice to define chance. Poincaré's definition depends on the scale of events in relation to human perception; similarly, despite its apparent objectivity, Cournot's account hinges on the consequences of the event from a human point of view. As Henri Bergson points out, if the tile simply fell to the ground, we would not feel the need to apply the term *chance* to the incident.[30]

Bergson's own reflection on the notion of chance, in *L'Évolution créatrice* (1907) and in *Les Deux Sources de la morale et de la religion* (1932), is in many ways a modern reformulation of Aristotle's definition. It allows us to move beyond both the determinism/indeterminism debate and the attempt to define chance as an objective reality. Bergson claims that the idea of chance results from the confusion between two orders, the automatic laws of the universe on the one hand and the order imposed by will on the other.[31] Chance is a relative notion, which simply objectifies the mental state of someone who expected one of the two types of order and instead encounters the other. Hence the difficulty of defining chance, as the mind oscillates between the idea of an absence of final cause and an absence of efficient cause.[32] Against Lucien Lévy-Bruhl's analysis of the "primitive" mentality, Bergson asserts that the distance between the idea of a world ruled by supernatural spirits and the "advanced" idea of chance is not as great as it might appear. Both cases reveal our tendency to seek in the cause of an event a human significance equal to the significance of the effect. Chance is therefore "le mécanisme se comportant comme s'il avait une intention" (mechanism behaving as if it had an intention).[33] Bergson thus recasts the modern notion of chance as the negative image of a residual, but perhaps ineradicable, superstitious view of the world, a projection of final causes onto unintended outcomes.

It is not necessary to accept Bergson's dualism—to believe that human will *in fact* belongs to an order of things other than the determinist laws of physics—to find this view persuasive. We need only acknowledge that human beings instinctively look for purposes and intentions in the world. This impulse accounts for the tendency to associate fortune and fate; both are hypothetical agents, to which people attribute events that occur independently of human projects. It also explains the inherent ambiguity of modern attitudes toward chance. Since chance, as Bergson defines it, implies the recognition of the absence of intention—that is, intentionality is perceived to be only apparent—this perspective explains why the notion of chance takes a central place in the work of contemporary philosophers who, in the Nietzschean tradition, deny the existence of transcendent meaning and divine purpose in the universe.[34] These efforts to overcome metaphysics by accepting chance nevertheless remain unstable, if we accept Bergson's account, for our perception of chance depends precisely on our enduring search for a hidden purpose in events. Chance thus marks a limit of thought and of representation. As such, it is at the crux of a specifically modern dilemma: the inability either wholly to believe in a meaningful universe or wholly to reject the quest for meaning.

Chance—even if it cannot be seen as an objective force subject to scientific description—names a crucial feature of the way in which human beings subjectively experience and interpret the world. Bergson's account of chance is distinct from efforts to equate chance and free will (as in Lucretius's notion of the clinamen). On the contrary, chance implies the *absence* of human agency, and our reluctance to come to terms with the fact of this absence. The idea of chance is therefore not necessarily incompatible with determinism as such. Nor is it exactly the equivalent of the related notion of contingency, since the latter does not necessarily exclude human choice. I will not dwell here on debates about free will, which would risk leading back to the determinism/indeterminism deadlock.[35] However, the opposition between chance and agency has ethical implications to which I will return in the course of this study. If many events have significant human consequences but no intentional agent—things simply *happen* to people—then human claims to self-sufficiency and moral self-determination face a severe challenge. As both Clément Rosset and Martha Nussbaum point out, there is much that is tragic in the idea of chance.[36]

However, the chance event can also be a positive source of unexpected possibilities. This is chance as the Greek *kairos,* "the right moment" or "the opportune."[37] We begin to see how chance may be associated with creativity, with the opening of a space for invention. Chance is also linked to the narrative structuring of time, to stories and their turning points, and to the literary representation of human destinies.

Chance and Literature

Although the figure of Fortune fades out of literature after the Middle Ages, the idea of chance remains a durable source of literary inspiration. The novel is particularly well suited to the literary exploration of chance. Of course, it is the case that all narrative, which presents us with temporal sequences, necessarily deals with matters of causation. However, the modern novel emerges precisely at a time when (from the scientific revolution to Hume's skepticism) cause-effect relations fall under intense epistemological scrutiny. In this context, some novels undertake their own form of philosophical investigation. In *Jacques le fataliste* (1773), for instance, Diderot overtly stages the tension between chance, fate, and freedom by playing on the gap between different narrative levels. The protagonist's fatalism (his belief that all events have already been "written") is set against—or perhaps vindicated by—the narrator's assertion of his own freedom to manipulate his story at will.[38] Here, the arbitrariness of authorial decisions becomes a means of exploring the question of the role of chance in the world. Furthermore, Diderot's text highlights the ambiguous status of chance in narrative, where it may stand as either a sign of realism or a mark of contrivance and authorial manipulation.

In the nineteenth century, precisely as science propounded strict determinism, the modern city intensified the experience of chance and contingency in everyday life. The figure of the flaneur (who wanders the streets of Paris randomly) and the chance encounter became key ingredients in French literature. Fascination with the contingency of everyday life is at the heart of the realist novel, with its focus on the complex determinations of individuals' lives by character and social environment.[39] Balzac claims in his preface to *La Comédie humaine* (1842) that chance, the source of human variety, is the origin of novelistic inspiration: "Le hasard est le plus grand romancier du monde" (Chance is the greatest novelist in the world).[40] This does not prevent Balzac from employing a whole host of causal justifications for his plot events,[41] a fact that points to the fundamental realist dilemma: the difficulty of representing the disorder of the world in literary form. The mimetic project, which requires an acknowledgment of contingency, comes into conflict with an emerging aestheticism that emphasizes the autonomy of the work of art. Flaubert asserts in a letter that the novel should be "plus logique que le hasard des choses" (more logical than the haphazardness of things).[42] From this point of view, as Henri Mitterand observes, the very notion of the "realist novel" is contradictory.[43] In another sense, however, artistic organization itself can be understood as a form of mimesis. Many critics have argued that the nineteenth-century novel gave meaning to apparently random events by embedding them in a larger historical and social order.[44]

In modernist literature, this totalizing order increasingly breaks down, while writers accord even more significance to the random occurrence in itself. In Marcel Proust's *À la recherche du temps perdu* (*In Search of Lost Time*), the accidental encounter with a material object brings back to life the lost past and makes available its essential meaning.[45] The surrealists seek access to the secrets of the unconscious and liberation from rational constraints in the surprising coincidences of daily life—a quest explicitly theorized by André Breton in terms of "hasard objectif" (objective chance; defined, paradoxically, as a manifestation of necessity).[46] As chance was increasingly exalted as a path to meaning, the novel began to draw criticism for its perceived arbitrariness and banality, as well as for its creation of a teleological vision of reality. Voiced overtly in Jean-Paul Sartre's existentialist novel *La Nausée* (*Nausea*), the latter criticism is echoed in the second half of the century by the novelists and critics of the "era of suspicion" (to borrow Nathalie Sarraute's phrase).[47] These writers, suspicious of the falsifications of narrative form, contrast the world in its supposedly "raw" state—accidental, inexplicable, fragmentary—with the orderly form that stories impose on it.[48] They convict traditional realism of ideological flaws. It is in this context that we should understand the French New Novel, with its accompanying pronouncements that the sources of novelistic inspiration are in need of renewal. Critics and philosophers, among them Paul Ricoeur and Frank Kermode, have since argued for a more positive view of narrative constructions of experience.[49] In French literature, Perec's works mark a departure from the avant-garde austerity of the New Novel and inaugurate a return to the pleasure of storytelling.

The notion of chance can help us to investigate different types of causal relation in literary texts. Two broad sets of issues emerge here. First, chance appears in literature as an explicit theme, since writers investigate its impact on experience. Second, literary forms aim to convey an impression of order or disorder. As the realist dilemma shows, these two dimensions of the text are intertwined: art creates forms of organization that may or may not correspond to the logic of life itself (and which came under scrutiny in the twentieth century for their ideological implications). We should add a third dimension (closely related but not equivalent to the second): chance may play a role in the writing process itself, both in the involuntary aspects of creation and as an inherent part of language. Where the creative process is concerned, one tendency in modern literature values the suspension of authorial intention. The romantic notion of poetic inspiration finds its successor in the surrealist praise of "automatic writing," believed to liberate the unconscious from the tyranny of will and reason. A different line of modernist poetics emphasizes the importance of arduous, fully conscious labor: Charles Baudelaire (who asserts that "there is no chance in art, no more than in mechanics")[50] and Gustave Flaubert fall into this category, as does Paul Valéry (although he is less dismissive of chance as a dimension of the creative process).

As for the place of chance in language itself, Stéphane Mallarmé's preoccupation with this question would have a profound influence on subsequent writers. In "Crise de vers," Mallarmé reflects on the imperfection of languages ("imparfaites en cela que plusieurs"—imperfect in that they are several) and his disappointment at "la perversité conférant à jour comme à nuit, contradictoirement, des timbres obscur ici, là clair" (the perversity that confers upon day and night, in contradictory fashion, a timbre that is here dark, there light).[51] For Mallarmé, poetic form has as its *raison d'être* the attempt to compensate for this flaw in language, "niant, d'un trait souverain, le hasard demeuré aux termes malgré l'artifice de leur retrempe alternée en le sens et la sonorité" (denying, with a lordly gesture, the chance that remains in terms despite the artifice of their alternate tempering in meaning and sonority).[52] Thus poetry denies chance but does not abolish it. Language's "perversity" here is the chance relationship between word and concept, which the linguist Ferdinand de Saussure would soon recast in different terms as the arbitrary relationship between signifier and signified within the linguistic sign. As the linguist Jean-Claude Milner points out, in labeling linguistic signs as conventional or arbitrary—a subject of philosophical speculation at least since Plato's *Cratylus*[53]—we essentially mean that the link between sound and meaning is based on chance, given the complexities of language development and use.[54]

In employing the term *arbitrary,* Saussure invokes the figure of an original legislator, yet this origin is a fiction: "le signifiant apparaît comme librement choisi" (the signifier appears to be freely chosen).[55] In Saussure's ambiguous use of the notions of choice and arbitrariness we find all the hallmarks of chance in the Bergsonian sense: the result of a complex set of causes resembles the consequence of a human intention. Significantly, the idea of chance provides the starting point for linguistic study but is simultaneously marked as that which linguistics cannot investigate. According to Saussure, the temporal process that fixes the signifier-signified relationship should not be the object of linguistics; linguists must look for precise rules, whereas the elements of language are modified spontaneously and accidentally.[56] (Thus, in contrast with nineteenth-century philology which concerned itself with the search for origins, Saussure establishes a strict distinction between the synchronic and diachronic perspectives.) While chance is in a sense the foundation of the system or its point of emergence, it seems itself to resist conceptualization. The inescapable presence of chance within language is the precondition for linguistic and literary creativity, but this point of origin itself remains mysterious and external.[57]

In the realm of poetry, Mallarmé's solution to this dilemma is to create an alliance of sound and meaning that motivates language while removing words from ordinary reference. The novel remains closer than poetry to the "universel reportage" scorned by Mallarmé;[58] its necessity lies in its organization of discourse and narrative. Both Mallarmean poetics and Flaubertian aesthetics nevertheless define literary art as the effort to eliminate chance. However, the opposition between art and chance was increasingly called into question during the twentieth century, as many writers and artists attempted to incorporate chance elements into their work. While the surrealists attempt to convert chance into necessity, the Dadaists enlist the negative force of blind chance as a means of attacking literature and language itself. Tristan Tzara's recipe for the Dadaist poem, produced using cut-up newspaper articles, is a case in point.[59] Chance may be exploited for a variety of purposes. After the Second World War, a widespread fascination with indeterminacy led many artists to incorporate chance procedures into either the artistic process or product, first in the field of music (the work of John Cage is perhaps the most familiar example), and then in other domains. Henceforth, the decision to eliminate or incorporate chance became tied to questions of philosophical attitude and aesthetic sensibility, and to efforts to redefine the category of art itself.

Perec and the Oulipo

It is in the context of this contemporary trend that we should situate the Oulipo's description of its approach as "anti-chance." In November 1960, the writer Raymond Queneau joined forces with the mathematician François Le Lionnais to form the Séminaire de littérature expérimentale (Seminar for Experimental Literature, abbreviated to Sélitex), a group that the following month was renamed the Ouvroir de littérature potentielle. The Oulipo began its days as a subcommission of the Alfred Jarry–inspired Collège de 'Pataphysique[60] before becoming an increasingly independent entity and gradually adopting a more public profile. Counting among its members such prominent writers as Queneau, Jacques Roubaud, and Italo Calvino, the Oulipo explores the use of rules or "constraints" in writing and is undoubtedly one of the most significant literary groups of recent years. It continues to exist to the present day (with its initial membership of ten writers, mathematicians, and academics having expanded to thirty-five by 2008).

Insisting that it is not a literary school, the Oulipo's claims are modest.[61] Unlike other literary groups of the twentieth century (such as the surrealists or its contemporary *Tel Quel*), it avoids adopting positions in political debates and does not impose a strict literary dogma on its members.[62] It is pluralist in its approach, and the sheer variety of possible constraints—mathematical, syntactic, metrical, lexical, "lettric," and semantic—makes generalizations about the group's work difficult. Yet despite their differences, the members of the group clearly share certain assumptions. Above all, the Oulipo reacts against "the post-romantic ideology of spontaneity, randomness, and innate, tumultuous genius."[63] The alternative proposed by the Oulipo is not neoclassicism; the group's collective goal is not to propose a set of general, authoritative rules for literature but rather to explore the creative possibilities of various literary forms.[64] Oulipian writers generally align themselves not with Racine but with the *grands rhétoriqueurs* of the fifteenth and sixteenth centuries, court poets who excelled in technical virtuosity and the use of such devices as acrostics and palindromes. As well as experimenting with existing forms such as the sonnet and the sestina, Oulipian writers have created new literary constraints and have also explored non-Western forms of constraint such as the Japanese haiku and tanka.[65]

The "fundamental principle" of anti-chance invoked by many of the group's members is at the heart of the group's anti-romantic, anti-surrealist stance.[66] Against the idea of spontaneous creation, the Oulipo insists on the importance of conscious control of the writing process. The expression *anti-chance,* introduced by Claude Berge during one of the group's early meetings,[67] has since been taken up by Jacques Roubaud, Noël Arnaud, Paul Fournel, Jacques Bens, and Georges Perec himself. Despite this insistence, some critics have associated the group with chance-based procedures. In chapter 5, I return to this debate in order to argue that Oulipian constraints do indeed involve chance in a certain sense. To recognize this, however, is not to side with the group's detractors and to condemn Oulipian writing as gratuitous, for chance may play a creative role. The group's self-definition of its project as "anti-chance" points to an anxiety at the heart of the exploration of forms and to a profound concern with what is at stake—psychologically, aesthetically, and epistemologically—in literary creation. While the preoccupation with chance appears in the works of many Oulipian writers (Marcel Bénabou, Italo Calvino, Jacques Roubaud), it finds its most explicit and complex expression in the works of Georges Perec.

Perec was born in 1936 to a family of Polish Jews who had immigrated to Paris. Perec's father, having joined the French Army, died on the battlefield in 1940. In 1943, when Perec was six years old, his mother was deported to Auschwitz and never returned. Perec himself escaped this fate by living with relatives and in boarding schools in the unoccupied zone. In the script for the documentary film he made with Robert Bober, *Récits d'Ellis Island* (1980), Perec stated that he owed his own life to chance and exile (*REI,* 58). As Régine Robin notes, it is by chance that French was his language, and the consciousness of this accident pervades his writing.[68] Chance appears in Perec's works both as a theme and as a problem of literary form. Although the young Perec asserted an optimistic vision of humankind's control over history, his literary works later emphasize the inescapable presence of chance in the world. His writings on what he terms the "infra-ordinary," for example, aim to capture the disordered background noise of everyday life. The notion of chance is at the center of Perec's human dramas: from his first novel *Les Choses* (*Things*) of 1965 to the unfinished *"53 jours"* (*"53 Days"*), posthumously published in 1989, his characters strive, but usually fail, to exclude chance from their actions. His texts also relate chance to a set of explicit or implicit epistemological concerns. In Perec's works, narrative itself becomes a means of investigating the questions of fate and chance. While his plots accumulate unexpected accidental reversals, numerous stories of false coincidences serve to test the proposition that narrative (as Roland Barthes suggests) is the language of destiny.[69]

Perec began writing at a time when French literature was starting to emerge from the postwar debate that opposed the ideal of political engagement (espoused by Jean-Paul Sartre) to the New Novel's insistence on formal innovation and rejection of supposedly outdated modes of storytelling. He emerged onto the literary stage in 1965 with his first published novel, *Les Choses,* which won the Prix Renaudot. Subtitled "A Story of the Sixties," *Les Choses* offers an acute analysis of the dilemmas facing a young couple in a consumer society obsessed with status. While this novel established Perec (somewhat to his chagrin) as a "sociological" writer, his later works display spectacular formal virtuosity without abandoning social and realist concerns. While Perec is notorious for his 1969 novel *La Disparition* (*A Void*)—a three-hundred-page tour de force that does not contain the letter *e*—it is his encyclopedic work *La Vie mode d'emploi* (1978; *Life A User's Manual*) that established his place as one of the greatest novelists of the twentieth century. Perec died in 1982 while working on *"53 jours."*

Perec joined the Oulipo in 1967. (His friend, the poet and mathematician Jacques Roubaud, had been elected to the Oulipo in 1966, at the time when Perec was working with Marcel Bénabou, another future Oulipo member, on the joint project of Production automatique de littérature française, or PALF.)[70] From this point on, as Perec himself states, almost none of his works is written without recourse to some kind of Oulipian constraint or structure ("NSC," 11). Perec even declared himself a "product" of the Oulipo, "97 percent Oulipian" in his existence as a writer.[71] In turn, Perec played a crucial role in establishing the Oulipo as a force in the literary world. As emerges clearly from such recent retrospective accounts as *Moments oulipiens* (*Oulipian Moments*),[72] Perec was the author who both validated and transformed the group's existence, convincing the reading public—and indeed the other members of the group—of the fruitfulness of the Oulipian approach to writing.

Of Perec's Oulipian works, the e-less *La Disparition* is the best known. An even more extreme example of Oulipian virtuosity is *Alphabets* (1976), a collection of 176 heterogrammatic poems: each poem is composed of eleven series of eleven letters (the ten most common letters in the French language, *E, S, A, R, T, I, N, U, L,* and *O,* plus an additional letter that differs for each section of the collection), and no letter is repeated until each letter in the series has been used.[73] The poems of *La Clôture* (1980; *The Enclosure*) are twelve-letter heterograms, using *E, S, A, R, T, I, N, U, L, O, C,* and an additional letter freely chosen for each line. "Beaux présents" and "belles absentes" are poems that are also based on combinations of particular letters.[74] *La Vie mode d'emploi* (1978) uses a combinatory system based on a ten-by-ten Greco-Latin bi-square, among other structures, to provide a list of elements that are the starting point for each chapter. Shorter experimental texts such as "81 fiches-cuisine à l'usage des débutants" ("81 Recipes for the Use of Beginners") and "Deux cent quarante-trois cartes postales en couleurs véritables" ("Two Hundred and Forty-Three Postcards in True Colors") also use combinations of elements, this time in a more noticeable way.

Perec is not only a member of the Oulipo, of course. It is hard to convey the extraordinary diversity of his writings. From 1965 to his premature death, he created novels, poems, plays, short experimental exercises, musical and filmic collaborations, and works with visual artists (Cuchi White, Jacques Poli, and Paolo Boni). *Espèces d'espaces* (1974; *Species of Spaces*) is a captivating reflection on the ways in which we occupy and think about the spaces in which we live. Perec's autobiographical works, such as *Je me souviens* (1978; *I Remember*) and the moving *W ou le souvenir d'enfance* (1975; *W, or the Memory of Childhood*), deal with memory as both a public and private phenomenon. The sheer variety of Perec's work, and his puzzling, paradoxical combinations—of realism and formal play, comedy and tragedy, fantastic narratives and minute descriptions of everyday reality—pose particular challenges for critics. Should we, as Perec himself suggests, divide his work into four "fields": sociological, autobiographical, Oulipian, and novelistic ("NSC," 9)? Scholars have emphasized particular aspects of his work: some approach his Oulipian works by studying the systems of constraint used to produce them; many privilege the autobiographical dimension of his work as a key to understanding the origin of his self-imposed formal restrictions.

This book follows a different thread in order to demonstrate the fundamental coherence of Perec's literary output. It offers a comprehensive account of Perec's approach to writing, doing justice to the importance of constraints in his texts without reducing his work to an Oulipian exercise. That being said, Perec's originality undoubtedly lies in the connection between his experimental writing methods, which harness chance for creative purposes, and his exploration of chance as an ethical and existential problem. His narrative works are most successful in bringing together formal experimentation, realist scope, and aesthetic achievement. It is also in these works that the tension between chance and anti-chance is particularly significant. My discussion of Perec's Oulipian works will focus on the two most remarkable cases: *La Disparition* and *La Vie mode d'emploi*. Perec's "non-Oulipian" works remain relevant to my discussion of Perec's writing practice and the question of chance; my main reference points here are the novels *Les Choses* and *Un homme qui dort* (1967; *A Man Asleep*), the autobiographical *W ou le souvenir d'enfance*, and the writings on the infraordinary (the "background noise" of everyday life). I will also consider Perec's poetry, his theater, his early essays, the unfinished novel *"53 jours,"* and the text for the documentary film *Récits d'Ellis Island*. While emphasizing certain texts, this study will situate Perec's thematic treatment of chance, and his aesthetics of anti-chance, in the context of his work as a whole.

Characterized by irony, linguistic play, and narrative flair, Perec's works are nonetheless incontestably poignant, bearing the mark of the writer's personal history. Perec belongs to a generation of writers whose work struggles directly with the war's individual and collective aftermath, presenting an often tragic vision of life. In his fiction and autobiography, Perec emphasizes the powerlessness of individuals faced with a future that is both unpredictable and seemingly inexorable. Unsurprisingly, the human confrontation with the arbitrary and uncontrollable aspects of existence takes on its most somber resonance in his autobiographical texts. I argue in this book that the vision of causality, chance, and fate that emerges from Perec's texts is inseparable from his aesthetic practice, including his use of Oulipian constraints. While Perec's literary procedures do function in part as an organizing, ordering principle, their complexity often creates an appearance of disorder. In exploring this paradox, I will show that Oulipian constraints allow Perec to play with the conventions of language and narrative, with results that are often comic or parodic. At the same time, this very playfulness is a means of engaging the reader in an investigation of chance and necessity. In Perec's texts, comedy and tragedy are intermingled, and both are tied to the intervention of chance. My investigation of the role of chance in Perec's work unites formal and thematic concerns in order to address the epistemological, ethical, and aesthetic implications of Perec's literary practice.

The book is organized by theme rather than by text. However, particular chapters sometimes revolve around one or two specific works, depending on the topic. The first four chapters focus on thematic and narratological analysis, while chapters 5 through 8 recast the discussion in light of Perec's literary constraints. While these two levels of textual construction are far from being independent and indeed often converge, this approach allows me to begin with an account of Perec's work that does not overemphasize the Oulipian texts or present him misleadingly as an esoteric, inaccessible writer. The first chapter offers a general overview of Perec's literary trajectory, from the point of view of his reflection on the place of chance in history. The political articles that Perec wrote when in his twenties introduce in straightforward form a set of themes and questions that receive a much more complex and nuanced treatment in his later texts. The optimism of these early texts stands in sharp contrast to the vision of history that emerges from Perec's literary works. The focal point of chapter 2 is a reading of *W ou le souvenir d'enfance,* which reveals the autobiographical and ethical dimensions of Perec's preoccupation with chance. The author's exploration of his own personal history provides the setting for an anguished reflection on the connection between chance, justice, power, and the possibilities of human action. Similar concerns appear in the fictional works, which often deal with characters' efforts to shape their own destinies. The role of chance events in Perec's stories and the relationship between chance and narrative genres are the subject of chapter 3, which centers on *La Vie mode d'emploi.* Chapter 4 extends this discussion to the theme of apparent coincidence: *La Disparition* and *"53 jours"* provide us with important insights into the epistemological implications of this problem.

Chapter 5 considers the Oulipian aesthetics of the constraint in terms of the often misunderstood notion of anti-chance. It also shows that the role of chance in artistic creation became an important issue in the twentieth century, sparking debates in the domains of the visual arts, music, and dance, as well as literature. Chapter 6 explores the relationship between constraint and final text in Perec's Oulipian writing, through close readings of specific examples from *La Disparition, Alphabets,* and *La Vie mode d'emploi.* Chapter 7 investigates the metaphorical and allegorical expression given to Oulipian anti-chance in the texts themselves, focusing on two figures: the labyrinth and the jigsaw puzzle. Finally, chapter 8 offers both a synthesis and a new perspective, by considering Perec's fascination with the infraordinary. This chapter brings together thematic and formal considerations in a discussion of the place of chance in representation.

I hope that this book will introduce readers unfamiliar with Perec to a writer whose engaging, playful, and moving works opened up new directions for literature in France and beyond. For those who already know his texts, I offer a new perspective that allows me to tackle some of the trickier philosophical and aesthetic problems that his writing raises, and to rethink some critical commonplaces. Above all, I believe that Perec is an exemplary figure in the history of twentieth-century literature, an author who, while detaching himself from avant-gardist squabbles, succeeded in inventing formal possibilities in order to better investigate and represent contemporary reality. His work points the way to a new understanding of the relationship between chance and form in literature.

No victor believes in chance.

—Nietzsche

1. Mastering History

History, Politics, and "La Ligne Générale"

"History," states James Joyce's Stephen Dedalus, "is a nightmare from which I am trying to awake."[1] Much of modernist literature shares this opinion, which later events of the twentieth century only serve to strengthen. This catastrophic vision finds a powerful embodiment in Walter Benjamin's figure of the angel of history, irresistibly propelled by a storm "into the future to which his back is turned, while the pile of debris before him grows skyward."[2] Georges Perec's pun, in *W ou le souvenir d'enfance,* on "l'Histoire avec sa grande hache" (History with its big ax/capital *H*) is no joke; it is the violence of history that cut Perec off from his origins, from his family, from any normal childhood memories (*W,* 17). However, this discourse of destruction and rupture is not necessarily the predominant one in post–World War II France. The political ideologies of the time continued to promise either possible or inevitable historical progress. Perec's works show the author's own transition from a somewhat forced optimism about the processes of history to a more pessimistic but also more nuanced view. This shift corresponds to his increasing acceptance of chance as an inescapable element in human lives.

In French intellectual circles, postwar debates on the philosophy of history generally set in opposition the proponents and critics of various forms of Marxist thought. In the years following the liberation of France, as the historian Tony Judt puts it, "a generation of French intellectuals, writers, and artists was swept into the vortex of communism."[3] Liberal thinkers (such as Raymond Aron) who resisted this trend were left on the fringes of French intellectual life largely because of "the postwar obsession with History, with the need to align oneself with the forces of progress and action, the premium placed on success and on victory."[4] Yet the Marxist doctrine of historical materialism also posed problems for those who wished to align themselves with "the forces of progress." In the case of Jean-Paul Sartre, for instance, this aspect of Marxist doctrine came into conflict with an existentialist thought that emphasized individual choice. In his *Critique de la raison dialectique,* Sartre criticizes the mechanical materialism of orthodox Marxism on the grounds that it denies the importance of individual freedom and creativity.[5] Rejecting the view of history as necessity, Sartre seems to accept the existence of chance. Yet he asserts that individual projects (by which we freely orient our lives and contribute to history) depend on a conception of possibility that to some extent excludes chance from the future.[6] Perec's early writings, as we shall see, express views that are fairly close to Sartre's.

Sartre's *Critique* appeared in 1960. After the dogmatism of the postwar decade, the late 1950s and early '60s marked something of a turning point in French leftist thought: writers such as Maurice Merleau-Ponty and Henri Lefebvre began to disengage themselves from their earlier opinions, and the gradual acknowledgment of Stalin's crimes led to various efforts to decontaminate Marxism.[7] The Algerian War and the end of the Fourth Republic also presented the French left with new challenges. It is in this context that we should understand the political commitments of the young Georges Perec, who was close to the intellectual Marxism of his time and milieu without belonging to any particular party. In 1959, at the age of twenty-three and six years before the publication of his first novel, *Les Choses,* Perec attended two meetings of the group Arguments, whose goal was to reconstruct a Marxist politics capable of dealing with contemporary problems such as the situation in Algeria.[8] In the same year, Perec and some of his friends (Roger Kléman, Claude Burgelin, Marcel Bénabou, Jean Crubellier, and Pierre Getzler, among others) decided to create a new review, "La Ligne générale" ("The General Line"). The group's name, taken from the title of a film by Sergei Eisenstein, indicates its ambitions: the project of forming a coherent theory that would unite politics and art. In 1960 the French Communist Party (PCF) refused to endorse the project, and the participants consequently abandoned their plans for publication. The group nevertheless continued to meet until 1964 and to publish articles, mostly in François Maspero's journal *Partisans,* with a few in the PCF-controlled *Nouvelle Critique* (the journal of communist intellectuals) and in *Clarté* (the journal of the Union des étudiants communistes).[9]

The group's desire to define a new direction in political thought and to win the approval of the PCF is typical of the political climate of the time, and not surprising for a group of young students and writers; such ambivalence was to be found even among heavyweight writers and intellectuals.[10] In some respects, the group attempted to remain close to orthodox Communism. It also borrowed elements from Sartre's existentialism and his doctrine of literary "engagement," or commitment. A further crucial influence, as Marcel Bénabou emphasizes, is the work of the Hungarian Marxist theorist Georg Lukács (first published in French translation in the 1950s and '60s).[11] "La Ligne générale" came into being at a time when the question of individual agency in history seemed particularly urgent, and when debates about the moral and political function of literature were heated. The articles that Perec wrote for the group tackle these issues head-on.

Perec's "Ligne générale" articles do not constitute a theoretical key to the author's literary works. Polemical and often simplistic, they provide us with a statement of the author's positions only at a particular point in time—the early 1960s, before the publication of his major works. That said, they should not be ignored. David Bellos rightly notes that these texts constitute "an essential exposition of Georges Perec's theoretical and ethical attitudes at the dawn of his career as a writer."[12] Since the role of chance in both history and literature is an explicit and central theme in these writings, the "Ligne générale" texts provide a useful starting point for examining what is at stake in these notions, before I turn to the much more nuanced and complex thematics of the literary texts. The most significant of Perec's "Ligne générale" texts, for the purposes of my argument, are four articles published in *Partisans* in 1962 and 1963: "Le Nouveau Roman et le refus du réel" ("The New Novel and the Refusal of the Real"), February 1962; "Pour une littérature réaliste" ("For a Realist Literature"), April/May 1962; "Engagement ou crise du langage" ("Commitment or Crisis in Language"), November/December 1962; and "Robert Antelme ou la vérité de la littérature" ("Robert Antelme, or the Truth of Literature"), January/February 1963.[13] At the heart of these essays is the effort to define literary realism in terms of the writer's engagement with history.

Commitment or Chance

In "Le Nouveau Roman et le refus du réel," Perec and coauthor Claude Burgelin acknowledge the twentieth-century crisis in realist representation, dismissing the popular literature that simply follows traditional models (*L.G.*, 30). However, they then attack the apparent solution proposed by the contemporary New Novel, arguing that a reactionary ideology underlies the aesthetic theories of such writers as Alain Robbe-Grillet, Claude Simon, and Nathalie Sarraute.[14] Ironically, the future member of the Oulipo does not hesitate to accuse these writers of "formalism" (*L.G.*, 40), even as he acknowledges that existing literary forms may no longer be adequate. While the article's insistence on political commitment reveals the influence of Sartre (who had formulated his argument for "littérature engagée" in "Qu'est-ce que la littérature?" ["What Is Literature?"] a decade earlier, in 1948), Perec and Burgelin's argument also draws heavily on Lukács's criticism of literary modernism.[15] A case in point is the claim that the New Novel expresses the inherent contradictions of Western capitalist societies but fails to explain and overcome these contradictions (*L.G.*, 39); this essentially repeats Lukács's judgment of such writers as James Joyce, Franz Kafka, and Samuel Beckett.[16]

Perec and Burgelin claim to reject the Sartrean model of "littérature engagée" (committed literature), arguing that it simply involves the insertion of the correct political intentions into conventional narrative structures. However, their essay is essentially a plea for commitment in literature: "L'engagement, aujourd'hui, c'est le respect total de la complexité du monde, la volonté acharnée d'être lucide, de comprendre et d'expliquer" (*L.G.*, 44–45) (Commitment, today, is the total respect for the world's complexity, the fierce determination to be lucid, to understand and to explain). Perec returns to many of the same arguments in "Pour une littérature réaliste," where he refers to the project of "littérature engagée" and the New Novel as the two great failures of the contemporary novel (*L.G.*, 47). Echoing Lukács once again, Perec affirms that literature's function is to be realist, and that realism aims at nothing less than the total explanation of history—and thus the demonstration of the necessity of social change. Conceived of in these terms, a realist literature would necessarily be revolutionary in nature. According to Perec, a socialist perspective is necessary for realism because it guarantees the correct understanding and portrayal of reality (*L.G.*, 61).

Even at his most dogmatic, Perec is clearly uncomfortable with the traditional terms of a debate that opposes committed, realist representation to formalist, nonrealist, noncommitted art—a distinction that is founded on the customary distinction between form and content. However, the "Ligne générale" articles do not articulate a clear alternative to this dichotomy. While Perec struggles to articulate his position on the question of form, his primary concern at this point is with the content of the realist text, with its status as a complete explanation of experience: "Le réalisme n'est pas un mot magique: il est un aboutissement; toute situation décrite d'un bout à l'autre nous y mène; il suffit de refuser les mythes, les explications trop faciles, les hasards, l'inexplicable" (*L.G.*, 65) (Realism is not a magic word: it is an end point; a complete description of any situation leads us to it; it is enough to reject myths, facile explanations, accidents, the inexplicable). Realism, according to this view, is a total description of a situation, and it is a refusal of chance. It is grounded in an underlying necessity that characterizes both the course of history and the actions undertaken by human beings: realism is possible because the future is predictable and controllable (*L.G.*, 66). The notion of chance has no place here; placed on the same level as myth, it is treated as a fiction, a symptom of our failure to understand causes. The goal of the realist writer is therefore to trace the necessary path from cause to effect, all the while rejecting both easy explanations and the refusal to explain.

Perec's argument in the "Ligne générale" texts rests on an understanding of the world, and of human history, as essentially coherent and comprehensible. On the one hand, this is a view that seems to presuppose an overarching order, even recalling the Hegelian view of history as the necessary course of the World Spirit. On the other hand, Perec accords an important place to human choices and actions in determining the movement of history. The influence of Sartre's existentialism is evident here, although it is unclear precisely how Perec reconciles historical determinism with his insistence on human choice. A similar ambiguity can be found in Lukács's *Meaning of Contemporary Realism.*[17] However, what is clear is that chance is excluded from Perec's account, as a notion that escapes both the idea of necessary causal chains and that of free choice. The young Perec's rejection of the idea of chance is closely linked to his insistence on the complete description of situations, to the emphasis on "totality" that Tony Judt identifies as a special characteristic of modern French Marxism, and which results from "an energetic desire to exorcize from the thing-to-be-explained all random, or contingent, or causally under-determined phenomena."[18] In this respect, the "Ligne générale" project presupposes the refusal of chance.

Conquering the World

The desire for moral and political certainty emerges strongly in Perec's "Ligne générale" writings. Language and reason, Perec affirms, are capable of connecting the individual to the course of history, thereby making freedom possible (*L.G.*, 114). One of the most striking aspects of these articles, viewed as a whole, is their optimism: confidence in the contribution of literature to future social change, faith in language and its ability to represent reality, and above all, belief in the individual's ability to master his or her destiny, and thereby the world itself. Throughout the articles, the words *conquête* (conquest) and *maîtrise* (command, mastery) recur. In their article on the New Novel, for example, Perec and Burgelin criticize Nathalie Sarraute's treatment of psychology because it allegedly implies that self-mastery is unthinkable (*L.G.*, 37), and the essay concludes that true literature is a sign of humankind's "conquest of the world" (*L.G.*, 45). The essay "Pour une littérature réaliste" repeats this notion that realism is defined by mastery of the real (*L.G.*, 53), and is even more emphatic in its claims for the power of reason: there are no phenomena that rationality and language cannot "conquer" (*L.G.*, 64–65). The article "Engagement ou crise du langage" reaffirms the belief that a correct perception of reality entails a conquest of that reality (*L.G.*, 85).

As we have seen, there seems to be little room for chance in this account of the three-way relationship between the individual, history, and representation. As becomes clear in the article "Robert Antelme ou la vérité de la littérature," the notion of chance stands in opposition to the principle of human freedom and mastery. Antelme's account in *L'Espèce humaine* (*The Human Race*) of his experience in a Nazi concentration camp is, according to Perec, exemplary both of literature's power to represent the real and of humanity's ability to triumph over even the most terrible circumstances:

> La survie est, bien sûr, une question de chance. Mais la chance n'explique finalement rien. Il y eut, dans la détention de Robert Antelme, des moments qu'il ne put contrôler. C'est à la veine, ou à un automatisme, pur et simple, ou au geste inespéré d'un autre, qu'il dut alors de ne pas mourir. Il en eut d'autres dont il resta maître. Alors il triompha de la mort. (*L.G.*, 103)

> Survival is, of course, a matter of luck. But luck ultimately explains nothing. There were, during Robert Antelme's detention, moments that

> he could not control. Then he owed his escape from death to a fluke or to a pure and simple reflex, or to the unhoped-for gesture of another. There were other moments of which he remained in command. Then he triumphed over death.

Here, Perec seems to acknowledge the existence of chance—understood not as an absence of causality, but as an aspect of experience that escapes our conscious control. However, he then attempts to diminish its consequences, claiming that the essential human moments are those in which luck plays no role. It is almost as if Antelme's symbolic triumph over death had more importance than the accidental fact of his actual survival.[19] Perec's insistence on Antelme's control of his own destiny recalls some of the more extreme formulations of existential freedom put forward by Sartre—for instance, the latter's assertion that the French had never been freer than under German occupation, since the constant threat of torture and death led to deeper self-knowledge and the discovery of the essence of liberty.[20] If Perec does not go quite this far, his attitude toward individual freedom seems similar.

Les Choses: Tensions and Tenses

Perec's *Partisans* essays do not amount to a sustained reflection on Marxist theory, but they do help us to situate the beginnings of Perec's literary career in relation to the literary and political debates of the period. If we turn from Perec's political essays to his literary texts, *Les Choses* (1965; *Things*) is closest in both chronological and ideological terms to the concerns of the "Ligne générale" project. It even concludes with a quotation attributed to Marx (*C*, 157).[21] Subtitled "Une histoire des années soixante" ("A Story of the Sixties"), *Les Choses* is the tale of a young couple who struggle to find happiness in the France of that era. It has been read as a "sociological" novel and as an attack on the consumer society of the post–World War II years known as the Trente Glorieuses (Glorious Thirty).[22] However, the novel does not present us with a clear political message.

While the "Ligne générale" articles present human freedom as the essential link between individual action and the course of history, *Les Choses* suggests a separation between destiny and history, between individual choices and their effects on the larger map of events. The novel's two characters, Jérôme and Sylvie (presented as an undifferentiated and typical couple of their time, rather than as psychologically complex beings), are unable to establish any real connection with history. They worry about political commitment (a question made particularly urgent by the Algerian War) but do not undertake any meaningful action. This inertia is due not only to their powerlessness when faced with the scale of the problem but also to a fundamental divergence in nature between their political concerns and the field of practice:

> Leur conscience politique, pour autant qu'elle existât en tant que telle comme forme organisée et réflexive [. . .] se situait, pensaient-ils, en deçà ou au-delà du problème algérien, au niveau de choix plus utopiques que réels, au niveau de débats généraux qui n'avaient guère de chances, ils le reconnaissaient tout en le regrettant, de déboucher sur une pratique concertée. (*C,* 85–86)

> Their political consciousness, insofar as they had any such thing as a structured and considered set of thoughts [. . .] was, they thought, already beyond or above the Algerian issue, engaged with alternatives that were more utopian than real, with general questions which, they conceded with some regret, had little chance of producing any kind of practical result. (*T,* 74)

The word *chances,* used here in the sense of "possibilities," appears only to be negated; political debates contain little potential for action. The narrator's ironic tone remains ambiguous: are Jérôme and Sylvie to be condemned, or are they right to believe that their political consciousness is incompatible with direct action? It is possible to read this statement as Perec's own wry comment on the "Ligne générale" project and its abstract political goals.

Besides these "utopian" choices, the characters face decisions that affect their practical lives but that may not in fact be a matter of free will at all: Jérôme and Sylvie become market researchers "by necessity and not by choice" (*C,* 29/*T,* 35). It is difficult to situate this claim, which may be either the narrator's judgment or Jérôme and Sylvie's own belief presented in free indirect style (Perec's principal intertextual model for this novel was Flaubert).[23] In this context, this appeal to necessity may be a strategy of disavowal. The characters' passivity is both a form of failure—a symptom of their absence of ambition, lucidity, and courage to follow their convictions—and a kind of liberation, since the necessity of the outcome absolves them of responsibility for the course of their lives: "L'histoire, là encore, avait choisi pour eux" (There again, history had chosen for them) (*C,* 29/*T,* 35). However, the forces of history cannot be defined solely in terms of opposition to individual ambitions, for the pressures that determine Jérôme and Sylvie's actions operate, partially at least, through the characters' projects. Choice and necessity do not appear as a straightforward dichotomy. Jérôme and Sylvie do in fact resist the social pressure to conform and to acquire the trappings of bourgeois existence. Yet, after attempting in vain to find happiness by leaving Paris (fleeing to Sfax, Tunisia), they eventually give in and play society's game.

On one level, *Les Choses* undoubtedly offers a commentary on contemporary consumer society (modeled in part on Roland Barthes' *Mythologies*). However, the novel's ambiguity tempers its ideological force. The tension between ironic impersonality and a tendency toward didacticism creates an unstable narrative voice. For the most part, the tone is neutral and distanced from the characters (a fact that bears witness, once again, to Perec's ambition to imitate Flaubert), but on more than one occasion the narrator intervenes directly to provide us with either positive or negative judgments on the characters—telling us, for example, that Jérôme and Sylvie are right not to like the film *L'Année dernière à Marienbad* (*C,* 60) or commenting disparagingly on their lack of lucidity (*C,* 23) and the shallowness of their political commitment (*C,* 80–81). Yet if the characters' actions (or inaction) are criticized, a form of historical necessity seems to determine their lives despite their attempts at resistance. The novel's exploration of contemporary society is thereby mapped onto an archetypal narrative schema, and the social forces pitted against individual freedom become an avatar of fate. This is not an external fate that strikes from above, but one that acts through the characters' desires and choices, in a complex intermingling of the social and the personal.

Les Choses ultimately transcends dogmatism in its exploration of causal complexity and of the subtle pressures that influence the characters' choices. Despite the various judgmental or ironic narratorial interventions, we cannot be sure whether Jérôme and Sylvie are to blame for their passivity or whether their history was already written in advance by the pressures that limit their field of action. The novel's use of verb tense contributes to this ambiguity; the first chapter is written entirely in the conditional, while the epilogue is in the future. As Harry Mathews points out, "Between those two 'unreal' time zones, the bulk of the story is related in the past definite and the imperfect in sentences of such Flaubertian inexorability as to exclude all possible alternatives."[24] The future tense of the final section also creates a sense of the inexorable, if we lend credence to the narrator's prophetic authority. The beginning of the epilogue exemplifies the novel's uncertain temporal structure:

> Tout aurait pu continuer ainsi. Ils auraient pu rester là toute leur vie. Jérôme, à son tour, aurait pris un poste. Ils n'auraient pas manqué d'argent. On aurait bien fini par les nommer à Tunis. Ils se seraient fait de nouveaux amis. Ils auraient acheté une voiture. Ils auraient eu, à la Marsa, à Sidi-Bou-Saïd, à El Manza, une belle villa, un grand jardin.
>
> Mais il ne leur sera pas si facile d'échapper à leur histoire. (*C*, 149)

> Things could have carried on in the same way. They could have stayed like that all their lives. Jérôme would have got a job for himself. They would not have been short of money. They would have got transferred to Tunis eventually. They would have made new friends. They would have bought themselves a car. At La Marsa, or Sidibou Saïd, or El Manza, they would have had a fine detached house, a big garden.
>
> But it will not be easy for them to escape from their own story. (*T*, 120)

The initial use of the past conditional tense affirms the existence of a set of possibilities yet simultaneously refuses these possibilities any actualization. The very category of the possible is then apparently negated by the jump to the future tense: time will inevitably bring Jérôme and Sylvie back to France. However, the narrator's position with respect to these events is not clear: is he recounting real possibilities and impossibilities, or simply the characters' daydreams of what might have been and what will be? To what extent are their lives determined by the "histoire" (history/story) in which they are finally caught up?

Despite these causal uncertainties, the world of *Les Choses* appears largely deterministic. This is a world in which neither chance nor agency seem to have much weight: "Ils écriront, pleins d'espoir, des curriculum vitae soigneusement pesés. La chance—mais ce ne sera pas exactement de la chance—sera pour eux" (Full of hope, they will write carefully pondered curricula vitae. Their luck—but it will not be luck exactly—will be in) (*C*, 154/*T*, 123–24). Multiple readings are possible here: in one sense, the reference to luck masks the role of free will: Jérôme and Sylvie find positions in part because of their own efforts. In another sense, the appearance of luck masks the predictability of the outcome; given the rules of the milieu in which they live, Jérôme and Sylvie are bound to find employment in accordance with their social status. The sense of inevitability is reinforced by the future tense. On yet another level, the characters' "luck" may be read as misfortune, since Jérôme and Sylvie have ultimately given in to the system that they attempted to flee. Thus the tension between chance, freedom, and determinism is never fully resolved.

If we judge by the characters' fate, *Les Choses* does not so much display as it calls into question the individual's ability to master history. Except perhaps in the epigraph[25] and envoi, we find little trace of Perec's earlier conviction that reason and language are all-powerful. Implicated by the Flaubertian ambiguity of the narration, the reader is not entirely free to feel superior to Jérôme and Sylvie. We sense in this novel a loss of political optimism that is seemingly confirmed, albeit on a humorous note, in Perec's next work, published in 1966, *Quel petit vélo à guidon chromé au fond de la cour?* (*Which Moped with Chrome-Plated Handlebars at the Back of the Yard?*). This short, playful, and parodic text, whose index lists the rhetorical techniques used by the author, is dedicated "à L.G. en mémoire de son plus beau fait d'armes (mais si, mais si)" (to the memory of L.G.'s finest feat of arms [and I'm not kidding you]) (*QPV,* 11/*WM,* 3). Recounting the failed attempt by a group of friends to save a particular individual (designated by the names Karamanlis, Karawo, Karawasch, Karacouvé, Karablast, Karawann, Karatruc, and further variations) from being called up to fight in Algeria, *Quel petit vélo* overtly mocks the aspirations of the "Ligne générale":

> [Henri Pollak] venait nous retrouver, nous ses potes, dans le café d'en face, où l'on parlait Lukasse, Heliphore, Hégueule et autres olibrii de la même farine, car on était tous un peu fêlés à l'époque, jusques à des heures aussi avancées que nos idées. (*QPV,* 18)

> [Henri Pollak would] come to meet us, his mates, in the café over the road, where we'd speak about Lukasse, Heliphore, Heygal and other oddbodkins tarred with the same brush, for we were all a touch cracked in those days, until the hour was as advanced as our ideas. (*WM,* 9)

As was the case in *Les Choses,* the characters' "advanced" political and philosophical ideas never have any substantial consequences, not even with respect to the relatively derisory task of saving one person from the draft.

Escaping History: *Un Homme Qui Dort*

With few exceptions, the characters of Perec's novels have seemingly abandoned the hope of intervening in history and turned instead toward more modest attempts to master the real. *Un homme qui dort* (1967; *A Man Asleep*) can be read as an allegory of the rupture between collective history and individual destiny. The novel's protagonist (addressed throughout in the second person singular) is a student who one day puts down his copy of Aron's *Leçons sur la société industrielle* and stops attending classes. No longer feeling connected to the world, his response is to intensify this alienation and become "celui sur qui l'histoire n'a plus de prise" (the one on whom history has lost its hold) (*UHD,* 95/*MA,* 189). If Joyce's Stephen Dedalus wishes to awake from the nightmare of history (but to awake to what?), Perec's character withdraws from history into indefinite slumber.

Intertextuality has a central place in *Un homme qui dort* for an important reason: in removing himself from time and history, the protagonist wishes to escape the preordained roles available to him. The problem is that all possible forms of revolt against convention have themselves been included in this repertory; they are all entirely predictable and banal:

> Tu ne vendras pas ton âme au diable, tu n'iras pas, sandales aux pieds, te jeter dans l'Etna, tu ne détruiras pas la septième merveille du monde. [. . .]
>
> Pourquoi grimperais-tu au sommet des plus hautes collines, puisque ensuite il te faudrait redescendre, et, une fois redescendu, comment faire pour ne pas passer ta vie à raconter comment tu t'y es pris pour monter? Pourquoi ferais-tu semblant de vivre? Pourquoi continuerais-tu? Ne sais-tu pas déjà tout ce qui t'arrivera? (*UHD,* 44)

> You won't sell your soul to the devil, you won't go clad in sandals to throw yourself into the crater of Mount Etna, you won't destroy the seventh wonder of the world. [. . .]
>
> Why climb to the peak of the highest hills when you would only have to come back down again, and, when you are down, how would you avoid spending the rest of your life telling the story of how you got up there? Why should you keep up the pretence of living? Why should you carry on? Don't you already know everything that will happen to you? (*MA,* 155–56)

The protagonist refuses to identify with a whole series of destructive and self-destructive antiheroes, both fictional and historical: Faust, who sold his soul to the devil; the Greek philosopher Empedocles, who allegedly threw himself into the crater of Mount Etna so that people would believe he had attained apotheosis; Herostratus, who burned the temple of Artemis at Ephesus in order to immortalize his name. The reference to climbing hills also evokes Sisyphus, the epitome of the "absurd hero," according to Albert Camus,[26] while the question "Why should you carry on?" might be addressed to Beckett's "unnamable" protagonist.[27]

The problem with this rejection of literary and cultural stereotypes, however, is that the act of negation has itself become a literary stereotype. Indeed, the "man asleep" inevitably reminds us of characters we have encountered elsewhere. For instance, he spends hours contemplating the leaves, branches, and roots of a tree (*UHD,* 40–41), bringing to mind the tree root that reveals the raw contingency of existence to Sartre's protagonist Roquentin, of *La Nausée* (*Nausea*).[28] This is not just a localized intertext; throughout Perec's novel, the protagonist's queasy fascination with the infinite, disorienting, and unnecessary forms of the world recalls Roquentin's existential crisis. However, instead of a retrospective first-person narration accompanied by philosophical reflections, as in *La Nausée,* Perec's novel consists of a second-person narration in the present tense, which simultaneously plunges us into the moment of the character's perceptions and creates the impression of a dislocated, alienated subjectivity (next to which the voice of Sartre's protagonist seems almost self-assured).

As John Pedersen has pointed out, *Un homme qui dort* draws from a wide variety of other authors, including Kafka, Antoine de Saint-Exupéry, Baudelaire, and Herman Melville.[29] However, the novel's existentialist overtones bring particular intertexts to the foreground. The protagonist's withdrawal from the world and his refusal to participate in society remind the reader not only of Roquentin, but perhaps even more forcefully of another existentialist hero, Meursault of Camus' *L'Étranger* (*The Stranger*). However, Perec's narrator denounces these literary precursors as no less dishonest than the view of the universe they purport to discredit, since they exalt the individual's refusal to the status of heroism. Absolute indifference seems the only form of escape that remains possible, although this attitude too has a forerunner in Melville's Bartleby, the man who would "prefer not" to do anything his employer asks of him, and whose story is summarized in Perec's novel (*UHD,* 136). As Perec reveals in interviews, this text was one of his principal inspirations for the work (*EC* 1:83, 91). Beyond this explicit intertext, there are also hints of the Stoic effort to become indifferent to external things, taken here to an extreme point of negation and withdrawal.

Crucially, the "man asleep" chooses indifference rather than revolt, because he views the former as a means of restoring order to the world, of attaining "une vie immobile, sans crise, sans désordre: nulle aspérité, nul déséquilibre" (a life without motion, without crisis and without disorder, a life with no rough edges and no imbalance) (*UHD,* 52/*MA,* 161). The novel's title suggests a lack of consciousness and thereby announces the protagonist's state of detachment; it also refers to the desire for control over time and space, via an intertextual allusion to Proust's phrase "Un homme qui dort tient en cercle autour de lui le fil des heures, l'ordre des années et des mondes" (A sleeping man holds in a circle around him the thread of the hours, the order of the years and worlds).[30] At one point in the novel, it seems that this paradoxical goal of combining both mastery and passivity has been attained; the protagonist believes that he has become "maître du temps, maître du monde" (the master of time itself, the master of the world) (*UHD,* 53/*MA,* 162). However, the novel ultimately rejects this vision of mastery: "Tu n'es plus le maître anonyme du monde, celui sur qui l'histoire n'avait pas de prise" (You are no longer the nameless master of the world, the one on whom history had lost its hold) (*UHD,* 144/*MA,* 221).[31] The protagonist cannot detach himself from history, yet his place in it remains undefined. The novel ends not with a confident re-engagement with the world, but rather on a note of uncertainty: "Tu attends, Place Clichy, que la pluie cesse de tomber" (You are waiting, on Place Clichy, for the rain to stop falling) (*UHD,* 144/*MA,* 221).

Chance and Circumstance

Characters in *La Vie mode d'emploi* (*Life A User's Manual*) also devise plans to master if not history as a whole, at least some aspects of reality. Bartlebooth's endeavor is a case in point. His initial ambition, and the basis for his whole elaborate scheme of creating, reconstituting, and then destroying jigsaw puzzles, is to grasp a fragment of the world:

> Face à l'inextricable incohérence du monde, il s'agira alors d'accomplir jusqu'au bout un programme, restreint sans doute, mais entier, intact, irréductible. (*VME,* 152)

In the face of the inextricable incoherence of things, he will set out to execute a (necessarily limited) programme right the way through, in all its irreducible, intact entirety. (*LUM,* 117)

Unlike the Perec of the "Ligne générale" days, Bartlebooth recognizes the impossibility of describing the world in its totality. He therefore takes on a compromised—but ultimately no less impossible—form of this task, treating the fragment as a microcosm of the whole of reality. Bartlebooth's effort to impose order on the "inextricable incoherence of things" involves a form of tyranny over others, requiring the participation of a number of people. Valène teaches Bartlebooth to paint watercolors, Winckler transforms the paintings into jigsaws, Morellet glues the pieces together again; others, including his servant Smautf, play an organizational role. Bartlebooth gathers these people around him (they all live in the same building), and their participation in his program shapes their lives. The project also requires a degree of indifference to historical events and circumstances that exceeds even that of the "man asleep." As Bartlebooth travels to produce the watercolors that he will then have made into jigsaw puzzles, World War II and subsequent regional conflicts become important only if they threaten the perfection and autonomy of his program—as when a bomb explodes in his hotel in Port Said but fortunately does not destroy his luggage (*VME,* 82). The search for coherence no longer implies attaining mastery over history, as it did in the "Ligne générale" essays, but almost complete lack of concern for the human consequences of historical events.

Indeed, few of the numerous characters of *La Vie mode d'emploi* attempt to participate actively in the larger events of history, although several—for example, Paul Hébert (who is deported to Buchenwald on flimsy evidence) and Célia Crespi's son (killed accidentally during the liberation of Paris)—are history's victims. We learn that Olivier Gratiolet was the only one of all the building's residents to join the Resistance and spent hours in the cellar receiving radio instructions from London (*VME,* 269, 365–66). Despite this former political commitment, chapter 58 describes Gratiolet as the victim of circumstances and as someone who has, like many of the novel's other characters, turned from the realm of pragmatic action to that of the unrealizable project: "Cet homme de cinquante-cinq ans, veuf et infirme, dont les guerres ont façonné le terne destin, est habité par deux projets grandioses et illusoires" (This fifty-five-year-old widower and invalid, whose shabby fate has been forged by wars, is obsessed with two grandiose and illusory projects) (*VME,* 333/*LUM,* 275). The degree of deterministic force implied by "destin" here is not entirely clear; while the wars that have shaped Gratiolet's existence are evidently the result of causes distinct from his will, the nature of his involvement in them was determined by voluntary actions. Grammatically, nevertheless, the above sentence places him in an entirely passive position in relation both to his past existence and current passions. In any case, the connection between individual destiny and collective history is represented as unstable, uncertain, and in many cases devastating for the individual.

It is this somber image of human destiny that predominates in Perec's works, despite the confident claims of the "Ligne générale" articles. Indeed, the insistent optimism of the early writings, and Perec's obsession with the need to master language and history, can be understood as compensatory mechanisms in the face of the cruel arbitrariness of history. (Catherine Dana suggests that the author's use of Oulipian constraints should also be read in this light.)[32] In Perec's autobiographical texts—in particular, *W ou le souvenir d'enfance*—history is associated with a set of forces that threaten the individual with irreparable damage and ultimately death. Of course, the violence that decimated Perec's family was the result not of an abstract force but of specific plans formulated by particular people, the Nazis. Yet the word *history* serves to designate a complex causal chain that has unpredictable consequences, from the point of view of the individual. It is impossible to know when or how events will strike, or how various human decisions and actions will interact: "Ma grand-mère paternelle, Rose, dut au seul hasard de ne pas être arrêtée: elle était chez une voisine quand les gendarmes vinrent chez elle" (My paternal grandmother, Rose, owed it to chance alone to have escaped arrest: she was at a neighbour's house when the gendarmes came) (*W,* 61–62/*WMC,* 41).

Chance here is not the absence of cause—viewed individually, all of the events narrated have explicable causes—but rather a term that designates the individual's lack of predictive power over events, resulting in a discrepancy between intention and result: Rose did not intend to save herself by visiting her neighbor. This thwarting of human projects can have positive effects, as with the police's failure to arrest Rose, or devastating ones, such as the absence of the runner who might have smuggled Cyrla Perec across the Loire into the unoccupied zone (*W,* 53). In these cases luck and chance indeed "explain nothing," as Perec stated in the essay on Antelme, but it is precisely for this reason that they are terrifying. The word *chance* occupies the space in which explanation becomes meaningless.

This space or gap that we call chance is a paradoxical one that conjures up both the infinite potentialities of the present and the arbitrary closing off of this sphere with each instant of time. This is the *clôture* (closing, enclosure) that gives its title to a collection of Perec's poems, and it creates an appearance of inevitability that Perec often calls the "irrevocable" (*W,* 26) or the "inexorable": "L'inexorable a construit son luxe icarien, sort là chu..." (The inexorable constructed its Icarian luxury, lot fallen there...).[33] The documentary film *Récits d'Ellis Island* (1980) reaches back into the lost possibilities of a potential future envisaged from the past. For Perec and the filmmaker Robert Bober, the island belongs to a "potential memory" and a "probable autobiography":

> nos parents ou nos grands-parents auraient pu s'y trouver
> le hasard, le plus souvent, a fait qu'ils sont ou
> ne sont pas restés en Pologne, ou se sont arrêtés,
> en chemin en Allemagne, en Autriche, en Angleterre ou en France.
> ce destin commun n'a pas pris pour chacun de nous la même figure.
> (*REI,* 56)

> our parents or grandparents might have been here
> it was mainly chance that decided whether they would stay
> or would not stay in Poland, whether they would stop
> on the way, in Germany
> or Austria or England or France.
> to each of us, this shared fate has appeared
> in a different light. (*EI,* 57–58)

As in *Les Choses,* the past conditional ("auraient pu") simultaneously evokes and negates the realm of the possible. It suggests, together with the reference to chance, that things could have been otherwise. Yet, as the text of *Récits d'Ellis Island* emphasizes, events suddenly seem inescapable as soon as they have taken place. The future of the emigrants who arrived at Ellis Island seemed to depend largely on chance, but Perec tells us that these people found themselves face-to-face with "l'inexorable" (*REI,* 52). In *Un homme qui dort,* the narrator asks the protagonist, "Pendant vingt-cinq ans, n'as-tu rien su de ce qui aujourd'hui est déjà l'inexorable?" (Did you never have an inkling, not once in twenty-five years, of that which, today, has already become inexorable?) (*UHD,* 28/*MA,* 144)—but at what point did this destiny become fixed and unchangeable? Referring to a passage from Malcolm Lowry's *Under the Volcano,* the philosopher Clément Rosset argues that all reality has the inherent property of being at once *somehow* and *anyhow.* Even if no necessity governs events, random happenings must come into being in a particular form; on the threshold of existence in the present, total indetermination and total determination are merged.[34] Perec's motif of the inexorable seems quite close to Rosset's conception.

We thus find in Perec's works a shift from an initial Sartrean position—that is, belief in absolute freedom of choice within a contingent situation—to a more pessimistic acknowledgment of the ways in which time and circumstance inevitably constrain our possibilities of action. A chasm opens up between the individual and history, but also between our sense of infinite possibilities and our powerlessness to determine which of them will be realized.[35] This is the "faille" (breach) that suddenly opens up in the protagonist's life in *Un homme qui dort* (*UHD,* 28) and leaves the individual both unable to participate in history and incapable of living in a state of detachment from the world. Faced with this double obstacle, Perec's characters—and Perec himself as autobiographical subject—can never attain the autonomous position of the Sartrean subject. They nevertheless adopt various plans and procedures for dealing with the uncertainties of destiny. Chapter 2 examines some of these tactics and their ethical implications.[36]

> C'est imprudence d'estimer que l'humaine prudence puisse remplir le rolle de la fortune. Et vaine est l'entreprise de celui qui presume d'embrasser et causes et consequences, et mener par la main le progrez de son faict.
>
> It is unwise to think that human wisdom can fill the role of Fortune. And vain is the undertaking of him who presumes to embrace both causes and consequences and to lead by the hand the progress of his affair.
>
> —Montaigne

2. Questioning Destiny

Power and Passivity

Perec's autobiographical work *W ou le souvenir d'enfance* consists of two alternating texts. One of these, in italics, recounts the fictional story of a journey undertaken by a character named Gaspard Winckler; the other, in roman type, deals with Perec's childhood and family history.[1] Despite its opening phrase, "Je n'ai pas de souvenirs d'enfance" (I have no childhood memories) (*W,* 17/*WMC,* 6), the autobiographical section does recount some of Perec's memories. This is particularly true of the second part of the text, which concerns the period after Perec's separation from his mother and begins, "Désormais, les souvenirs existent" (From this point on, there are memories) (*W,* 97/*WMC,* 68). However, Perec claims to lack the reference points that would anchor these recollections in a chronological narrative: "Les souvenirs sont des morceaux de vie arrachés au vide" (Memories are scraps of life snatched from the void) (*W,* 98/*WMC,* 68). This uncertainty impinges on time, places, and people:

> On ne posait aucune question. On attendait que le hasard fasse revenir la tante, ou, sinon cette tante-là, l'autre tante, en fin de compte, on se fichait pas mal de savoir laquelle des deux tantes c'était et même on se fichait qu'il y ait des tantes ou qu'il n'y en ait pas. (*W,* 98–99)
>
> You didn't ask any questions. You waited for fate to bring auntie back, or if not that aunt, then the other—in the end you didn't much care

> which one it was and anyway you didn't really care whether there were any aunties at all or not. (*WMC,* 69)

The impersonal subject pronoun *on* here masks the point of view of the young Perec, who holds chance responsible for the appearance of one aunt or the other. This causal judgment hinges on the child's ignorance of, and indifference to, the factors that determine the visits. The author's necessarily retrospective point of view further complicates his account; from the adult writer's perspective, the unreliability of memory exacerbates the impression of randomness.

Chance is primarily a subjective concept in this context: the child perceives events as random because he is powerless to change the situation and therefore adopts a passive attitude. The text is understated with respect to his emotional response to his situation; its colloquial constructions combined with the impersonal pronoun ("on se fichait pas mal") distance the text from pathos and yet also suggest, in their abruptness, the underlying shock and hostility that lie behind the child's apathetic stance. The young Perec's isolation from his surroundings is paralleled, in the fictional part of the work, by the autistic state of the deaf and mute child Gaspard Winckler (whose name has been appropriated by the adult narrator of this section). On the intertextual level, we detect an echo of the protagonist's deliberate indifference in *Un homme qui dort.*

The passivity that acts as a defense mechanism for the young Perec is elsewhere suggested to be potentially dangerous. In chapter 8 of *W ou le souvenir d'enfance,* Perec suggests that his mother allowed her fate to be determined by chance events:

> Elle tenta plus tard, me raconta-t-on, de passer la Loire. Le passeur qu'elle alla trouver, et dont sa belle-sœur, déjà en zone libre, lui avait communiqué l'adresse, se trouva être absent. Elle n'insista pas davantage et retourna à Paris. On lui conseilla de déménager, de se cacher. Elle n'en fit rien. (*W,* 53)

> I've been told that later on she tried to cross the Loire. The runner she called on, who was to smuggle her across, and whose address had been passed on by her sister-in-law who was already in the free zone, turned out to be away. She didn't make a fuss and returned to Paris. She was advised to move house, to hide. She didn't bother. (*WMC,* 33)

Perec's detached tone thinly veils his bitterness. Implicit criticism marks the text's account of Cyrla Perec's response to the occupation—her belief that her status as a war widow would guarantee her safety; her decision to remain in Paris; and finally her presumed lack of comprehension when deported to Auschwitz: "Elle revit son pays natal avant de mourir. Elle mourut sans avoir compris" (She saw the country of her birth again before she died. She died without understanding) (*W*, 53/*WMC*, 33). Perec's laconic assertions deny his mother a final moment of lucidity that might give heroic dignity to her tragic confrontation with fate—just as he also refuses any heroic status to his father's death on the battlefield (*W*, 48). Such statements undoubtedly express the orphan's anger and sense of abandonment (a theme made explicit in the fictional part of *W*, in which we learn that Caecelia Winckler may have abandoned her young son, Gaspard). At the same time, we detect an echo of the "Ligne générale" texts and, in particular, of Perec's insistence that knowledge allows individuals to master situations. Perec suggests that the passive acceptance of events, allowing oneself to be the plaything of chance and history, constitutes an ethical failure.

Chapter 8 of *W* in fact consists of a montage of texts, including two in bold type which predate by more than fifteen years the rest of the chapter (*W*, 45–46), and which are subsequently commented on by notes that exceed in length the original texts. Perec's explanations allow us to date the earlier texts to 1959 or 1960. The chapter's endnotes question not only several details given by the younger Perec but also the earlier manner of telling the story: "Je ne dirais évidemment plus les choses de cette manière aujourd'hui" (I would not put things that way now, obviously) (*W*, 60/*WMC*, 39). The textual montage and the tone of the later segment attenuate the underlying aggressiveness of the text in bold type and implicitly cast doubt on the earlier description of Cyrla Perec's passivity. In the context of the chapter as a whole, it is clear that a complete comprehension of her dangerous position cannot have been available to her. Her belief that she would be safe was irrational only in relation to the greater irrationality of the Nazi plan. Nor is it certain that an awareness of the risks could have saved her. Despite the illusion of hindsight, we have no more knowledge of what might have been than she had knowledge about the future.

This reflection on the limits of knowledge clearly has implications for Perec's autobiographical project. No written relation of events, Perec acknowledges, can be the definitive one. Retrospection distorts our understanding of the past, and memory is intermittent and aleatory—as is Perec's writing process itself: he claims to assemble various details "complètement au hasard" (completely at random) (*W,* 61/*WMC,* 40). However, this randomness does not diminish the necessity of the individual's link to his or her past. In choosing to write of his personal history, Perec rejects his own earlier passivity, his sense that he had been released from the obligation of telling his story because history "had answered the question in my stead" (*W,* 17/*WMC,* 6). Perec's decision to explore his personal history through writing is a challenge to the violence and irrationality of history, which threatens to rob the individual of agency. In this sense, *W ou le souvenir d'enfance* is itself a repudiation of the fatalistic attitude that views events as inevitable and therefore refuses to examine and question them: "Je n'ai pas d'autre choix que d'évoquer ce que trop longtemps j'ai nommé l'irrévocable; ce qui fut, ce qui s'arrêta, ce qui fut clôturé: ce qui fut, sans doute, pour aujourd'hui ne plus être, mais ce qui fut aussi pour que je sois encore" (I have no alternative but to conjure up what for too many years I called the irrevocable; the things that were, the things that stopped, the things that were closed off—things that surely were and today are no longer, but things that also were so that I may still be) (*W,* 26/*WMC,* 13).

Coming to terms with the "irrévocable" is crucial to Perec's autobiographical project. The fictional section of *W* is in part an allegory of his search for identity through exploration of the past (in the first part of the text in italics the narrator, Gaspard Winckler, is sent in search of the child whose name he has adopted). It also raises the question of human knowledge of the future. The passengers and crew of the *Sylvandre,* having undertaken a voyage in the hope of curing the young Gaspard, place their hopes almost entirely in chance; they drift aimlessly across the ocean, convinced that an accidental miracle will lead them to a place where anything is possible (*W,* 42). This belief in the powers of chance transforms itself into a dangerous fatalism. The site of possibilities that the characters envisage does not materialize—or does so only in the nightmarish form of the island, W, described in the second half of the fictional text.[2]

Chance and the Law

The description of the island of W reveals the reversibility of the chance/fate opposition in the starkest of terms. Life on W is entirely devoted to the pursuit of sport and is founded on a system that distributes prizes and penalties. This system initially seems to be governed by strict hierarchies and fixed rules. Laws regulate the different types of sporting trials and competitions and clearly differentiate winners from losers. At first glance, W is a predictable world in which the best contender will necessarily win on each occasion. Even if its values, based entirely on physical prowess, are evidently questionable, W nevertheless seems to function as a just society according to its self-imposed values; it combines the Aristotelian principle of distributive justice with the ethics of sport to form a particular meritocratic model.[3]

However, as the narrator's account of life on W progresses, uncertainty gradually creeps into the picture. First of all, we learn that the consequences of winning or losing are extreme and that they depend on completely arbitrary factors:

> *Le triomphe réservé au vainqueur d'une Olympiade, et plus particulièrement à celui qui aura gagné la course des courses, c'est-à-dire le 100 m, aura peut-être comme conséquence la mort de celui qui sera arrivé le dernier. C'est une conséquence à la fois imprévisible et inéluctable. Si les Dieux sont pour lui, si nul dans le Stade ne tend vers lui son poing au pouce baissé, il aura sans doute la vie sauve et subira seulement les châtiments réservés aux autres vaincus [. . .]. Mais si un seul spectateur se lève et le désigne, appelant sur lui la punition réservée aux lâches, alors il sera mis à mort; la foule tout entière le lapidera.* (*W,* 148)

> *The triumphal celebration laid on for an Olympic winner, and most specially for the winner of the race of races, that is to say the 100 metres sprint, may result in the death of the man who comes last. This outcome is both unpredictable and inexorable. If the Gods are for him, if no one in the Stadium shows a clenched fist with the thumb pointed down, he will probably save his skin and undergo only the same punishment as the other losers [. . .]. But if one single spectator rises and points to him, calling down upon him the punishment meted out to the cowardly, then he will be put to death; the whole crowd will stone him.* (*WMC,* 110–11)

The pair of adjectives *imprévisible et inéluctable* (*unpredictable and inexorable*) aptly captures the tension between the random and the determined that is at the heart of the system. Gradually, we learn that this kind of arbitrariness intervenes at every level of the competition, and is in fact essential to the organization of W: "*Il faut savoir que le hasard fait aussi partie de la règle*" (*You have to know that chance is also one of the rules*) (*W,* 158/ *WMC,* 118). Chance determines not only the nature of the prize or penalty but also the outcome of the competitions. The best athlete cannot be sure of winning, for luck is more important than merit (*W,* 158). The principle of chance thus intervenes decisively in a world that is ostensibly based on the principle of skill.

Theories of play often set skill and chance in opposition. According to Roger Caillois' typology of play principles, for example, *agon* (rivalry based on skill or strength) and *alea* (chance) are fundamentally different in their moral implications: *agon* is considered "an active and fecund factor," *alea* "a passive and ruinous element."[4] Nevertheless, they may also be complementary—many types of games include elements of both; both principles call for rules and calculations. This coexistence is, in Caillois' view, a positive force because it creates hope for the weaker player:

> [Le vaincu] n'aurait plus rien à attendre, s'il ne lui restait, pour équilibrer son humiliation, la compensation, d'ailleurs infiniment improbable, d'un sourire gratuit des puissances fantasques du sort, inaccessibles, aveugles, implacables, mais qui, par bonheur, ignorent la justice.[5]

> The loser would have nothing more to hope for, if to counterbalance his humiliation he did not retain the—for that matter infinitely improbable—compensation of an unwarranted smile from the capricious powers of fate, which are inaccessible, blind, implacable, but which, happily, are ignorant of justice.

This passage would not be out of place in *W,* although in Perec's text the capricious powers of fate are much more sinister. The Officials who rule W—the "Gods of the Stadium"—are indeed inaccessible, blind, and implacable. On the island, the paradoxical alliance between *alea* and *agon* creates an "organized injustice" (*W,* 149/*WMC,* 111). In sporting competition, the worth of each participant should in principle be determined by performance according to a fixed set of rules. On W, however, this distributive principle can be violated: on occasion the weakest athlete may win, or the strongest may lose. The presence of arbitrary and unjust elements in the system is not motivated here by the wish to "give everyone a chance," as the narrator at one point ironically suggests (*W,* 158) and as is the case in Caillois' theory.[6] On the contrary, collusion with chance is intended to make the law of W all the more powerful and all the more oppressive:

> *La Loi est implacable, mais la Loi est imprévisible. Nul n'est censé l'ignorer, mais nul ne peut la connaître. Entre ceux qui la subissent et ceux qui l'édictent se dresse une barrière infranchissable. L'Athlète doit savoir que rien n'est sûr; il doit s'attendre à tout, au meilleur et au pire; les décisions qui le concernent, qu'elles soient futiles ou vitales, sont prises en dehors de lui; il n'a aucun contrôle sur elles.* (*W,* 157)

> *The Law is implacable, but the Law is unpredictable. The Law must be known by all, but the Law cannot be known. Between those who live under its sway and those who pronounce it stands an insurmountable barrier. The Athlete must know that nothing is certain; he must expect anything, the best outcome or the worst. Decisions concerning him, whether they be trivial or vital, are taken without reference to him; he has no control over them.* (*WMC,* 117)

A dream narrative recorded by Perec in May 1968 anticipates his description of W. In the dream, Perec narrowly avoids torture but realizes that this lucky escape itself proves that he is in a concentration camp: "Ce qui me sauve, c'est seulement l'indifférence du tortionnaire, sa liberté de faire ou de ne pas faire; je suis entièrement soumis à son arbitraire" (*BO,* no. 1) (The only thing that saves me is the torturer's indifference, his freedom to act or not to act; I am entirely subject to his whims). The same logic is at play in W, where the Athlete must live each day under the "scornful and sarcastic eyes" of his Judges (*W,* 218/*WMC,* 159).

In the final pages of Camus' *L'Étranger,* Meursault bemoans the lack of proportion between the arbitrariness of the judgment that condemned him and the inevitable chain of events it set in motion. This absurdity might be tempered, he thinks, by reforming the law to include chance: "L'essentiel était de donner une seule chance au condamné. Une seule sur mille, cela suffisait pour arranger bien les choses" (The most important thing was to give the condemned man a chance. Even one in a thousand was good enough to set things right).[7] In Perec's dystopian vision, however, the intervention of chance simply confirms the arbitrariness of the judgment without compensating for it. The notion of an inaccessible, unknowable law, to which individuals are nonetheless subject, is more reminiscent of Kafka's works, where, as Gilles Deleuze and Félix Guattari argue, "la justice n'est pas Nécessité, mais au contraire Hasard" (justice is not Necessity, but on the contrary, Chance).[8] At the same time, the attribution of a special place to apparent chance within a utopia can be traced back to Plato's *Repub-*

lic. In order to arrange the breeding of the guardian class according to the rulers' decisions, for example, Socrates asserts that "some ingenious kind of lots" should be arranged so that the less worthy men and women "will accuse their own ill-luck and not the rulers."[9] There are other points of similarity between Perec's Athletes and the guardians of Plato's Kallipolis: in Plato the braver and better guardians have first choice of women and may have more wives and are also rewarded with a larger share of food and drink; they have to undergo a series of trials and tests of their physical and psychological strength; children, like the offspring of Perec's Athletes, are removed from their parents and placed in separate quarters.[10] However, whereas in Plato the use of deceitful strategies as well as laws is justified by the rulers' concern for the happiness of the city as a whole (the rulers' lies are likened to a medicine),[11] in Perec's allegory, those in power are far from acting for the good of the Athletes. Their very impartiality and indifference are sinister symptoms of their unjust power.[12]

Life as Lottery: Perec and Borges

Critics have explored other intertextual connections, for instance, between *W ou le souvenir d'enfance* and the works of Jules Verne.[13] I will pause here to consider another link: Perec's treatment of the themes of chance and necessity echoes Borges's story "The Lottery in Babylon" (a text with which Perec was certainly familiar).[14] Borges's narrator describes a society that functions entirely on the basis of chance: everything is decided by a lottery in which all inhabitants participate. We learn of the lottery's gradual progression from an innocuous game (people could win small prizes by drawing a ticket) to a complete system of government: the lottery distributes lucky and unlucky numbers that have incalculable consequences, ranging from promotion and the fulfillment of various wishes to mutilation and even death.[15]

As in Perec's text, chance becomes the basis for law and is transformed into necessity. While *W* describes this form of arbitrary distribution as organized injustice, Borges's narrator suggests that it is in fact more just than any other system since all people, regardless of wealth or status, are subject to the same arbitrariness. Indeed, the people of Babylon themselves campaign to make the lottery "secret, free of charges, and open to all," and in this they achieve their "generous objectives."[16] Although this presentation of the lottery as a democratic model is ironic, it nevertheless reminds us that the impersonality of chance is a guarantee of fairness in many a game, and that this equality is the guiding principle for lotteries. The logic of games of chance, their form of "justice," is not that of meritocracy but that of equal probabilities for each player at the outset of play; thus a lottery is unfair if somebody is chosen for a particular reason. In Borges's story, chance establishes a perverse type of equality between individuals. In *W,* the combination of chance and competition, *agon* and *alea,* has the effect of distorting all values and rendering any form of justice impossible. In both cases, the game becomes deadly serious. The Babylonians and the W Athletes live in a constant state of hope and fear, rendered powerless by the uncertainty that touches every moment of existence.

The most troubling dimension of both stories is doubtless the alliance of chance with arbitrary power. The law of chance is ideally an impersonal principle, producing unmotivated decisions independent of human influence. However, in both *W ou le souvenir d'enfance* and "The Lottery in Babylon" (as in Plato's *Republic*), chance events are in fact controlled, and indeed generated, by those in power. On the island of W, chance becomes synonymous with the will of the Officials. Perec uses chiasmus to emphasize the equivalence between two forms of arbitrariness:

> *Ils peuvent laisser faire, comme ils peuvent interdire; ils peuvent entériner le choix du hasard ou lui préférer un hasard de leur choix; ils peuvent décider, et revenir à tout instant sur leur décision.* (*W,* 209–10)

> *They can sanction, just as they can veto; they can uphold the choice of fate, or choose a different fatality, at random; they make the decisions, and they can change them at any time.* (*WMC,* 154)

Similarly, Borges's Babylonian lottery is governed by a sinister Company that holds total authority. The Company acts secretly, but its actions cannot be criticized because they all take place in the name of chance; errors in the system can only be a corroboration of the founding principle.[17] Like the rulers of the stadium in *W,* the Company possesses godlike power. The apparently accidental events on which everything depends come to be seen as the actions of an all-encompassing fate that knowingly but secretly manipulates individual lives. Fate, chance, and the decisions of the Company all ultimately merge into a terrifying unity, in the face of which the Babylonians remain generally uncurious: "They obey the dictates of chance, surrender their lives, their hopes, their nameless terror to it, but it never occurs to them to delve into its labyrinthine laws or the revolving spheres that manifest its workings."[18] They thus remain passive in the face of the powers that govern their lives.

Perec's Athletes adopt a similar attitude toward their destiny:

> *Immergé dans un monde sans frein, ignorant des Lois qui l'écrasent, tortionnaire ou victime de ses compagnons sous le regard ironique et méprisant de ses Juges, l'Athlète W ne sait pas où sont ses véritables ennemis, ne sait pas qu'il pourrait les vaincre et que cette Victoire serait la seule vraie qu'il pourrait remporter, la seule qui le délivrerait. Mais sa vie et sa mort lui semblent inéluctables, inscrites une fois pour toutes dans un destin innommable.* (*W*, 218)

> *Submerged in a world unchecked, with no knowledge of the Laws that crush him, a torturer or a victim of his co-villagers, under the scornful and sarcastic eyes of the Judges, the W Athlete does not know where his real enemies are, does not know that he could beat them or that such a win would be the only true Victory he could score, the only one which would liberate him. But his own life and death seem to him ineluctable, inscribed once and for all in an unspeakable fate.* (*WMC*, 159–60)

Here the narrator departs from his habitually detached stance to comment on the Athlete's ignorance and to suggest that his fatalistic belief in an "ineluctable," unspeakable destiny is an illusion. We are reminded of Perec's remarks on his mother's lack of awareness of her situation. The implied judgment is rather puzzling: how can the Athlete know the laws that oppress him when these laws are subject to constant and arbitrary alteration? Could he necessarily conquer his true enemies even if he recognized them? Does the conditional tense ("pourrait les vaincre," "pourrait remporter," "délivrerait") designate a real potentiality? It is difficult to see what kind of victory the narrator envisages, when the path to knowledge and power has been cut off. Nevertheless, the Athlete apparently stands accused of naive passivity. Instead of seeking understanding of the situation, "*il préfère croire à son Étoile. Il attend que la chance lui sourie*" (*he would rather believe in his Star. He waits for luck to smile on him*) (*W*, 218/*WMC*, 160). The cruelty of the text's irony is striking: what the Athlete takes as the symbol of luck—his "Star"—is evidently, in this context, the very sign that marks him out for destruction. Luck will always be on the side of the "Gods of the Stadium." In another reversal that transforms a sign of good fortune into the indication of a terrible destiny, the crowning moment of an Athlete's career—the honor of being elected to carry the Olympic Flame to the "Central Pyre" (ibid.)—takes on sinister meaning as it evokes the crematory ovens of the concentration camps.

Despite his ignorance and culpable passivity, the W Athlete remains curious about his destiny:

> *L'un des traits ultimes de la société W est que l'on y interroge sans cesse le destin: avec de la mie de pain longtemps pétrie, les Sportifs se fabriquent des osselets, des petits dés. Ils interprètent le passage des oiseaux, la forme des nuages, des flaques, la chute des feuilles. Ils collectionnent des talismans: une pointe de la chaussure d'un Champion olympique, un ongle de pendu. Des jeux de cartes ou de tarots circulent dans les chambrées: la chance décide du partage des paillasses, des rations et des corvées. Tout un système de paris clandestins, que l'Administration contrôle en sous-main par l'intermédiaire de ses petits officiels, accompagne les Compétitions.* (*W*, 218–19)

> *One of the ultimate features of W society is that fate is constantly being questioned: with bits of bread laboriously rolled between their fingers, Sportsmen make themselves dibs or little dice. They read the meaning of the flights of birds, of the shapes of clouds and puddles, of falling leaves. They collect talismans: a spike from an Olympic Champion's running shoe, a hanged man's fingernail. Sets of playing cards and tarot cards go the rounds of the barracks: games of chance settle the share-outs of bedding, of rations and of chores. A whole system of clandestine gambling, deviously controlled by the Administration through its petty officials, is attached to the Competitions.* (*WMC*, 160)

Games of chance here represent an effort not only to deal with the unbearable nature of experience, but also to attain knowledge of the future—to discover whether or not luck, or the Gods, are on one's side. As with Borges's Babylonians, the notions of chance and destiny are merged, and the outcome of a particular game is treated as a premonition. The various games of chance become the equivalent of superstitious practices: the construal of natural occurrences as portents of the individual's destiny, the use of random objects as talismans. On one level, these practices rest on a rejection of chance: everything is believed to possess a meaning, if only it can be correctly interpreted. Yet these games and superstitions are also, paradoxically, based on the assumption that the future is uncertain, on the hope that a miracle could occur at any moment and put an end to the Athlete's suffering. This form of optimism is almost tantamount to complicity with the system. Although the Athlete does seek knowledge of this destiny, he remains trapped by the illusion that he can gain access to the law and predict its decisions in order to win the game. But the Gods to whom he appeals are none other than the Officials, whose goal is not to save but to destroy. Chance does not offer the Athletes the possibility of escape since it is itself used as a means of oppression and has been entirely incorporated into the system, "*cette machine énorme dont chaque rouage participe, avec une efficacité implacable, à l'anéantissement des hommes*" (*this huge machine, each cog of which contributes with implacable efficiency to the systematic annihilation of men*) (*W,* 220/*WMC,* 161).

At this point, Perec's allegory is at its most transparent—the island becomes a concentration camp—but also at its most problematic in its apparent emphasis on the complicity of the victims and their victimization of each other. However odd this representation may seem, charges of Jewish passivity and failure to resist were in fact aired in the years when Holocaust consciousness first emerged. As Hannah Arendt reports, the prosecutor in the Eichmann trial of 1961 repeatedly asked witnesses the "cruel and silly question" of why they did not revolt.[19] In France, the preoccupation with passivity versus heroism became an object of controversy in 1966, when Jean-François Steiner published an account of the revolt organized by the prisoners at the extermination camp of Treblinka. Steiner, the son of a Holocaust victim, spoke in a notorious interview of his earlier sense of shame that Jews had been led "like lambs to the slaughter."[20] The Treblinka revolt also raised the question of Jewish participation in the functioning of the camps—anticipating another controversy in the same year following the appearance in France of Hannah Arendt's *Eichmann in Jerusalem,* which criticized the collaboration of the Jewish councils with the Nazis. In addition, Steiner's book provoked debate by insisting on the particularity of the Jewish fate during the war.[21]

Perec does not directly mention these debates. Yet it is surely significant that between his "Ligne générale" essay on Robert Antelme and the writing of *W ou le souvenir d'enfance* lies what Samuel Moyn calls a pivotal moment between "two major regimes of memory of French postwar life"—the first dominated by a *résistancialiste* discourse of deportation that assumed the unity of Nazi criminality, and the second by an increasing emphasis on the specificity of Jewish victimhood.[22] Nevertheless, Perec's main source of information on the camps seems to be *L'Univers concentrationnaire* (*The Universe of the Concentration Camp*), published in 1946 by David Rousset, a Resistance fighter who had been imprisoned at Buchenwald. Beyond Perec's own childhood fantasy of an island dedicated to sport (*W,* 17–18), and the association with Leni Riefenstahl's film of the 1936 Berlin Olympics (the source of the phrase "the Gods of the Stadium" that appears twice in Perec's text; *W,* 161 and 219),[23] Perec finds justification for the sports analogy in a passage from Rousset's text, quoted toward the end of *W.* Rousset describes life in the camp as an intensely competitive struggle for survival; the camp's organization pits victim against victim precisely by implicating them in the system. Although the SS officers themselves exercise control from the outside, they do so by creating divisions among the prisoners that make any kind of unified opposition impossible.[24] While Perec's description of the W Athlete echoes Rousset's account, it is important to note that Rousset (one of Steiner's antagonists in the *Treblinka* controversy) does not see the victims' lack of resistance as a moral failing: the hierarchies and divisions of the camp are an inherent, inescapable part of the system. Nevertheless, solidarity is presented as a central moral problem in another Resistance deportee's account of the camps, Robert Antelme's *L'Espèce humaine,*[25] and Perec focuses on this point in his laudatory article of 1963 (*L.G.,* 100–101).[26]

The moral dimension of the concentration camp experience is thus a key concern. However, if Perec prefers the universalist discourse of a David Rousset to the Jewish particularism articulated by Jean-François Steiner,[27] this also suggests that the allegory of W lends itself to multiple readings. Indeed, in the final sentence of *W ou le souvenir d'enfance,* Perec explicitly extends the meaning of this story to other periods of history: "Les fascistes de Pinochet se sont chargés de donner à mon fantasme une ultime résonance: plusieurs îlots de la Terre de Feu sont aujourd'hui des camps de déportation" (Pinochet's Fascists have provided my fantasy with a final echo: several of the islands in [Tierra del Fuego] are today deportation camps) (*W,* 222/*WMC,* 164). The island of W can stand for other forms of totalitarianism, and also for the entire organization of societies, as well as for the places in which they imprison their victims. As Manet van Montfrans has noted, Perec's description of W parallels Hannah Arendt's discussion of totalitarianism as constituted by a contradiction between the omnipresence of the law and its incessant transgression.[28] Perec's implicit allusion to Leni Riefenstahl's documentary reminds us of the Nazi preoccupation with sport and physical prowess, and Hans Hartje has pointed out the connections between some elements of *W* and French life under the occupation, in particular the promotion of sport in Vichy France.[29] Other historical events, such as the Vél'd'Hiv roundup of Jews in 1942 or the more recent terrorist massacre of Israeli athletes at the 1972 Munich Olympic Games, are also in the background of *W.*[30] Sport is almost always presented as politically dubious in Perec's works. In *"53 jours,"* for example, the city of Grianta is chosen to be the host of the "Panafrican Games," but when the corrupt and dictatorial government starts to build a stadium (an enterprise partially funded by a lottery), the construction collapses and kills eleven people (*"53J,"* 68).

In this context, we should not read Perec's account of the W Athletes simply as an indictment of the victims' passivity; it has a more general application to those who fail to resist corrupt systems. The comparison with Borges's "Lottery in Babylon" further illuminates the universalizing dimension of Perec's text. The Officials of W, like Borges's Company, are the "Gods" who maliciously control human existence, implementing a Law that is both inexorable, since their power enforces it, and uncertain, since it is based on chance. The logic of W and that of Babylon thereby implements an extreme version of fate, which is made to coincide with chance: unpredictable events strike without warning, transforming the individual into the passive instrument of those in power. Of course, there are key differences between the two texts. In Borges's story, it is never entirely certain that the Company actually exists, for it could simply be a projection of the Babylonians' belief in destiny.[31] *W,* on the other hand, explicitly links its fiction to the reality of a specific historical moment, and it is the total oppression implemented by the "Gods of the Stadium" that creates the particular existential situation in which fate and chance are merged.[32]

Thus there is at the heart of *W ou le souvenir d'enfance* a tension between the generalizing drive of allegorical description and the concrete particularity of a historical situation—a tension that dramatizes the impossibility of representation itself. A sense of descriptive failure hovers over not only the fictional section of Perec's text but also the autobiographical account that can never encompass the truth of the past. The text's ethical judgments, including its speculation on the possibility of resistance or escape, present themselves as provisional and unreliable, situated at the limits of moral imagination and historical understanding. Chance has an ambiguous status in this context, standing as both a pretext for avoiding responsibility and a true limit to human possibilities.

Possibilities

Reading *W ou le souvenir d'enfance* in conjunction with Borges's story sheds light on the broader significance of chance, destiny, and freedom in Perec's work as a whole. Michel Viegnes points out that games of chance in the European literary tradition can be identified either with fatalistic passivity or with revolt.[33] Perec's works thematize this ambiguity, as is evidenced by the futile attempts of the W Athletes to manipulate their destinies through play. In the fictional section of *W*, for example, games occur on two levels: on the one hand, agonistic competition is gradually transformed into a game of chance through the arbitrariness and uncertainty of the rules; on the other hand, games of chance (the dice fabricated by the Athletes) have a secondary role and are used as a means of predicting the outcome of the first type of game (the athletic competitions) and thereby of examining—or even hoping to change—destiny itself.

Although the stakes may be lower in Perec's other works, games of chance are always presented as inherently ambiguous. In *Les Choses*, Jérôme and Sylvie are drawn to the uncertainty and promise of such play. Admittedly, they do not take great risks in order to obtain the wealth they covet. They fantasize about stealing money but do no such thing;[34] they are too passive—or perhaps too rational—even to buy a lottery ticket. However, they invest in their poker games "un acharnement qui, à certains instants, pouvait paraître suspect" (a relentlessness which at times could look suspicious), even if the stakes involved are very low (*C*, 104–5/*T*, 87). If they win, they feel themselves to be almost heroic (*C*, 105). The essence of this experience lies not so much in the magnitude of the risk or of the prize, as in the sense that "ils avaient forcé la chance" (they had pushed lady luck their way) (*C*, 105/*T*, 87). Of course, this sense of control over their fortunes is really an illusion. Similar in this respect to the Athletes of *W*, Jérôme and Sylvie choose the wrong means of examining their destinies: their poker games create a sense of infinite possibilities, but these possibilities remain within the system they are attempting to dominate. Neither material gain nor the euphoria of winning would take them outside the circle of desire and acquisition that controls their lives. The poker games also serve as a substitute for risks the characters do not take elsewhere (in political action, for example). They are a pseudoactivity, for chance is expected to intervene on the couple's behalf. Jérôme and Sylvie live in a perpetual state of waiting: "Ils attendaient de vivre, ils attendaient l'argent" (They were waiting to live, they were waiting for money) (*C,* 28/*T,* 34). They do appear to break out of this passivity at the end of the novel, but only by resigning themselves to being players in a different kind of game, one which will bring them not sudden fortune but comfortable earnings. Happiness, on the other hand, may have eluded them.

It is perhaps too easy to condemn Jérôme and Sylvie for their illusions of power and possibility. Whereas Roger Caillois emphasizes the separation between games and everyday life, other thinkers, such as Henri Lefebvre and Serge Moscovici, insist on their close connection. According to Lefebvre, games of chance allow consciousness of and imagined domination over a human situation that is experienced as inherently double: "On the one hand chance, the non-domination of nature (and of one's own nature); on the other hand freedom (but empty freedom, the freedom to benefit from chance)."[35] Moscovici argues that the psychology of the lottery is not irrational but involves a strategy to open up closed situations and create a world of possibilities: "We play chance against determinism, the extraordinary against the ordinary, saying to ourselves, once again: 'Why not me?'"[36] Indeed, despite the narrator's ironic tone in *Les Choses,* the characters' fascination with games of chance is not entirely irrational: it represents the presence of hope, the constant expectation of the exceptional, and is therefore a comprehensible attitude toward the future.

In *La Vie mode d'emploi,* David Marcia similarly turns to games of chance as a strategy after a series of failures. Having had to renounce, in succession, motorcycling, car racing, record production, the direction of a holiday village, and the organization of a theater festival, David uses his income (from his mother's antiques business) to finance his new passion, games of chance and specifically roulette, at which he loses from 350 to 1,000 francs nearly every evening (*VME,* 433/*LUM,* 365). In other words, his path begins with a type of game dominated by the principle of *agon* but eventually moves to the sphere of *alea,* the pure chance of roulette, where success and failure no longer depend on his own talents.[37] And still he loses. Lino Margay is more successful when he takes a gamble based on the same principle: "Il avait confié au hasard le soin de choisir sa destination ultime; il avait ouvert un atlas et sans le regarder avait planté une épingle sur une carte du monde; le hasard, après être plusieurs fois tombé en pleine mer, avait fini par désigner l'Amérique du Sud" (He had left it to fate to decide his final destination; he had opened an atlas and had stuck a pin in a map of the world without looking: fate, after falling a few times into the ocean waves, had in the end indicated South America) (*VME,*

423/*LUM,* 355–56). The pin's initial indications demonstrate the absurdity of Margay's appeal to chance, yet in another sense his action is not at all senseless. Having been horrifically injured in a bicycle accident and then abandoned by his wife, Margay has little to lose, and it matters little if chance's "choices" are illogical. Chance is a substitute for his own will, and he entrusts his future to it, hoping to open up a new, unexpected set of possibilities that will allow him to find a way out of a desperate situation. The strategy is successful: he makes his fortune in South America as a gangster, has plastic surgery to restore his good looks, and wins back his wife. This story is in fact a rewriting of "Beauty and the Beast": the couple "belle" and "bête" is one of the hidden constraints used for this particular chapter of *La Vie mode d'emploi.* (Even if the reader is not aware of this, the ending of Margay's story, along with the explicit mention of *La Belle et la bête* that precedes it [*VME,* 416], function as clues for the reader.) Although good luck rarely produces such happy consequences in Perec's stories, its intervention here creates the preprogrammed, if improbable, fairy-tale ending.

Games of Anti-Chance

Un homme qui dort works in a different narrative mode—one where such solutions are inaccessible. For the protagonist, openness to future possibilities is replaced by apathy. Significantly, the protagonist's withdrawal from society is evoked metaphorically using terms that refer to games of chance: "Tu retires du jeu tes billes et tes épingles. Tu ne mets aucune chance de ton côté, aucun œuf dans nul panier" (You're getting out while the going's good. You're not stacking any odds in your favour or putting any eggs in any baskets) (*UHD,* 45/*MA,* 156). The "man asleep" refuses to play, or rather chooses only solitary games such as pinball (*UHD,* 106) or patience, a game in which "la chance ne joue presque aucun rôle" (chance has virtually no role to play) (*UHD,* 72/*MA,* 174).[38] Although he spends hours doing this, very little seems to be at stake, for he does not believe that victory has any significance: "Ce n'est pas la victoire qui t'importe, car, que voudrait dire ta victoire, et s'il ne s'agit que d'avoir avec toi les dieux, il y a tellement de façons plus faciles de s'attirer leur bienveillance" (Winning doesn't matter to you, for what would winning mean to you anyway, and if it's just a question of having the gods on your side, there are easier ways of inducing them to look kindly on you) (*UHD,* 73/*MA,* 174).

Even if the protagonist allows himself to drift through the streets of

Paris "au hasard"—at random, without goal or method (*UHD,* 62)—this action is symptomatic not of receptiveness to unexpected possibilities but rather of a willed rejection of these possibilities as irrelevant. His attempt to retreat from society recalls the Stoic project of self-sufficiency and indifference to external things—the attempt to reach a state of *ataraxia.* Yet the novel also presents this refusal to engage with others as an ethically problematic escapism. The same observations apply to Grégoire Simpson, a character whose story, recounted in chapter 52 of *La Vie mode d'emploi,* is an abbreviated, third-person version of *Un homme qui dort.* Grégoire Simpson (whose name recalls the Gregor Samsa of Kafka's *Metamorphosis*) is a student who begins to spend his days wandering through Paris: "Il se laissait dériver, allait au hasard, plongeait dans la cohue des sorties de bureaux" (He let himself wander, going wherever the whim took him, plunging into the five-o'clock bustle of office workers) (*VME,* 290–91/*LUM,* 237). Eventually, he renounces even this activity and shuts himself away in his room before disappearing without a trace. These characters are apparently not enthralled by the workings of chance. Their passivity is not that of Jérôme and Sylvie, governed by hope for a stroke of luck, but one that sees all events and choices as equivalent. Their intention is to create a world with no possibilities and no surprises. This willed attempt to suspend the will recalls Nietzsche's analysis of the ascetic ideal: human beings "will rather will nothingness than not will."[39]

There is a fine line, in *Un homme qui dort,* between the acceptance and the rejection of chance. The fact that the "man asleep" continues to play games—and sometimes to cheat[40]—indicates that he still believes, on some level, that the outcome is tied to a higher necessity. Far from being indifferent to his destiny, he in fact attempts to control it, and his choice of games of skill over games of chance is a response to this need. For the same reason, his apparent submission to chance eventually gives way to a desperate attempt to create order and exclude chance, as he invents rules to govern his budget, his movements, his meals, indeed his every action:

> Tu règles ta vie comme une montre, comme si le meilleur moyen de ne pas te perdre, de ne pas sombrer tout à fait, était de te livrer à des tâches dérisoires, de tout décider à l'avance, de ne rien laisser au hasard. Que ta vie soit close, lisse, ronde comme un œuf, que tes gestes soient fixés par un ordre immuable qui décide tout pour toi, qui te protège malgré toi. (*UHD,* 120)

> You set your life like a watch, as if the best means of saving yourself, of avoiding going under altogether, were to set yourself derisory tasks, to decide everything in advance, to leave nothing to chance. Let your life be closed, smooth, rounded and full, let your actions be dictated by a fixed, immutable order which decides everything on your behalf, which protects you against yourself. (*MA,* 204)

By replacing chance with rules, the protagonist attempts to eliminate unpredictability and enclose his life in a fixed, predetermined order. However, in order to establish the system that will supposedly govern his existence for him, he needs constantly to multiply his rules, making increasingly arbitrary decisions: "Tu t'imposes des interdits puérils. Tu ne marches pas sur l'intersection des pavés au bord des trottoirs. Tu respectes les sens giratoires, les stationnements interdits. Tu ne supportes pas d'être en retard ou en avance. Tu voudrais allumer tes cigarettes toutes les quarante-cinq minutes" (You impose childish constraints on yourself. You do not step on the cracks between the paving slabs near the kerbside, you go the right way around traffic islands, you observe parking restrictions. You cannot stand being late or early. You would like to light your cigarettes at intervals of precisely forty-five minutes) (*UHD,* 121/*MA,* 205).

According to Isabelle Dangy-Scaillierez, the majority of Perec's characters are "orphans of the law."[41] This is certainly true of the protagonist of *Un homme qui dort,* who responds to this absence by attempting to construct his own law. This compulsive rule maker does not in fact construct an impersonal system but rather asserts a desire for mastery, since the system is founded on an act of will. In formulating rules, the protagonist is also motivated by an obscure desire for transgression: "Comme si, à tout instant, tu attendais du moindre de tes fléchissements qu'il t'entraîne tout de suite trop loin" (It is as if you were living with the constant dread that the slightest weakening of your resolution might, all at once, take you too far) (*UHD,* 121/*MA,* 205). This kind of rule making is both a form of resistance to what Johan Huizinga sees as the true spirit of play—the acceptance of pure fortuitousness[42]—and a species of game in its own right, founded on the anxious need to eliminate chance. We are closer here to Freud's notion of the game as the compulsive enactment of an instinct for mastery, and as a means of dealing with overpowering experiences, than to Huizinga's "merry play mood."[43]

While the protagonist of *Un homme qui dort* most clearly exemplifies the obsessive side of play and the ambiguity of the impulse to abolish chance, *La Vie mode d'emploi* contains numerous characters who elaborate compulsive systems of rules. One such system is the methodical avarice that governs Adèle Plassaert's existence in its most minute details, leading her to record every household expense each day "avec une précision qui ne laisse rien au hasard" (with an exactness that leaves nothing to chance) (*VME,* 306/*LUM,* 251). Another is the complex scheme developed by the antiques dealer Madame Marcia to govern the transfer and exchange of furniture and other objects between the four rooms of her apartment and store; her rules are illustrated in the text by a diagram that parodies Greimas' semantic square (*VME,* 136). Most significantly, the refusal of chance and the formulation of strict rules are essential to Bartlebooth's project:

> Excluant tout recours au hasard, l'entreprise ferait fonctionner le temps et l'espace comme des coordonnées abstraites où viendraient s'inscrire avec une récurrence inéluctable des événements identiques se produisant inexorablement dans leur lieu, à leur date. (*VME,* 153)

> All recourse to chance would be ruled out, and the project would make time and space serve as the abstract coordinates plotting the ineluctable recursion of identical events occurring inexorably in their allotted places, on their allotted dates. (*LUM,* 118)

Bartlebooth aims for nothing less than the conversion of disorder into order, the reduction of the real to an abstract schema, entirely governed by his project. At first view, this enterprise begins successfully and in accordance with its principles: Bartlebooth finds a painter (Valène) to teach him the art of watercolor, and a talented jigsaw-maker (Winckler) to cut up his canvases; he travels the world and paints his seascapes. He nevertheless involves chance in his project from the outset, in apparent violation of his principles, when he chooses the places to represent in his seascapes: "Les ports furent choisis plus ou moins au hasard par Bartlebooth qui, feuilletant des atlas, des livres de géographie, des récits de voyages et des dépliants touristiques, cochait au fur et à mesure les endroits qui lui plaisaient" (The ports were chosen more or less at random by Bartlebooth, who thumbed through atlases, geography books, travellers' tales, and tourist brochures and ticked off the places that appealed to him) (*VME,* 80/*LUM,* 52). Chance sometimes enters into the project for reasons beyond Bartlebooth's control, for example due to the contingencies of his travels which compromise the temporal progression of the program (*VME,* 462). In other respects, however, this randomness is a constitutive element of the system. Why paint seascapes and not landscapes, for example, and why precisely five hundred watercolors in twenty years? The complete exclusion of chance is an impossible ideal: in order to attain it, each principle that Bartlebooth establishes (such as the number of ports to be painted) would require another to justify it, leading to infinite regression. This is precisely what occurs in *Un homme qui dort,* where the protagonist tries to exclude chance from his life through existential constraints; instead of tranquilly living a life in which everything is decided in advance, he constantly and compulsively invents new rules.

Through games of chance on the one hand and rule-governed systems on the other, Perec's characters attempt to confront and control reality. From the examples discussed so far, Perec's perspective—and certainly the view of many of his characters—seems close to Roger Caillois' judgment that chance is a "passive and ruinous element." While the passive fascination with chance is often symptomatic of an ethical failure (*Les Choses, W*), the invention of rules that work against chance represents an active effort by the individual to control his or her destiny. However, this effort poses its own problems, often taking on obsessive and megalomaniacal proportions (the "man asleep," Bartlebooth). Furthermore, just as *agon* is compromised by *alea* in *W,* rules never completely succeed in eliminating chance.

Fortune and Fate

The themes of struggle with or acceptance of chance in Perec are further complicated by the frequent association of chance with some kind of transcendent force: destiny or the will of the "Gods of the Stadium" in *W* and "the gods" again in *Un homme qui dort.* As occurs in *W,* games of chance are associated with superstitious practices, providing a means by which characters try to obtain signs and portents regarding the future. *La Vie mode d'emploi* provides us with another example in the story of Sven Ericsson's vengeful pursuit of Elizabeth de Beaumont. Having sought Elizabeth systematically, multiplying his traps but failing to find her, Ericsson has a dream:

> Installé à côté d'un immense tableau noir couvert d'équations, un mathématicien finissait de démontrer devant une assistance houleuse que le

fameux théorème dit "de Monte-Carlo" était généralisable; cela voulait dire que non seulement un joueur de roulette misant au hasard avait au moins autant de chances de gagner qu'un joueur misant selon une martingale infaillible, mais que moi-même j'avais autant sinon davantage de chances de découvrir Elizabeth en allant prendre le thé chez Rumpelmayer le lendemain à seize heures dix-huit minutes qu'en la faisant rechercher par quatre cent treize détectives. (*VME,* 187)

> Standing beside a huge blackboard covered in equations, a mathematician was concluding his demonstration, in front of a turbulent audience, that the celebrated "Monte Carlo theorem" was generalisable; that meant not just that a roulette player placing his stake on a random number had just as much chance of winning as a martingale player systematically doubling his stake on the same number on each loss in order to recoup eventually, but that I had as much if not more chance of finding Elizabeth by going to Rumpelmeyer's for tea next day at sixteen hours eighteen minutes precisely than by having four hundred and thirteen detectives looking for her. (*LUM,* 146–47)

After Ericsson accordingly looks for Elizabeth at 1618, to no avail, one of his detectives then suggests that he has misinterpreted the dream: "413 était évidemment l'inverse de 314, c'est-à-dire du nombre π: c'est à 18 h 16 qu'il se serait passé quelque chose" (413 was obviously the inverse of 314, that is to say of the number π: something would have happened at 18 hours 16 minutes) (*VME,* 187/*LUM,* 147). As a result Ericsson falls into mysticism, appealing to the "épuisantes ressources de l'irrationnel" (the exhausting resources of the irrational) (*VME,* 187/*LUM,* 147) by wearing various rings and magnets and consulting magicians and witches who, among other activities, throw dice (*VME,* 188). Interpreting every accidental event as meaningful, he treats chance as only an appearance that disguises a hidden order—an order that the individual must uncover and exploit. Is there a causal relationship between Ericsson's gestures and the "coup de théâtre" that occurs shortly afterward, when one of his detectives finally tracks down Elizabeth (*VME,* 187–88)? The novel does not confirm or contradict this hypothesis, but in any case Ericsson is henceforth able to trace his victim's movements and to carry out his planned revenge. Elizabeth, in turn, comes to accept the inevitability of her death, writing to Ericsson that "la chance et l'argent ont été et seront toujours de votre côté" (you will always have luck and money on your side) (*VME,* 190/*LUM,* 149). From Elizabeth's point of view, the dice have been fixed; chance, destiny, and Ericsson's wishes are one and the same.

As Serge Moscovici remarks, "[Chance] carries with it a demonic image of a force that works against you, that prevents you from doing as you wish, that can ruin your efforts."[44] The vision of chance as a capricious power can be traced back to the ancient and medieval figure of Fortune. Perec, for his part, does not often invoke Fortune, although *Les Choses* plays on the double meaning of the word: "Ils savaient tout de l'ascension de ces chéris de la Fortune: chevaliers d'industrie, polytechniciens intègres, requins de la finance, littérateurs sans ratures" (They knew all there was to know about the rise of such men kissed by Fortune—captains of industry, incorruptible, glittering prize-winners from Ecole Polytechnique, financial wizards, men of letters without a smudge) (*C,* 99/*T,* 83). Chance is also sometimes identified with fate, as in the following passage from *La Vie mode d'emploi:*

> Au cours d'une réception que donnait le duc de Crécy-Couvé [. . .] [Laurelle de Dinteville] porta un toast à sa future belle-famille en vidant d'un trait une coupe de champagne et en la lançant dans l'air. La fatalité voulut qu'elle se trouvât alors juste au-dessous d'un gigantesque lustre qui provenait du célèbre atelier Baucis de Murano. Le lustre se rompit, provoquant la mort de huit personnes [. . .]. François de Dinteville, oncle de Laurelle, qui assistait à la réception, émit l'hypothèse d'une "amplification pendulaire enclenchée par les phases vibratoires antagonistes de la coupe de cristal et du lustre," mais personne ne voulut prendre cette explication au sérieux. (*VME,* 78)

> During a reception given by the Duke of Crécy-Couvé [. . .] [Laurelle de Dinteville] drank a toast to her future in-laws, emptying her champagne glass in a single draught, and then flung the glass in the air. Fate determined that she should be standing immediately beneath a gigantic chandelier, which came from the famous workshop of Baucis at Murano. The chandelier snapped and caused the deaths of eight people [. . .]. François de Dinteville, Laurelle's uncle, who was present at the reception, put forward the theory of "pendular amplification produced by the conflicting vibratory frequencies of the crystal glass and the chandelier" but no one took this explanation seriously. (*LUM,* 51)

Of course, it is possible to trace a causal chain: Laurelle decided to throw her champagne glass into the air; she had placed herself underneath a large chandelier; in accordance with certain physical laws (which François de Dinteville attempts to uncover), the force of the glass led to the fall of the chandelier; a certain number of people were, like Laurelle, close enough to be killed or injured by its fall. What is shocking, in these circumstances, is the suddenness and the unpredictability of this sequence, the interruption of human projects by unintended consequences, and above all the disproportion between the initial action (giving a toast) and the effect (the death of eight people).

In such a case, we are not interested in purely mechanical efficient causes (such as those presented in François de Dinteville's explanation) but are tempted to seek a hidden intention or force behind events.[45] The reference to fate is an instinctive response to a situation where we find only trivial causes but catastrophic consequences. Above all, the concept of fate suggests a lack of human control and thus absolves individual human beings of responsibility for the chain of events. The word *fatalité* (fate), with its romantic connotations, does not appear frequently in Perec's writings.[46] Almost as rare is the word *sort* (lot, fate, destiny) used to refer to an imaginary power that determines events. In chapter 73 of *La Vie mode d'emploi,* the cyclist Albert Massy blames the "injustice du sort" (*VME,* 419) (the injustice of fate), or again "un sort inique" (*VME,* 421) (an iniquitous fate) for the fact that his world record is never ratified; what is evidently an accident resulting from several combined causes—military service, schedule problems, and the absence of a judge—is attributed to an abstract entity.

Much more common in Perec's works are the terms *chance* and *hasard,* particularly the latter. The adverbial expressions *par hasard* or *au hasard* (by chance; at random) indicate the absence of intention behind a particular event or action—in the case of *au hasard,* a deliberate lack of intention or method. Expressions such as "le hasard lui avait fait ouvrir" (chance made him open), "la chance fut pour nous" (chance was on our side), "le hasard voulut que" (chance would have it that) suggest the presence of some other agency, since they place chance in the position of grammatical subject. These figures of speech do not necessarily imply belief in an actual transcendent force. Nevertheless, the concept of chance functions as a substitute for an absent intention, and in this sense it can come very close to notions of destiny and fate.[47] In speaking of either chance or fate, in other words, we project finality onto events while simultaneously acknowledging this finality to be an illusion.

Above all, these notions have in common the fact that they imply a degree of human helplessness in the face of events. Retrospectively, we may be able to untangle the causes of events (as François de Dinteville attempts to do in the case of the chandelier catastrophe), but foreseeing and controlling the future consequences of present facts and actions is more complicated. In *La Vie mode d'emploi,* Blunt Stanley and Ingebord Skrifter claim to be capable of doing this, but their exercises in divination are nothing more than circus tricks (*VME,* 371). It is perhaps no accident that Perec attributes to a detective novel, in chapter 32 of the same novel, the title *Clocks and Clouds.* While the disguised allusion to a work by György Ligeti obeys the constraint "contemporary music," Ligeti's title itself refers to the distinction, proposed by the philosopher Karl Popper, between two conceptions of phenomena. The first of these is deterministic and considers that events are governed by a rigorous order that is inherently predictable. The second conception, more meteorological in nature, accepts that the evolution of some systems cannot be predicted.[48]

If we adopt Popper's terms, the universe of Perec's novels is rather cloudy. However, unpredictability does not necessarily imply indeterminism, or leave room for human freedom: events might be both unpredictable and inevitable, or they might merely be perceived as inevitable (the word *inéluctable* is a leitmotif in Perec's works) by people who did not expect or intend them. The notions of chance and fate are therefore bound up with problems of power and subjective observation. Their ambiguity is intensified by the fact that chance, in Perec's works, often seems to merge with the sinister and inscrutable workings of human power—whether totalitarian power in *W* or the economic power wielded by Sven Ericsson in *La Vie mode d'emploi.* In another story of *La Vie mode d'emploi,* Ursula Von Littau, captive in an Algerian harem, is condemned to death for attempting to escape: "La pauvre prussienne avait subi le sort réservé aux femmes infidèles: cousue dans un sac de cuir, elle avait été jetée à la mer du haut de la forteresse" (The unfortunate Prussian girl had suffered the fate reserved for unfaithful wives: she had been sewn into a leather sack and thrown into the sea from the top of the fortress) (*VME,* 449/*LUM,* 379). The reference to "le sort" followed by the use of the passive voice obscures the question of agency; however, it is evidently a specific set of human laws, based on a particular set of social norms, that determines Ursula's fate.[49] In *La Disparition,* the sinister fate that hangs over the heads of all the characters is ultimately traced to the actions of one particular character, the "barbu" who sets out to murder his own descendants.

The idea that chance can be controlled by shadowy "others" surfaces in one of Perec's dream narratives, dating from 1971:

> Une autre fois, j'ai joué à un jeu de hasard et j'ai gagné énormément d'argent (plusieurs milliers de nouveaux francs). Les perdants n'ont pas l'air très contents mais ils ne font pas de difficultés particulières pour me payer. Néanmoins, juste avant de quitter la table de jeu, on recommence à jouer et je perds une somme minime, disons 100 francs. Cela a l'air de vouloir dire: Nous pouvons te faire gagner mais nous pouvons aussi te faire perdre quand nous voulons et tu ne dois pas l'oublier. (*BO*, no. 85)
>
> Another time, I played a game of chance and won an enormous sum of money (several thousand new francs). The losers don't look very happy, but they pay me without much demur. Nevertheless, just before leaving the playing table, we begin to play again and I lose a minor sum, let's say 100 francs. That seems to mean: we can have you win but we can also have you lose when we wish and you must not forget it.

Later, in *Récits d'Ellis Island,* Perec refers to his Jewish identity in negative and passive terms, first as "un silence, une absence, une question," then as the certainty "d'avoir été désigné comme juif, / et parce que juif victime, / et de ne devoir la vie qu'au hasard et à l'exil" (of having been labeled a Jew, / Jew therefore victim, / and so beholden for being alive to exile and luck) (*REI,* 58/*EI,* 60). What is obscured, in this opposition between the mark of fate ("avoir été désigné comme") and chance, is the agency that operates the identification of "juif" with "victime." In fact, chance saved Perec from a specific historical situation that made survival improbable but not impossible. Similarly, when Perec tells us that for the emigrants on Ellis Island "le destin avait la figure d'un alphabet" (fate appeared in the guise of an alphabet) (*REI,* 49/*EI,* 51), this destiny also has a human face, in the form of the immigration officers who mark the arrivers with chalk letters to divide the healthy from the ailing. These individuals are representatives of the law—but this in fact consists of a set of particular national laws, the details of which remain obscure in Perec's account. By connecting the officials' actions with the kabbalistic legend of the Golem (ibid.),[50] Perec assimilates earthly and divine power. Such is the complexity of the factors that influence the individual's destiny, that they appear as transcendent forces rather than the consequences of human actions.

In addition, Perec cites the Golem legend as an allegory of the power of writing: in a very real sense, the officers on Ellis Island shape the immigrants' destinies simply by tracing letters. The fixity of writing is a common metaphor for determinism or fate, exploited to great effect in such works as Diderot's *Jacques le fataliste,* with its references to "le grand rouleau où tout est écrit" (the great scroll where everything is written).[51] This analogy between writing and the world implies that narratives can mirror the processes of history. It also places the writer in the position of God in respect to his fictional universe. In this respect, the author's causal construction of events in a story necessarily implies a particular vision of causality, determinism, and chance. This observation leads me to the subject of chapter 3: the relationship between chance and narrative structure in Perec's works.

> Le procureur a rétorqué que le hasard avait déjà beaucoup de méfaits sur la conscience dans cette histoire.
>
> The prosecutor retorted that chance already had a lot of misdeeds on its conscience in this case.
>
> —Camus

3. Cause and Effect

Incidents and Accidents

One of the indexes of *La Vie mode d'emploi* enumerates "some of the stories narrated in this work." The tales mentioned here number 107, while the "Compendium" of chapter 51 lists 179 characters.[1] The book's subtitle, "Romans" ("Novels"), emphasizes this plurality. The first chapter evokes both the ideal separation between the multiple lives of the building and the way in which these existences may nevertheless intermingle:

> De ce qui se passe derrière les lourdes portes des appartements, on ne perçoit le plus souvent que ces échos éclatés, ces bribes, ces débris, ces esquisses, ces amorces, ces incidents ou accidents qui se déroulent dans ce que l'on appelle les "parties communes," ces petits bruits feutrés que le tapis de laine rouge passé étouffe. (*VME,* 21)
>
> What happens behind the flats' heavy doors can most often be perceived only through those fragmented echoes, those splinters, remnants, shadows, those first moves or incidents or accidents that happen in what are called the "common areas," soft little sounds dampened by the red woollen carpet. (*LUM,* 3)

The narrative structure of the novel attests to both the efficacy and the fragility of these barriers. While each of the chapters begins with a description of a particular room, this account is the starting point for the narration of stories that involve movement between spaces and interaction between characters. The individual is never entirely separated from others, nor the private from the public.[2] As the setting for the first chapter, the staircase marks this impossible boundary; it contains the traces of existence that escape from the enclosed, private space of the apartments into the public arena. It is the space in which lives come into contact, and in which stories come into being. From the strictly separated, silent space of each room, the stories of *La Vie mode d'emploi* emerge as a form of disorder, as noise that is not entirely absorbed by the red wool carpet of the staircase. It is often apparently insignificant "incidents et accidents" that disrupt boundaries and tie lives together.

The construction of causal links is arguably the driving force in all narrative. E. M. Forster deems it a measure of novelistic value, distinguishing between a "story," which merely arranges events in their time sequence, and a "plot," which emphasizes causality and thereby makes demands of intelligence and memory.[3] More skeptical of causal claims, Roland Barthes defines narrative as the systematic application of the *post hoc ergo propter hoc* fallacy, which confuses consecutiveness and consequence.[4] Reformulating the seventeenth-century writer Jean-Baptiste-Henri de Valincour's remarks on *La Princesse de Clèves,* Gérard Genette characterizes narrative texts in terms of the determination, not of effects by causes, but of causes by effects.[5] It is precisely this form of reverse determination that constitutes the arbitrariness of narrative. On the other hand, Genette gives the name of "motivation" to those causal explanations by which authors (in particular "realist" authors such as Balzac) try to naturalize narrative and hide its artificial, finalist determination.[6] Similarly, Philippe Hamon states that the psychological motivation of characters in realist discourse functions as an *a posteriori* justification of the narrative's functional construction.[7]

Forster's distaste for unmotivated stories suggests that ruptures in the novel's causal construction transgress our expectations of the serious novel. He echoes Flaubert's assertion that the novel must be more logical than the haphazardness of real life.[8] It is essentially in the name of a particular realist tradition, which emphasizes causal coherence as a condition for the reader's adherence, that Flaubert and Forster assert the necessary link between plot and character. However, the structuralist analyses of Barthes, Genette, or Hamon can be linked both to Russian formalist theories (for example the functional account of narrative put forward by Vladimir Propp) and to suspicions of narrative causality that had already found stark expression in modern French literature earlier in the century. In Camus' *L'Étranger,* for example, the prosecutor is the voice of narrative motivation: unconvinced by the assertions of both Meursault and his friend Raymond that "le hasard" (or perhaps the sunlight) was responsible for Meursault's crime, he constructs a more plausible sequence of causes and effects (which the reader nevertheless knows, from Meursault's account, to be false).[9] In Sartre's *Nausée,* Roquentin comes to think of storytelling itself as a widespread form of bad faith, used to transform banal events into adventures.[10] Life and narrative are ultimately incompatible; the teleological logic of our storytelling falsifies the meaningless succession of hours and days: "Les événements se produisent dans un sens et nous les racontons en sens inverse" (Events happen in one direction and we narrate them in the opposite direction).[11]

Barthes therefore remains close to Sartre's Roquentin when he describes the French *passé simple* tense as "le temps factice des cosmogonies, des mythes, des Histoires et des Romans" (the fictitious tense of cosmogonies, myths, Histories and Novels) and defines narrative as the language of destiny.[12] While Genette emphasizes the autonomy of narrative's reverse determination in relation to the causality of real life, novelists such as Camus and Sartre question the ways in which narrative affects our daily understanding of experience. Camus' use of the French *passé composé* tense in *L'Étranger* and Sartre's organization of *La Nausée* in the form of a journal each generate narrative forms that strive to avoid the kind of causal construction that the novels criticize. (We are very far here from Proust's claim that the underlying unity of life is discovered precisely through memory and the retrospective projection of meaning.) The experiments of the "Nouveau Roman" ("New Novel")—for example, the circular temporal structure of Robbe-Grillet's *Les Gommes*—often push causal chains to their breaking point. In doing so, however, they may dissolve any trace of referential illusion and thus preclude the kind of epistemological exploration of causality found in Camus and Sartre.

Taking up Genette's distinction between *histoire* (story; the narrative "content"), *récit* (the discourse or narrative text itself), and *narration* (the narrative act that produces the text),[13] Roy Jay Nelson points out that functional accounts such as Genette's privilege the backward logic of the *narration* over the forward logic of the *histoire.* However, the interference between different narrative levels can be read as a creative tension rather than as a masking of "true" narrative causality with the "false" (but verisimilar) causality of motivation.[14] This is an important insight for my reading of Perec. Characterized by an almost static temporality or by discontinuity and fragmentation (or both), Perec's narratives manifest a degree of resistance to conventional narrative causality. Nevertheless, rather than dismantling cause-effect relationships, they produce meaning by exploiting the causal tensions between different narrative levels.

Chance has an ambiguous status in this context. When given as the explanation for an event or situation, the reference to chance is partly a form of "motivation," in Genette's sense—albeit a negative motivation, as it obscures the event's actual cause. In chapter 66 of *La Vie mode d'emploi,* the narrator describes in detail a variety of animated watches, both those that are present in Madame Marcia's boutique and some that belong to other collectors. We subsequently learn that it is by chance—"par hasard"—that Madame Marcia has come to possess eight watches of this kind. The narrator then elaborates on the locution by explaining that Madame Marcia initially had no intention of becoming a collector; she has simply accumulated the watches in the course of her work (*VME,* 387). Structuralist narrative models might suggest that the true function of Madame Marcia's collection is to permit the lengthy description of the watches contained in the chapter (and also, perhaps, to fulfill some of the stipulated constraints, which I will discuss later). The narrator's subsequent explanation then provides causal "motivation" by justifying the character's accumulation of these heterogeneous and bizarre objects. However, in a sense our example reverses this functionalist model: whereas for Genette motivation is an invasion of the narrative construction proper (*récit*) by a self-justifying discourse (*discours*),[15] here it is the narrative that motivates, *a posteriori,* the descriptive discourse that opens the chapter. Indeed, *La Vie mode d'emploi* is structured primarily by the organization of fictional space, and the time of the narration is suspended, occupying only the few minutes that precede Bartlebooth's death: "C'est le vingt-trois juin mille neuf cent soixante-quinze et il est près de huit heures du soir" (It is the twenty-third of June nineteen seventy-five, and in a moment it will be eight o'clock in the evening) (*VME,* 577/*LUM,* 497). It is only through the narrative "motivation" of description that this static time opens up into the dynamic time of the various stories.

In this sense, the locution "par hasard" (by chance) in the above example constitutes the motivation of a motivation. Yet it has a function beyond that of simply creating a "reality effect" (if this were all, it would be gratuitous, for it is not particularly unlikely that Madame Marcia, a specialist in animated watches, might own some of them). It takes on significance in the context of a broader thematic network: in *La Vie mode d'emploi,* many characters are collectors (Smautf, James Sherwood, Rémi Plassaert, Gaspard Winckler, to name but a few), and Madame Marcia, who accumulates things only accidentally, is a variation on this type. Her relative indifference to her possessions, however, contrasts with other characters' often obsessive fixation on them (and, on an intertextual level, with the passion for acquisition portrayed in *Les Choses*). Perhaps because her trade consists in placing objects in a state of constant circulation, her desires reach an equilibrium: "[Elle] vend volontiers des objets avec lesquels elle a longtemps vécu, sûre d'en retrouver d'autres qu'elle aimera au moins autant" (She is quite willing to sell items she has lived with for years, never doubting she will find others of which she will grow just as fond) (*VME,* 387/*LUM,* 323). She therefore exemplifies an openness to chance, a willingness to accept and adapt to the unexpected, that is rare in Perec's novels.[16]

Reversals and Recognitions

Madame Marcia's unplanned watch collection is apparently without great consequence in the larger scheme of events. In other cases, however, an accidental occurrence represents the dramatic turning point of a particular story. Many of these events are attributed explicitly to chance.[17] For example, Sam Horton undergoes a sex-change operation after happening upon an article on the subject (*VME,* 229). A more central character, Doctor Dinteville, harbors the modest ambition of becoming a good country doctor until the day when "une découverte fortuite modifia le cours tranquille de son existence" (a chance discovery altered the tranquil course of his life) (*VME,* 555/*LUM,* 474). After accidentally discovering a book by his ancestor, Rigaud de Dinteville, in a collection of old papers, Dinteville devotes years of research to producing a critical edition, only to have his work plagiarized by a professor to whom he had turned for advice. In yet another case of accidental reading, the art critic Beyssandre learns of Bartlebooth's project by chance ("par hasard") while preparing to light a fire with an old newspaper (*VME,* 507). Beyssandre's subsequent fascination with Bartlebooth's project leads him to commit arson and even murder.

As narrative motivations, these references to chance account for a sudden reversal of the situation; in Aristotelian terms, they bring about the peripety (*peripeteia*). In the *Poetics,* Aristotle defines this notion as the change from one set of affairs to its opposite and argues that it is one of the essential parts of the tragic plot (*muthos*). According to Aristotle, the reversal of the action should be unexpected, yet take place not by accident but according to the demands of probability and necessity. Events that do occur by accident are most marvelous when they seem intentional: Aristotle gives the example of the statue of Mitys falling on the man who had caused Mitys's death.[18] Here, we detect a degree of ambiguity, since Aristotle's definition of chance in the *Physics* rests on the possible resemblance between accident and design. The same ambiguity is present in Perec; thus Christelle Reggiani affirms that peripety implies the intervention of a transcendent force, possibly in the guise of Fortune or Providence.[19] However, chance does not necessarily have this transcendent status in *La Vie mode d'emploi.* While Perec's novel stages multiple human tragedies, they often seem to be governed by arbitrariness rather than necessity. In the cases of Hortense, Dinteville, and Beyssandre, the peripety results from an intersection of circumstances. Furthermore, these events are not necessarily surprising or unpredictable in themselves, but only in relation to the individual's reaction to them: the disproportion between cause and effect is a powerful motor of narrative.

Chance often plays the role of *anagnorisis,* to adopt another term from Aristotle; that is, it provokes the passage from ignorance to knowledge through the recognition by a character of a particular state of affairs.[20] The archivist Zaccaria is about to cement his fame by publishing his discoveries on the naming of the New World when he receives a letter from Florentin Gilet-Burnachs, who has learned—by chance, of course—of Zaccaria's hypothesis (*VME,* 456). Unfortunately for Zaccaria's reputation, Gilet-Burnachs is able successfully to defend a completely different hypothesis regarding the historical documentation. In another story, Paul Hébert and Laetizia Grifalconi correspond for several months before "le hasard voulut que le brouillon d'une de ses lettres à elle tombât entre les mains de son mari" (by chance a draft of one of her replies was found by her husband) (*VME,* 156/*LUM,* 120). Similarly, it is thanks to chance that Léon Salini can piece together, purely on the basis of written traces, his account of Elizabeth de Beaumont's fate: "Cette fois-ci la chance fut pour nous: dans l'*Express and Echo* d'Exeter du lundi quatorze juin 1953, nous lûmes [un] fait divers navrant" (In the Exeter *Express and Echo* of Monday the fourteenth of June 1953 we read this heartbreaking story) (*VME,* 180/*LUM,* 141). The sources of the discovery sometimes lie in the interaction between a set of psychological factors and external circumstances; this is the case with the Danglars' kleptomania, an urge which is revealed to them "d'une manière tout à fait fortuite" (quite by chance) during a shopping excursion (*VME,* 472/*LUM,* 399). Elsewhere, recognition can depend on an encounter between people: "C'est grâce au jeune Riri, qui le rencontra par hasard en mille neuf cent soixante-dix, que l'on sut, au moins partiellement, ce qu'était devenu Paul Hébert" (It was thanks to young Riri, who ran into him by chance in 1970, that something at least was learned about Paul Hébert) (*VME,* 160/*LUM,* 124).

Paul Ricoeur, in his account of the Aristotelian model, argues that *peripeteia* and *anagnorisis* represent the integration of the accidental with narrative necessity: "Ce sont ces incidents discordants que l'intrigue tend à rendre nécessaires et vraisemblables. [. . .] C'est en incluant le discordant dans le concordant que l'intrigue inclut l'émouvant dans l'intelligible" (It is these discordant incidents the plot tends to make necessary and probable. [. . .] By including the discordant in the concordant, the plot includes the affecting within the intelligible).[21] In the stories of *La Vie mode d'emploi,* however, the accidental often overwhelms the concordant and the necessary. In this respect, the novel's accidental reversals do not entirely conform to the Aristotelian model—unless we shift levels and attribute the intentionality behind chance not to the actors in the story, but to the author himself. Terence Cave has discussed the "scandalous" aspect of recognition plots, which draw attention to themselves as a contrivance,[22] and Perec's multiple recognition scenes often have the effect of highlighting the artificial nature of the narrative. Recognition, Cave argues, brings together formal questions of plot structure, the theme of knowledge, and the problems of interpretation; he also suggests that today, it may only be possible to write "a parody of recognition plots."[23] While *La Vie mode d'emploi* has a significant parodic dimension, Perec's recognitions are not without dramatic and pathetic impact. As Cave notes, the scandal of recognition at its most effective affords "a glimpse of the failure of human order, the triumph of accident and coercion."[24]

The novel's reversals and recognitions often involve the accidental encounter between a text and a reader,[25] and the chance diffusion of information sometimes allows the reconstruction of a story by one of the characters. This is true of Léon Salini's reading of the Exeter *Express and Echo,* for example, or young Riri's meeting with Paul Hébert, where the reader's knowledge coincides with that of the characters. In the first case, we learn with Salini that Eric Ericsson drowned while in the care of Elizabeth de Beaumont (this is the "fait divers" reported in the newspaper), but we never know whether this was simply an accident; in the second, we learn something of Paul Hébert's ultimate fate (selling charcuterie and cider in Bar-le-Duc) but not the entire sequel to the Paul Hébert–Laetizia Grifalconi love story. Such cases of incomplete stories do not occur only when there is an intradiegetic narrator, such as Salini, or indirect narration, as in the case of young Riri.[26] The narrative undermines its own claims to omniscience and thereby casts doubt on the possibility of fictional totalization. In this respect, the stories of *La Vie mode d'emploi* relativize Perec's earlier view of the novel (expressed in his "Ligne générale" days) as a complete understanding and explanation of the real (*L.G.*, 45, 53). The presence of a metanarrative level raises questions about knowledge in general, emphasizing our dependence on subjective point of view and on accident.

Chance and Calamity

The interventions of chance are not isolated narrative units in *La Vie mode d'emploi* but fit into a larger set of patterns and themes. "La vie est-elle apparue par hasard?" ("Did Life Begin by Chance?") asks the religious magazine touted by the salesman in chapter 42 (*VME*, 232/*LUM*, 184), posing, although in a derisory way, the central question of life's necessity or contingency. The novel as a whole suggests an affirmative answer, contrary to the magazine's religious perspective. In this secular context, chance is not necessarily a negative concept but can be the equivalent of the ancient notion of *kairos;* as Sabine Hillen points out, chance can constitute an opportune moment, a stroke of luck, a discovery.[27] Occasionally, *La Vie mode d'emploi* hints at this view of chance as positive potentiality:

> Le hasard voulut qu[e] [Madame Orlowska] arrivât à Paris au plus fort des événements de Mai 68. Dans ce déferlement d'ivresses et de bonheurs, elle vécut une passion éphémère avec un jeune Américain, un chanteur de folk-song qui quitta Paris le soir où l'Odéon fut repris. (*VME*, 326)

> Fate determined that her arrival in Paris coincided with the height of the student revolt in May '68. In that great wave of intoxication and joy she had a fleeting and passionate affair with a young American folk singer, who left Paris on the night the police reoccupied the Odéon theatre. (*LUM*, 269)

Yet Madame Orlowska's love affair is brief, and in other cases where "le hasard" begins by opening up possibilities, its ultimate consequences are usually disastrous. In the second-degree narrative of chapter 78, "un hasard bénéfique" (an advantageous stroke of chance) does save Carel Van

Loorens from otherwise certain death in the desert (*VME,* 447), yet he ultimately succeeds neither in the mission which Napoleon has entrusted to him nor in his plan to save Ursula von Littau, the Eagle's captive. Chance's good deeds are equally ambiguous in the story of the young Marquiseaux, who are suddenly liberated from the personal and financial constraints that weighed on their lives in an unexpected manner, and through the misfortune of their parents:

> Madame Echard, un jour, s'étrangla avec une arête; Monsieur Echard, qui n'attendait que cela depuis dix ans, se retira dans le tout petit cabanon qu'il avait fait construire à côté d'Arles; un mois plus tard, Monsieur Marquiseaux se tua dans un accident de voiture, laissant à son fils un héritage confortable. (*VME,* 174–75)

> One day Madame Echard choked on a fish bone; Monsieur Echard, who'd been waiting for that day for ten years, retired to a tiny shack he had put up near Arles; a month later Monsieur Marquiseaux killed himself in a car accident and left his son a comfortable inheritance. (*LUM,* 137)

Numerous other unintentional calamities punctuate the novel: David Marcia is injured in a motorcycle accident (*VME,* 388), while Michel Claveau is killed in another (*VME,* 205); Lino Margay is horribly disfigured when he falls from his bicycle during a competition (*VME,* 421); Morellet loses three fingers, and later his job, from carrying out a chemistry experiment (*VME,* 47). We can add to this list Laurelle de Dinteville's mortal chandelier accident. These misfortunes are not entirely unpredictable, given the risks associated with the characters' respective activities. They nevertheless remain "accidents" because they do not result from any individual intention but from a causal chain that the characters trigger involuntarily. Faced with this catalogue of disasters, we can agree with Hillen that Perec refuses *kairos* in favor of the apocalyptic version of chance.[28]

Such a multiplication of catastrophes, extreme situations, and random twists of fate has implications for the text's generic status and literary affiliations. Christelle Reggiani is surely correct to see Perec's use of plot reversals as one aspect of a recent "retour au romanesque" (return to the novelistic) following the modern perception of a crisis in the novel.[29] However, the novelistic is in Perec's case a hybrid category. With its descriptive detail, attention to story, and the treatment of the apartment building as a microcosm of Parisian society, *La Vie mode d'emploi* is in some respects a homage to the nineteenth-century realist novel.[30] It also draws both on conventional tragic situations and on the melodramatic imagination. At the same time, the discrepancy between the events of the *histoire* and the almost neutral tone of the *narration* creates a constant (although understated) irony. The account of the accidents that befall the Echards and the Marquiseaux provides us with a characteristic example: Perec presents the events in swift succession through a series of paratactic clauses, conveying their suddenness and their impact while simultaneously de-dramatizing them. This is a chronological sequence of the type derided by E. M. Forster as mere "story": Madame Echard dies, then Monsieur Echard leaves, then Monsieur Marquiseaux dies. The events here are not linked by an unbroken causal chain but by a point of view and an interest—the fact that they combine to change the existence of the young Marquiseaux. This "and then— and then—" sequence is not simply a case of careless narrative construction (as Forster's opposition between "story" and "plot" implies); it is a deliberate and blatant device that is used frequently in the novel and which heightens the sense of arbitrariness and even randomness.

In order to revitalize the twentieth-century novel, Perec ironically revisits forms of narrative that predate nineteenth-century realism. The "chronotope" (spatio-temporal matrix) of *La Vie mode d'emploi* corresponds in some respects to that of the ancient Greek adventure novel, in which chance is the principal governing force.[31] Another important model for Perec's narratives, as Warren Motte points out, is provided by eighteenth-century works such as *Les Liaisons dangereuses, Jacques le fataliste,* and *Tristram Shandy.*[32] *La Vie mode d'emploi* also plays with the narrative conventions of "paraliterary" genres, in particular the adventure novel, the detective story, and even fairy tales (Josette and Lino Margay as Beauty and the Beast).[33] It contains allusions to popular novels—two characters are named Danglars, after one of the villains in Alexandre Dumas' *Le Comte de Monte Cristo*—and also mimics their plots. According to Thomas Pavel, the entire novel is constructed on the conjunction between Perec's realist attention to descriptive detail and the derealized stories inspired by popular fiction.[34] The accumulation of chance events in the plot has a central role in creating this impression of unreality.

The emotional impact on the reader of the chance event hovers precariously on the border between realism and parody, between the shock of the unexpected and the recognition of familiar plot devices. Other works by Perec more clearly cross the line into the ironic or the absurd. This is true of *La Disparition,* as we shall see. Perec's play *La Poche Parmentier* (1974) is constructed entirely on the basis of clichés, presenting us with a set of anonymous characters whose only role is to rehearse various preexisting scenarios. The play assembles an array of theatrical conventions and stories, complete with reversals and recognitions. In this context, references to chance and fate are elements of well-known stories and are mocked as such, as in the case of the "pure young girl" saved by chance alone from being seduced by a rich nobleman.[35] As the other characters soon point out, they have heard all this before; her account is in fact a version of the Don Juan story.[36] While chance events can be used as a device to create surprise and novelty—and to provoke an emotional response on the part of the spectator, they become banal through overuse. In Perec's works, the excessive presence of chance pushes plots toward marginalized literary genres as well as the realm of parody.

La Vie mode d'emploi also amasses novelistic devices and clichés. The multiple interventions of chance in the plot contribute to the impression of excess, as does the fragmentation of the narrative's causal chains (the transformation of a "roman" [novel] into the plural "romans"). Yet the novel negates its own narrative excess through irony, through its static "hyperrealist" descriptions, and by counterbalancing its exuberant proliferation with images of absence and nothingness: Bartlebooth's dissolved watercolors, Valène's blank canvas. The work does not fall entirely into the realm of caricature, and narrative excess does not ultimately cancel out the poignant resonance of many of the novel's stories. Rather, the comic and the tragic are intertwined. Even the impression of narrative contrivance is bound up with the sense of an arbitrary fatality that governs human life; as Harry Mathews puts it, it "is as if human life was confined by a syntax as unyielding as language itself, as if life were the outcome of some arbitrary, abstract, formal constraint."[37] Chance and necessity merge in this catastrophic vision.[38]

Stories Without Event

The interference between narrative levels is crucial in determining the reader's response to *La Vie mode d'emploi.* On the level of the plot, chance occurrences belong to a fictional universe loaded with potential calamity; on the level of narration, however, chance opens up areas of creativity and surprise. In this respect, chance functions as *kairos.* Works such as *La Vie mode d'emploi* and *La Disparition,* with their digressive, chance-laden plots, contrast strongly with *Les Choses* and *Un homme qui dort,* which play down the place of the event. It is perhaps not surprising that chance does not seem to play a major role in the narrative of *Les Choses.* The latter is not a novel of dramatic twists and turns; instead, it cultivates a sense of slow inevitability in its account of the protagonists' lives. The reverse side of this ordinary universe is the virtual world of the characters' imaginations, made up of perfect objects and expressed by the conditional. Here, too, surprises and reversals are scarce. Where chance might play a role is in the possible connection between the two worlds: "Et puis soudain, brutale, échevelée, inattendue, éclatant comme un tonnerre: la fortune!" (And then, suddenly, brutally, wildly, unexpectedly, like a thunderclap: fortune!) (*C,* 100/*T,* 84). The characters imagine various improbable ways in which this sudden change in circumstances might occur, either accidentally—the discovery of oil or uranium in their garden, or an unexpected inheritance—or through their own efforts: the writing of a play, the theft of paintings or diamonds. But while such events would not be out of place in *La Vie mode d'emploi,* they can only be dreamed of in the universe of *Les Choses.*

The plot of *Les Choses* contains very few "events." Noting the predominance of the imperfect and conditional tenses in the work, Dominique Duquesne even calls into question its status as a narrative text. However, he concludes that a plot does exist, structured by the emergence, growth, and eventual loss of Jérôme and Sylvie's illusions, and with them the illusions of a whole generation in France.[39] The novel's causal architecture is perceptible if we consider the progression of the novel as whole, yet is often hard to trace in the process of reading. As Duquesne also emphasizes, the use of the imperfect tense and parataxis link *Les Choses* to Flaubert's *L'Éducation sentimentale,* in terms of both style and narrative construction: neither novel recounts a structured adventure with dramatic turning points and a clear beginning, middle, and end.[40]

The predominance of iterative scenes over series of singular causes and effects, the emphasis on repeated microevents—the window shopping, the poker games, the visits to restaurants and cinemas—evoke, in their apparent insignificance, both the randomness and the repetition of daily life. However, the impression of randomness on the local level is subordinated to an overarching necessity that determines the course of the characters' existence. Explicit references to chance in *Les Choses,* unlike those in *La Vie mode d'emploi,* generally appear in iterative sequences, designating chance events that occur regularly, but without necessarily opening up new possibilities. Such references are also fairly rare, occurring only in limited thematic contexts. For example, they indicate the uncertainty, precariousness, and even superficiality of the characters' friendships. Accidental meetings can lead to possible friendships (*C,* 44), while fortuitous incidents also reveal the fragility of such relationships (*C,* 53). But it is above all in the second part of the book, which recounts the protagonists' life in Sfax, that chance seems increasingly to dominate their actions. It intervenes in the form of the random event that occasionally livens, albeit in a minor way, a life of monotony: the characters' Sunday evenings are dull, "à moins que, par hasard, un film ne les attirât" (unless, by chance, there was a film to attract them) (*C,* 133/*T,* 109).

In this context, a character's receptivity to chance can be a sign of freedom but also of passivity and absence of purpose: "Jérôme allait à la bibliothèque municipale, lisait des livres au hasard: Borges, Troyat, Zeraffa" (Jérôme went to the City Library, read books at random: Borges, Troyat, Zeraffa) (*C,* 139/*T,* 113). The couple move to Sfax in order to escape the stifling determinism of their life in France, and in a sense they succeed. However, they replace it with a sense of meaninglessness and emptiness, of not belonging. As Stella Béhar has noted, the triangle of desire, whereby the characters' relationship to objects is always mediated by cultural images, no longer functions in a society whose mechanisms Jérôme and Sylvie do not understand.[41] They therefore return to France, unable to "escape their own story" ("histoire") (*C,* 149). "Histoire" takes on a double meaning here: on the level of the plot, Jérôme and Sylvie's story is governed by a set of social pressures that influence them (and within which their margin to maneuver seems very small). On the level of the narration, however, the necessity is that of the narrative's teleological movement. The characters are trapped both in the history of their generation and in Georges Perec's story.

Perec described *Un homme qui dort* as the "somber side" of *Les Choses* (*EC,* 1:44) and its narrative construction is in some respects similar. Once again, we can trace a chronological progression in the plot—the moment of withdrawal from the world, the passage through different attempts to attain complete indifference, and finally the recognition that "l'indifférence est inutile" (indifference is futile) (*UHD,* 140/*MA,* 219). However, this occurs on the global level, while the detail of the text creates little sense of dynamic movement. The novel's use of the present tense has a similar iterative function to the imperfect of *Les Choses:* "Tu traînes dans les rues, la nuit, le jour. Tu rentres dans les cinémas de quartier où flotte l'odeur insistante des désinfectants, tu manges des sandwiches à des comptoirs, des frites dans des cornets, tu traverses les fêtes foraines, tu joues au billard électrique" (You drift around streets, by night, by day. You go into local cinemas where the insistent stink of disinfectant hangs in the air, you eat sandwiches standing at the counter, chips in paper cones, you walk through fun-fairs, you play pinball) (*UHD,* 76/*MA,* 176). The protagonist's goal is to live in a permanent present, to suspend time. In this he inevitably fails:

> Les cloches de Saint-Roch, l'alternance des feux au croisement de la rue des Pyramides et de la rue Saint-Honoré, la chute prévisible de la goutte d'eau au robinet du poste d'eau sur le palier, n'ont jamais cessé de mesurer les heures, les minutes, les jours et les saisons. (*UHD,* 141)

> The bells of Saint-Roch, the changing traffic lights at the intersection between Rue des Pyramides and Rue Saint-Honoré, the predictable drip from the tap on the landing, never ceased to signal the hours, the minutes, the days and the seasons. (*MA,* 219–20)

Time has passed, its passage marked by these numerous "infraordinary" signs, yet "rien ne s'est passé: nul miracle, nulle explosion" (nothing has happened: no miracle, no explosion) (*UHD,* 141/*MA,* 219).

The narrative of *Un homme qui dort* is built not on significant events but on the accumulation of the insignificant. The protagonist, paradoxically, attempts to give a particular type of meaning to this meaninglessness, just as he hopes that his suspension of time will lead to some kind of event (whether miracle or disaster). The novel privileges a sense of randomness over causal chains. As John Pedersen points out, this is in one sense an "anti-histoire," despite its citation of multiple stories by other authors.[42] It is only at the end of the novel that the protagonist is called back to time and causality—to the predicable fall of the water droplet. Chance in *Un homme qui dort* is the all-pervading randomness of the everyday nonevent, not the catastrophe that suddenly intervenes in a causal chain to cause a dramatic reversal of circumstances.

Retrospection and Rupture

In the case of autobiographical texts, the role of chance can be linked to specific debates about the genre's narrative conventions. Autobiography, at least according to Philippe Lejeune's famous definition,[43] implies the transformation of the writer's existence into a story, a sequence of causes and effects recounted from the retrospective perspective of the time of narration. It is for this reason that Jacques Roubaud describes the genre as "un des derniers refuges du déterminisme mécaniste" (one of the last refuges of mechanical determinism).[44] Determinism, perhaps, but above all teleology: autobiography looks back at the causes from the point of view of the effects. In fiction, retrospective construction tends to be (more or less) disguised by the opposite causal direction of the plot, while in autobiography the antichronological dynamic is more apparent. However, a concern for veracity or authenticity leads some writers to question conventional narrative's capacity to convey the complexity of experience and memory. This preoccupation is behind many of the formal choices and innovations of twentieth-century autobiographers, such as Michel Leiris's networks of associations in the four volumes of *La Règle du jeu* (1948–76; *The Rules of the Game*) or Nathalie Sarraute's use of dialogue in *Enfance* (1983; *Childhood*).

In *W ou le souvenir d'enfance,* only the text in roman type can be said to correspond to traditional autobiography, and then only in part. Perec does present some episodes of his childhood as being significant moments in the history of his personality. In chapter 31, for example, Perec's account of his childhood readings of Jules Verne and Alexandre Dumas provides an origin and an explanation for his interest in literature (*W,* 193–95). The text nevertheless remains laconic on many aspects of Perec's personal history: we do not know at what point he learned of his mother's death, for example, or his reaction to the exhibition about concentration camps to which his aunt Esther accompanied him (*W,* 215). Generally, Perec's childhood memories are presented as a series of disconnected episodes rather than as a continuous narrative. In many cases, we do not even find the structure of E. M. Forster's primitive "story" ("and then— and then—"), but rather "une fois— une fois— une autre fois—"; "plus tard— plus tard—" or "un soir—" (one time— one time— another time—; later— later—; one evening—), markers that cast doubt on the chronological sequence of events (*W,* 139, 141, 214, 215). Even when the reference to chance is not explicit, the narrative structure of *W* conveys the confused nature of both the child's perception of events and the adult's memory that attempts to recall these events.

Although Perec tells us that his original *W* fantasy constituted "sinon l'histoire, du moins une histoire de mon enfance" (if not the story of my childhood, then at least a story of my childhood) (*W,* 18/*WMC,* 6), the fictional section of *W ou le souvenir d'enfance* is less a narrative than a description of the way in which the Olympic island functions. Chance plays an important role in this section, but it does not bring about a specifically narrative development. The progression from utopia to dystopia is not a chronological one on the level of the plot, but a gradual revelation on the part of the narrator. As Philippe Lejeune points out, the text remains curiously silent on the question of the author's relationship to the invented story of his childhood, the function of this Olympic fantasy for the thirteen-year-old boy.[45] The gaps in explanation that we find in *W* and the division of the text's narrative into a set of micronarratives indicate the rupture that intervened in Perec's history, the lack of continuity in the child's existence, and the weight of the unsayable.

Bernard Magné describes this narrative fragmentation as the founding gesture of *W*, a biographical mark that gives literary form to the violence of history.[46] Jeanne Bem offers a more radical conclusion, arguing that Perec "detests narrative" because narrative is concerned with chronology, with an ideal sequence of events that has been mastered by memory.[47] However, while it is undoubtedly true that Perec cannot anchor his memories in a secure chronology, it is not the case that he entirely rejects narrative. In this respect, the autobiographical section of *W ou le souvenir d'enfance* differs greatly from another form of autobiographical writing adopted by Perec, that of *Je me souviens*. This text abandons narrative altogether in order to gather, in seemingly random order, isolated fragments all beginning "Je me souviens..." (I remember...). The enumerated memories range from the advertising slogan—"Je me souviens de 'Dop Dop Dop, adoptez le shampooing Dop'" (I remember "Dop Dop Dop, use Dop shampoo," no. 63)—to momentous historical events—"Je me souviens du jour où le Japon capitula" (I remember the day when Japan surrendered, no. 40).[48] The text's cover page suggests a process whereby banal details from the past are miraculously rescued from contingency:

> Il arrive pourtant qu[e] [les choses oubliées] reviennent, quelques années plus tard, intactes et minuscules, par hasard ou parce qu'on les a cherchées, un soir, entre amis: c'était une chose qu'on avait apprise à l'école, un champion, un chanteur ou une starlette qui perçait, [. . .] un geste, ou quelque chose d'encore plus mince, d'inessentiel, de tout à fait banal, miraculeusement arraché à son insignifiance, retrouvé pour un instant, suscitant pendant quelques secondes une impalpable petite nostalgie.[49]

> It nevertheless happens that [forgotten things] come back, some years later, intact and minute, by chance or because you have sought them,

> one evening, among friends: it was something you learned at school, a champion, a singer, or a starlet making their big break, [. . .] a gesture, or something even flimsier, inessential, entirely banal, miraculously wrested from its insignificance, rediscovered for a moment, generating for a few seconds a small, impalpable wave of nostalgia.

While there are echoes of Proust here, Perec's miracle of memory is confined almost to the instant in which it comes to light, creating only a fleeting sense of nostalgia that immediately fades. The operation of involuntary memory does not, as in Proust, provide access to the essence of the self or allow the different moments of the past to be incorporated into a coherent narrative whole.[50]

In *W ou le souvenir d'enfance,* the technique of montage certainly creates ruptures.[51] However, this discontinuity is compensated for by mechanisms that ensure the coalescence of the two texts; for example, the repeated motifs that Bernard Magné calls "sutures."[52] Within each of the juxtaposed texts, narrative continuity is also present (with the notable exception of the break between Gaspard Winckler's story and the description of the island). Unlike *Je me souviens, W ou le souvenir d'enfance* does tell a story, albeit one with gaps and silences. Significantly, the chapter on Perec's childhood reading expresses a desire for narrative:

> Les mots étaient à leur place, les livres racontaient des histoires; on pouvait suivre; on pouvait relire, et, relisant, retrouver, magnifiée par la certitude qu'on avait de les retrouver, l'impression qu'on avait d'abord éprouvée: ce plaisir ne s'est jamais tari: je lis peu, mais je relis sans cesse, Flaubert et Jules Verne, Roussel et Kafka, Leiris et Queneau; je relis les livres que j'aime et j'aime les livres que je relis, et chaque fois avec la même jouissance, que je relise vingt pages, trois chapitres ou le livre entier: celle d'une complicité, d'une connivence, ou plus encore, au-delà, celle d'une parenté enfin retrouvée. (*W,* 195)

> The words were where they should be, and the books told a story you could follow; you could re-read, and, on re-reading, re-encounter, enhanced by the certainty that you would encounter those words again, the impression you had felt the first time. This pleasure has never ceased for me; I do not read much, but I have never stopped re-reading Flaubert and Jules Verne, Roussel and Kafka, Leiris and Queneau; I re-read the books I love and I love the books I re-read, and each time it is the same

enjoyment, whether I re-read twenty pages, three chapters, or the whole book: an enjoyment of complicity, of collusion, or more especially, and in addition, of having in the end found kin again. (*WMC,* 143)

Fictional stories provide the security of a chronologically anchored sequence, fixed forever by the stability of the words on the page. They become a substitute for Perec's personal history and for his lost family, providing an existence removed from uncertainty. This pleasure is magnified by the act of rereading, which necessarily diminishes the unpredictability of the reader's first impressions. And yet, an element of unpredictability—and the desire to discover how the plot unfolds—must have been partly what motivated the child, initially, to devour, "couché à plat ventre sur [s]on lit" (lying flat on his stomach on his bed) (*W,* 193/*WMC,* 141), the still unknown books.

Texts such as *La Disparition* and *La Vie mode d'emploi* clearly respond to this need for narrative—as does the first half of the fictional segment of *W,* for that matter, with its echoes of Jules Verne (one of Perec's childhood favorites). *La Disparition* stands at the opposite end of the spectrum from the narrative sobriety of *Les Choses, Un homme qui dort,* and even *Quel petit vélo à guidon chromé au fond de la cour*—texts whose plots revolve around the insignificance, repetitiveness, and monotony of the everyday, in a universe governed by both randomness on the local level and an inescapable determinism in the general scheme. In Perec's lipogrammatic novel, on the other hand, we find countless extraordinary occurrences, surprises, and reversals. In short, we find a return to the event. It is significant that of all Perec's texts, *La Disparition* contains by far the most frequent uses of the word *hasard.*

Digression and Damnation

La Disparition explicitly compares itself to models of digressive or excessive narrative. As the character Amaury Conson notes,

> On croirait parcourir un roman à tiroirs, un roman noir à l'instar d'un Mathurin [*sic*], d'un Jan Potocki, d'un Hoffmann, d'un Balzac avant Vautrin, Goriot, Pons ou Rastignac. (*D,* 217)
>
> I can't stop thinking that I'm in a sort of *roman à tiroirs,* a thick, Gothic work of fiction with lots of plot twists and a Russian doll construction, such as Mathurin's *Monk,* Jan Potocki's *Manuscript Found at Saragossa*

> and just about any story by Hoffmann or Balzac (Balzac, that is, prior to Vautrin, Goriot, Pons or Rastignac). (*V,* 198)

Most of the authors mentioned here are associated with genres of nineteenth-century popular fiction. The Irish writer Charles Robert Maturin (1782–1824) is the author of the gothic novel *Melmoth the Wanderer* (1820) (and not of *The Monk,* as Gilbert Adair's translation would have it, although this is indeed the title of a gothic novel by Matthew Gregory Lewis).[53] Jean Potocki's *Manuscrit trouvé à Saragosse* (1722) contains multiple short narratives embedded in a larger frame; Hoffmann wrote fantastic tales; as for Balzac "avant Vautrin, Goriot, Pons ou Rastignac," this is the young Balzac who wrote little-known "noir" novels rather than the canonized, realist author of the *Comédie humaine.*[54] This self-referential passage emphasizes both continuity and discontinuity, both the presence of a plot ("un fil narratif") and the impression of "un hasard divaguant puisant, dirait-on, son inspiration dans un choix aussi discontinu qu'inconstant, aussi gratuit qu'instinctif!" (an inspiration so capricious and inconstant, so gratuitous and instinctual) (*D,* 217/*V,* 198).

Perhaps even more frequently than in *La Vie mode d'emploi,* the chance transmission of knowledge drives the narrative's progress in *La Disparition.* To cite just a few examples: Olga discovers, "par hasard," Anton Voyl's talisman, which resembles "a scrap of typography" perhaps in the shape of the letter *e* (*D,* 206/*V,* 187); Voyl later tells her that he has found out, "tout à fait par hasard" (totally haphazardly), that Tryphiodorus is Douglas Haig's father (*D,* 207/*V,* 188);[55] after Voyl leaves Olga she learns, again "par hasard," several details about his situation (*D,* 209–10). By chance again, in the main plot Amaury Conson finds a photograph of the mysterious bearded man in Arthur Wilburg Savorgnan's closet, only to perish shortly after this discovery. As in *La Vie mode d'emploi,* the narrative turning points attributed to chance often correspond to moments of recognition, as the characters attempt to learn about the "damnation" that hangs over them. However, the knowledge brought by chance in these cases is not only bad news, it is also dangerous. Indeed, chance is predominantly disastrous, as is emphasized by the adjectives that usually accompany it: it is accursed ("un hasard maudit" [*D,* 47]), bad ("un mauvais hasard" [*D,* 105, 153, 244, 264, 281]), or wicked ("un hasard malfaisant" [*D,* 272]).

Nevertheless, a more positive version of chance sometimes seems to intervene, closer to the notion of *kairos:* on several occasions we find the expression "un hasard opportun" (*D*, 259, 269, 272) (a lucky opportunity). However, as in *La Vie mode d'emploi*, these examples of apparent good fortune are undermined by future developments, precipitating the final disaster. A stroke of luck serves to alleviate Aloysius Swann's misfortune: "Il chut dans un ravin, qu'un hasard opportun n'avait pas fait trop profond" ([his car] would skid into a ditch, a ditch that, luckily for both, was fairly shallow) (*D*, 225/*V*, 207). As we later discover, however, Aloysius Swann is on a mission to exterminate the other characters. The fortunate absence of the murderous bearded man (*barbu*) at the moment of his sons' births does not ultimately prevent their deaths. When Savorgnan, abandoning his wife in the desert in order to seek help, places his hopes in a "hasard miraculant" (*D*, 276) (a miraculous bit of luck), his belief that he will be able to save her and his unborn children proves to be an illusion.

Despite its multiple events, or rather because of the very excessiveness of these events, *La Disparition* gives little space to causal motivation, except through frequent references to chance or to the ineluctable "damnation." Few concessions are made to verisimilitude. The plot's numerous deaths and disasters fall into the realm of dark comedy. Of all Perec's works, *La Disparition* not only contains the most numerous references to chance, but it also creates the most insistent sense of fatality as the characters are killed off one by one. When chance always acts in a particular way, it is transformed into necessity, as evidenced by Savorgnan's statement that a continuous shared fortune ("un hasard continu") has always and will always unite him to Conson (*D*, 109). By definition, chance is discontinuous and uncertain in its results, yet in *La Disparition* it becomes inseparable from the "damnation" that destroys the characters: "Or j'avais, à tout instant, l'intuition d'un mauvais hasard nous poursuivant" (Now, at that point, fairly constantly, I had an intuition of bad luck pursuing both of us) (*D*, 264/*V*, 243). While leading all the characters to their inevitable end, Perec's lipogrammatic narrative continually startles the reader with unexpected digressions and outrageous events along the way. Explicitly placing the themes of chance and necessity in an epistemological and aesthetic framework, *La Disparition* is both a parody and a defense of narrative manipulations of causality:

> On conçoit sans mal qu'il fallut un hasard tout à fait hors du commun (d'aucuns y ont vu aussitôt l'infini doigt du Tout-Puissant: à coup sûr, ils n'ont pas tort, mais la Narration contraint à offrir, au moins, l'illusion

du pas tout à fait fatal; sinon à quoi bon discourir?) tout à fait hors du commun, donc, pour qu'Aignan, sous un climat aussi cordial, soit toujours vivant dix-huit ans plus tard. (*D,* 46)

Thus you wouldn't go far wrong in supposing that only miraculous odds (I fancy a Christian would put it down to God working in mystical ways and is probably right to do so; but fiction has an intrinsic duty to contradict[, if only by illusion, such a notion] of propitiatory fatality; for if not, what's its point?)—in supposing, as I say, that only miraculous odds could account for Aignan's surviving up to and including his 18th birthday. (*V,* 30; translation modified)

Such narratorial interventions are reminiscent of Diderot's *Jacques le fataliste,* with its reflection on arbitrariness, chance, and determinism. In this case, the author, as omnipotent deity ("Tout-Puissant") in his fictional universe, ultimately determines everything that takes place in the text. Yet the novel insists that chance, or at least the perception of randomness, plays an essential role in the pleasure of narrative. Consequently, the movement of the story should not appear to obey an ineluctable determinism or overwhelming finality, even if it in fact does so. Part of the author's task is therefore to deceive the reader by creating the impression of causal uncertainty. The different levels of narrative construction disguise one another and manipulate the reader's perceptions of accident and intention. Chapter 4 addresses this association of chance with illusion and its connection with the themes of ruse and machination in Perec's narrative texts.

Hasard ou machination, qui sait?

Fortuitous or calculating, who can say?

—Georges Perec

4. Traps and Machinations

Hidden Signals

The plot of *La Disparition* hinges on a double enigma: the puzzle of the missing letter and the disappearance of Anton Voyl. The mystery surrounding the missing *e* is linked to the diabolical scheme set up by a sinister bearded man in order to destroy all of the characters. As events unfold, numerous machinations disguise themselves in the cloak of chance. It is easy enough to see through this appearance if we know the schemer's motives; thus the narrator explicitly tells us that it is "pas par hasard" (not haphazardly) that the murderous Maximin happens to be passing by his brother Optat's home at an opportune moment to finish him off (*D,* 249–50/*V,* 229).[1] In other cases, distinguishing coincidences from determined events is not such a simple matter. Ottaviani and Conson, for example, have no means of knowing whether the meeting with Hassan Ibn Abbou at the zoo is a case of chance or calculation (*D,* 75), although the reader suspects the latter. Chapter 2, which contains a lipogrammatic amalgamation of *Moby-Dick* and *Robinson Crusoe,* emphasizes that the ascription of events to chance depends on subjective judgment. Ismaïl finds himself stranded on an island and believes that it is by chance ("par hasard") that no dangerous animals populate the island (*D,* 32–33). The expression "par hasard" in this example is almost a mark of free indirect discourse; the narrator cites part of the character's thoughts.

In some cases, the suddenness and unpredictability of the event may make it appear accidental—or at least unconnected to the curse that hangs over the characters—before its real causes are eventually revealed. This is true in particular of the events recounted by Savorgnan in chapters 22 through 24, for example, the murder of the Ankara lawyer and the kidnapping of two of Savorgnan's infant sons, which Savorgnan initially ascribes to pure chance (*D,* 272, 283). These cases of false chance all thematize the ways in which narrative finality is disguised by the appearance of infinite possibilities. The text reflects not only on its own construction of causality but also on that of narrative and the novel in general. Occasionally the shift from the narrative to the metanarrative level is explicit: Savorgnan proclaims that the elimination of chance words is "quasi la Loi du roman d'aujourd'hui" (a paradigm, a matrix, if you wish, for all works of fiction of today) (*D,* 217/ *V,* 199). In Anton Voyl's novel about Aignan and Sibylla—a version of Thomas Mann's *Holy Sinner,* which itself rewrites elements of the Oedipus myth—the transcendent force that determines Aignan's destiny is described as the "Tout-Puissant," the All-Powerful (*D,* 46). While the expression evokes, in this context, an apparently benevolent Providence, the Oedipus story is an exemplary case of individual destinies condemned by an inevitable fate despite their efforts to escape it. This absolute power also belongs to the *telos* of the narration, and in this case it is Anton Voyl, the writer/transposer of this micronarrative, who plays the role of the "Tout-Puissant" in relation to his characters. On yet another level, the novel's mysterious bearded man reminds us of Georges Perec himself.

As Gérard Genette notes of metalepsis (the shift between narrative levels), its most troubling aspect lies in the suggestion that the extradiegetic is perhaps always already diegetic and that perhaps we ourselves are merely characters in some narrative.[2] In *La Disparition,* the problem of interpreting appearances is explicitly linked to the role of texts in the plot and thereby to the difficulties of reading. For example, Voyl's friends notice that some poems he has transcribed occasionally allude to some of the character's own obsessions—"l'obscur, l'immaculation, la disparition, la damnation" (obscurity, immaculation, vanishing, and damnation)—yet they attribute this conjunction between Rimbaud and Voyl to pure chance (*D,* 116/ *V,* 100). They therefore miss the clear indication of the nature of their predicament contained, for example, in the lipogrammatic version of Rimbaud's poem "Voyelles" ("Vowels")—rewritten here as "Vocalisations." Of course, the characters are not in a position, as Perec's readers are, to recognize the textual manipulation; since the universe of the diegesis does not contain a single *e,* the poem is presumably not a transformation at all for the intradiegetic readers. This discrepancy between our knowledge and that of the characters creates an ironic distance yet also hints at a troubling affinity, since the characters are presented as readers.

In other instances, the characters are well aware that texts and signs are not mere accidents, but obstacles to interpretation nonetheless remain. This is the case when Haig notices some marks on the billiard table[3] and instantly recognizes them as a significant clue: "non pas un signal au hasard, mais, au plus fort du mot, un signal signifiant" (not a random but a *signifying* sign) (*D*, 156/*V*, 138). Before attempting to decipher this "inscription," Anton Voyl compares it to a novel that features mystified characters: "cinq ou six individus s'affrontant, s'abordant sous l'action d'un fatum qu'ils croiront jusqu'au bout dû au hasard, l'illusion du fortuit masquant, mais masquant mal l'absolu du fatal" (a handful of individuals in conflict, in confrontation with a curious sort of fatality, imagining, right up to its last paragraph, that this fatality is actually a fortuity, a product of nothing but downright bad luck) (*D*, 196/*V*, 177). The confusion belongs to the characters on one level but to the readers on another: "l'insinuant fil tramant la narration tissant un tapis aux motifs si confus qu'on n'aura jamais la vision d'un croquis abouti, qu'il nous paraîtra vain d'y vouloir voir un signal" (a haunting strand of plot working its way through a mosaic of motifs so confusing that you and I can't possibly summon up a vision of its totality from A to Z, its organic unity, so confusing that our wish to find a significant sign in it is simply an illusion) (*D*, 196/*V*, 177).[4]

Means and Ends

Voyl's metatextual digression suggests that chance masks necessity on two levels: in the story, the appearance of chance disguises from the characters the inevitability of their fate, while in the narration, the illusion of randomness and disorder obscures from the reader, at least initially, the fact that the novel is justified by the "law" of the constraint. The connection between chance and fate in the plot is thus paralleled by the relationship between text and constraint on the level of the narration. Two types of necessity—narrative and linguistic—converge on the thematic level, since the general "damnation" that hangs over all of the characters refers not only to the destruction plotted by the bearded man but also to the omission of the taboo letter. *La Disparition* is in fact founded on a triple tension: between Oulipian anti-chance—"il n'y a pas un mot fortuit" (not any word of ours is fortuitous) (*D*, 217/*V*, 198)—and ordinary language; between narrative anti-chance (its movement toward a predefined goal) and the need for an appearance of uncertainty; and, finally, the interaction between these two levels of the text.

Narrative chance has an ambiguous status in *La Disparition;* it both provides the causal motivation for the improbable twists, turns, and digressions of the plot and is undermined by the text's emphasis on machinations, inevitability, and "damnation"—the ultimate "machination" being the construction of the text itself. As Warren Motte points out, we are faced with a spectacle of "generalized and apparently aleatory carnage," and yet there are certain patterns: a law of retribution; death bound up in the letter.[5] In one sense, chance and the aleatory have in fact been removed from the world of *La Disparition.* Nevertheless, the presence of an inescapable curse—the "damnation" to which the characters refer—does not entirely exclude chance from the universe of the novel. This point is illustrated in a darkly humorous mode in the novel's final chapter: Aloysius Swann enumerates various improbable ways in which he could kill Savorgnan, mentioning, among other possibilities, an exploding pineapple, a radioactive bird, a game of Go, and a falling sculpture. In each case he specifies the exact situation in which these scenarios could function. When Savorgnan objects that none of these methods is feasible in the present circumstances, Swann summarily draws out a "Smith-Corona" to shoot his victim dead, or rather (since a Smith-Corona is actually a brand of typewriter not a firearm) to "cross him out" (*D,* 303). All of the potential plot sequences enumerated by Swann thus become relatively unimportant, and ultimately derisory, narrative "motivations" for the inevitable result: Savorgnan's death.

Jacques Roubaud claims that "le roman est mangé par sa et ses fins" (the novel is consumed by its end and ends),[6] and this certainly seems true of *La Disparition.* According to Gérard Genette, it is precisely this teleological logic that constitutes what is often called the arbitrariness of the novel.[7] This combination of the arbitrary and the ineluctable is particularly conspicuous in *La Disparition,* which often either omits causal motivation altogether or refers to the absent agency of chance as it traces the inevitable destruction of the characters. Critics have interpreted *La Disparition* as an allegory of Perec's personal loss and trauma, particularly in light of the French homophony between *e*—the letter—and the word *eux*—"them," the lost parents (significantly, *W ou le souvenir d'enfance* is dedicated "Pour E").[8] This interpretation links the lipogrammatic constraint to the problem of narrative ends and to the theme of catastrophe. More generally, the novel's emphasis on death as the goal of narration can be read as a commentary on narrative form; Peter Brooks suggests that plot is "the internal logic of the discourse of mortality."[9]

However, the insistence on death as the novel's conclusion (*D*, 305) in itself no way implies that this goal must be reached by one path rather than another. In fact, the paths that the novel could have taken to reach the characters' ends are potentially infinite in number; the narrative can sustain its multiple digressions and twists while still emphasizing the inevitable doom that will strike everyone. In this sense, chance and destiny cease to be contradictory. Furthermore, as Clément Rosset points out, the sense of a fatality that hangs over existence is not necessarily incompatible with belief in contingency: "L'inéluctable [. . .] ne désigne pas ce qui serait nécessaire de toute éternité, mais ce à quoi il est impossible de se dérober dans l'instant même" (The ineluctable [. . .] does not designate what would be necessary for all eternity, but what it is impossible to avoid at this very moment).[10] The arbitrariness of narrative here gives us access to what Rosset calls the "idiocy of the real": reality's existence as a singularity, and its character of being at once "somehow" and "anyhow" (in Perec's novel, Swann's approach to Savorgnan's killing is a case in point).[11] Aloysius Swann uses the metaphor of the labyrinth to evoke this ultimate compatibility of chance and fate:

> Voici parcouru jusqu'au bout, jusqu'au fin mot, l'insinuant circuit labyrinthal où nous marchions d'un pas somnambulant. [. . .] Chacun, s'avançant plus loin dans l'obscur du non-dit, a ourdi jusqu'à sa saturation, la configuration d'un discours qui, au fur qu'il grandissait, n'abolissait l'hasard du jadis qu'au prix d'un futur apparaissant sans solution, à l'instar d'un fanal n'illuminant qu'un trop court instant la portion d'un parcours, lors n'offrant au fuyard qu'un jalon minimal, fil d'Ariana toujours rompu, n'autorisant qu'un pas à la fois. Franz Kafka l'a dit avant nous: il y a un but, mais il n'y a aucun parcours; nous nommons parcours nos dubitations. (*D*, 304)

> This circuitous labyrinth, through which all of us would drift with a somnambulist's languorous gait, driving our plot forward with our contribution to it, our participation in it, moving on and on, braving its paralysing taboo, concocting out of that taboo, to a point of saturation, a story which, with all its manifold ramifications, would abolish what you might call its random factor only at a cost of our giving up any claim to a solution, similar to a lamp illuminating, and fitfully, only

> part of our path, according us only a hint, an inkling, of what is lying in front of us, of what is awaiting us—it is, I say, fast approaching its conclusion, its last word. But Franz Kafka said it first: you know what your goal is but you don't know of any path to that goal and what you call a path is only your own blind, groping doubt. (*V,* 277)

The existence of a goal—here a narrative final cause—does not in itself determine the path taken to this goal. The abolition of chance by the progression of writing and narrative, which fixes words on the page as it settles the characters' destinies, corresponds to the retrospective illusion of inevitability created by the irreversibility of time.[12] Necessity always exists in the past, in what is already written, but chance is always reborn in the contingency of the future. Narrative, with its double causal direction (efficient causes on the level of plot, final causes on the level of narration) becomes a means of expressing and exploring our ambiguous experience of time as both chance and destiny.

Schemes and Disguises

The status of narrative chance in *La Vie mode d'emploi* is similarly ambiguous, although explicit references to its role are less frequent here than in *La Disparition.* Once again, the distinction between the determined and the accidental is complicated by the various machinations and schemes involved in the various stories. Repeatedly, apparent accidents are later revealed to be traps set for a particular character by another. Like the "truly" accidental events of the story, the numerous false coincidences often represent the peripety or reversal in a particular story. Due to what the narrator initially calls a "coïncidence sublime" (a sublime coincidence), for example, Longhi returns to inform the collector James Sherwood of his sighting of Mandetta/Van Schallaert, the supposed thief of the holy vase that Sherwood seeks to acquire (*VME,* 123). We later learn that the whole affair of the Grail has been constructed by Van Schallaert and the false Shaw in order to trick Sherwood into buying a forgery; Longhi is simply a minor character in a carefully elaborated drama where apparent chance intervenes to create an illusion. In this case, the reference to coincidence functions as a form of narrative focalization and thus creates a degree of irony; it is from Sherwood's point of view that Longhi's reappearance is a "coïncidence sublime." However, a final twist in the story suggests that perhaps Sherwood was not fooled after all. He may have paid for the fake vase with forged money, and willingly entered into the game of false coincidences. Like the reader of a novel, perhaps, he suspends disbelief in order to enjoy the illusions of narrative. The reference to chance thus becomes doubly ironic.

In the story of Ingeborg Skrifter and Blunt Stanley, who become fortune-tellers and tricksters, apparent chance has the same mystifying function: "Blunt, en fakir, devinait diverses choses à partir de chiffres apparemment choisis au hasard" (Blunt, dressed as a fakir, would guess various things from numbers chosen apparently at random) (*VME,* 371/*LUM,* 309). The use of the adverb *apparemment* here functions as an ironic signal of the narrator's judgment. Similarly, and more significantly for the outcome of the novel's main plot, Gaspard Winckler uses the appearance of chance as a ruse: at first, the traces of glue that remain on the puzzle pieces seem to offer Bartlebooth helpful clues for the reconstitution of his jigsaws, but in fact they only lull him into a false sense of security:

> C'est seulement quand cette habitude fut prise, et suffisamment ancrée pour que s'en débarrasser devînt désagréable, que Bartlebooth se rendit compte que ces "heureux hasards" pouvaient parfaitement être piégés à leur tour, et que le faiseur de puzzles n'avait laissé, sur une centaine de jeux, cette mince trace servir d'indice—ou plutôt d'appât—que pour mieux l'égarer ensuite. (*VME,* 402)

> It was only when this habit had been acquired and had grown sufficiently ingrained that it would be unpleasant to give it up that Bartlebooth realised that these "happy chances" could themselves perfectly well be booby trapped and that the puzzle-maker had allowed this tiny trace to serve as a clue—or rather, as a bait—on a hundred jigsaws or so only in order to mislead him the more later on. (*LUM,* 336)

In this case, quotation marks hint at the falsity of Bartlebooth's initial judgment, even before the narrator elaborates on Winckler's trick. Bartlebooth must not only be alert to the traps set for him by Winckler, but also has to thwart Beyssandre's schemes to obtain one of the watercolors. In this case he does not mistake design for coincidence: "Divers incidents qui pouvaient difficilement passer pour des coïncidences montrèrent [. . .] que Beyssandre n'abandonnait pas" (Various incidents that could not easily be ascribed to chance proved nonetheless that Beyssandre had not given up) (*VME,* 509–10/*LUM,* 434). These occurrences include a burglary, an arson attack, and finally an "inexplicable" car accident that kills Rorschash's camera crew (*VME,* 510).

As in Hume's skeptical solution to the problem of causal induction, the frequency of events is a key factor in inferring the relationship between them. The coincidence surprises by its rarity, and too many coincidences awaken suspicions. Coincidences and apparent coincidences are variously accompanied by the adjectives "sublime" (*VME,* 123), "admirable" (*VME,* 255), "extraordinaire" (*VME,* 459)—the event is marked out as notable, from the point of view of a particular individual. Yet the word *coïncidence* may also point to the insignificance or irrelevance of an event or correspondence—*mere* coincidence. In *La Vie mode d'emploi,* as in *La Disparition,* false coincidences fit into a broad network of themes related to deception, illusion, and ruse. They also represent one point of contact with the conventions and structures of the detective plot, present in numerous micronarratives of *La Vie mode d'emploi.* The detective narrative is well placed to explore the epistemological problem of appearance and interpretation: how do we distinguish between incriminating evidence and an accidental connection? In the story of the Danglars and their kleptomania, for instance, Inspector Blanchet examines the records of thefts committed during society soirées and notices that the couple appear on twenty-nine of the thirty-four invitation lists, but for the police prefect this is a case of "simple coïncidence" (*VME,* 474).

The coincidence is something inherently insignificant because it does not itself result from an intention or design, yet it takes on significance because of its consequences (which are then all the more surprising, curious, or sublime because they result from the nonagency of chance). This ambiguous status of the coincidence—as simultaneously significant and meaningless—creates particular interpretative problems. Even the peritextual notice at the beginning of the novel highlights this question, offering a variation on a stereotyped formula that emphasizes the unintentional nature of certain connections: "L'amitié, l'histoire et la littérature m'ont fourni quelques-uns des personnages de ce livre. Toute autre ressemblance avec des individus vivants ou ayant réellement ou fictivement existé ne saurait être que coïncidence" (Friendship, history, and literature have supplied me with some of the characters of this book. All other resemblances to living persons or to people having lived in reality or fiction can only be coincidental) (*VME,* 13/*LUM,* n.p.). Perec transforms the traditional affirmation of fictitiousness (more common in film than in literature) into a tautology. All that is not intentional is accidental, but how is the reader to tell the difference?

Chance and Detection

In the fictional section of *W ou le souvenir d'enfance,* as we have seen, the Athletes are at the mercy of "divers systèmes *apparemment* fondés sur le seul hasard" (various systems *apparently* based on pure chance) (*W,* 208/*WMC,* 153; emphasis added). The Officials of W deliberately cultivate the ambiguity between chance and design so that it is impossible to tell the difference between "le choix du hasard" and "un hasard de leur choix" (*W,* 209–10) (the choice of chance and a chance of their choice). This uncertainty serves only to make more inevitable the final goal of the system—the destruction of the Athletes (*W,* 220)—all the while disguising this knowledge from the victims themselves. On the other hand, the illusion of coincidence can be used as a protective ploy, as shown by one of Perec's childhood recollections:

> Nous arrivâmes dans une clairière, où nous attendait un groupe de maquisards. Nous leur donnâmes nos musettes. Je me souviens que je fus très fier de comprendre que cette rencontre n'était pas du tout le fait du hasard et que la promenade habituelle du jeudi n'avait été cette fois que le prétexte choisi pour aller ravitailler les Résistants. (*W,* 153)

> We got to a clearing where a group of partisans awaited us. We gave them our satchels. I remember being very proud to grasp that the meeting had not happened by chance and that our usual Thursday walk had this time been cover for getting supplies to the Resistance. (*WMC,* 114)

Subjective judgment, understanding, and recognition are at stake in the distinction between the presence and absence of agency. The notion of chance—and in this case its usefulness as a disguise—is therefore bound up with epistemological and ethical questions. In Perec's works, it is also tied to the theme of textual interpretation and thus to the reader's horizon of expectations. Many of Perec's narratives exploit self-reflexivity and play with generic conventions not merely as "postmodern" ploys but as a way of staging and exploring the problem of chance.

While chance events play an important role in the adventure story, the theme of *apparent* chance as illusion takes on particular significance in detective fiction. While often identified as a popular or "paraliterary" genre (distinct from great art, according to Tzvetan Todorov, because of its attachment to its own norms),[13] the detective story had considerable influence on many twentieth-century literary works. Robbe-Grillet's *Les Gommes,* Michel Butor's *L'Emploi du temps* (1956; *Passing Time*), and Umberto Eco's *Name of the Rose* (1980) are notable examples. Unsurprisingly, given the genre's ludic character and emphasis on conventions (as formulated, for instance, in S. S. Van Dine's twenty rules for writing detective fiction), the Oulipo has taken a particular interest in the classic, enigma-based model of the crime story. According to Todorov, this form (as distinct from the later noir version) involves two distinct temporal series: the story of the detective's inquiry and the (retrospective, reconstructed) story of the crime. The story of the inquiry has a particular status, since it recounts the construction of the narrative as a whole.[14] Such a narrative becomes a game between writer and reader and lends itself well both to the constraint-driven manipulations of the Oulipo and to metanarrative manipulation.[15]

As for Perec, his fascination with the detective genre is indicated by the preprogrammed allusions to Agatha Christie in *La Vie mode d'emploi* and by the multiple detective stories in that novel, from the absurd tale "L'Assassinat des poissons rouges" ("The Murder of the Goldfish") to the story of the fire in the Danglars' apartment. *La Disparition* is, in Jeanne Ewert's words, a novel that "deals more destruction to truth seekers than perhaps any other metaphysical detective story" and "screams its detectives' incompetence from every page; it hurls the missing *E* in its reader's face."[16] Unsurprisingly, a key intertext for this novel is Edgar Allan Poe's "The Purloined Letter"; just before his disappearance Anton Voyl reads a version in which Dupin fails to find the crucial manuscript (*VME,* 53–54). In the more successful quest of *Les Revenentes* (Perec's complement to *La Disparition* in which the only vowel is the letter *e*), the protagonists have no difficulty in using Dupin's methods to discover the Bishop's jewels: "Te rémembères les 'Lettres Menquentes': le meyer recette de céler est de sembler lesser en éveedence!" (Remember 'The Fleeced Letters'? The best secret's when we leeve the key reveeled!).[17] However, it is Perec's last novel, the unfinished *"53 jours"* (1989; *"53 Days"*) that comes closest to the detective model in its overall structure.

In detective fiction, chance generally features only as a deceptive appearance. As Sabine Hillen points out in her discussion of the "fait divers" (incident) in *La Vie mode d'emploi,* the notion of chance is connected to that of the enigma: faced with the causal complexity behind a particular situation, we use the word to name our confusion.[18] The mystery novel generally offers a reduction of this complexity by eventually providing the solution to the enigma. In this sense, it offers a reassuring epistemological vision. In fact, it is perhaps the detective novel that most systematically applies the *post hoc ergo propter hoc* fallacy to causality. Citing Conan Doyle's fictional detective Sherlock Holmes, for whom it is "unthinkable" that the universe is ruled by chance, Peter Brooks suggests that the detective novel is symptomatic of a historically conditioned need for narrative form: "The urgency of narrative explanation in modern times is [. . .] well represented in that nineteenth-century invention, the detective story, which claims that all action is motivated, causally enchained, and eventually comprehensible as such to the perceptive observer."[19] In "The Mystery of Marie Rogêt," Edgar Allan Poe's detective Auguste Dupin proclaims that it is necessary to "make chance a matter of absolute calculation."[20]

Following Howard Haycraft, Patricia Merivale and Susan Elizabeth Sweeney give the name of "metaphysical detective story" to "a genre of largely twentieth-century experimental fiction" distinguished by the "profound questions that it raises about narrative, interpretation, subjectivity, the nature of reality, and the limits of knowledge."[21] Chance, causality, and motivation are among the epistemological themes that such texts address. Borges's "Death and the Compass" is a case in point: the detective Lönnrot comes to believe that a series of murders are linked to kabbalistic symbolism; however, it is eventually revealed that the first murder was an accident (a case of mistaken identity) and that the murderer Scharlach has used the others to ensnare the detective in a trap.[22] Narrative self-reflexivity is a key element in Borges's text: Dominique Jullien argues that the crimes become works of art authored by Scharlach, who places Lönnrot in the role of commentator while transforming the latter's commentary into creation.[23]

There are some striking parallels here with Perec's *"53 jours."* In the first part of Perec's novel the murderer is an author who uses his story and the detective-narrator's commentary on it to frame the detective for a murder. However, the final irony of Borges's story is the fact that the perfect crime depends on an initial chance event, a mistaken identity; furthermore, the police superintendent does reach a correct hypothesis about the first murder, but only by chance. As Jeanne Ewert notes, Lönnrot (unlike Poe's Dupin) fails in his identification with the other, "or rather, Lönnrot fails because he has attempted to identify with the wrong adversary; the Other is not any human agent, but chance itself. The solution for which he searches is purely aleatory, and he fails to double his adversary because the aleatory cannot be mirrored."[24] In the first half of Perec's text, on the other hand, the murderer's machinations seem perfectly crafted from beginning to end, excluding chance. Nevertheless, the conventions of the detective narrative are disrupted by mirroring devices and narrative embedding, which leave the reader in perpetual doubt as to how to judge appearances, how to decide which apparent coincidences conceal motivations and meanings.

Clue and Coincidence

The narrative of *"53 jours"* is structured by two principal mysteries that revolve around texts. The story of the first section is set in a fictional African country, Grianta, which is governed by a dictator. The author Robert Serval goes missing and the narrator, Veyraud,[25] seeks the key to the enigma in Serval's incomplete detective novel, *La Crypte* (*The Crypt*), which in turn contains another detective story, *Le Juge est l'assassin* (*The Magistrate Is the Murderer*); later, a spy novel, *K comme Koala* (*The Koala Case Mystery*) will be revealed as another source for the novel. It is eventually revealed that Veyraud is simply a pawn in an elaborate scheme set up by Serval, who succeeds in framing him for murder. The second part of the novel, titled "Un R est un M qui se P le L de la R" ("Un roman est un miroir qui se promène le long de la route"—"A Novel Is a Mirror Walking Along a Road"),[26] is unfinished, but Perec's notes allow us to gather that it shifts Veyraud's narrative onto a secondary diegetic level. Now referred to as *53 jours,*[27] the story of Veyraud's inquiry functions as a piece of evidence in another mystery, the murder or suicide of another Robert Serval, which is investigated by the detective Salini.

"53 jours" contains a set of embedded narratives and multiple *mises-en-abyme* that both echo and undermine one another; as Michel Sirvent states, the core of the enigma is "this virtually infinite, metadiegetic, digressive, and reflexive structure through which the narrative progresses."[28] At first view, the role of chance in the plot conforms to the conventions of the detective narrative. Nothing is what it seems, and what appear to be chance events usually merit special attention, signaling vital clues to the text's solution. Isabelle Dangy-Scaillierez sees Veyraud as a model of the inadequate reader who ignores the coincidences that could alert him to the artificial nature of the mystery.[29] However, Veyraud does recognize that any good reader of detective novels will be suspicious of "coincidences" in the plot: "L'hypothèse d'un accident (à laquelle aucun lecteur ne croirait sérieuse-

ment) n'est émise que pour être aussitôt écartée" (The supposition of a road accident [which no reader would seriously entertain] is only made in order to be shot down forthwith) (*"53J,"* 40/ *"53D,"* 24).

Constantly attentive to the possibility of encrypted references, Veyraud also hesitates to attribute to mere coincidence the associations that can be made between *La Crypte* and the political reality of Grianta. He concludes, for example, that the similarities between the chief of Grianta's secret police, Blabami, and the character Fly of *Le Juge est l'assassin* (a text that serves as a clue in *La Crypte*) cannot all be coincidences; some must be intentional, even if he cannot decipher the meaning behind them (*"53J,"* 96). Similarly, he notes a possible allusion in Serval's text to the scandal surrounding the theft of a statue in Grianta; this affair involves, among other people, a certain Joseph Boss, an antiques dealer who specializes in walking canes: "Dans *Le Juge est l'assassin,* la machination contre Fly s'appuie sur une histoire de collectionneurs de cannes. Est-ce une coïncidence?" (In *The Magistrate Is the Murderer,* the sting is built around Fly being a collector of walking-sticks. Coincidence?) (*"53J,"* 127/ *"53D,"* 91). The narrator's alertness to possible machinations behind apparent coincidences is not focused only on the text, but also on the political spectacles of Grianta. He comments ironically on the method used to distribute the findings of Grianta's archeological dig: "Le hasard attribua on ne peut plus opportunément la statue de Dioclétien au musée du Louvre, ce qui permit de faire exactement coïncider sa mise en place avec la visite officielle que le Président-à-Vie devait effectuer en France à la mi-mars 1980" (The luck of the draw most conveniently attributed the statue of Diocletian to the Louvre, which allowed its first showing to coincide exactly with the President-for-Life's official visit to France, scheduled for mid-March 1980) (*"53J,"* 123/ *"53D,"* 88).

Where Veyraud fails to be sufficiently suspicious, however, is in his interpretation of connections between the text and his own life. He therefore dismisses as mere "coincidences" the crucial clues that point to his own role in the drama. It is this weakness that ensnares him in Serval's machination—for it is in fact Serval, the apparent victim, who has engineered the whole mystery. Veyraud recognizes similarities between the places that play a role in Serval's plot and those that he frequents in Grianta, but dismisses this as a "strange coincidence" rather than a clue to Serval's machinations (*"53J,"* 65). In another incident, Veyraud discovers that Serval's text was typed using an Olivetti typewriter. This seems to be a stroke of luck, for he happens to know ("par un véritable coup de chance"—by a splendid stroke of luck) the Olivetti representative in Grianta (*"53J,"* 75/ *"53D,"* 52).

Again, he realizes too late that the author has manipulated him, choosing the brand of typewriter precisely for this reason (*"53J,"* 138).

In other words, Veyraud positions himself only as reader, and does not recognize that he is also a character in Serval's machination—and, of course, in Perec's novel. In adopting this attitude he is playing the expected role of the detective in the classic enigma-based model where, as Todorov notes, nothing can happen to the detective.[30] Although it may be tempting to distinguish the figure of the "bad reader" (Veyraud) from that of the "good reader"—possibly represented by Salini[31]—who can trace the logical connections that link events,[32] the situation is more complicated. Furthermore, Veyraud reads *La Crypte* exactly as the author intended him to read it. On another level, the readers of Perec's text are in a position to recognize Veyraud's universe also as a diegetic one, as is Salini in the second half of *"53 jours."* Veyraud's dilemma is troubling because it undermines the usual boundary that separates valid interpretations—of texts and of events—from paranoid or superstitious overinterpretations.[33] It calls into question the difference between internal and external events that is crucial for distinguishing the accidental from the meaningful.

Red Herrings

While Veyraud is wrong to attribute some things to chance, in other cases he overinterprets both texts and events. Serval's machinations add a further twist to this problem: a resemblance between text and reality may be too striking to be a mere coincidence, but the narrator's recognition of this fact may not lead him any closer to the truth. A case in point is the encrypted presence of Grianta's secret police, the Main noire (Black Hand), in Serval's *La Crypte.* Veyraud is probably not mistaken in concluding that these references are not the result of his imagination or of chance (*"53J,"* 101), and yet it does not occur to him that the false coincidence may be designed precisely to awaken his suspicions and set him on the wrong track. This narrative pattern is repeated. Robert Serval, just before his disappearance, refuses to recount to the Consul the recent events that have troubled him, citing the possibility that they are "de simples coïncidences" (*"53J,"* 24). When Serval disappears, the Consul assumes that the threat must have been real, but it is later revealed that Serval's conversation with the Consul and his disappearance were part of an act. In the second part of the text, when Salini notices elements that connect the second Serval (i.e., the murder victim in this section) to the characters Robert Serval and the Consul in *53 jours,* he is rightly suspicious:

> L'auteur de *53 jours* multiplie les fausses pistes; c'est ainsi que Robert Serval sert de modèle, non seulement au personnage de Robert Serval, mais au consul et au narrateur: Serval, comme le consul, était né à Rouen sans être d'ascendance normande; comme le narrateur, il était allé plusieurs fois en vacances à Veulle-les-Roses; il y avait trop de détails de ce genre pour que ce soient des coïncidences. (*"53J,"* 147)

> The author of *53 Days* lays many false trails. For instance, Robert Serval is the model not only for the character of Robert Serval, but for the Consul and the narrator too. Like the Consul, Serval was born at Rouen without being of Norman ascent; like the narrator, he had spent several holidays at Veulle-les-Roses. There were too many details of this kind for them all to be coincidences. (*"53D,"* 108)

Another false path is the one that links *53 jours* to Stendhal and his novels, for example via allusions to the colors red and black, or by the Consul's choice "comme par hasard" (as if by chance) of Stendhal's favorite meal (*"53J,"* 149/*"53D,"* 110).[34] Once again, apparently insignificant details of the narrative are revealed to be important, but not in the way that one might think. Thus Salini believes that the disguised allusions to Stendhal point to Serval's betrayal of his fellow Résistants at a place called La Chartreuse (the Charterhouse) while in fact (at least as far as we can tell from the unfinished novel) the motivations of Serval's murderers have nothing to do with this. On these occasions, the reference to chance functions as a double bluff: the reader thinks he has cleverly deciphered the text's code by recognizing the appearance of chance as an illusion—"par hasard" as only "comme par hasard" (by chance; as if by chance)—while in fact his perspicacity leads him to fall all the more blindly into the intended trap. This trick resembles the strategies used by Humbert Raffke in *Un cabinet d'amateur,* who succeeds in making fake paintings appear authentic by making copies of them, and by Lord Ashtray in *La Vie mode d'emploi,* who hides his real passions behind false obsessions (*VME,* 531–32). Bernard Magné has referred to this as the strategy of the "double cover" and pointed out its importance in Perec's works.[35] The appearance of chance is particularly difficult to interpret since it may function as either a cover or a double cover.

The movement from detecting an apparent coincidence to hypothesizing a motivated connection is nonetheless an important part of the reading process. Another of Perec's texts, the short story *Le Voyage d'hiver* (*The Winter Journey*), presents this development as relatively unproblematic. In this allegory of the Oulipian notion of "anticipatory plagiarism,"[36] the academic Vincent Degraël[37] finds a text by a nineteenth-century writer, Hugo Vernier, who seems at first to be a plagiarist but in fact turns out to be a precursor of all the great modernist poets. Degraël notices several intertextual similarities, which he initially discounts as partly accidental: "Peut-être pouvait-on prendre en compte les rencontres fortuites, les influences affichées, les hommages volontaires, les copies inconscientes, la volonté de pastiche, le goût des citations, les coïncidences heureuses" (Perhaps it should be put down to a fortuitous convergence, to a parading of influence, a deliberate homage, unconscious copying, wilful pastiche, a liking for quotation, a fortunate coincidence) (*VH,* 17/*WJ,* 8). However, he soon recognizes that these correspondences are too numerous to be true coincidences, and moves from the hypothesis of accident to the hypothesis of intentionality. After looking at the date of publication, he then realizes that this intention to plagiarize must be attributed not to Vernier but rather to his successors—Rimbaud, Mallarmé, Lautréamont, Gustave Kahn, Verlaine (*VH,* 18/*WJ,* 9).

In *"53 jours,"* the use of apparent coincidences as red herrings places the would-be interpreter in a more complex and delicate position. This problem becomes vertiginous when the search for clues is extended from the text's manifest "content"—plot elements, descriptions, etc.—to its form, for example when the reader manipulates letters to form new signifiers. In one such instance, Veyraud discovers the name "Blabami" in the form of an anagram that connects several words of the text. He does have doubts about this method of reading, noting that it is possible to become obsessed with anagrams and logogriphs: "on peut faire tout dire, par définition, aux vingt-six lettres de l'alphabet" (By definition, the twenty-six letters of the alphabet can be made to mean anything you want) (*"53J,"* 95/*"53D,"* 67). This form of exegesis implies that the distribution of letters cannot simply be discounted as a chance consequence of the arbitrariness of the linguistic sign. The second part of the novel further suggests that such approaches can be valid, for it reveals that the *53 jours* text contains a diagonal that spells "La Chartreuse." Yet once these readings are acknowledged, are we to conclude that all of the text's formal features are potentially meaningful? What are the limits of interpretation, and on what level can aspects of the text be attributed to chance?

Both the "Blabami" and "Chartreuse" paragrams seem to be ploys to set the intradiegetic readers (Veyrand and Salini) on the wrong track. Since Salini knows the outcome of *53 jours* (the first part of the book), he is necessarily aware of the dangers of this method of reading—"cette fastidieuse et interminable *explication de texte*" (this endless, pernickety *explication de texte*)—and yet he identifies with Veyraud as he himself struggles to find a path in a "réseau de miroirs trompeurs" (gallery of distorted mirrors) (*"53J,"* 158/*"53D,"* 119). A paradox emerges here: even the most subjective manipulations of the text by the reader somehow do not escape the author's control, for everything plays a part in the preplanned machination. Similarly, in the first part of the novel, Serval and his accomplice Lise are able to incorporate into their plans possible future events that they cannot entirely control. Thus they predict and make use of the violent protests and subsequent repression that mark the twenty-fifth anniversary of Grianta's independence (*"53J,"* 138). Serval's text *La Crypte* is an effective machination because it succeeds in abolishing or at least incorporating chance.

In the dizzying, potentially infinite game of mirrors that is *"53 jours,"* it is difficult to establish criteria for distinguishing between the true and the false. While the traditional detective narrative also leads the detective on false paths, they ultimately allow him to arrive at the truth; "the status of the false solution is epistemologically internal to the detective's final, true solution."[38] This is not clearly the case in *"53 jours."* Nor does the detective story offer an unequivocal lesson as an allegory of reading. Veyraud's fate seems to warn Salini of the dangers inherent in interpretation, but given the logic of the narrative and the theme of deceptive reflections, even this interpretation might be a trap. As it happens, it seems that Salini comes close to the truth, but the embedded structures of Perec's text put this reading into doubt. As Michel Sirvent notes, it seems that "no story can explain the puzzle that initiates it *on its own level*"; rather, a metadiegetic transfer may be necessary to resolve the enigma.[39] Since the novel is unfinished, however, it is hard to know what degree of narrative closure it would have offered.

Text and World

The different diegetic levels in *"53 jours"* allow not only a self-referential investigation of narrative mechanisms but also a reflection on the relationship between epistemology and hermeneutics, between the interpretation of the world and the interpretation of texts. In this context, the theme of chance relates questions of narrative focalization to more general problems of perception. What seems to be coincidence from one character's perspective may not be from another. In the case of Veyraud's first-person narration, the reader is initially in the same position of ignorance as the narrator. Even if the second part of the novel exists only in note form, Salini appears as the focal character. Veyraud's failure, and Salini's potential success, point to both the powers and the limits of the detective novel as a model for the human quest for knowledge. This observation lends weight to Marcel Bénabou's view that the movement from ignorance to knowledge is a general rule in Perec's works; the false and the fake offer a warning to the reader of the traps of representation while ultimately functioning as an instrument for the discovery of the truth.[40] In *Un cabinet d'amateur,* for example, the elaborate scheme set up by Hermann Raffke initially fools both Perec's reader and the art collectors of the story, but we eventually learn that all the paintings described are fakes. While Perec's *characters* may be completely deceived, the *reader's* quest for knowledge is never entirely thwarted by machinations or subject to chance.

However, the structure and themes of *"53 jours"* also undermine the reader's claim to final knowledge. As Bernard Magné suggests, Salini's uncovering of the mechanisms at work in the first part of the novel—the Stendhalian intertext, for example—might have functioned, in Perec's unwritten final version, as a disguise for other intertextual presences in the second part.[41] Like Veyraud, in other words, we might not realize that we too are players in the textual game. Even where Perec's detectives succeed, Isabelle Dangy argues, Perec transforms the epistemological optimism of the detective story into despair, since the reversals are not really the reward for the detective's previous efforts, but only the results of luck or chance.[42] Perec's texts thus present us with two different but perhaps equally disquieting epistemological models. In some cases, knowledge is created and manipulated by malevolent individuals (Serval and Lise). In others, it is made possible only by chance.

Like Borges's "Death and the Compass," Perec's tales of intrigue and machination can be considered allegories of authorial control; both narratives suggest the presence of a secret order that directs the plot. In *La Disparition,* a shadowy power deceives characters (who are also readers), with the illusion of chance (*D,* 46). *La Vie mode d'emploi* also has disturbing implications for the practice of reading. No matter how many chance events disrupt Bartlebooth's plans and influence the way he completes the puzzle, Gaspard Winckler's vengeance remains perfectly defined and circumscribed; he has seemingly foreseen every future contingency. In *"53 jours,"* the intradiegetic reader Veyraud is similarly manipulated into becoming a pawn in the author's game. The representation of artistic creation as akin to the divine act is not uncommon; it suggests a romantic conception of the artist that also owes much to the Platonic notion of the divine artificer.[43] However, Perec's author-God, at least as represented within the texts, seems more akin to Descartes' hypothesized evil genius than to a benevolent deity. Perec's texts thus raise the specter of radical skepticism: textual universes and even the actual world may be designed to deceive. The problem of chance adds another layer of complexity, since it suggests that some aspects of the text (or of the world) escape design altogether. Yet between chance and machination, the apparent divide often seems to be small.

While chance appears as an explicit theme in Perec's works, it is also explored through the medium of narrative form: through the causal links between events on the level of the plot, the structuring and motivating of these events on the level of the narrative, and the teleological movement of the narration. Playing on the tension between different narrative levels, with their different forms of causal organization, Perec's works foreground and question the finality of their own logic. In a self-reflexive gesture, the narrative investigates the powers and limits of its own mode of constructing causality. However, this reflexivity is never an end in itself. Perec's stories can never be divorced from the writer's effort to shape experience and come to terms with history.

"53 jours," as far as we may judge from the novel's unfinished state, both stages and forestalls the epistemological closure of the detective plot. Borrowing conventions and techniques from various genres, *La Disparition* and *La Vie mode d'emploi* emphasize the teleological movement of their narratives. Yet these novels are complicated by discontinuities, digressions, and stories within stories, to the point that arbitrariness and fragmentation seem to dominate. The multiple references to chance events accentuate this disjunction of causality. Significantly, it is with *La Disparition* that Perec first turns to chance-driven plots after the exploration of very different territory in *Les Choses* and *Un homme qui dort.* (This is not to say that these earlier texts do not investigate causality; however, they do not offer the same spectacular staging of narrativity.) This fact highlights a point that I will explore in subsequent chapters: the link between Perec's narrative explorations, his fascination with chance, and his adoption of Oulipian constraints.

Inspired by and assimilating numerous literary traditions, the digressions of *La Disparition* and the encyclopedic accumulation of stories in *La Vie mode d'emploi* represent both a homage to the novelistic tradition and a resistance to linear narrative. In some respects, these novels belong to the category of "beguiling narration" that Ross Chambers has called "loiterature," where the accidental "has become the rule," and which has its modern beginnings in Sterne's *Tristram Shandy*.[44] However, Perec's use of constraints and structures works against the formal looseness associated with such works. Significantly, Perec does not go to such extremes of narrative discontinuity as some of his contemporaries, such as Julio Cortázar or Maurice Roche, whose respective works *Hopscotch* and *Compact* he admires but considers insufficiently systematic (*EC* 1:103). As Warren Motte points out, "Perec takes position both against the preceding forms *and* against those of his contemporaries, such as Michel Tournier and J. M. G. Le Clézio, who, undoubtedly discouraged by the *apparent* bankruptcy of novelistic experimentation, chose to return to more traditional narrative modes."[45]

La Vie mode d'emploi is particularly successful in negotiating a new path between narrative discontinuity and unity. It presents itself as an exuberant encyclopedia of narrative possibilities, while at the same time problematizing narrative through dramatic excess and through the plurality and fragmentation of the various stories. The teleological movement of the novel is thematized by the multiple false coincidences of the plot, and the narrative of *La Vie mode d'emploi* indisputably has as its "final cause" the moment when Bartlebooth holds between his fingers a jigsaw piece that, instead of fitting the remaining X-shaped hole, has the form, "depuis longtemps prévisible dans son ironie même" (*VME,* 579) (long predictable in its very irony), of a W. Harry Mathews contends of this ending that "the abundance of stories, the multiplicity of lives, have brought us to a conclusion empty of life and possibility; all we have now read collapses in a hopeless finality."[46] Yet for whom was this collapse predictable? Does this "longtemps" refer to the chronological time of the story, the *histoire* (as reconstituted by the reader, for it has been scattered among different chapters of the novel), or is it what Genette calls the "pseudo-time" of the narrative (*récit*) as we read it? The irony of this moment lies partly in the gap between the predictability that governs the level of the *narration* and the unpredictability of Bartlebooth's life on the level of his own diegetic existence. On one level he is the plaything of chance and of Gaspard Winckler; on another he is the victim of his inevitable destiny, caught in Perec's own machination. Jacques Roubaud suggests that Bartlebooth's death is an allegory of the novel form itself, destined for effacement because it must end. Bartlebooth's project of self-effacement nevertheless fails, suggesting the novel's desire to defer its own end.[47] Perhaps this conclusion is not so final after all.

In fact, the novel emphasizes from the beginning the arbitrariness of its own order: "Oui, cela pourrait commencer ainsi, comme ça" (Yes, it could begin this way, right here, just like that) (*VME,* 21/*LUM,* 3). Other beginnings, other versions of the novel would have been possible. (Although the phrase echoes Céline's "Ça a débuté comme ça" [It started off like that] in *Voyage au bout de la nuit,*[48] it also contrasts with it, emphasizing hesitation and slowness.) The novel's epigraph, borrowed from Paul Klee, nevertheless tells us that the reader's response to the text is governed by a certain necessity: "L'œil suit les chemins qui lui ont été ménagés dans l'œuvre" (The eye follows the paths that have been laid down for it in the work) (*VME,* 17/*LUM,* n.p.). The form of *La Vie mode d'emploi* thus realizes Perec's ambition, voiced in his 1967 lecture "Écriture et mass-media" ("Writing and Mass Media") to find new models of narrative discontinuity without abandoning literary form to randomness. The solution, according to Perec, lies in the elaboration of "un code des contraintes et des subversions permettant de définir les limites de l'œuvre entre le trop aléatoire et le trop déterminé" (*EC* 1:103) (a code of constraints and subversions that allows you to set the limits of the work between the overly random and the overly determined). It is to this question of constraints that I turn in chapter 5, which aims to situate Perec's fascination with chance in the context of the anti-aleatory aesthetics of the Oulipo.

Car il y a et il n'y a pas de hasard.

For there is and is not chance.

—Mallarmé

5. A Challenge to Chance: The Poetics of the Oulipo

Since its founding in 1960, the Ouvroir de littérature potentielle (Workshop for Potential Literature) has defied attempts to characterize its goals and creative work. Unlike other literary groups of the twentieth century (such as the surrealists or *Tel Quel*), it avoids adopting positions in political debates and keeps a skeptical distance from contemporary intellectual trends. Focusing on practice rather than theory, the group quickly abandoned the pedagogic and scientific implications of its initial name—Séminaire de littérature expérimentale (Seminar for Experimental Literature)—in favor of the more modest notion of an "ouvroir" (workshop, but with the secondary meaning of "sewing circle"). The Oulipo is not easily labeled an avant-garde movement, since it insists less on novelty than on its debt to tradition.[1] At the same time, the authority of the literary past is undermined by the group's emphasis on the arbitrary constraint rather than the normative aesthetic rule.

The difficulty of defining an Oulipian poetics is compounded by the transformations that have marked the group during almost fifty years of existence. As Jacques Roubaud points out, the term *contrainte* (constraint), now a key term in the group's theoretical writings, is conspicuously absent in early texts.[2] François Le Lionnais' first manifesto (1961) emphasizes two directions of research: an analytic tendency that focuses on the exploitation of existing structures, and a synthetic tendency that aims to create new forms and formulas.[3] Yet the notions of "structure," "form," and "formula" remain rather imprecise here, amalgamating linguistic and mathematical notions. (In his second manifesto of 1973, Le Lionnais wryly coins the term *structurEliste* to differentiate the Oulipian perspective from the then-fashionable *structurAlisme.*)[4] The gradual shift toward the term *constraint* has not brought further clarity, for the notion is almost impossible to circumscribe. Oulipian constraints are not always purely formal, as is often assumed; their sheer variety—mathematical, syntactic, metrical, lexical, "lettric," semantic—makes generalizations about the group's work difficult. The notorious "S+7" (N+7) method—which consists in replacing every noun in a given text with the seventh one following it in a dictionary[5]—is very different from the semantic manipulations of Perec and Bénabou's Production automatique de littérature française (Automatic Production of French Literature), or PALF,[6] which in turn is unlike the complex combinatorics that governs the narrative structure of Perec's *La Vie mode d'emploi* or Italo Calvino's *Se una notte d'inverno un viaggiatore* (*If on a Winter's Night a Traveler*). Furthermore, the status of Oulipian textual experiments often remains unclear. The group's initial goal, as stated in early texts, was not to write Oulipian literature but more modestly to fabricate tools for use by writers and to offer brief illustrations of these tools.[7] While the Oulipo continues to insist on the virtue of the short illustrative exercise (such as the texts published in the Bibliothèque Oulipienne series) in demonstrating a particular constraint, the emergence of significant Oulipian works by such writers as Perec, Calvino, and Roubaud has amplified the group's ambitions. Suspicious of dogma, the Oulipo does not propound a coherent theory of literature. The Oulipo member Hervé Le Tellier wryly states in *Esthétique de l'Oulipo* that there is no Oulipian aesthetics; that is, there exists no Oulipian concept of the beautiful.[8] If I refer here to Oulipian "poetics," this term should be taken in a broad sense, since one of the Oulipo's achievements is to apply traditionally poetic constraints to prose genres and in particular to the novel. Even allowing for this breadth of application, Oulipian poetics resists definition. Oulipo members express widely divergent views on such questions as the meaning of "potentiality," the need to hide or display the constraint, and the role of mathematics in the group's project. Nevertheless, the members of the group clearly share certain assumptions, which may be summarized as two related principles. First, the Oulipo counters the post-romantic notion of innate genius with an emphasis on techniques and rules of writing.[9] The second idea, and the main focus of this chapter, was first voiced by Claude Berge in the Oulipo meeting on April 12, 1962: "Nous sommes essentiellement anti-hasard"

(We are essentially anti-chance). Significantly, Queneau expressed doubts about this turn of phrase: "Nous ne sommes peut-être pas tellement 'anti'. Je préférerais dire que nous manifestons une certaine méfiance à l'égard du hasard" (We are perhaps not so very 'anti.' I would prefer to say that we display a certain suspicion with regard to chance). Berge then reformulated his claim in terms of a challenge to chance: "Nous lançons un défi au hasard" (We throw down a challenge to chance).[10] Queneau's objection notwithstanding, the term *anti-hasard,* "anti-chance," has almost become the group's motto. Noël Arnaud cites anti-chance as the main point of "theoretical unanimity" within the Oulipo,[11] and the expression appears under the heading "chance" in the *Oulipo Compendium.*[12] Hervé Le Tellier asserts that the group members have in common the rejection of chance, in the absence of any particular aesthetic theory.[13] The abolition of chance through constraint is a central theme in Georges Perec's *La Disparition,* and Jacques Roubaud, Jacques Bens, and Marcel Bénabou all refer to anti-chance as a principle.[14]

The Oulipo today has gained an international influence that reaches far beyond the number of its actual members. In the ensuing poetic and critical context, and especially when judged from outside France, the group is often identified with the broad set of tendencies that Marjorie Perloff has termed "procedural poetics."[15] Under this rubric, the Oulipo writers are often seen as French counterparts of John Cage, Jackson Mac Low, or the Fluxus poets.[16] The existence of cross-cultural affinities cannot be denied. Nevertheless, the Oulipo's apparent rejection of chance-based operations, along with its ambivalent attitude toward avant-gardism in general, set it apart from many other procedural approaches. The notion of anti-chance, with all its attendant ambiguity, offers a key to understanding the elusive poetics of the Oulipo.

Chance and the Oulipo's Critics

Chance is a central and contested term in debates about the Oulipo's value and status. Despite the Oulipo's insistence that it is "anti-chance," attacks on the group have often claimed precisely the opposite. Provoking indignant responses from Oulipians, the critic Gérard Genette has argued that Oulipian writing is "a game of chance, like roulette," and a variation on the surrealist word-collage game known as the "cadavre exquis" (exquisite corpse).[17] Focusing on "mechanical" constraints such as the S+7 method, Genette claims that the Oulipian approach involves no semantic intention and that any resulting meaning is therefore accidental.[18] The Oulipo's fierce reaction to Genette's characterization reiterates the anti-chance principle and emphasizes the distance between Oulipian practices and surrealist automatic writing.[19] But Genette's apparent misunderstanding is a common one. Under the heading "aléatoire," the Robert dictionary cites the "theories of the Oulipo" to illustrate the notion of the aleatory work of literature. Nor is Genette alone in disputing the group's claims to literary seriousness. Adopting a more virulent tone, the poet and critic Henri Meschonnic attacks the Oulipo's "ludic mathematization," which uses chance and calculation to produce "une caricature, par son volontarisme, de la contrainte interne que doit exercer un poème sur lui-même, sur les autres poèmes, sur le sujet écrivant et lisant, pour être un poème" (a caricature, in its voluntarism, of the internal constraint that a poem should exert on itself, on other poems, on the writing and reading subject, in order to be a poem).[20] Poetics, according to Meschonnic, should not precede poetry, and the predetermined exercise of will—the "volontarism" of the Oulipian constraint—should not be confused with the inner necessity of the poem.

Leaving aside the questionable validity of the ludic/serious distinction, the key terms in this debate are subjectivity, intention, and automatism. Although Meschonnic's idiosyncratic poetics rests on his own particular conception of the subject's relationship to language and rhythm, his objection and Genette's both rest on the place of the subject and intention in the writing process. Where Genette sees an absence of semantic intention, Meschonnic complains that the constraint embodies excessive, external intentionality with regard to form. Both argue that a split between form and content ultimately leads to the evacuation of the subject from the text. The critic Laurent Jenny voices a similar objection, arguing that the Oulipo furthers a contemporary tendency—inaugurated by the surrealists, once again—toward an "automatisation of speech," creating a form of communication that is ahistorical, cut off from the circumstances of discourse.[21] For the group's detractors, the Oulipian constraint engenders a form of automatism that eliminates subjectivity from the writing process, thus producing a form of chance. The central point of confusion here is that for others such as Jacques-Denis Bertharion and Warren Motte, the pre-elaborated systems of constraint are precisely what constitute Oulipian *anti*-chance.[22] The disagreement stems in part from the familiar confusion between two conceptions of chance: chance as absence of intention on the one hand, and chance as indeterminism on the other. However, to delve more deeply into this problem, we need to take a closer look at the Oulipo's insistence on "anti-chance."

Voluntary Literature: Oulipian Anti-Surrealism

At first glance, the anti-chance formula simply encapsulates the Oulipo's "theoretical anti-surrealism,"[23] its insistence on conscious control of the writing process. Chance in this context is associated with the haphazard outpourings of the unconscious, and in particular with the automatic writing advocated by the first surrealist manifesto.[24] Yet the surrealist concept of chance is double-edged. André Breton was, after all, an admirer of Freud, who refused to consider chance as a determining element in psychic life.[25] When Breton defines surrealism as an "automatisme psychique pur" (pure psychic automatism) that, in the absence of any intervention of reason, expresses "le fonctionnement réel de la pensée" (the real functioning of thought),[26] it is clear that this inner reality is not considered wholly random. Indeed, from the surrealist point of view, rational, moral and aesthetic preoccupations represent a set of exterior accidents that obscure and disrupt the essential operation of the mind. This reversibility of chance and necessity is most evident in *L'Amour fou* (1937; *Mad Love*), where Breton develops the notion of "objective chance." Having reviewed several different definitions of chance, from Aristotle to Freud, Breton settles on the definition of chance as the "la forme de manifestation de la nécessité extérieure qui se fraie un chemin dans l'inconscient humain" (the form of manifestation of exterior necessity which clears itself a path in the human unconscious).[27] The difference between this account and the Aristotelian definition is that the internal finality, for Breton, may exist in the unconscious. Breton goes on to posit the necessity of such encounters, overtly praising the paranoid faculty of overinterpretation: the forms that we see in the clouds are in no way accidental, but augural.[28] Italo Calvino argues convincingly that Breton's formula "did away with the irrationality of chance."[29] Objective chance, illuminated and motivated by surrealist logic, is no longer chance at all.

Raymond Queneau, cofounder of the Oulipo with François Le Lionnais in 1960, was a member of the surrealist group in the 1920s. His bitter rupture with the group, on both ideological and personal grounds, colors the theoretical critique of surrealism that he develops from the 1930s onward. Significantly, Queneau does not so much reproach the surrealists for surrendering to absolute chance as he criticizes them for being slaves to psychological determinism: poetic inspiration, if it consists in blindly obeying impulses, is really a form of enslavement. The classical tragedian who obeys a certain number of given rules is freer than the poet who, writing everything that comes into his mind, is subject to "other rules which he does not know."[30] Rather than setting up a dichotomy between chance and constraint, Queneau contrasts conscious and unconscious constraints. The need to maximize conscious control of the writing process is a key principle behind Queneau's use of numerical constraints in his early novels[31] and the Oulipo's later promotion of systematic, rule-governed writing. "Il n'y a de littérature que volontaire" (The only literature is voluntary literature), announced Queneau in one of the group's early meetings.[32] "We want to predict what we are doing," claims Georges Perec in an interview.[33] Jacques Bens goes even further, stating that the Oulipian writer tries to foresee all possible meanings of the text—thus extending the ideal of authorial control to the consequences of the reading process.[34] Bens's extreme position, while not necessarily shared by all Oulipians, rests on a valorization of hyperintentionality that is not uncommon in reflection on literature and art. Yet the precise status of intention—and its relationship to literary form—is subject to historical and ideological variation.

Oulipian anti-surrealism should therefore be set in a wider post-romantic context. Its roots can be traced to the backlash against the romantic emphasis on genius, inspiration, and spontaneity, and an increasing emphasis on form as the locus of authorial control over meaning. In French literature, the formalism of the Parnassian poets and Baudelaire's praise of the sonnet,[35] as well as Flaubert's emphasis on the work of writing, are just a few instances of this, as is Paul Valéry's interest in "*poïetique*"—in the making (*poïein*) of the poem as intellectual process and mobilization of particular means and techniques.[36] In the debate surrounding verse constraints in particular, the idea of chance is frequently invoked as a critical concept. Master of the variable-length verset line, Paul Claudel is close to the romantic sensibility when he complains of the immobile, airless monotony of traditional French verse, attributing this formal rigidity to "l'horreur du hasard" that is part of the French national character.[37] On the other hand, romanticism's critics insist on the haphazard nature of much "inspired" writing as well as on the value of traditional constraints.[38] This is not to say that these writers entirely discount the role of chance in the creative process; Valéry's *Cahiers,* for example, contain a rich reflection on the writer's capacity to exploit the possibilities opened by chance.

Despite Perec's claim that literary history deliberately ignores "l'écriture comme pratique, comme travail, comme jeu" ("HL," 79) (writing as practice, as work, as play), Oulipo writers are clearly not alone in emphasizing the importance of form, of difficulty, and indeed of the struggle against chance. Yet their work is perceived as fundamentally different from that of Flaubert or Valéry, who are never accused of playing roulette or of being unserious writers. To understand the provocative nature of Oulipian experiments, it is first worth noting that despite the group's predilection for formal rules, Oulipo writers in general do not share the classicist sensibility of a Valéry.[39] According to the Oulipo writer Jacques Jouet, "classicism has chiseled out a fairly constraining form that it considers natural."[40] The Oulipo, on the other hand, aims not to propose a set of general, authoritative rules but rather to explore the creative possibilities of various literary forms. In this sense, its approach is similar to that of the *rhétoriqueur* poets who, according to Paul Zumthor, assert the rights of virtuosity and technical mastery for their own sakes.[41] In its admiration for the *rhétoriqueur* tradition, the Oulipo associates itself with an often-denounced tendency in literature, one that E. R. Curtius traces back to the sixth century and labels "formal mannerism." Among the examples of the "systematic affectation" that Curtius condemns as "unnatural" are the lipogram—a text that omits a particular letter of the alphabet—and the pangram—a sentence that uses every letter of the alphabet at least once.[42] Both forms have been adopted by Oulipians.

The Oulipo calls into question the distinction, implicit in Curtius's account, between the natural rule, which is an acceptable part of literary technique, and the artificial, mannerist constraint.[43] It insists on the arbitrary dimension of even the most time-honored forms, such as the sonnet. This is not to say that all literary rules are automatically Oulipian. An example offered by Raymond Queneau illustrates this point: Flaubert's effort to avoid repeating words in close proximity might be considered an Oulipian rule, according to Queneau, but in order for it to be truly so, a writer would have to avoid a word for exactly "15 lines, or 17, or 16."[44] We witness a shift here from an aesthetically motivated principle (the avoidance of repetition) to a constraint that presents an exceptional and to some extent arbitrary challenge: why fifteen or seventeen lines rather than any other number? Of course, fixed poetic forms such as the sonnet or sestina have long imposed such restrictions in number, although the insertion of these forms into a literary tradition attenuates our sense of the arbitrary. The Oulipian approach, while it does not reject tradition, foregrounds and accentuates the arbitrary dimension of constraint. This move is at the heart of the controversy surrounding Oulipian anti-chance: the group's emphasis on conscious control of the writing process is closely tied to the arbitrariness of the constraint, but it is this very arbitrariness that its critics identify with chance.

Aleatory Art

The problem of the interaction of chance, rules, and the arbitrary extends beyond literature. Attempts to give chance a role in the creative process can be traced back to the avant-garde works of the early twentieth century. In the visual arts, the use of chance procedures is perhaps exemplified in its purest conceptual form by Marcel Duchamp's *Trois stoppages étalon* (1913; *Three Standard Stoppages*), created by dropping three threads onto three canvases then varnishing them into place. Kurt Schwitters's collages of bus tickets, rags, and other discarded materials transform apparently random, insignificant fragments into works of art. Preceding surrealist experiments in automatic writing and meditations on "objective chance," Blaise Cendrars's *Prose du Transsibérien* (*Prose of the Transsiberian*) of 1913 presents in stream-of-consciousness form, espousing the rhythm of a train journey, the poet's sporadic impressions and thoughts. But it is in the second half of the twentieth century that the fascination with disorder, chance, and indeterminacy reached its apogee. Notable examples in the visual arts include Robert Rauschenberg's assemblages (or "combines") of disparate objects and his silkscreen collages of media images.[45] Jackson Pollock's action painting, Francis Bacon's practice of flinging paint or a sponge at the canvas, Jean Dubuffet's *art brut,* and Pierre Soulages' *tachisme* all incorporate chance to a degree, and to very different aesthetic effects.

A consideration of developments in twentieth-century music is particularly useful in illuminating the complex relationship between chance and constraints, setting it in the framework of the tension between the "automatic" aspects of a system and intentional composition. While the Western musical tradition has always established strict rules of modes and harmonies, the twentieth century saw the creation of new systems for composition, in particular the serial technique inaugurated by Schoenberg's twelve-tone music. On the other hand, composers in the second half of the century increasingly introduced elements of indeterminacy into their music. As Suzanne Winter points out, this is in part a reaction to a perceived crisis in strictly serial music in the 1950s, resulting largely from the irreducible conflict between rigidity of organization and the chance effects that are perceived to emerge from this very rigidity.[46] Pierre Boulez describes in an interview the total serialism of his own *Structures* for two pianos (1951–52) as an instance where the "automatism" of musical relations is pushed to the point of absurdity, the complexity of the mechanism both reducing the role of individual invention and generating an excess of order that was equivalent to disorder.[47] Boulez is concerned here primarily with the composer's creative control over an increasingly autonomous system. Conversely, the composer Iannis Xenakis points out the limits of serialism from the point of view of the *listener:* to the ear, the enormously complex structures of such music are often indistinguishable from a random mass of notes.[48] Xenakis's solution is to introduce probability calculations to composition.

It is in this context that the adjective *aléatoire* (aleatory) began to be applied to certain musical works after 1955. Boulez, for his part, invoked the principle of *alea,* chance, as one remedy to the excessive rigidity of serial music. In his Third Piano Sonata (1955–57), the five movements (except for the third, which must be central) can be combined in different ways according to the choice of the performer. However, the composer most famous for incorporating chance procedures into his work is undoubtedly John Cage. In composing *Music of Changes* (1951), a piece inspired by the Chinese *I-Ching,* Cage flipped coins to determine tempos, the number of simultaneous layers, dynamic levels, pitches, and sound categories.[49] His *Imaginary Landscape no. IV* (1951) uses twelve radio receivers, whose wavelengths and dynamic levels are based on chart positions derived from coin tosses. The composer has no knowledge of what will be broadcast on the given frequencies at the time of performance.[50]

In fact, the term *aleatory* is used in music criticism to designate different kinds of procedure, and the same imprecision ensues when it is transferred to other artistic domains. It is therefore worth pausing to untangle some of the various ways in which chance may intervene in the construction of a work of art. Of course, no work is purely aleatory in any of the ways outlined in the typology below; conversely, it is difficult to imagine a work that could entirely exclude all forms of chance. The presence of one or more of these types (whether in the creative process or in the mobility of the work's structure) should be understood in terms of a dialectical relationship between form and openness. Chance is understood here as a relative concept, defined by an absence of authorial intention (and not an absence of cause). What these categories all have in common is a certain suspension or displacement of the creator's control over the process, whether in favor of internal or external forces, mechanical procedures, or the intervention of other agents.

a. The chance of the dice throw, coin flipping, or random-number generators may be used as part of the process of creation, for example, in Cage's *Music of Changes* or Iannis Xenakis's stochastic music. In literature, works that involve chance in the writing process itself include Tristan Tzara's randomly generated Dadaist poems and William S. Burroughs's "cutups." In the 1950s, the German poet Theo Lutz—a member of Max Bense's group at the Technische Hochschule in Stuttgart—experimented in stochastic texts based on probability distributions.[51] From the simple coin flip to complex stochastic processes, these gestures all involve and integrate into the finished work laws of probability exterior to the creator's intentions.

b. Free rein may be given to "pure psychic automatism" as a creative force, as in some surrealist productions. Such automatic writing is conceived of as a way to allow a liberation of thought and to explore psychic reality. Chance is involved here in the sense that such writing requires a certain suspension of authorial intention and control.

c. The composition process may involve a form of automatism that is not psychological but mechanical. The ambiguity of this automatism lies in the fact that it is deterministic, but nevertheless escapes the creator's control or the reader's/listener's perception. This mechanical form of chance plays a role in the construction of Perec's *La Vie mode d'emploi,* where themes, plot elements, and literary allusions, among other things, are combined by a particular algorithm, producing unforeseen configurations that are then incorporated into the final text.

d. The form of the "work in movement," to adopt Umberto Eco's term,[52] is established or modified in the moment of performance (in the case of musical compositions or dance) or of reading (in the case of literary texts). Such works do not possess a single finished form. Musical examples include Boulez's Third Piano Sonata and his Mallarmé-inspired *Livre pour quatuor* (1948–49). In Stockhausen's *Klavierstück XI* (1956), the elements are recombined in performance to create one of billions of possible sequences. In literature, an important forerunner is Mallarmé's unfinished project of "Le Livre" ("The Book"), which would be subject to permutation and actualized in different "performances."[53] Perhaps modeled in part on Mallarmé's ideas but also inspired by Nouveau Roman experiments in narrative fragmentation, Marc Saporta's *Composition no. 1* (1962) is an unbound novel whose pages may be shuffled. A lesser degree of indeterminacy is found in another nonlinear novel, Julio Cortázar's *Hopscotch* (1966), which offers two paths for the reader. As for Oulipian works, Raymond Queneau's combinatory poem book *Cent mille milliards de poèmes* (1961; *One Hundred Trillion Poems*) is a collection of ten sonnets whose lines can be combined to produce the number of poems stated in the title (10^{14}). The reader may select particular lines for a particular reason, open the book at random, or use a formula to determine the choice of lines. Perec's "Un peu plus de quatre mille poèmes en prose pour Fabrizio Clerici" ("A Little More Than Four Thousand Prose Poems for Fabrizio Clerici") offers a more modest number of combinations: the work consists of eight prose poems each divided into four sections, which can be combined to produce, in theory, 4,096 poems. Perec also created a musical score in collaboration with the composer Philippe Drogoz: "Souvenir d'un voyage à Thouars" ("Memory of a Journey to Thouars") is a fugue in E-major written for four groups of instruments, with a duration of thirty temporal "units," each of which lasts approximately ten seconds. The score, composed of a set of graphic signs rather than conventional notation, can be realized in an infinite number of ways: the performer can decide on the significance of each sign, provided that each time the sign is repeated within one performance the same "value" recurs.

The term *aleatory*, applied first to music then by extension to the other arts, is used to designate both cases a and d above, the intervention of chance in either the conception or the execution of the work. Hence the Robert dictionary's misleading but not entirely unfounded reference to the Oulipo's "theories" of aleatory literature:[54] Oulipian writing often involves chance in sense d, and also in sense c, but generally avoids cases a and b. In defining itself as "anti-chance," the group aims to distinguish itself primarily from surrealism (case b). However, when Queneau states that the Oulipo "n'est pas de la littérature expérimentale ou aléatoire" (is not experimental or aleatory literature), the foil is less surrealism than the contemporary experiments of Max Bense's Stuttgart school (whose stochastic experiments fall under heading a above).[55] Although the Oulipo too was interested in the use of technology, it was concerned less with stochastic processes or the machine's linguistic capabilities than with the possibilities of the computer as a combinatorial machine (often leading to the mechanical automatism of case c).[56] It is nevertheless clear that works such as *Cent mille milliards de poèmes*—Queneau's inaugural Oulipian text—can be compared to other experiments in creating "open" or "virtual" works.[57] And it is no accident that the title of Perec's musical score ("Souvenir d'un voyage à Thouars": "Je suis *allé à Thouars*" ["*I went to Thouars*"], i.e., *aléatoire*) is a punning reference to the contemporary fascination with the aleatory.[58]

Controlling Chance

Clearly, it is too simple to establish a binary opposition between the "anarchic aesthetic" of Dada, surrealism, and Cage on the one hand and the use of constraints as an effort to return to "premodernist" conditions by eliminating chance on the other.[59] The Oulipo, especially in its early days, explores the possibilities of works that incite the reader's participation.[60] It also has recourse to certain forms of mechanical automatism, the results of which may ultimately escape authorial control. There is a tension in Oulipian poetics between the exploration of potentiality—which often involves opening up the text to the possibilities of the unexpected and unintended—and the group's emphasis on conscious control of the writing process. Jean Queval, for example, expresses a misgiving that anticipates Gérard Genette's account: "Il ne faudrait pas substituer à l'automatisme psychique des surréalistes un automatisme mécanique où le hasard aurait autant de part" (We should not replace the psychic automatism of the surrealists with a mechanical automatism where chance would have just as much a part).[61] Jacques Bens tries to resolve this problem by distinguishing between uncertainty and randomness.[62] However, while the unpredictability of the dice throw (which results from the inability to control the gesture of throwing and therefore its results) is indeed different from the unpredictability of a system whose parameters are known to us, it is difficult to conclude, as Bens does, that the notion of chance can only be applied to the first type of unpredictability.

Some critics who are otherwise sympathetic to the Oulipo lament the group's apparent self-contradiction in this regard.[63] Both defenders and detractors assume that "chance" has purely negative connotations in this debate; the ideological clashes over the Oulipian project, by establishing a simplistic opposition between anti-chance and chance-based operations (Genette's "roulette"), have obscured the point that the intervention of chance is not always aesthetically destructive. When Harry Mathews states that the Oulipian approach "guarantees that the unforeseen will happen and keep happening,"[64] he indicates that constraints can generate a form of chance that may be a more powerful liberating force than surrealist spontaneity. The Oulipo's preference for a "mechanical," determined form of automatism over the psychological automatism of surrealism testifies to the group's desire for a rigorous, systematic exploration of "potential" literature, an exploration that reaches beyond the limits of individual psychology and intention.

However useful the above typology in illuminating the Oulipian position may be, it is worth emphasizing the wide range of possible practices contained in each category. Each of these forms of chance admits of different degrees, and of very different kinds of aesthetic purpose. The dice throw or cutup, for example, may be an aggressive anti-art gesture (as in Tzara's Dada poems) or part of a quest for impersonality or nonintention (as in the case of Cage, who was inspired by Zen Buddhism to adopt a quasi-mystical attitude to chance). The relationship between chance and constraint also varies widely within each category. Type d, for example, includes Boulez's Third Sonata, a work whose mobility is limited and circumscribed within a relatively small number of possibilities, and Stockhausen's *Klavierstück XI*—where the number of possible combinations is finite but nevertheless so large as to make realization of all possibilities improbable. Cage's *Imaginary Landscape no. IV* has an infinite number of possible actualizations.

If we consider all these forms of chance procedure together, we may distinguish very broadly between two sets of aesthetic attitudes. The difference is perhaps clearest in music, where it is exemplified by the disagreement between Pierre Boulez and John Cage on the correct uses of chance. For Boulez, Cage's coin flipping is both unnecessary and risky: unnecessary because other aspects of the compositional process already introduce unforeseen elements that are sufficient for the purposes of producing an original work, and risky because the "unknown" that results from absolute chance is insufficiently controlled.[65] Yet Boulez argues that chance is acceptable if it is directed or "absorbed" by the work, and if it is used to create a mobile and renewable form of musical complexity.[66] Both Boulez and Cage, in fact, turn to forms of chance in order to correct the excessive rigidity of musical structure and avoid falling into conventional patterns. Where they differ is in their attitude to the finished work: Boulez's musical labyrinth may have many paths, but it is a figure of completeness and closed form. Michael Nyman groups Boulez among the "avant-garde" composers who search for coherent systems, contained and constrained; Cage, on the other hand, belongs to an "experimental" tendency concerned not with "prescribing a defined time-object" but with "outlining a situation in which sounds may occur, a process of generating action (sounding or otherwise), a field delineated by certain compositional 'rules.'"[67]

In the literary sphere, many Oulipo members hesitate between two stances. As Oulipians, their role is to generate a field of potentiality; as writers, they want to create coherent literary works. According to Christelle Reggiani, the Oulipo remains caught between two contradictory aspirations: between a "rhetorical regime" concerned with process and openness and a "scholastic ideology" that emphasizes the unity of the text.[68] While this may be true on the theoretical level, I believe that many Oulipians successfully negotiate, in practice, the tension between openness to possibility and aesthetic closure. As Umberto Eco notes, the very notion of the "work" of art sets limits to indeterminacy; even the mutability of "open works" "is always deployed within the specific limits of a given taste, or of predetermined formal tendencies, and is authorized by the concrete pliability of the material offered for the performer's manipulation."[69] The work of John Cage points toward a dissolution of the work, in its aspiration to "let sounds be themselves" rather than a vehicle for human expression.[70] In this sense, as the music critic Paul Griffiths puts it, Cage's "intention of non-intention," his quest for self-withdrawal from his work, has as its logical conclusion the silence of *4′33″* (1952).[71] But the Oulipo does not aim for such withdrawal, nor for the conflation of literature and life. The paradox and strength of the Oulipian constraint is that it is at once an organizing principle and—in its arbitrariness and in the complexity that it may generate—an embodiment of chance.

Chance and Language

To this general characterization of Oulipian poetics, it is time to add a more specific account of the group's linguistic incorporation and control of chance. Prior to any deliberate efforts to introduce chance into the writing process, chance is at the heart of the linguistic sign itself, forming the link between signifier and signified. Although Saussure famously calls this connection "arbitrary," there is no original arbiter: rather, the result of a complex historical development resembles the outcome of a deliberate choice. Writers, linguists, and literary theorists have often defined literature, or at least poetry, in terms of the attempt to limit this form of chance by motivating the sign.[72] Roland Barthes suggests that all writers necessarily adopt a Cratylian attitude toward the relationship between names and essences.[73] Taking up Barthes' remark, Gérard Genette proposes a distinction between primary and secondary Cratylism: the first considers that the words of language are truly mimetic, whereas the second believes that language is potentially mimetic but not always constituted according to this capacity.[74] This second attitude, then, applies itself to correcting the failings of language, by linking sound and meaning.

This attitude of "secondary Cratylism" is perhaps most obvious in texts that focus explicitly on the signifier, defining and redefining words and thereby echoing the speculative etymologies of Plato's dialogue. Examples include Proust's fascination for proper names and Michel Leiris's *Glossaire j'y serre mes gloses.*[75] In these cases, writers transform accidental similarities between signifiers into relationships based on meaning; they redistribute the differential relationships of language and disrupt the fundamental duality of the sign. Warren Motte has suggested that the Oulipian enterprise is a search for an "original language," where there is no split within the sign and all elements of discourse are fully motivated.[76] Some statements by Oulipo writers support this claim: the Oulipo member Jacques Jouet argues that a "quasi-Cratylic" affirmation is essential to the definition of an Oulipian oeuvre,[77] and Marcel Bénabou claims that his procedure of "surdéfinition" (superdefinition) can awaken the writer's (and the reader's) inner Cratylus.[78] This, then, might be another way of understanding the notion of anti-chance. From this point of view, the members of the Oulipo inherit Mallarmé's conception of poetry. In "Crise de vers" ("Crisis in Verse"), Mallarmé states that verse offers a remedy for the inadequacy of language, "niant, d'un trait souverain, le hasard demeuré aux termes malgré l'artifice de leur retrempe alternée en le sens et la sonorité" (denying, with a lordly gesture, the chance that remains in terms despite the artifice of their alternate tempering in meaning and sonority).[79] The simultaneous necessity and impossibility of abolishing chance is at the heart of Mallarmé's poetics. For Mallarmé, chance remains part of words ("demeure aux termes") even as poetry denies it; indeed, this fundamental chance gives poetry its reason to exist. A paradoxical gesture, the dice throw is grounded in chance but also appropriates chance in order to negate it. Chance is the foundation for the poetry that denies it, making verse both possible and necessary. It is no accident that explicit and implicit references to Mallarmé abound in Oulipian writing, from Queneau's truncated versions of the poet's sonnets[80] to the echoes of Mallarmé's diction in Perec's *Alphabets* poems.

If the Mallarmean quest for a purified poetic language is apparently tempered in Oulipian practice by an emphasis on deliberate artifice, the seeds of this approach may be found in Mallarmé's own poetics (for example, in the use of highly constrained rhyme schemas in such poems as his "Sonnet on X"). Indeed, I argue that it is precisely through its manipulations of a heightened sense of artifice that the Oulipo continues the Mallarmean struggle between chance and anti-chance. (The next chapter will discuss a specific case of Oulipian engagement with Mallarmé: one of Perec's *Alphabets* poems.) The sense that poetic artifice is ultimately powerless to abolish the original chance of language ("un coup de dés jamais n'abolira le hasard"—a dice throw will never abolish chance) is of course an eminently Mallarmean sentiment but reappears in different forms in the work of later modernist writers. Michel Foucault, writing on Raymond Roussel (one of the Oulipo's "anticipatory plagiarists"), highlights the capacity of highly artificial procedures to both unmask and organize the arbitrariness of language itself. Roussel's Procedure,[81] according to Foucault, "consiste justement à purifier le discours de tous ces faux hasards de 'l'inspiration', de la fantaisie, de la plume qui court, pour le placer devant l'évidence insupportable que le langage nous arrive du fond d'une nuit parfaitement claire et impossible à maîtriser" (consists precisely in purifying discourse of all those false hazards of "inspiration," of fantasy, of the freely moving pen, in order to place it before the unbearable evidence that language reaches us from the depths of a night that is perfectly clear and impossible to command).[82] This is the night of the original chance from which words emerge, and which Oulipian texts both reveal and confront.

Mysticism, Mathematics, Meaning

The Oulipo, again like Mallarmé, is fascinated with the idea of the total Book. In "Histoire du lipogramme" ("History of the Lipogram"), Perec invokes the linguistic mysticism of the kabbalah to justify his own use of the lipogram ("HL," 73). Given its emphasis both on textual necessity and on the endless multiplicities of meaning present in language, it is not surprising that the kabbalah has held a particular fascination for writers, even if they do not subscribe to the mystical beliefs that ground it. Michel Leiris, for example, invokes in *Biffures* the kabbalists' sacred view of written language to justify his poetic treatment of the linguistic sign.[83] The critic Jürgen Ritte argues that the literary obsession with kabbalism can be traced back to romanticism—to the moment when literature becomes self-reflexive and secularizes the mystical as a language game.[84] In this context, the kabbalah represents both the displacement of an origin—divine law becomes a rule of the game—and a form of poetic self-justification. In his essay on the lipogram, Perec cites Borges's account of the kabbalistic conception of Scripture as a figure of the absolute text, one that unites letter and meaning and therefore excludes chance ("HL," 73).[85] In its conception of a language that unites form and meaning, the kabbalist approach is close to the "Cratylist" attitude outlined earlier, but its methods of uncovering hidden meanings are even more complex and dizzying. Both presuppose that language has a metaphysical source that makes its forms meaningful, but the kabbalah emphasizes the infinite multiplicity of meanings rather than a single, stable interpretation. Paradoxically, the belief in the absolute unity of truth and language opens up an infinite process of interpretation. Perec recognizes, however, that once deprived of metaphysical grounding, the artifice of the lipogram can only offer a faint echo of kabbalist preoccupations ("HL," 74).

A similar ambiguity marks the Oulipian preoccupation with mathematics; the latter can be seen as further evidence of the Oulipo's "quest for an order of the real," as Christelle Reggiani puts it,[86] or alternatively as a purely formal pursuit. In fact, the Oulipo often seems to hesitate between a Pythagorean conception of number and a formalist conception of axiomatics as play. Queneau's fascination with number and form often has mystical overtones, for example, in the surprising conclusion to a 1937 essay:

> Il n'y a plus de règles depuis qu'elles ont survécu à la valeur. Mais les formes subsistent éternellement. Il y a des formes du roman qui imposent à la matière proposée toutes les vertus du Nombre et, naissant de l'expression même et des divers aspects du récit, connaturelle à l'idée directrice, fille et mère de tout les éléments qu'elle polarise, se développe une structure qui transmet aux œuvres les derniers reflets de la Lumière Universelle et les derniers échos de l'Harmonie des Mondes.
>
> Rules cease to exist once they have outlived their value, but forms live on eternally. There are forms of the novel which impose on the suggested topic all the virtues of the Number. Born of the very expression and of the diverse aspects of the tale, connected by nature with the guiding idea, daughter and mother of all the elements that it polarizes, a structure develops, which transmits to the works the last reflections of Universal Light and the last echoes of the Harmony of Worlds.[87]

On the other hand, the Oulipo explicitly models itself on Bourbaki, a group of French mathematicians who rejected mathematical realism and even claimed to treat axiomatics as a set of formal games.[88] The reference to Bourbaki provides the Oulipo with a partial justification for the arbitrariness of the literary constraint. Just as mathematics, from a Bourbakian perspective, is a serious game, writing can operate as a game of constraints and yet remain rigorous in its practice. In this sense, the Oulipo offers us a paradoxical poetics of necessity grounded in arbitrariness.

The place of the subject in such a poetics is problematic. In the kabbalist model cited by Perec, God's authority founds all possible interpretations of the text. The mathematical model suggests a fully coherent formal and logical system. Oulipian texts, however, are composed of linguistic and not mathematical signs, and they are produced by the finite human author. We are therefore faced with most fraught questions of literary criticism: the problem of authorial intention as source and stabilizer of meaning. (It is the perceived absence of intention, we have seen, that is at the root of many attacks on the Oulipo.) Since Plato, writing has been viewed as problematic precisely because it cuts off language from its origin in the speaker.[89] Twentieth-century literary theory picks up the same theme, but rather than denouncing writing's inherent mobility it often exalts the opening up of texts to endless interpretation. Roland Barthes, for example, bases his famous argument about the "death of the author" on the notion that writing destroys all voice, all origin.[90] Where Barthes and Derrida both associate the idea of a stable signified with metaphysical and even theological assumptions,[91] the kabbalist attitude evoked by Perec apparently rests on just the opposite idea: the association of metaphysics and multiplicity—God as the guarantor of endless readings. This leads to a paradox: if nothing can be pinned to authorial intention (following Barthes' view), interpretation is infinite; but we reach exactly the same conclusion if, on the contrary, everything in the text is assumed to be intentional.

Although constraints such as the lipogram arguably engage the writer's intention at every point, the merely mortal Oulipian author cannot possibly motivate all aspects of language. Furthermore, certain forms of Oulipian automatism seem to replace authorial intention with a mechanical principle. Hence Genette's claim that meaning in Oulipian texts is largely accidental, because it is not attached to a semantic intention. Oulipo members themselves offer very different views on the relationship between intention and meaning. Some (notably Jacques Bens) insist that the author should control the reading process. Italo Calvino, on the contrary, suggests that a combinatorial machine could easily replace the author, since the system could produce new meanings independently of, and perhaps even more effectively than, any authorial intention:

> At a certain moment things click into place, and one of the combinations obtained through the combinatorial mechanism itself, independently of any search for meaning or effect on any other level—becomes charged with an unexpected or unforeseen effect which the conscious mind would not have arrived at deliberately: an unconscious meaning, in fact, or at least the premonition of an unconscious meaning.[92]

The author's unconscious—the concern of the surrealists—is replaced here by the collective unconscious of the reading public, accidentally (in the mechanical sense) activated by the text.

In reading Oulipian texts we are inevitably confronted with the problem of the limits of interpretation: how do we distinguish between the accidental and the meaningful? In his critical account of literary theory's central postulates, Antoine Compagnon argues that only the hypothesis of intention can allow us to distinguish random coincidences from significant parallels of meaning and structure within a given text or group of texts.[93] Yet this argument risks becoming circular (if there are parallels, then we hypothesize that they are intentional, and if there are intentions, then there must be parallels). This question takes on particular importance when it comes to Oulipian texts. Perec's work in particular tends to inspire interpretations of almost kabbalistic character (especially the discovery of paragrams or of special numbers that structure aspects of the text). It is clearly not the case, as Jacques Bens claims, that the Oulipo eliminates chance by predicting and controlling the reader's responses. On the contrary, the reader's knowledge of a text's Oulipian status exacerbates the tendency to overinterpret. Oulipian texts invite us to uncover hidden meanings and thus to engage in reading tactics that may or may not mirror the author's strategy.[94] However, the Oulipian approach does not entail the elimination of intention, but rather its displacement or temporary suspension. For the Oulipo, Queneau remains the author of each of the hundred trillion poems of his book.

Method and Mechanism: S+7

Oulipian constraints are a form of external "programming" of the text that appears, at first view, to be an impersonal principle. And we may concede to Genette that the Oulipo's exploration of mechanical structures does indeed introduce a particular kind of chance. Yet the mechanical automatism involved has its origin in an intention. This is true even of the "S+7" (henceforth N+7) method, so often dismissed as frivolous even by those who admire the Oulipo.[95] It is true that N+7 seems to reduce the role of the author to a minimum: the choice of the text to be transformed and of the dictionary to be used for the transformation. In a sense, the arbitrariness of the constraint (why the number 7, rather than any other?) colludes here with the arbitrariness of the sign—the constraint depends on the order of words in the dictionary, which is arbitrary in relation to these words' meanings. However, we need to be precise about the nature and extent of the uncertainty involved. Rather than exploring the functioning of thought, as the surrealists claim to do, the Oulipo investigates the possibilities of language, in order better to exploit its possibilities. The substitutive procedure of N+7 respects the syntactic structure of the original sentence, and thus reveals both the importance and the limits of syntax in the production of meaning.

The Oulipo adds supplementary constraints to a linguistic system which is already, necessarily, governed by rules, and the resulting tension between these elements can itself generate "potential literature." This type of experimentation depends on an interaction between several factors: the systematic and rule-governed aspect of language (the condition for ordinary linguistic creativity, in the Chomskyan sense); the linguistic sign's arbitrary nature; and the combination of chance and rule in the mechanical application of a chosen constraint. Would the procedure be equally effective if the substitutive nouns were selected from the dictionary at random, instead of following a formula? In other words, is there a significant difference between the absolute chance of the dice throw or roulette wheel and the "automatic chance" of the arbitrary constraint? In the case of N+7, the constraint imposes the choice of a substitute which is close to the original word in the alphabet, with a more predictable result than a dice throw would give. Especially when the constraint is used to transform a well-known text, the results can be both humorous and uncanny. The proximity of the substituted signifiers to the original ones means that the nouns are familiar and yet unexpected, as in this parodic version of the beginning of Genesis by François Caradec:

> Au commencement, Dieu créa les ciguës [ciel] et la terreur [terre]. La terreur était informe et vide, et l'essaim [esprit] de Dieu se mouvait au-dessus des ébarbures [eaux]. Dieu dit: Que le lundi [la lumière] soit! Et le lundi fut. Dieu vit que le lundi était bon, et il sépara le lundi d'avec les tennis [ténèbres].[96]

> In the beginning, God created hemlocks and terror. The terror was formless and empty, and the swarm of God hovered over the burrs. God said: let there be Monday! And there was Monday. God saw that Monday was good, and he separated Monday from the tennis courts.

What is perhaps most disquieting about N+7 is the way in which it unveils the "mechanical" aspect of language itself—that is, language's capacity to produce meaning independently of human intention. Most important, however, is the constraint's role in converting chance into literary potentiality. When the constraint is applied several times, the resulting text suggests a journey through language, a quest that both centers on the original meaning and moves away from it. The following excerpt, taken from a poem by Caradec, apparently presents the results in reverse order, leading us back to the original, generative—and banal—phrase, while simultaneously destabilizing this site of origin:

> Pour moi,
> Cette justesse-là était discobole,
> Ce juron était dirigeable,
> ce jurançon était direct,
> Cette jujube était diphtongue,
> Ce judo était dingue,
> Cette jouvence était dindon,
> Pour moi
> ce jour-là, c'était dimanche[97]
>
> For me,
> That accuracy was a discus-thrower,
> That oath was dirigible,
> That Jurançon was direct,
> That jujube was a diphthong,
> That judo was daft,
> That youth was a turkey,
> For me
> That day was Sunday

The chance element of this procedure is limited and controlled to some extent, even if the result remains unpredictable. This observation can be extended to other constraints that have proved to be fruitful starting points for literary creation. In the case of combinatorial procedures, such as those used by Perec to write *La Vie mode d'emploi,* the constraint ensures that all of the system's possibilities are explored in a way that is rigorous, not random, and yet remains largely unpredictable. Initially, the constraint creates a form of purposeless play that, free from personal intention, opens up new possibilities. The order of words in the dictionary, for example, while arbitrary from a semantic point of view, is often motivated by a textual construction.

In the case of N+7, the intervention of constrained chance does not block meaning but produces a semantic drift within a fixed syntactic form. The method depends on the combination of order and chance, the familiar and the unexpected. While it might be tempting to relegate this particular constraint to the group's early days, before the development of more sophisticated methods and approaches, Oulipian writers have in fact repeatedly returned to it and developed it in other directions. One extension is the "eclipse," a text composed in two parts, the first being the N-7 of the second and the second the N+7 of the first.[98] Harry Mathews's "Example of an Eclipse" offers both an illustration and a defense of the method:

> The principle governing the procedure known as N+7 is respected by replacing each noun in a given text with another one found by counting seven nouns down in a previously chosen lexicon; and the priority governing the procurer known as N+7 is respected by replacing each nub in a given theme with another found by counting seven nubs down in a previously chosen liberator. Why should we be restricted to the confessions of our predetermined likings? Why should we be restricted to the confines of our predetermined limitations. Let's nourish our outgrowths. Let's nourish our outlooks.[99]

This application of the N+7 rule to its own definition literally transforms the *lexicon* into a *liberator.* The syntactic repetitions and alliteration encourage us to discover semantic echoes between the parallel clauses, and the resulting associations are rather compelling: a *noun* in a *text* may indeed be a kernel of meaning (*nub*) in a larger thematic network. The word *procurer* raises the problem of authorial intention, suggesting that the procedure displaces the author and allows meaning to be secured by someone else. Yet the following two sets of questions and exhortations emphasize the liberating effects of this displacement. The rule frees the author from the restrictive effects of habit, since our "likings" may be "limitations" and our "confessions"—our attempts to use literature to express personal emotions—can be "confines." The N+7 rule, on the other hand, allows us to move beyond personal intentions, providing us with new "outgrowths" and "outlooks"—both terms emphasizing the broadening of artistic scope and vision. Mathews has not mechanically applied the formula but has carefully juxtaposed phrases to produce a surprising degree of semantic coherence. The repeated structures serve to increase the rhetorical impact of his exhortation to try out the constraint.

Christelle Reggiani suggests that the Oulipian work is "biphasic": the first phase being the formulation of the constraint, and the second its application.[100] I propose a slight modification of this model, in three stages: first the invention and/or definition of the constraint; second, the exploration of the possibilities that it creates; finally, a process of ordering, selection, and elimination based on these possibilities and leading to the actualization of the final text. Of these phases, it is only the second that may temporarily suspend authorial intention and control. The constraint serves to generate poetic and narrative material that is then shaped by the writer. Harry Mathews's *Selected Declarations of Dependence,* for example, combines well-known proverbs to create new formulations (which Mathews calls "perverbs"),[101] such as "Time and tide gather no moss."[102] These combinations then serve as the foundation for poetic development. Not all Oulipian constraints transform existing texts or phrases, but they all involve, to some degree, the retrospective motivation of an initially arbitrary constraint. The lipogrammatic method of *La Disparition,* for example, takes as its starting point chance relationships between signifiers—it is accidental, from a semantic point of view, that certain words contain the letter *e* while others do not. However, as I will show in more detail in the next chapter, these resemblances are then justified by a narrative and thematic construction.

Chance may then be involved at two levels of the Oulipian approach: first in the arbitrariness of the constraint itself, then in the more or less "automatic" functioning of this constraint. What, then, becomes of the Oulipian challenge to chance? The Oulipian constraint, in fact, both represents chance and works against it. This position is presented most clearly by Jacques Roubaud, who both reasserts the common claim that the Oulipo's work is a form of anti-chance and qualifies this statement. Roubaud notes that Queneau was fascinated by arithmetic series, such as the series of prime numbers, that "imitent le hasard tout en ressortissant à une loi" (imitate chance while obeying a law).[103] The Oulipo's rejection of surrealist automatism, according to Roubaud, does not imply the elimination of all mechanical procedures, but rather the recognition that all literature is subject to automatisms. In this context, anti-chance signifies a rejection of "la croyance mystique selon laquelle la liberté peut naître de l'effacement au hasard des contraintes" (the mystical belief according to which freedom can be born from the random elimination of constraints).[104] Roubaud's example of the series of prime numbers represents the whole problem of constraint and chance in microcosm; the series is a clearly defined system governed by deterministic laws, and yet mathematicians remain unable to predict the next element in the series. The Oulipo is intrigued by such apparent points of convergence between order and disorder, law and its absence, chance and necessity.

In offering this general account of Oulipian poetics, this chapter has not done justice to the richness and variety of Oulipian constraints. While different Oulipian authors employ particular styles of constraint for their own aesthetic ends (and often in more developed literary works than the brief exercises I have focused on here), I have tried to shed light on what I believe is the key principle that these writers share. I have also situated the group's work in the context of more general tendencies in literature and the arts. Of course, the retrospective justification of the aleatory is not the province of the Oulipo alone. According to Pierre Boulez, all creation entails the transformation of the unpredictable into necessity.[105] Louis Aragon claims that the "explained accident," the retrospective legitimation of an encounter of words or sounds, is the starting point for all his novels.[106] The Oulipo's originality lies in the systematic use of constraints that simultaneously incorporate, produce, and control chance. Anti-chance is "le hasard reconnu donc apprivoisé" (chance acknowledged and therefore tamed), as Roubaud puts it;[107] similarly, Perec describes the constraints of *La Vie mode d'emploi* as "une programmation du hasard" (*EC* 2:166) (a programming of chance). The creativity of Oulipian constraints depends precisely on their capacity to generate the accidental and the unexpected—to enable the writer to take chances—while at the same time pointing the way to order and aesthetic closure. The next chapter examines this dialectical operation of constraints in some of Perec's Oulipian works.

Il n'y a pas de "génie" purement inconscient. Mais l'homme de génie est au contraire celui qui sait mettre à profit les figures jetées par le hasard. Il en tire une ressource infinie, vaste comme le monde.

There is no purely unconscious "genius." But the man of genius is on the contrary the one who knows how to take advantage of the figures thrown by chance. He draws from them an infinite resource, vast as the world.

—Paul Valéry

6. Perec's Constraints: Combination, Coincidence, Clinamen

Perec's references to the role of chance in the creative process are usually interpreted as entirely ironic. "Je ne demande qu'au hasard cette fable en prose vague" (I ask only of chance this fable in vague prose), reads one line from a poem addressed to the Oulipo.[1] At first view, the line is an antiphrasis; not only does it appear in a poem rather than in vague prose, but this poem refers to its own constraints in its second line: "J'ai désiré vingt-cinq flèches de plomb" (I desired twenty-five arrows of lead). For this is a poem written in the Oulipian "belle absente" form: each line of the poem uses all the letters of the alphabet except one of the letters from the addressee's name (although, since Perec allows himself to omit the letters *k, w,* and *x,* the reference to twenty-five letters is somewhat deceptive).[2] Yet on another level, this poem does have an important chance component, since it submits the distribution of letters to rules that at the outset are independent of meaning. This accidental aspect is creative in its initial undoing of the "field" of writing, which then opens up a set of new possibilities—possibilities of which the actual poem is only a "relic," as the last two lines suggest: "Vestige du charme déjà bien flou qui / Défit ce champ jusqu'à la ligne brève" (Relic of the already loose spell that / Untied this field up to the brief line). Perec's *Alphabets* poems also refer to chance in this semiserious manner: one poem, for example, refers to "zanzi" (*A,* 169), which Marc Lapprand glosses as a possible abbreviation for "zanzibar," a game of chance played with two or three dice.[3]

This ironic acknowledgment of chance is at the heart of Perec's poetics. In his 1967 lecture on writing and mass media, Perec speaks of the need to define the limits of the work between two extremes: the excessively aleatory and the excessively determined (*EC* 1:103). The same pair of adjectives reappears in an article on free jazz written the same year: Perec notes that it is impossible for a work to be entirely aleatory or entirely determined, despite twentieth-century efforts to produce works that are nothing but constraints (Roussel), or on the other hand nothing but chance ("informal art" in painting) ("LC," 59). He concludes that chance should only play a role in an aesthetic structure if subordinated to a choice, a rule, a sensibility, or a framework; the only solution is to establish the right relationship between freedom and constraint ("LC," 59, 61). This formulation is appealing but ambiguous: freedom seems to signify both chance and choice, while constraint can be imposed by a subjective preference or a mechanical framework. In order to offer a more complete account of Perec's poetics, this chapter analyzes some of the different kinds of choice-chance-constraint relationships at work in Perec's own Oulipian texts.

To this end, I will undertake close readings of excerpts from three texts that Perec wrote using Oulipian constraints. In *La Disparition, Alphabets,* and *La Vie mode d'emploi,* knowledge of the initial constraints is available to the reader, albeit in different ways. In *La Disparition,* as we have seen, the absence of the letter *e* becomes the novel's subject matter. In *Alphabets,* the constraints are visible in the text itself. During his lifetime, Perec partially disclosed the constraints of *La Vie mode d'emploi.*[4] Readers now have access to the posthumously published *Cahier des charges*—a set of "project specifications," the portion of Perec's manuscripts that comprise the book's "programs," in other words, the tables and lists used to write the novel. The constraint of *La Disparition* is simplest in terms of its formulation, while the rules of *Alphabets* are more complex and those of *La Vie mode d'emploi* highly intricate. However, this complexity of formulation does not correspond in any direct way to the difficulty of the constraint, as the example of *La Disparition* demonstrates.

La Disparition: Codes and Clichés

We have already seen that the opposition between chance and fate in *La Disparition* fits into a larger thematic network: this novel contains a reflection not only on human destinies but, above all, on its own construction. However, the relationship between the lipogrammatic constraint and the novel's narrative structure is not straightforward. The gap between these different levels is itself thematized at many points in the novel. In the following passage, Anton Voyl describes his attempt to decipher an "inscription," which clearly stands for the novel that we are reading:

> —Il y aura ainsi trois instants du discours: d'abord, nous croirons voir un galimatias confus, capharnaüm insignifiant, constatant pourtant qu'il s'agit d'un signal affirmatif, sûr, soumis à un pouvoir codifiant, à l'appropriation d'un public qui l'a toujours admis: un outil social assurant la communication, la promulguant sans infraction, lui donnant son canon, sa loi, son droit. [. . .]
>
> Il y aura donc d'abord un pouvoir du Logos, un "ça" parlant dont nous connaîtrons aussitôt l'accablant poids sans pouvoir approfondir sa signification. Ainsi, s'il s'agit d'un roman, il y aura, ipso facto, l'autour commun, connu, banal, dont nous tirons la conviction qu'il s'agit, trait pour trait, d'un roman [. . .]. Un mort, puis trois, puis cinq, puis six, puis tous, puis l'insinuant fil tramant la narration tissant un tapis aux motifs si confus qu'on n'aura jamais la vision d'un croquis abouti, qu'il nous paraîtra vain d'y vouloir voir un signal.
>
> Mais, plus tard, quand nous aurons compris la loi qui guida la composition du discours, nous irons admirant qu'usant d'un corpus aussi amoindri, d'un vocabulariat aussi soumis à la scission, à l'omission, à l'imparfait, la scription ait pu s'accomplir jusqu'au bout.
>
> Abasourdis par l'inouï pouvoir marginal qui, contournant la signification tabou, la saisit pourtant, la produit pourtant par un biais subtil, la disant plus, l'ultradisant par l'allusion, l'association, la saturation, nous garantirons, lisant, la validation du signal sans tout à fait pourtant l'approfondir.
>
> Puis, à la fin, nous saisirons pourquoi tout fut bâti à partir d'un carcan si dur, d'un canon si tyrannisant. Tout naquit d'un souhait fou, d'un souhait nul: assouvir jusqu'au bout la fascination du cri vain, sortir du parcours rassurant du mot trop subit, trop confiant, trop commun, n'offrir au signifiant qu'un goulot, qu'un boyau, qu'un chas, si aminci, si fin, si aigu qu'on y voit aussitôt sa justification. (*D*, 195–96)

"Actually, I would count on a trio of distinct strata of clarifications: "First, you and I look at it casually and think of it as just confusing poppycock, foolish mumbo jumbo—noticing, though, that, as a signal, it's obviously not random or chaotic, that it's an affirmation of sorts, a product of a codifying authority, submitting to a public that's willing to admit it. It's a social tool assuring communication, promulgating it without any violation, according it its canon, its law, its rights. [. . .]

"Thus, first of all, is Logos and its primacy, that talking 'it' of our inscription: putting it baldly, you and I know that it's talking to us but still don't know what it's saying. Now, assuming that it's a fictional work, or part of a fictional work, what I must look for is a group of banal, common, familiar signs surrounding it, by which I can start assuming, unambiguously, that a work of fiction is in fact what it is [. . .]. An individual is slain, now two, now four, and now all six, with a haunting strand of plot working its way through a mosaic of motifs so confusing that you and I can't possibly summon up a vision of its totality from A to Z, its organic unity, so confusing that our wish to find a significant sign in it is simply an illusion.

"But, gradually, with our starting to grasp that a law is structuring its composition, this initial confusion of ours will turn to admiration—admiration at how, with such a niggardly grammatical, syntactical and punctuational construction, with a vocabulary cut down to a minimum by so many constraints of scission, omission and approximation, such an inscription can still contain so much information.

"Dumbstruck by this amazing capacity that it has—whilst outwardly avoiding a signification which it knows is taboo—to affirm it anyway, articulating it by a cunning bias, shouting it out as if from a rooftop, formulating it by association, by allusion, by saturation—dumbstruck, as I say, you and I, although still not totally grasping at this point what it's saying to us, can at last boast of proving its validity as a signal, as a communication.

"From which point it's but a hop, skip and a jump to grasping why so much was built on so rigorous a constraint, so tyrannical a curb. It was born out of a mad and morbid whim: that of wholly satisfying a fascination with linguistic gratuity, with proscription and subtraction, that of avoiding any word striking its author as too obvious, too arrogant or too common, of according its *signifiant* just a gap, a slit, a loop, so narrow, so slim and so sharp, that you instantly grasp its justification." (*V*, 176–77)

Offering an account of our own reading process, this passage presents the causal tensions of the narrative as merely one "signal" in a complex process of interpretation, broken down here into three stages. The first step is the recognition that the confused text we are reading is not simply noise (in the information theory sense) but contains a coded message. The reader identifies the genre of this discourse as that of a fictional work through familiarity with novelistic conventions. Yet this recognition of codes and clichés turns once again to confusion as the narrative weaves a tangled thread of confused motifs. A second moment of reading takes the reader beyond the narrative to the detection of the constraint (the law "structuring its composition"), which first of all awakens admiration at the perceived overcoming of difficulty. In a final stage, the reader's understanding of the text's meaning will deepen as he or she grasps the underlying justification behind the constraint: "sortir du parcours rassurant du mot trop subit, trop confiant, trop commun" (avoiding any word striking its author as too obvious, too arrogant, or too common). In other words, the constraint permits the writer to escape from linguistic habits and opens up new creative paths.

The passage aims to describe the lipogrammatic language of which it is also a characteristic example. With a few lexical exceptions (the neologisms "vocabulariat," "scription"), the rules of language have largely been respected here. However, certain syntactic constructions, expressions, and turns of phrase are likely to strike readers as strange: the abundance of present participles ("l'insinuant fil tramant la narration tissant un tapis"; "nous irons admirant qu'usant d'un corpus"), the use of Latin locutions ("ipso facto") or of neologisms. All of these linguistic detours point to the absence of more familiar terms. Despite the text's insistence on restricting the means of expression, this supposedly constrained discourse is subject less to lack than to proliferation.[5] The necessity of replacing forbidden words with synonyms and paraphrases seems to provoke a dizzying lexical "saturation"—things are "ultra-said" (to borrow two terms from Voyl). Perec is almost never content, in this text, to choose one word where he can use two or three. Not only in this excerpt but in the text as a whole synonymic triads are plentiful. Examples here are: "son canon, sa loi, son droit" (its canon, its law, its rights); "commun, connu, banal" (banal, common, familiar); "n'offrir au signifiant qu'un goulot, qu'un boyau, qu'un chas, si aminci, si fin, si aigu" (according its *signifiant* just a gap, a slit, a loop, so narrow, so slim and so sharp). As Voyl puts it, the constraint gives rise to an amazing creative power that produces an abundance, even an excess, of language. The constraint is therefore far from functioning as a law of the "mot juste" or of brevity. Even if there is no random word in this text, since all are consciously selected (*D,* 217), *La Disparition* seems to demonstrate that there is no necessary word either. As Anton Voyl notes in his journal (adapting Mallarmé in lipogrammatic form), "nul discours jamais n'abolira l'hasard" (no amount of prolix circumlocution, brilliant as it may sound, can abolish flip-of-a-coin fortuity) (*D,* 50/*V,* 36).[6]

If the primary effects of the constraint occur on the level of language, what are the consequences of this lexical proliferation for the narrative? The linguistic level is not unconnected to the convoluted narrative threads that complicate the initially common, familiar, banal unfolding of the plot to produce "un tapis aux motifs si confus qu'on n'aura jamais la vision d'un croquis abouti" (a mosaic of motifs so confusing that you and I can't possibly summon up a vision of its totality) (*D,* 196/*V,* 177). The rule that ultimately gives the text its meaning is thus, paradoxically, precisely what produces confusion and chaos on the surface level. The narrative, thematic, and linguistic levels are inextricably bound together in *La Disparition.* While the lipogram seems at first view to be a purely formal constraint, the absence of the letter *e* does not function only on the level of the form of expression.[7] In his study of the manuscripts for *La Disparition,* Marc Parayre has shown the direct role played by the lipogram, and associated linguistic manipulations, in the development of the novel's plot and themes. For example, one character dies of suffocation as a result of Perec's play on the homophony between "sans air" (without air) and "sans r" (without *r*),[8] and a similar (although necessarily unspoken) play on "*e*" and "œufs" (eggs) is the origin of a set of motifs associated with birds and their nests; for example, Aloysius Swann proposes the use of an "oisillon radioactif" (a radiating bird) as a murder weapon (*D,* 303/*V,* 276). The lipogram becomes a powerful source of narrative, as well as linguistic, invention.

The chaotic proliferation initially provoked by the constraint is motivated, therefore, at the thematic and narrative levels, although the reader's sense of disorder and excess is never completely eliminated. We find further evidence of this dialectical tension in the novel's treatment of determinism and fate. At first glance, the lexical detours used to address these themes may appear rather arbitrary: there is no *destin* (destiny) and no *fatalité* (fate) in the novel, but we do find the rarer terms *fatum* and the adjective *fatal;* the noun *sort* (fate, lot) appears elsewhere, as does the Latin *fatalitas* (*D,* 283). However, these terms have the effect of drawing the reader's attention precisely to the absence that determines the destiny of the characters. Elsewhere, the impossibility of using the words *récit* (narrative) and *histoire* (story) is compensated for by the use of metaphors of threads and weaving ("l'insinuant fil tramant la narration tissant un tapis"—literally: the insinuating thread plotting the narration weaving a rug) that clearly have metatextual significance. Similarly, when the word *roman* (novel) is substituted for the expected but forbidden *histoire* (story), the word choice accentuates the self-referential dimension of the novel: "Tu connaîtras un jour mon roman" (You'll soon know my story), says Savorgnan to Conson (*D*, 99/*V*, 83). The constraint functions as a stimulus for literary creation, as the writer works both with and against its arbitrary and random effects.

Alphabets: Chaotic Language

I pointed out earlier that Oulipian practice puts into play two systems of constraint: the rules of language and the Oulipian rule or rules. In *La Disparition,* but to an even greater extent in *Alphabets,* the two systems come into conflict. To compose the poems of *Alphabets,* Perec uses the ten most frequent letters in the French language and adds a supplementary letter (a "joker") for each section of the work. The letters are arranged in eleven "verses" of eleven letters, with no repetitions of any letter within each verse. This is a method that can be compared to the serial technique in music, with the use of letters corresponding to that of notes.[9] *Alphabets* openly displays its basic constraint system to the reader; we see on the same page the initial "onzain" (an eleven-line stanza, in fact eleven series of eleven letters) and, in a different typographical arrangement, the resulting text.

The success of *Alphabets* arguably rests on a wager: given the frequency of the given letters in the French language, it is probable that combinations of these letters will allow the formation of meaningful syntactic units. By limiting the possibilities in this way, the probability of repetition is also increased. In *Alphabets,* this leads to the creation of a set of motifs: two words that recur are *art* and *rat,* for example (the significance of the first word is obvious; I will return to the second in chapter 7). Although the heterogrammatic constraint pushes the rules of language to their limits, even to their breaking point, the resulting poems are nevertheless not entirely unreadable. The following example demonstrates this point.[10] (Even setting the constraint aside, the grammatical ambiguities of the poem are an obstacle to translation. For the purposes of commentary, my English version is literal and ignores the heterogrammatic restriction.)

ABOLIUNTRES	*Aboli, un très art nul ose*	Abolished, a null very art dares
ARTNULOSEBI		
BELOTSURINA	*bibelot sûr, inanité (l'ours-babil:*	a certain trinket, sonorous (the bear-babble:
NITELOURSBA		
BILUNRATESO	*un raté…) sonore*	a dud…) inanity
NORESAUTLIB		
ERANTSILBOU	*Saut libérant s'il boute*	Liberating leap if it drives out
TELABUSNOIR	*l'abus noir ou le brisant*	dark misuse or the breaking
OULEBRISANT	*trublion à sens:*	meaning-troublemaker:
TRUBLIONASE		
NSARTEBLOUI	*Art ébloui!*	Dazzled art!

(*A*, poem 2)

The poem describes a movement, a liberating leap ("saut libérant") from artistic failure ("art nul," "inanité," "un raté"—null art, inanity, a dud) to apparent success: the dazzled art ("art ébloui") of the final line. It is framed by the two extremes of this process, "aboli" and "ébloui" (abolished, dazzled). Art faces the risk of abolition but also the danger of becoming inane chatter ("babil"). The line "Aboli bibelot d'inanité sonore" (Abolished trinket of sonorous inanity), borrowed from Mallarmé's "Sonnet on X"[11] provides a matrix for the first three lines of the poem.[12] The allusion refers not only to another text written using constraints (the rules of the sonnet and the letter-based rhyme scheme) but also to a conception of poetry as pure sonority, lacking any utility (hence the "inanity")—language abolishing itself in the act of utterance. More generally, the Mallarmean parallels in *Alphabets* can be and have been read as a refusal of chance.[13] Indeed, Perec's *Alphabets* poems radicalize the Mallarmean view of poetry. They separate language from its normal referential usage; we are very far from "l'universel reportage" (universal reportage) of ordinary language derided by Mallarmé in "Crise de vers." However, the starting point for these poems is the visual unit of the letter rather than the pure musicality of sound.[14] From this point of view, the reference to the "bibelot d'inanité sonore" has a certain irony. The Mallarmean intertext is also deflated by the commentary in parentheses; the "bibelot d'inanité sonore" apparently becomes mere babble ("babil"), a poetic failure ("un raté") that will be transcended by the leap evoked in the second "strophe."

The constraint system of *Alphabets* reduces the probability of certain types of traditional poetic devices, such as the construction of metrical units, regular rhyme, or rhythmic schemes. Perec's poems, once they have been transcribed from the initial *onzain* stanza into their final form on the page, look very close to free verse. However, the combinatorial process makes other kinds of effects more probable, such as the repetition of particular sounds (although the possibilities are also limited by the rule of the series). The restricted set of consonants means that alliteration is frequent; in the above example, the *b* (the "joker" letter added to the initial series of *E S A R T I N U L O*) stands out prominently, appearing four times in the second line ("bibelot [. . .] babil") and reinforcing the parallel between these trivializing descriptions of art, as trinket and as chatter. The repetition of vowel sounds establishes an important parallel—while also emphasizing the opposition—between "aboli" and "ébloui" (abolished, dazzled), both past-participle adjectives modifying "art."

Although the poem does allow for interpretation, syntactic and semantic ambiguities remain. First of all we find "un très art nul," rather than "un très nul art" or "un art très nul" as we might expect, creating doubt as to the grammatical status of "art" and "nul." As for "bibelot sûr," is it the object of "ose" (dare) or does it stand in apposition to "art"? If the "abus noir" (dark misuse) and the "brisant trublion à sens" are a double risk to be pushed out, what exactly are they? Alternatively, we might interpret "brisant" as a noun (reef or breaker) rather than as a present participle (breaking), and separate it from the troublemaker ("trublion")[15]—a reading encouraged by the typographical layout of the poem—and see the second as being in apposition to the "il" (it) of two lines earlier. But does this "il" refer back to "saut" (leap) or to the earlier "art"? This solution does not greatly facilitate interpretation. Is it by liberating itself from meaning (driving it out as a troublemaker) that the abolished art becomes "art ébloui," or by creating a new kind of troublesome meaning? As for the curious "ours-babil" of the second line, it becomes less obscure if we accept Bernard Magné's interpretation of the word "ours" in Perec as the equivalent of "règle" (rule).[16] In this case, we can read the poem either as praise or criticism of the Oulipian constraint: the rule can be the babble that fails to produce anything worthwhile, or it can allow the leap of poetic liberation. The final "art ébloui" is itself ambiguous, appearing to be a triumphant exclamation while also suggesting that art has been overpowered, dazzled by something rather than dazzling the reader.

We can understand this irreducible ambiguity as both the result of the constraint, which threatens semantic and syntactic coherence, and part of a reflection on this very problem. The poems of *Alphabets* occasionally strike us as a creative dislocation of language, while at other times they appear to be chaotic chatter, an art that has been dazzled and even blinded by the virtuosity of its procedures. The strength or weakness of the poems of *Alphabets,* in short, seems to depend largely on chance: it happens to be the case that a particular combination allows, in the above poem, an allusion to Mallarmé and a description of artistic creativity through constraint. In this sense, the highly codified and rigid constraint does not eliminate chance but, paradoxically, creates it—generating chaotic results, founded on the arbitrariness of the sign and dependent on the strokes of luck that produce meaningful combinations.

La Vie Mode D'Emploi: Combination and Clinamen

For the third case study of this chapter, I turn to *La Vie mode d'emploi.* This novel is in many ways an exemplary Oulipian text, given the complexity and importance of the constraint system and the aesthetic success of the final text. I will therefore discuss it at some length here. The system of constraints used to write this novel is based on a table of 420 elements, divided into forty-two lists of ten elements each. These forty-two categories specify, at least in theory, the function of each element in a given chapter. Under the heading "sentiments" (feelings), for example, we find: indifference, joy, sorrow, boredom, anger, anguish, surprise, hatred, love, and ambition; these indicate the emotion to be attributed to one or more character(s) in a particular chapter. Other categories concern descriptive details (walls, floors, furniture, etc.), formal aspects of the text (such as length of chapter), plot elements (epoch, activity, position, role, and motivation), and intertextual references (notably the allusion to at least two authors in each chapter). The forty-two lists are then divided into twenty-one pairs, and the elements within each list are combined using a ten-by-ten orthogonal Greco-Latin bi-square—a matrix that distributes pairs of elements in such a way as to ensure that no pair is repeated and that no individual element appears more than once in the same column or row of the table.[17] The resulting twenty-one squares distribute the elements of the general table (for example, one square determines the combination of the elements of the two lists "flowers" and "trinkets," so that one chapter will contain both "Japanese garden" and "crystal," another "shrub" and "bronze," and another "green plants" and "mineral," without any of these pairings ever being repeated; each individual element, on the other hand, appears ten times).

Perec varies the application of this combinatorial algorithm by using a "pseudo-quenine d'ordre dix" (a pseudo-quenina of the tenth order). This is a permutation based on the poetic form of the sestina, which Queneau generalized to make it applicable to poems of a different number of lines (baptized "queninas" after the author).[18] In Perec's version, the permutation does not change the pairs themselves but rather the position of each pair in the table, with the result that the table's structure is made less rigid, more complex, and less predictable. The one hundred squares of each bi-square are superimposed onto the model of the apartment building that is the setting for Perec's novel. The narrator's movement in the building—and therefore in the distributive bi-square—is determined by the knight's tour constraint: the movement of a knight around a chessboard in such a way that it lands on each square once and once only (the chessboard in this case is a modified one of ten-by-ten squares). This system allows Perec to establish a list of forty-two elements for each chapter, and it is this set of lists that constitutes the *Cahier des charges* proper. In addition to this basic system, some supplementary constraints are applied to each chapter: the use of a two-figure number corresponding to the coordinates of a particular room in the building's chessboard layout; an allusion to an event that occurred during the writing of the chapter; an allusion to special documents or particular objects; and an allusion to another of Perec's works.[19] I will limit myself here to discussing those constraints that are detailed in the *cahier* itself.

In its first stages (the table of lists and the bi-square), Perec's system operates on the basis of chosen, motivated elements. The initial table allows us to glimpse certain essential aspects of the novel's conception; it is no accident that the list "ressort" (narrative mainspring or motivation) contains the elements "plot revenge," "create," and "pursue a pipe-dream," or that the "games and toys" list contains "jigsaw puzzle," to cite a few examples. That being said, the system also has a mechanical, nonintentional element, since the distribution of elements is determined by a combinatorial algorithm. Troubled by this dimension of the writing process, scholars of the Oulipo, and of Perec in particular, have tended to insist on the role of the clinamen—the swerve or error in the system—as a countermechanical principle.

As I noted in my introduction, the term *clinamen* has its origin in ancient physics: in order to create a place for free will in Democritus's atomist theory, Lucretius argued that atoms can deviate spontaneously and accidentally during their fall. The Lucretian clinamen thus seems to conflate chance and freedom. The Oulipo's co-opting of the clinamen is just one of several twentieth-century reworkings of the notion.[20] While the Collège de 'Pataphysique (College of Pataphysics) borrowed Alfred Jarry's idea of the clinamen as a force that produces chaos,[21] the *Oulipo Compendium* defines it as "a deviation from the strict consequences of a restriction."[22] However, the Oulipo's collective works do not propose any coherent theory of the clinamen. Rather, the notion is invoked by some Oulipian writers, in particular Perec and Calvino, in order to justify or praise the transgression of constraints.[23]

In *La Vie mode d'emploi,* supplementary constraints disrupt the initial constraint system. First of all, the novel has only ninety-nine chapters, whereas the bi-square and the apartment building have a hundred cells/rooms. The knight's move "jumps" the cellar situated in the lower left-hand corner of the plan, which should, in theory, have corresponded to chapter 66. Another type of clinamen is integrated into the system itself, in the form of two "metaconstraints": the categories "manque" (lack) and "faux" (false). These two constraints intervene in the functioning of the lists, either to eliminate one of the other elements (manque), or to replace an element with another from the same category (faux). Other forms of clinamen appear on the local level: as we shall see, Perec does not always respect all the constraints in a given chapter.[24]

Encouraged by some of Perec's own statements,[25] critics often assert that the clinamen's disruption brings creative freedom into a system that is too well programmed. They also often identify it with chance.[26] Among the critical accounts, Christelle Reggiani offers what is perhaps the most thorough and persuasive discussion of the clinamen, arguing convincingly that there is a tension in the Oulipo between the exaltation of the machine as an operator of order and the awareness that the machine's automatic aspect can establish a reign of the aleatory—in opposition to the Oulipian "challenging" of chance.[27] The Oulipo's ambivalence toward the machine is grounded in a tension between two valorizations: one of expression and one of an order that transcends the human.[28] According to Reggiani, the clinamen negotiates this tension, not by introducing absolute chance into a fully controlled system, but on the contrary, by functioning in opposition to this "mechanical aleatoriness" of the constraint. It thus represents a rejection of "mechanographic" writing and an assertion of authorial control.[29]

Reggiani's notion of "mechanical aleatoriness" corresponds to Pierre Boulez's idea of "hasard par automatisme" (chance by automatism) discussed in my previous chapter. In this context, the clinamen that disrupts the mechanism does indeed represent a form of anti-chance. Although the constraints of *La Vie mode d'emploi* constitute a deterministic system, we have seen that determinism and chance are not simple opposites. A complex system—even if it is deterministic in principle—can produce coincidences, from the author's point of view, through the unforeseen intersections it produces. In the case of the *Cahier des charges,* the 420 basic elements are combined in unpredictable ways, independently of the author's will. However, I believe that critics—and even some Oulipo members themselves—attribute too much importance to the clinamen by seeing it as the guarantor of subjective invention. This is not to deny that clinamens such as "manque" and "faux" in *La Vie mode d'emploi* involve authorial choice; furthermore, these two constraints are characteristic in that they transform two of Perec's existential themes—falsification and lack—into aesthetic principles.[30] However, it is hard to argue that such clinamens play more than a peripheral role in the system and in the final form of the novel. It is possible to imagine *La Vie mode d'emploi*'s system of constraints without their intervention. The effects of these kinds of clinamen are actually fairly limited when compared to other forms of freedom that Perec allows himself, and indeed, when compared to the freedom that the constraints themselves permit, by their very nature.

Rather than contrasting the supposedly "mechanical" constraints to the freedom, expressivity, or randomness permitted by the clinamen, we should perhaps consider the expressive possibilities of the constraints themselves. First of all, they are chosen by the writer. Once chosen, they do not mechanically determine the finished text. Sydney Lévy invokes the notion of emergence, an irreversible temporal process, to account for this underdetermination of the text by the constraint.[31] However, such emergence does not occur automatically, but involves the intervention of a whole set of uncodified intentions and rules during the writing process. As Jacques Neefs notes, the system is a prior condition of the text's possibility but cannot "explain" the text that ultimately liberates itself from the system.[32]

From List to Text

While we should guard against reducing *La Vie mode d'emploi* to the author's initial set of "specifications," it is important to examine the effects of the combinatorial system on the novel's form. A brief example, chapter 16 of *La Vie mode d'emploi,* will serve this purpose. What I offer here is not a full account of the chapter's genesis[33] but a reflection on the nature of the relationship between the initial list of constraints and the final text. Table 1 displays, in the center column, the forty-two "preprogrammed" elements of the chapter.[34] The left-hand column shows the category to which each of these elements belongs in the original "table of lists" (published in the *Cahier des charges*). The right-hand column shows the text of the chapter in its entirety.[35]

We see immediately that Perec actualizes the constraints in very different ways. In the simplest of cases, the original element is inserted directly into the chapter as a narrative or descriptive element. In chapter 16, this happens with the constraints "bed," "hatred," "wool," "grey," and "medals." The word can undergo a minimal semantic change: for example, "faire-part" (announcement) becomes "bristol" (calling card) and "water" becomes "lake." In the case of the element "Laurel" (which originates as the "couple" Laurel and Hardy in the initial table), the status of the word is altered from proper name to the plant, via the English term.

In theory, the *Cahier des charges* ascribes particular functions to particular elements: thus the constraint "a few lines" determines the length of the chapter. In other cases, Perec displaces or manipulates his own functional categories. For example, the constraints which dictate, in principle, the position and number of characters in chapter 16 are not applied to the primary diegetic level: only one person, Mademoiselle Crespi, is in this room, and the position "monter" (rise, go up) does not apply to her, since she is sleeping. The three people and the stipulated position appear in her dream instead (the figures are climbing a path). The role of the initial elements is therefore not entirely fixed. Some elements are more open by their nature and serve as the starting point for a narrative or descriptive development. This occurs with the "preprogrammed" quotation from Thomas Mann; in theory, this constraint allows Perec to use any passage, long or short, from any place in this writer's oeuvre. In this case, Perec has chosen a quotation from chapter 5 of *The Magic Mountain:* a description of an Alpine landscape with three characters walking toward a cemetery.[36] The writing process can expand the initial element, as occurs here or with the constraint "have a dream," which constitutes the kernel of the entire chapter. In other cases we see the converse movement of condensation and overdetermination, when Perec unites several elements of the list in one element of the chapter. The Mann quotation, for example, also fulfills the constraints "water," "pasture," "rise," and "three people"; the reference to the battle of Stalingrad integrates the elements "Russia" and "2nd War."

From this example alone, it is clear that the system of constraints does

Table I

Category	List
position	monter
activité	manger
citation 1	Leiris
citation 2	Mann
nombre	3 personnes
rôle	fournisseurs
3e secteur	faire-part
ressort	faire un rêve
murs	peinture brillante
sol	moquette [M]
époque	2e guerre
lieu	Russie
style	Regency
meubles	lit
longueur	quelques lignes
divers	1 couteau [faux: militaire]
âge & sexe	vieille femme
animaux	chat
vêtements	blouson
tissus (nature)	à pois
tissus (matière)	laine
couleur	grise
accessoires	chaussures
bijoux	médailles
lectures	livre d'art
musiques	musique romantique
tableaux	Carpaccio
livres	100 ans de solitude
boissons	eau
nourriture	gâteaux
petits meubles	cendriers
jeux et jouets	dés
sentiments	haine
peintures	aquarelle
surfaces	rond
volumes	hémisphère
fleurs	plante grasse
bibelots	pierre semi-précieuse
manque	manque in 3
faux	faux in 4
couples	Laurel
	pâturage

Chapter 16 (Chambres de bonne, 6; Mademoiselle Crespi)

La vieille mademoiselle Crespi est dans sa chambre, au septième, entre le logement de Gratiolet et la chambre de bonne de Hutting.

Elle est couchée dans son lit, sous une couverture de laine grise. Elle rêve: un croque-mort aux yeux brillants de haine se tient en face d'elle, debout, sur le pas de la porte; de sa main droite à demi levée il présente un bristol bordé de noir. Sa main gauche supporte un coussin rond sur lequel reposent deux médailles dont l'une est la Croix des Héros de Stalingrad.

Derrière lui, au-delà de la porte, s'étend un paysage alpestre: un lac dont le disque, entouré de forêts, est gelé et couvert de neiges; derrière sa rive la plus éloignée les plans inclinés des montagnes semblent se rencontrer et au-delà des pics couverts de neige s'étagent dans le bleu du ciel. Au premier plan, trois personnes gravissent un sentier menant à un cimetière au centre duquel une colonne surmontée d'une vasque d'onyx jaillit d'un massif de lauriers et d'aucubas.

Table 1, continued

Category	List
position	rise
activity	eat
quotation 1	Leiris
quotation 2	Mann
number	3 people
role	suppliers
3rd sector	announcement
[plot] mainspring	have a dream
walls	glossy paint
floor	wall-to-wall carpet [L]
era	2nd War
place	Russia
style	Regency
furniture	bed
length	a few lines
miscellaneous	1 knife [false: military]
age and gender	old woman
animals	cat
clothes	jacket
fabric (nature)	polka-dotted
fabric (material)	wool
color	grey
accessory	shoes
jewelry	medals
reading	art book
music	Romantic music
pictures	Carpaccio
books	100 Years of Solitude
drinks	water
food	cakes
small furnishings	ashtrays
games and toys	dice
feelings	hatred
painting	watercolor
surfaces	round
volumes	hemisphere
flowers	succulent plant
trinkets	semi-precious stone
lack	lack in 3
false	false in 4
couples	Laurel
	pasture

Chapter 16 (Servants' Quarters, 6; Mademoiselle Crespi)

Old Mademoiselle Crespi is in her room on the seventh floor, between Gratiolet's flat and Hutting's maid's room.

She is lying in bed, beneath a grey woollen blanket. She has a dream: an undertaker, eyes gleaming with hatred, stands opposite her in the doorway; in his half-raised right hand he proffers a pointed, black-edged card. His left hand supports a round cushion on which two medals lie, one of which is the Stalingrad Hero's Cross.

Below him, beyond the doorway, lies an Alpine scene: a lake, a frozen and snow-covered round, bordered with trees; the mountains seem to slope directly down to its further shore, while beyond there again show unfamiliar peaks, all in full snow, overtopping each other against the blue sky. In the foreground, three young people are climbing a path which leads to a cemetery, in the middle of which a column surmounted by an onyx basin rises from a clump of oleander and aucuba trees.

not exclude authorial choice. Perec is free to obey, transform, or ignore each individual element. Some modifications of the initial list are required by the system; this is true of the nonfulfillment of the element "wall-to-wall carpet," subjected to the constraint "lack," and the replacement of "knife" by "soldier" because of the application of the "false" rule. However, several other elements of the list apparently do not appear in the chapter. On the manuscript page, Perec circled in red ink the constraints he used, and added an indication that only twenty-eight of forty-two constraints had been respected. A reading of the chapter seems to confirm this: there is apparently no quotation from Leiris, no art book, nor any allusion to romantic music, for example. Nevertheless, a degree of ambiguity remains: the element "glossy painting" seems to have been omitted, yet the adjective appears in the form of the "gleaming" eyes of the undertaker. The presence of this "croque-mort" (undertaker, but literally "eater of the dead") could be the result of a transformation of the "eat" constraint. These associations can be taken further: even if there is no "romantic music" as such in this chapter, and no "art book," the Alpine landscape perhaps combines these two elements in a romantic tableau. The operations through which the initial element might "cross over" into the chapter are in theory so numerous (metaphoric transformation, manipulation of the signifier, semantic association) that there will always be an element of uncertainty. The system's mobility relativizes the very notion of "constraint," which can hardly be conceived in wholly deterministic terms.

The constraints of the *Cahier des charges* operate paradoxically since they are a principle of distributive organization, but also create a kind of disorder. While the system functions on the basis of elements chosen by the author, the combinatory system creates unpredictable configurations that escape authorial control to a certain degree. Of course, this unpredictability is not as extreme as that of a dice throw, for Perec knows the initial position of all the elements and the rules that govern their distribution. However, knowledge of the system's rules does not mean that the author can predict all its results. Given these limits of intentional control, I believe it is not inaccurate to speak of a form of chance in this case—this is "automatic chance," as described in my previous chapter.

Coherence and Multiplicity

At the heart of Perec's novel is a formal and thematic tension between coherence and unity on the one hand and multiplicity and fragmentation on the other. The constraints embed this struggle in the writing process itself. In the novel's numerous stories, for example, the impression of heterogeneity is diminished by the expansive movement of narrative logic. The book's narrative construction is nevertheless discontinuous: each chapter is based on a different list of constraints and also deals with a different room in the apartment building, and therefore with different characters and their stories. The knight's tour constraint governs the order of the chapters, yet this order is not obviously systematic from the reader's point of view and contributes to the impression of narrative discontinuity and indeed randomness.[37] Once again, the constraint works as a midpoint between chance and order. Danielle Constantin observes that the fragmentation of the novel's narrative structure is a direct consequence of the constraint system and its effects on the writing process: Perec could quickly attach textual fragments to particular chapters and work on chapters in any order, even simultaneously.[38]

The Latin square permutation has a similar function; in a letter to the mathematician Indra Chakravarti, Perec characterizes it as "the most adequate expression of a determined randomness."[39] On the level of individual chapters, the text unifies the multiple, heterogeneous elements of the *Cahier des charges* by different means and to differing degrees. In chapter 16, the text unites the undertaker, the medals, the visiting card, the Alpine scene, and the other constraints to form an enigmatic whole. However, the presence of these incongruous elements is justified by the particular logic of Célia Crespi's dream. Thematic coherence emerges from the different elements, which become motifs of war, death, and mourning. These function not only on the local level but fit into a broader thematic construction: we learn later in the novel that Célia Crespi's son died during the Second World War—although not as a hero in battle, but accidentally, during the Liberation struggles, while he was still a child (*VME,* 479). In other cases, Perec combines the juxtaposed elements of the *Cahier* to produce stories that verge on the absurd or the fantastic. An extreme example of this is the story of the "murder of the goldfish" in chapter 50, a model of narrative excess. In this summary of a detective novel, a set of incongruous characters (a man in uniform, a woman dressed as a Quaker, a middle-aged man in a medieval fool's suit, another dressed as a baby, and a little shepherd girl) are all involved in an equally improbable plot: a man who is preparing to commit suicide falls victim simultaneously to three separate murder plots, each of which shows a different motive (*VME,* 272–78).

In the novel's descriptions, which often take the form of enumerations, the juxtaposition of disparate elements contributes to the "list effect" that is characteristic of Perec's works. Yet even in chapters whose elements are linked and absorbed by a plot or thematic construction, the impression of heterogeneity is never completely abolished. The heterogeneity of the initial list helps to fulfill the novel's totalizing ambition. The *Cahier des charges* requires, for example, the inclusion of references to different eras (from antiquity to the post-1945 period), the use of quotations and allusions drawn from numerous sources (musical, literary, and pictorial), and the incorporation into the text, through the category "troisième secteur," of forms of writing that are normally considered to be nonliterary (recipes, bibliographies, pharmaceutical brochures, etc.). The combinatory distribution of elements produces this diversity, while at the same time guaranteeing a level of coherence and continuity thanks to the repetition of the elements of the general table. In theory (although not necessarily in practice, as we have seen), each element should be used ten times in the course of the book. The system thus creates a network of motifs that are linked in constantly changing configurations. The constraint "serial music," for example, is actualized in several different ways; two instances of this are the story of the singer Véra de Beaumont—who, having been Schoenberg's pupil, introduced the vocal compositions of the Vienna School to French audiences (*VME,* 41)—and a photo of "Pierre Boulez, en frac, [. . .] lors de la première de *Wozzeck* à l'Opéra de Paris" (Pierre Boulez, wearing a tuxedo, [. . .] at the première of *Wozzeck* at the Paris Opera) (*VME,* 198/*LUM,* 156). Occasionally the element is hidden; thus one character is called Peter Mond (*VME,* 418), a name that is in fact a rough German translation of "Pierrot lunaire" and a disguised allusion to Schoenberg's composition of that title. Each point in the constraint system is mobile and can be actualized in various ways. Yet this mobility remains relative, since a degree of fixity is also necessary in order for the constraints to be effective, and perceptible, in the final text. The different elements can take on more or less significance in the larger construction of the text. While the theme of vengeance, inscribed in the *Cahier des charges,* is central in the finished novel, other constraints remain largely invisible. However, an attentive reader will perhaps notice the repeated, albeit discreet, reference to certain things (such as miniature trees, walls lined with cork, cats) that form the "infra-ordinary" background of the novel.

Since it is the combinatoric algorithm, rather than a direct authorial decision, that determines the presence of a particular element or conjunction of elements in a particular place, informed readers may have doubts about the status of any thematic connections they discern in *La Vie mode d'emploi.*[40] However, Perec's retrospective integration of the accidental results of the constraint is precisely the dialectical movement that I defined as "anti-chance" in the previous chapter, and an example of what Paul Valéry calls the genius's ability to take advantage of the figures thrown by chance.[41] Even if Perec did not initially predict the possibilities that would arise from the distribution of a particular element, when transforming the list of constraints into the final text he chose to actualize the possibilities of the list in a particular way. Ultimately, of course, the reader can never be sure that every meaning found in a text was foreseen and intended by the author. This is not to say that "the hazards of programming"[42] have no consequences for the form of *La Vie mode d'emploi.* While I do not believe that the intervention of chance in one phase of the writing process suffices, in itself, to destabilize thematic interpretation, the *effects* of the combinatory system on the final text nevertheless create an impression of randomness and even incoherence. The constraints, although they are an organizational principle, also create fragmentation and unpredictability that remain perceptible on the surface of the text.

The operations of the *Cahier des charges* illustrate Oulipian anti-chance, while they are also characteristic of Perec specifically, since they are founded on the list form and favor the elaboration of an encyclopedic novel. The presence of the aleatory within the system is due less to the intervention of the clinamen than to the nature of the constraints themselves; the writing process uses and organizes chance. Thus, while Perec's Oulipian methods can certainly be ascribed in part to a "quest for formal symmetry and purity,"[43] this is only part of the story. The constraint is also a powerful agent of chaos, mimicking the dice throw. The dialectical tension between chance and necessity is played out on the level of structures that can be perceived by the reader, even if this reader does not have access to the published manuscripts. The constraints, a paradoxical "programming" of chance, embody the tension between order and disorder, unity and fragmentation, life and its *mode d'emploi*—its means of use—that is at the heart of Perec's novel.

Form Versus Diagram

Most accounts of the Oulipo describe the constraint as entirely "formal" in nature.[44] However, the above analysis suggests that this characterization is not always accurate. Furthermore, it becomes difficult to distinguish between the "mechanical" and "expressive" aspects of Oulipian creation. How, then, to better describe the functioning of Perec's constraints? I believe that the notion of the "diagram" developed in the philosophical and aesthetic writings of Gilles Deleuze provides one possible conceptual model. Although Deleuze himself does not discuss, to my knowledge, the question of the Oulipian constraint—nor do the members of the Oulipo often refer to his work—his work offers a sustained reflection on the role of limitations, whether imposed from the outside or self-imposed, in creating new possibilities.[45]

While less familiar than other Deleuzian concepts (deterritorialization, the rhizome, minor literature, the nomadic), the notion of the diagram appears in several of Deleuze's works, receiving slightly different (although not incompatible) definitions in each case. Deleuze first borrows the term from Foucault's *Surveiller et punir* (*Discipline and Punish*), where Bentham's Panopticon is described on one occasion as "le diagramme d'un mécanisme de pouvoir ramené à sa forme idéale" (the diagram of a mechanism of power reduced to its ideal form).[46] In a piece on Foucault, Deleuze describes the panoptic diagram as pure matter and pure function, a kind of machine that can be applied to visible matter (in the form of workshops, schools, hospitals, or prisons) while also traversing all utterable (énonçables) functions.[47] Mobile and unstable, the bearer of the forces that are temporarily stabilized in particular forms, the diagram makes history by undoing preceding realities and meanings (it is history's "outside" [dehors] rather than being outside history), constituting points of emergence or creativity, unexpected conjunctions, and improbable continuums.[48]

In *Mille Plateaux,* Deleuze and Guattari use the term *diagramme* in a semiotic and linguistic context, partly in order to attack the Chomskyan idea of language as a homogenous system composed of constants or universals. The problem with such models, they argue, is not that they are too abstract but on the contrary that they are not abstract enough: generative linguistics situates the mechanism of language on the level of syntax, whereas "une véritable machine abstraite se rapporte à l'ensemble d'un agencement: elle se définit comme le diagramme de cet agencement. Elle n'est pas langagière, mais diagrammatique et surlinéaire" (a true abstract machine pertains to an assemblage in its entirety: it is defined as the diagram of that assemblage. It is not language based but diagrammatic and superlinear).[49] Thus, the "diagrammatic" abstract machine exists prior to any distinction between content and expression, prior to the formation of what Deleuze and Guattari call "regimes of signs" that are situated on strata or territories. Although the diagram governs the distribution of signs among different strata, it is in itself destratified and deterritorialized, without form or substance, only functions and matters.[50] It is only in concrete assemblages (*agencements*), not in the diagrams that govern them, that the distinction between content and expression makes sense.[51]

Deleuze does not confine the notion of the diagram to a particular sphere but argues that each thing has its own geography, cartography, and diagram.[52] While diagrams are not necessarily creative, they are potentially so.[53] It is in *Francis Bacon: Logique de la sensation* that Deleuze uses the term *diagramme* to describe the process of artistic creation, using it to translate the English word *graph* found in interviews with Francis Bacon. Explaining the role of chance in his artistic process, Bacon describes the way in which involuntary brushstrokes can form a kind of "graph," in which the painter can see "the possibilities of all types of fact being planted."[54] Deleuze uses this account of the graph/diagram as the basis for a general theory of the creative process. According to Deleuze, the diagram is defined as a set of lines and zones, of asignifying traits and color-patches, that appears at a particular stage of artistic creation.[55] Chance plays an important role in this act; the lines of the diagram are "irrationnels, involontaires, accidentels, libres, au hasard" (irrational, involuntary, accidental, free, random).[56] Deleuze cites Bacon's example of a brushstroke that reveals that the mouth of a portrait could cut across the entire face, suddenly increasing the sense of distance and transforming the human face into a kind of "Sahara." The diagram's function is to disrupt and break up those figurative and probabilistic givens which pre-occupy the canvas and to allow the emergence of a new world. Although it is a kind of catastrophe that appears on the canvas, it contains a germ of order or rhythm.[57] It therefore exists on the boundary between preparatory work and the act of painting proper, allowing the painter both to confront chaos and to overcome it. The diagram should not be an end in itself: rather, its chaos must be transformed into a new form of figuration. Deleuze calls this the Figure, which must emerge from the diagram and "porter la sensation au clair et au précis" (make the sensation clear and precise).[58]

However different these various accounts of the diagram may seem, it is no accident that Deleuze applies the same term to Bacon's "graph" and to Foucault's descriptions of power mechanisms.[59] In both cases, the diagram exists at an abstract level which is not itself formal; rather, it is a site of potentiality that provides the conditions of possibility for the creation of forms. The function of the artist's diagram is to create an initial movement of deterritorialization, blurring and disrupting what is given in order to make possible the emergence of new "facts." A subsequent process of reterritorialization allows the work of art to come into being, as the lines, points, or marks of the diagram are transformed into a form of expression.[60]

Constraint and Chaos

It may seem paradoxical to argue that the Oulipian constraint functions as a diagram, in Deleuze's sense: while the diagram that Bacon uses is the product of accidental, chaotic brushstrokes, the constraint seems at first glance to be a principle of order, a manner of sidestepping chaos. However, in many respects the constraint's effects are similar to those of Bacon's diagram/graph. In fact, Harry Mathews explicitly compares the results of constraint to Bacon's description of his painting as "accident engendering accident."[61] The constraint, like Bacon's graph and Deleuze's diagram, traces a set of potentialities that are later actualized in concrete form.

In this chapter, I have considered three very different kinds of constraint used by Perec: the lipogram of *La Disparition,* the heterogrammatic combinations of *Alphabets,* the complex combinatoric system of *La Vie mode d'emploi.* Deleuze's concept of the diagram allows us to depart from the prevailing tendency to see Perec's constraints as purely formal or syntactic. In *La Disparition,* the interplay between the lexical constraint and the semantic level provides a strong degree of motivation for the text, while the accumulation of plot elements nevertheless creates an impression of arbitrariness and indeed randomness. On the level of language, Perec's lipogrammatic writing has a disconcerting force, even if its prolixity can also irritate. Since the pleasure of this novel depends to a large extent on Perec's play with the reader's expectations, the metatextual level comes to outweigh other dimensions of the text, including the narrative. As we see in the passage analyzed earlier, *La Disparition* often presents the constraint as an end in itself, as the goal to be attained once the reader has seen past the superficial surface of the text.

The lipogrammatic constraint of *La Disparition* can be situated somewhere between the explicit and rigid "lettric" constraints of *Alphabets* and the inherently mobile system used to write *La Vie mode d'emploi.* In the case of *Alphabets,* the conflict between the combinatoric system and the rules of syntax pushes language to the limits of readability. Using the Deleuzian model, we might describe *Alphabets* as a work that often remains at the stage of the diagram instead of moving beyond it. In a movement of deterritorialization, the constraint undoes normal syntax and creates what Deleuze would call a "ligne de fuite" (line of flight/escape). It then falls to the author to "reterritorialize" the text by choosing among the possibilities of the combinatory system, and eliminating the impossibilities (the combinations that would not function as language). However, the risk is that the necessary reterritorialization might not occur, that the poet might not always recreate signifying configurations. In this sense, there is insufficient distance between the constraint and the text, the diagram and its concrete actualization.

The *Cahier des charges* of *La Vie mode d'emploi* contains a set of constraints that, although they begin with particular word elements, essentially operate on the level of narrative. The constraints serve both to organize the narration on a global level (programming the narrator's movement through the space of the fictional building) and to distribute recurrent local effects (such as citations, allusions, and motifs). The conventional components of the novel—stories, descriptions, characters—are first of all broken, fragmented, and redistributed by a combinatory system independent, at least in an initial stage, of the movement of writing. The logic of the constraint therefore disrupts the linearity of narrative development, while in a later phase narrative coherence is woven from the various elements. The final text preserves an ironic distance from the narrative clichés that it both reconstructs and disrupts.

In the case of *La Vie mode d'emploi,* Deleuze's description of the diagram as a set of nonhierarchical, deterritorialized materials and functions seems particularly relevant. The functions of the constraint system communicate with, yet remain distinct from, the structure of the final text. Rather than being purely formal or semantic, the constraints are abstract possibilities that are actualized as form and content in the writing process. The elements coexist in the same list before they are distributed between the different levels of the novel (the various narrative levels, the description of space, the attributes of the characters, etc.). This stratification takes place only with the movement from constraint to text. As we saw in the case of chapter 16, the nonactualization of a particular element is also one of the possibilities of the system. Instead of concluding that Perec cheats at his own game, we should view the constraint as a generator of potentialities, only some of which will be actualized in concrete form.[62]

Perec's most successful exploitations of constraints are those that take a narrative form. Here, an additional level is added to the initial tension between constraint and language, and Perec allows himself a greater freedom in transforming his constraints. *La Vie mode d'emploi* most effectively negotiates the relationship between constraint and narrative, in part because the constraints operate on the macrostructural and microstructural levels, organizing the novel's structure while offering inspiration for its particular stories. In *La Vie mode d'emploi,* the constraints have a direct effect on the level of narrative and thematic coherence, while in the case of *La Disparition,* it is more difficult to motivate the relationship between linguistic and narrative construction—although the text does attempt to do this on the thematic level. With *La Vie mode d'emploi,* the aesthetic effect of the constraints is no longer dependent on the metatextual staging of these constraints (which is not to say that the metatextual level is unimportant, but that it does not take primary place). Rather, the novel's narrative discontinuity and plurality, to which the constraint system contributes, find a strong justification in the scope of Perec's epistemological concerns and aesthetic ambitions.

Even if it is inadequate to make the decryption of constraints the focus of reading, the reader's knowledge of the constraints may contribute to a work's aesthetic effects. Oulipian writers adopt varying approaches to this aspect of the text; some (Queneau, Mathews) tend to hide their constraints and even consider them mere "scaffolding";[63] others (Perec, Roubaud, Jouet) reveal them wholly or partially, setting up a game with the reader on this basis. The constraint for Perec is not simply a means or starting point. It is not only a matter for so-called genetic criticism, concerned with the stages of the writing process; it also enters into the reading process thanks to various metatextual devices, and in particular to the pervasive presence of constraint as a theme in Perec's major works. I will argue that this self-referentiality enables Perec to investigate the problem of chance precisely by foregrounding the ambiguities of literary constraints. To this end, the next chapter examines Perec's thematic exploration of the place of chance in creation.

A man sets out to draw the world. As the years go by, he peoples a space with images of provinces, kingdoms, mountains, bays, ships, islands, fishes, rooms, instruments, stars, horses, and individuals. A short time before he dies, he discovers that that patient labyrinth of lines traces the lineaments of his own face.

—Borges

7. Labyrinths and Puzzles

In Perec's works, two recurring figures thematize the role of Oulipian constraints: the labyrinth and the jigsaw puzzle. Both are spatial images that complicate the relationship between the local and the global. Both also have a temporal dimension, since they give rise to creative and problem-solving processes: in an initial phase, there is the task of creating the maze or puzzle; next, from the point of view of the solver, there is the problem of finding the center or exit, or of completing the jigsaw. In this double movement and in their implication of both space and time, the labyrinth and the jigsaw puzzle function as allegories for the interaction between reader and writer and as metatextual clues to the complex interplay between order and disorder, chance and constraint.

Literary Labyrinths

As Penelope Reed Doob observes, labyrinths "simultaneously incorporate order and disorder, clarity and confusion, unity and multiplicity, artistry and chaos. They may be perceived as path (a linear but circuitous passage to a goal) or as pattern (a complete symmetrical design). They are dynamic from a maze-walker's perspective and static from a privileged onlooker's point of view."[1] The labyrinth is a familiar motif in literature, especially so in the twentieth century. James Joyce's Stephen Dedalus is named after the architect of the labyrinth at Knossos—an allusion underscored in the epigraph of *A Portrait of the Artist,* and also by references in *Portrait* and *Ulysses* to the "fabulous artificer" of mythology.[2] Daedalus stands here as an archetypal figure both of creation—the construction of labyrinths and the invention of human flight—and of escape and exile. By implication, given the semiautobiographical status of Stephen, Joyce's text itself is the equivalent of the labyrinth, the result of magnificent artifice. The labyrinth is an even more central figure in the work of another author much admired by Perec, Jorge Luis Borges. In "The Garden of Forking Paths," for example, the labyrinth is an image of the world, as well as of the book whose narrative structure imitates the infinite potentialities of time.[3] Similarly, "The Library of Babel" describes the universe as a vast, and possibly infinite, labyrinthine library.

Umberto Eco, having paid ironic homage to Borges's library in *The Name of the Rose,* reflects in his postscript to that novel on the modern fascination with the labyrinth. Eco distinguishes between three types of labyrinth, the first being the labyrinth of Greek mythology with its entrance, center, and exit. Terror is created in this case by the presence of the Minotaur in an unknown location rather than by the labyrinth itself, which is essentially navigable by the hero (Theseus): "The classical labyrinth is the Ariadne's-thread of itself." The second type is the mannerist maze, a treelike structure with blind alleys, "a model of the trial and error process." The third is the net or rhizome (Eco adopts Deleuze and Guattari's term), which has no center, no periphery, and no exit, because it is potentially infinite.[4] Eco's distinction, to which I will return, usefully underscores the different epistemological implications that the labyrinth may take on in different contexts. It also indicates that the labyrinth, as both a metaphor for the text and an allegory of the subject's relationship to the world, engages the question of the connections between knowledge, representation, and literary form.

From Joyce to Kafka to Garcia Marquez, the labyrinth—especially of the rhizomatic type defined by Eco—has become a commonplace of the modernist imagination and a figure of epistemological crisis. In French literature, Alain Robbe-Grillet's *Dans le labyrinthe* (1959; *In the Labyrinth*) has as its subject an anonymous soldier who wanders through the maze of streets in an unknown city. The labyrinth refers, once again, to the act of artistic creation and to the text itself, yet it also symbolizes the confusion experienced by the subject in a simultaneously claustrophobic and disorienting world. This vision is in accordance with Robbe-Grillet's claim in his theoretical writings that the universe can no longer be perceived as stable, coherent, and decipherable.[5] Despite Perec's professed dislike of Robbe-

Grillet's works,[6] there are some striking parallels between *Dans le labyrinthe* and Perec's *Un homme qui dort.* Robbe-Grillet's wounded soldier contemplates cracks in the furniture and ceilings as he lies in bed, and these fissures are associated with the creative movement of the text itself.[7] In *Un homme qui dort,* too, ceiling cracks are associated with the generation of images, and the metatextual significance of this labyrinth is signaled by the series of words that the protagonist conjures in order to stabilize (if only temporarily) the forms he observes and imagines. Yet Perec's novel ultimately distances us from this solipsistic form of creation.[8]

The Rat in the Maze

An image of contained, controlled chance, the labyrinth motif in *Un homme qui dort* operates on several levels: as a metaphor for the protagonist's existential situation, for his effort to construct rules, and for the text itself. Echoing the existentialist literature of individual crisis, *Un homme qui dort* also offers a portrait of the artist. It can even be read, albeit with some caution, as an portrait of the Oulipian author. In a humorous, self-deprecating definition to which I will return later, Oulipians describe themselves as "rats qui ont à construire les labyrinthes dont ils se proposent de sortir" (rats who must construct the mazes from which they propose to escape).[9] Although Perec was not yet a member of the group in 1966, the figure of the rat in the maze has an uncannily central place in *Un homme qui dort.* Indeed, the novel anticipates the future direction of Perec's work by foregrounding his preoccupation with constraint. The labyrinth in this context marks the convergence of the existential struggle against chance and the aesthetic function of constraints as a form of anti-chance.

There is a moment in *Un homme qui dort* when the protagonist has apparently attained his goal of passive, indifferent existence. The second-person narration conveys this state of suspended consciousness through a series of similes:

> Tu survis, sans gaieté et sans tristesse, sans avenir et sans passé, comme ça, simplement, évidemment, comme une goutte d'eau qui perle au robinet d'un poste d'eau sur un palier, comme six chaussettes trempées dans une bassine de matière plastique rose, comme une mouche ou comme une huître, comme une vache, comme un escargot, comme un enfant ou comme un vieillard, comme un rat. (*UHD,* 77)

You survive, without joy and without sadness, without a future and without a past, just like that: simply, self-evidently, like a drop of water forming on a drinking tap on a landing, like six socks soaking in a pink plastic bowl, like a fly or a mollusc, like a cow or a snail, like a child or an old man, like a rat. (*MA,* 177)

A metonymic logic governs the initial comparisons, as the character's identity merges with elements of his immediate surroundings (the water droplet, his socks). There follows a set of animal and human motifs that reappear at other points in the novel: the reference is to creatures that apparently exist in an unproblematic, unconscious way, free from emotions and, above all, free from history. The protagonist's identification is a symptom of his desire to escape from human consciousness, while his obsession with the rat (an animal considered to be vermin) also suggests self-revulsion. His transformation, although merely metaphorical, is in this sense akin to the metamorphosis of Kafka's Gregor Samsa—and indeed the "man asleep" reemerges as "Grégoire Simpson" in *La Vie mode d'emploi.*

However, the rat motif becomes the basis of a larger and more complex metaphorical construct. Elsewhere in *Un homme qui dort,* the protagonist is compared not just to rats in general but more specifically to a laboratory rat, the subject of a scientific experiment that involves confinement in a maze:

Vie sans surprise. Tu es à l'abri. Tu dors, tu manges, tu marches, tu continues à vivre, comme un rat de laboratoire qu'un chercheur insouciant aurait oublié dans son labyrinthe et qui matin et soir, sans jamais se tromper, sans jamais hésiter, prendrait le chemin de sa mangeoire, tournerait à gauche, puis à droite, appuierait deux fois sur une pédale cerclée de rouge pour recevoir sa ration de nourriture en bouillie. (*UHD,* 94)

It is a life without surprises. You are safe. You sleep, you walk, you continue to live, like a laboratory rat abandoned in its maze by some absent-minded scientist, and which, morning and night, unerringly, unhesitatingly, follows the path to its food dispenser, turning left, turning right, pressing down twice on a pedal ringed in red in order to receive its portion of homogenised feed. (*MA,* 188)

Perec's image of the laboratory labyrinth corresponds in some respects to the "mannerist maze" identified by Umberto Eco, since it is a complex space within which the rat must find its way by trial, error, and memory. Yet the latter's task is not to escape but to survive by maneuvering within the maze, finding the correct pedal, and performing a particular set of actions to receive sustenance. The classical and mannerist mazes, to adopt Eco's distinction, imply a movement toward a singular and ultimate goal (finding the center of the labyrinth, or the hidden monster, then finding the exit), even if this process necessarily entails repetitions and false moves. For Perec's laboratory rat, on the other hand, repetition is the essence of the activity, and the labyrinth's unpredictability is eliminated by habit.

The figure of the rat thus ironically undermines the mythological associations of the labyrinth archetype. A debased version of the heroic Theseus, the novel's protagonist is also described as a semihuman monster: "Tu ne sors qu'à la nuit tombée, comme les rats, les chats et les monstres" (You only go out after nightfall, like the rats, the cats and the monsters) (*UHD,* 25/*MA,* 142). He is both Theseus and Minotaur, hunter and hunted. Yet the figure of the laboratory rat ultimately dissolves both of these identities and replaces agency with conditioned behavior. The role of the forgetful scientist, on the other hand, suggests the figure of an absent god who has created and then abandoned a world that continues to function even in the absence of any overriding necessity. Of course, this negligent scientist can also be identified with the author, who creates a universe in which his characters' actions and the possible outcomes are limited. On yet another level, the protagonist of *Un homme qui dort* is himself the researcher, carrying out an experiment on himself by attempting to live the unconscious, perfectly conditioned life of a laboratory rat. The gap between the protagonist and the second-person narrator corresponds to this split between the character's two roles: the scientist who manipulates and observes, and the passive object of his experiment.

The walls of the labyrinth initially appear to create a reassuring and protective space of possibility rather than a confining one. The rat's maze becomes a paradoxical image of freedom; the protagonist wishes to be "libre comme une vache, comme une huître, comme un rat!" (as free as a cow, as a mollusc, as a rat!) (*UHD,* 105/*MA,* 195). The rat is even capable of transforming the constraints of his existence into a form of creation:

> Le rat, dans son labyrinthe, est capable de véritables prouesses: en reliant judicieusement les pédales sur lesquelles il doit appuyer pour obtenir sa nourriture au clavier d'un piano ou au pupitre d'un orgue, on peut obtenir de l'animal qu'il exécute convenablement "Jésus que ma joie

> demeure" et rien n'interdit de penser qu'il n'y prenne un plaisir extrême. (*UHD*, 138–39)

> The rat, in his maze, is capable of truly heroic feats: by judiciously connecting the pedals he has to press in order to obtain his food to the keyboard of a piano or the console of an organ, the animal can be persuaded to give a passable rendition of "Jesu Joy of Man's Desiring," and there is no reason to doubt that he takes great pleasure in doing so. (*MA*, 218)

Yet this is a passive form of prowess, which requires the intervention of the scientist (the "on" who links the pedals and manipulates the animal's behavior). From the point of view of the rat, which intends only to obtain food, the emergence of the tune and the accompanying aesthetic pleasure are merely accidental consequences of its principal project. The musical collaboration of scientist and rat suggests a split within the persona of the artist, a division that entails both the necessity of control (the scientist's manipulation) and an element of chance (the rat's wanderings in the labyrinth and unintentional execution of the master's plan).

Ultimately, the book's ending demolishes the metaphorical construct that has been founded on the rat/scientist analogy: "Mais les rats ne cherchent pas le sommeil pendant des heures. Mais les rats ne se réveillent pas en sursaut, pris de panique, trempés de sueur. Mais les rats ne rêvent pas et que peux-tu faire contre tes rêves?" (But rats don't spend hours trying to get to sleep. But rats don't wake up with a start, gripped by panic, bathed in sweat. But rats don't dream and what can you do to protect yourself against your dreams?) (*UHD*, 105/*MA*, 195). In other words, the protagonist has failed to become as "free as a rat," in the sense of being free from human fears and aspirations. Yet in another sense, he is freer: "Mais toi, pauvre Dédalus, il n'y avait pas de labyrinthe. Faux prisonnier, ta porte était ouverte. Nul garde ne se tenait devant, nul chef des gardes au bout de la galerie, nul Grand Inquisiteur à la petite porte du jardin" (But, poor Daedalus, there never was a maze. You bogus prisoner! your door was open all the time. There was no warder posted outside, no head-warden stationed at the end of the corridor, no Grand Inquisitor waiting at the garden gate) (*UHD*, 139/*MA*, 218). The name Dédalus has a double reference here, alluding of course to Daedalus the maze builder (who, according to some versions of the myth, was eventually imprisoned in his own creation as a punishment for Theseus's success).[10] Yet the spelling Dédalus (rather than "Dédale") points to James Joyce's character Stephen Dedalus, as becomes clear on the following page: "Tu ne pars pas, pour la millionième fois, rechercher la réalité de l'expérience ni façonner dans la forge de ton âme la conscience incréée de ta race" (You are not going to encounter for the millionth time the reality of experience and to forge in the smithy of your soul the uncreated conscience of your race) (*UHD*, 140/ *MA*, 219). Here, the penultimate sentence of Joyce's *Portrait* is transposed into the second-person singular as well as the negative.[11] Perec's narrator rejects Stephen Dedalus's search for life and experience, along with a series of other novelistic endings. These include Kafka's story "Before the Law" (also recounted to Joseph K. in *The Trial*), which relates a man's encounter with a guard who blocks his access to the law.[12] In Kafka's text the prohibition may or may not be absolute. Perec's narrator, on the other hand, asserts that neither guard nor prohibition exist for the "man asleep," just as this "poor Daedalus" has no labyrinth. The protagonist, rather like the typical existentialist hero, is now faced with a purposeless and terrifying freedom.[13] The disappearance of the labyrinth does not lead to an epic ending with the hero striding out into freedom (for departure has lost its meaning when there is nothing to escape), but with an ambiguous opening onto an uncertain future.

Ceiling and City

The labyrinth is a figure of freedom within constraint, affording the rat the possibility of achieving various feats within a protective—or stifling—circumscribed space. It stands for an ideal of controlled chance, both because the rat unintentionally carries out the scientist's intentions, and, in a more general sense, because the paths of the labyrinth demarcate a certain number of possible paths, without determining exactly which one the explorer will take. This reading of the labyrinth metaphor is confirmed by several recurring motifs in *Un homme qui dort:* in particular those of the ceiling and the city. The protagonist spends large amounts of his time contemplating his ceiling, whose cracks trace "un improbable labyrinthe" (*UHD*, 30). Or rather, he himself creates this labyrinth (thereby adopting the role of Daedalus) by transforming the set of initially random, disordered markings into an organized structure or shape:

> La conjonction des ombres et des taches et les variations d'accommodation et d'orientation de ton regard produisent sans effort, lentement, des dizaines de formes naissantes, organisations fragiles que tu ne peux saisir

> qu'un instant, les arrêtant sur un nom: vigne, virus, ville, village, visage, avant qu'elles ne se disloquent et que tout ne recommence: l'apparition d'un geste, d'un mouvement, d'une silhouette, ébauche de signe vide que tu laisses grandir, hasard qui se précise: un œil qui se fixe, un homme qui dort, un remous, léger balancement de voiliers, bout d'arbre, rameau explosé, préservé, retrouvé, de l'intérieur duquel émerge en se précisant point par point l'amorce encore d'un visage, à peine différent de l'autre tout à l'heure, plus sombre peut-être, ou plus attentif, visage en suspens où tu cherches sans les voir les oreilles, les yeux, le cou, un front, ne retenant, ne retrouvant, pour les perdre aussitôt, que l'empreinte d'un sourire ambigu, l'ombre d'une narine que peut-être prolonge la trace—infamante ou glorieuse, qui sait?—d'une cicatrice. (*UHD,* 70)

> The conjunction of shadows and stains, and the variations of adjustment and orientation of your gaze, produce effortlessly, slowly, dozens of nascent shapes, fragile coalitions that you are able to grasp only for a fleeting second, fixing them on a name: vine, virus, town, village, face, before they disintegrate and everything starts all over again: the sudden appearance of a gesture or movement, of an outline or the merest suggestion of an empty sign which you allow to develop, a chance meeting which grows into a firm acquaintance: an eye staring back at you, a man asleep, an eddy-pool, the gentle rocking of sail-boats, the tip of a tree, a branch shattered, preserved, recovered, and from which emerges with growing precision the beginnings of another face, hardly different from the last one, perhaps a little more grim or attentive, a face in abeyance, in which you search in vain for the eyes, the neck, the forehead. But all that you are able to retain, or find, only to let slip again immediately, is the impression of an ambiguous smile, the shadow of a nostril, prolonged, perhaps, by the trace—ignominious or glorious, who can say?—of a scar. (*MA,* 172)

First, the set of random lines takes on the shape of a labyrinth as the cracks become paths and organizations of paths. Then the ceiling explodes into multiple forms before being stabilized, once again, as a partial portrait of the protagonist himself: the sleeping man, or the face marked by the presence of a scar.[14] The scar that marks the protagonist's own face (*UHD,* 134) and the cracked mirror in which he often observes himself (*UHD,* 50, 89) are signs of a fractured identity, and the organization of the ceiling lines can thus be seen as an attempt at reparation. Yet the boundary between order and disorder is fragile: each image is born of chance ("hasard qui se précise") and its stability is only momentary, before it is dissolved and replaced by other images.

Words play a similar role here to the vision of the scarred face: both represent the protagonist's attempt to fix the fleeting images by naming them, even if only through spontaneous associations. Both the alliterative series "vigne, virus, ville, village, visage" (vine, virus, town, village, face) and the sequence of images (eye, sleeping man, eddy, sailing boat, tree, root, face) move toward and settle on the unstable, incomplete, and fragmented self-portrait at the heart of the labyrinth. The link between linguistic production and the formation of the image suggests the movement of writing that creates a portrait of the artist. However, the creative potential of the labyrinth gives way to an overproduction of images and words that quickly lose their meaning, dissolving as quickly as they are formed:

> Tu apprends à regarder les tableaux exposés dans les galeries de peinture comme s'ils étaient des bouts de murs, de plafonds, et les murs, les plafonds, comme s'ils étaient des toiles dont tu suis sans fatigue les dizaines, les milliers de chemins toujours recommencés, labyrinthes inexorables, texte que nul ne saurait déchiffrer, visages en décomposition. (*UHD*, 56)

> You learn to look at paintings in art galleries as if they were bits of wall or ceiling, and how to look at the walls and ceiling as if they were paintings whose tens and thousands of paths you follow untiringly, endlessly retracing your steps, as if they were merciless labyrinths, or a text that no-one will ever decipher, or decaying faces. (*MA*, 164)

The protagonist attempts to place all his perceptions on the same level, to stop distinguishing between works of art and ceilings. Rather than attaining the desired indifference, however, he becomes trapped in a vicious circle, moving from chaos to order and back to chaos. The random markings of the ceiling turn into images and words, and images and words are changed in turn into random markings: "Tu lis à voix haute, tout le jour, en suivant du doigt les lignes du texte, comme les enfants, comme les vieillards, jusqu'à ce que les mots perdent leur sens, que la phrase la plus simple devienne bancale, chaotique" (You read aloud, all day long, following the lines of text with your finger, like a child or an old man, until the words lose their meaning, until the simplest phrase becomes cock-eyed and chaotic) (*UHD*, 46/*MA*, 157). Under the protagonist's gaze, images are endlessly composed and decomposed, fragmented and reassembled; texts are written and unwritten. Every surface, every object, every landscape can be subjected to the same treatment as the ceiling. Similarly, during the Sartrean episode in which the protagonist contemplates a tree, the face, the city, and the labyrinth ("dédale") reappear in the shapes of the branches and roots (*UHD*, 40–41).

When not staring at the ceiling, at paintings, at texts, or at trees, the protagonist spends large amounts of time exploring the labyrinth composed by the streets of Paris. The network of streets is less chaotic than the cracks in the ceiling, in that it corresponds to a more or less fixed pattern that can be mapped. However, it still includes a multiplicity of potential paths, a set of indeterminate possibilities. When it comes to choosing between these potentialities, the recourse to chance apparently obeys the principle of indifference: "Tu marches encore, au hasard, tu te perds, tu tournes en rond" (Still you keep walking, wherever your feet take you. You get lost, you go round in circles) (*UHD*, 62/*MA*, 167). This indicates, once again, the ambiguity of the protagonist's attitude to chance, for, as the philosopher Clément Rosset notes, there is no such thing as completely random wandering.[15] Sure enough, the "man asleep" chooses his paths in order to avoid some potential events: "Tu ne marches plus guère dans les rues où tu pourrais [. . .] rencontrer [tes amis]. Tu évites les questions, le regard de celui que le hasard met parfois sur ton chemin, tu refuses la bière ou le café qu'il t'offre" (Now, you rarely ever frequent the streets where you might run into them. You avoid the questions and the eyes of [those] whom chance occasionally places in your path, you refuse the beer or the coffee they offer you) (*UHD*, 27/*MA*, 143). The character oscillates between rule-governed and random itineraries, between choice and chance. Initially he wanders aimlessly, then he begins inventing rules to negotiate the maze of streets: "Tu inventes des périples compliqués, hérissés d'interdits qui t'obligent à de longs détours" (You devise complicated itineraries, bristling with rules which oblige you to make long detours) (*UHD*, 69/*MA*, 172).

At first glance, the protagonist's exploration of Paris emulates the random urban wanderings of the nineteenth-century flaneur, and, as the novel explicitly points out, of the surrealists (*UHD*, 87). Critics from Walter Benjamin onward have noted the parallels between the flaneur and the gambler, who both submit themselves to the positive or negative potentiality of chance.[16] David F. Bell associates chance and flanerie with the topography of the labyrinth, yet claims that the experience of the city as labyrinth "stops short of a radical confrontation with the real viewed as a manifestation of chance"—for the maze remains an ordered form and contains a possible law.[17] In a sense, the protagonist of *Un homme qui dort* attempts to attain this "radical confrontation" with chance and the real precisely by breaking away from the form of the labyrinth. Thus the model of flanerie is soon rejected because of the consciousness of time that it entails: "Seuls peuvent flâner ceux qui volent le temps de le faire, les précieuses minutes qu'ils s'ingénient à gratter sur leurs horaires" (The only people who can stroll are those who snatch the time to do so, those who contrive to fiddle a few precious moments off their schedules) (*UHD*, 86/*MA*, 183). The narrator criticizes the rule-governed approach to Paris as a form of heroic posturing—"tu imaginais des périples compliqués qui prenaient malgré toi des allures de voyages d'Ulysse" (you devised complicated itineraries, which, despite yourself, began to resemble the voyages of Ulysses)—and as a way of organizing space and time (*UHD*, 86–87/*MA*, 183).

The protagonist's enterprise of indifference implies a rejection of spatial or temporal measurements. Unlike the flaneur, he does not conceive of chance as *kairos* (the opportune moment); his project of indifference seems to exclude the possibility of the encounter or even of the event. Rather, he wants to suspend time. However, he is ultimately not able to escape the need for measurement, nor indeed his desire for events. He is therefore faced with a dilemma: chance represents an impersonal principle in accordance with his desired attitude of indifference, but it does not provide the reassuring structures that he also obsessively seeks. Yet Perec's novel also offers the disquieting suggestion that the order of the labyrinth is itself based on chance. The protagonist's self-imposed rules and prohibitions are founded on a set of arbitrary choices that both contravene the principle of indifference and elude absolute control.

Overcome by panic in the face of this realization, the protagonist of *Un homme qui dort* becomes an obsessive labyrinth builder, imposing ever stricter existential constraints on his life while all the time seeking an exit. Thus his card playing is motivated by the hope of finding "l'improbable solution d'un labyrinthe informe" (the unlikely exit from a shapeless labyrinth) (*UHD*, 111/*MA*, 199), and he moves around Paris "comme un prisonnier, comme un fou dans sa cellule. Comme un rat dans le dédale cherchant l'issue" (like a prisoner, like a madman in his cell. Like a rat looking for the way out of his maze) (*UHD*, 118/*MA*, 203). He finds a glimpse of the desired exit in the ceiling patterns: "Une petite bestiole noire vraisemblablement irréelle ouvre une brèche insoupçonnée dans le labyrinthe des fissures du plafond" (A tiny, black insect, quite possibly unreal, opens up an undreamt-of breach in the labyrinth of cracks in the ceiling) (*UHD*, 76/*MA*, 176). Paradoxically, however, the protagonist's sense of physical and psychological confinement is self-imposed; his frantic search for order leads him to construct, from his own existential rules, a personal labyrinth as a protective space. The eventual disappearance of the labyrinth announced in the final chapter is in one sense a liberation, yet the protagonist's real fear is not so much imprisonment as the absence of the labyrinth and its limits, the dissolution of order.

Simultaneously a figure of chance and order, the labyrinth is also an object of desire in *Les Choses.* The figure appears in the novel at the precise moment when Jérôme and Sylvie's daydreams reach their apotheosis: "Des labyrinthes inépuisables résonnaient de musiques suaves; une salle aux formes extravagantes n'avaient d'autres fonctions, semblait-il, que de déclencher d'interminables échos; le sol d'une autre, selon les heures du jour, reproduisait le schéma variable d'un jeu très compliqué" (Inexhaustible mazes echoed with sweet music; one room with an outlandish shape served no other purpose, it seemed, than to set off unending echoes. The floor of another room represented at different times of the day the different stages in a very complicated game) (*C*, 112/*T*, 91–92). Once again, the maze is an enclosed and therefore protective space, but nevertheless contains an infinite number of paths and possibilities. It is limited yet inexhaustible, just as the complicated floor patterns are both fixed and changeable. In short, the labyrinth does not abolish chance but contains and controls it, promising both security and variation. However, this image of complicated harmony can reach a state of only temporary stability. It is constantly threatened by disintegration and eventually collapses under the weight of its own complexity: "Les images s'estompaient, se brouillaient; ils n'en pouvaient retenir que quelques bribes, floues et confuses, fragiles, obsédantes et bêtes, appauvries" (The visions blurred, became jumbles; they could retain only a few vague and muddled bits, tenuous, persistent, brainless, impoverished wisps) (*C*, 115/*T*, 93). Like the "man asleep" imprisoned in a labyrinth of his own making and terrified of its inevitable collapse, Jérôme and Sylvie are constantly threatened by the disintegration of their world of images, yet unable to escape from it. In this context (via the common metaphorical locution "être fait comme un rat"—to be trapped, to have no way out), we once again find the figure of the imprisoned rat: "Ils se sentaient enfermés, pris au piège, faits comme des rats" (They felt locked in, trapped, [ensnared like rats]) (*C*, 69/*T*, 62; translation modified).

Verbal Ruses and Oulipian Rats

In *Les Choses* and to a greater extent in *Un homme qui dort,* the labyrinth represents a way of life that is both desired and feared. It is also a metaphor for the text. Just as they are prisoners of the seductive images that surround them, Jérôme and Sylvie are trapped in the paths of the text that determines their future. In the case of *Un homme qui dort,* as David Bellos notes, the protagonist's goal of suspending time itself renders a traditional linear narrative problematic.[18] Perec's solution to the problem is not complete discontinuity and fragmentation; in his own words, he creates a narrative "in the vague form of a labyrinth, dwelling upon the same words, repeating the same gestures, representing again and again the same paths" (*EC* 1:151–52). The character's obsessive actions are reflected on the stylistic level by the iterative mode that dominates the novel's tenses, and by lexical repetitions—for example, the sequence "comme une vache," "comme une huître," "comme un rat" (like a cow, like an oyster, like a rat) or the phrase "tu traînes" (you drift) (*UHD,* 77, 105; 25, 59, 69, 76, 86). Perec's narrative traces a set of meandering paths, which always take the narrator back to his starting point: the small room with its cracked ceiling, bed, and pink plastic basin (*UHD,* 77). The protagonist's story therefore aspires to the status of a maze without goal or exit, both mobile and immobile, caught in the temporality of the eternal return. Nevertheless, it is time that finally offers a way out of the labyrinth, as indicated in an unattributed quotation from Sophocles: "Le temps, qui veille à tout, a donné la solution malgré toi" (Time, which sees to everything, has provided the solution, despite yourself) (*UHD,* 143/*MA,* 221).[19] The protagonist's experiment and the labyrinth of phrases must come to an end with the text, and the reader, too, must leave the maze.

In many respects, Perec's own verbal labyrinths are a positive counterpart to the mazes constructed by his characters. In *Espèces d'espaces,* Perec associates his creative process with the contemplation of ceiling labyrinths: "J'aime les plafonds, j'aime les moulures et les rosaces: elles me tiennent souvent lieu de muse et l'enchevêtrement des fioritures de stuc me renvoie sans peine à ces autres labyrinthes que tissent les fantasmes, les idées et les mots" (I like ceilings, I like mouldings and ceiling roses. They often serve me instead of a Muse and the intricate embellishments in the plasterwork put me readily in mind of those other labyrinths, woven from phantasms, ideas and words) (*EE,* 36/*SS,* 18). However, this euphoric view of imaginative and verbal productivity that we find in *Espèces d'espaces* should be set against the ambivalence of "Les Lieux d'une ruse" (1977; "The Scene of a Stratagem"), a short text in which Perec describes his experience of psychoanalysis and in which the ceiling labyrinth figures prominently: "Pendant ces quinze mois, j'ai rêvassé sur ces mots-méandres, comme, pendant quatre ans, sur le divan, j'ai rêvassé en regardant les moulures et les fissures du plafond" (During those fifteen months, I daydreamed over those verbal meanderings just as, for four years, on the couch, I had daydreamed as I gazed at the mouldings and the cracks in the ceiling) ("LR," 61/"SS," 162). The meandering verbal paths that Perec produces during the analysis are explicitly assimilated with the act of writing, and the analyst's ceiling with the writer's blank page. The analysand speaks because that is his role, producing connections, interpretations, and meanings at will:

> Je parcourais allégrement les chemins trop bien balisés de mes labyrinthes. Tout voulait dire quelque chose, tout s'enchaînait, tout était clair, tout se laissait décortiquer à loisir, grande valse des signifiants déroulant leurs angoisses aimables. Sous le miroitement fugace des collisions verbales, sous les titillements mesurés du petit Œdipe illustré, ma voix ne rencontrait que son vide. ("LR," 67)

> I travelled cheerfully down the too clearly marked-out paths of my labyrinths. Everything meant something, everything was linked together, everything was clear, everything allowed itself to be dissected at leisure, a great waltz of signifiers unrolling their pleasing anxieties. Beneath the ephemeral glitter of these verbal collisions, the measured titillations of this little illustrated Oedipus, my voice met only its own emptiness. ("SS," 166)

Perec's labyrinth making functions here as a substitute, a mask for the true expression of his distress, even as it enacts a desperate search for meaning. While this solution is ultimately glimpsed at the end of the analytical process, most of these episodes have now merged in "le souvenir de cette attente plafonneuse, le désarroi de mon regard cherchant sans trêve dans les moulures des ébauches d'animaux, des têtes d'hommes, des signes" (the memory of waiting beneath that ceiling, of my troubled gaze as I searched unremittingly among the mouldings for the outline of an animal, or a man's head: for signs) ("LR," 71/"SS," 168). As in *Un homme qui dort,* the verbal labyrinth is both refuge and prison. The apparent solution to the problem—the exit from the labyrinth—also has an uncertain status. The spoken words that finally allow Perec to tell his analyst what he was trying to say are again equated with writing: "Il fallait d'abord que s'effrite cette écriture carapace derrière laquelle je masquais mon désir d'écriture" (First, the carapace of writing behind which I had concealed my desire to write had to crumble) ("LR," 71/"SS," 168). Yet the final, supposedly authentic utterance is left unsaid in "Les Lieux d'une ruse," perhaps because it cannot be voiced outside the context of the analysis: "De ce lieu souterrain, je n'ai rien à dire" (Of this subterranean place I have nothing to say) ("LR," 72/"SS," 168).

Claude Burgelin suggests that "Les Lieux d'une ruse" voices Perec's anger toward the verbal "gymnastics" of the Oulipo.[20] It is true that Perec expresses concern about linguistic inauthenticity both here and elsewhere, notably in the early "Ligne générale" articles, but also later in "Les Gnocchis de l'automne" ("The Gnocchi of Autumn"—the title is a pun on the Greek *gnoti se auton,* "know thyself," the motto carved on the temple at Delphi). In this short text, first published in 1972, Perec seems to posit a form of sincere speech that is opposed to his own ingenious but defensive use of writing.[21] However, he later affirms in *W ou le souvenir d'enfance* that the problem lies not in his false use of language, but in his autobiographical project itself:

> Ce n'est pas, comme je l'ai longtemps avancé, l'effet d'une alternative sans fin entre la sincérité d'une parole à trouver et l'artifice d'une écriture exclusivement préoccupée de dresser ses remparts: c'est lié à la chose écrite elle-même, au projet d'écriture comme au projet de souvenir. (*W,* 62–63)

> It is not—as for years I claimed it was—the effect of an unending oscillation between an as-yet undiscovered language of sincerity and the subterfuges of a writing concerned exclusively with shoring up its own defenses: it is bound up with the matter of writing and the written matter, with the task of writing as well as with the task of remembering. (*WMC,* 42)

At the same time, Perec distances himself from the common contemporary attitude (found in such writers as Blanchot) that impossibility and failure are inherent to writing itself; he adds in a significant parenthesis that "l'indicible n'est pas tapi dans l'écriture, il est ce qui l'a bien avant déclenchée" (the unsayable is not buried inside writing; it is what prompted it in the first place) (*W*, 63/*WMC*, 42). The difficulty lies not in language itself but in the historical and psychological reality with which it attempts to grapple.

All of this suggests that Perec's linguistic "ruses" should not be interpreted in wholly negative terms. Significantly, "Les Lieux d'une ruse" first appeared in a special issue of *Cause commune* on the subject of "la ruse" (ruse or stratagem) inspired by Marcel Detienne and Jean-Pierre Vernant's 1974 work on the Greek concept of *mètis* (guile, ingenuity).[22] The ruse of Perec's verbal gymnastics, in this context, might be understood as a necessary means of circumventing psychological resistance. Similarly, it is reductive to view Perec's use of Oulipian constraints as merely a symptom or defense mechanism.[23] Yet these constraints are ambiguous, since they are associated thematically with both with negativity (as with the "maldiction"—"curse" and "false diction"—of *La Disparition*)[24] and with creativity. Similarly, the labyrinth is at once a figure of ruse, deception, and obstacle, and a positive image of the complexities of creation.

In literature as a whole, according to Stephen Bold, "the labyrinth represents the dangers, twists, and intricacies of invention itself."[25] The labyrinth nevertheless takes on another layer of meaning in the light of the Oulipo's description of Oulipians as rats who must escape their self-constructed mazes. The phrase reminds us of the myth of Daedalus imprisoned in his own construction; indeed, according to Ovid, Daedalus's skill was attested to precisely by the fact that he himself could *not* navigate the labyrinth he had himself constructed.[26] However, the Oulipian rat is an even more paradoxical figure since he chooses imprisonment of his own will. He is also, like the protagonist of *Un homme qui dort,* reduced from a mythological hero to an animal in laboratory, the subject of a behaviorist experiment.

This Oulipian self-definition suggests a curious split within the writing subject with significant implications for our understanding of Oulipian creativity, intentionality, and chance. It points to the gap between constraint and text, between the speculative invention of forms and the actual act of creation represented by the "rat's" movements. In the type of scientific experiment alluded to here, the labyrinth itself—the system of constraints—provides a framework for conditioning the rat's behavior, which we do not necessarily need to attribute to a particular intention. However, the Oulipian is both the architect/scientist outside the labyrinth and the explorer/rat inside it. This observation calls into question the notion that the rat is passively constrained by the labyrinth and that its creativity is therefore accidental. As Jacques Bens notes, the group's self-definition is a sly one, for the easiest maze to escape from is precisely the one constructed by one's own hand.[27] Yet those critics who lament the "mechanical" nature of Oulipian constraints have arguably overlooked this fact. Furthermore, the call for *escape* from the labyrinth suggests that a text written within constraints must ultimately transcend these constraints.

Complications

Unsurprisingly, many of Perec's Oulipian texts are labyrinthine in their construction. This is most obviously true of *L'Augmentation* (*The Increase*), a play in which constraint coincides with narrative structure. The subject of the play is an employee's attempt to request and obtain an increase in salary from the head of his department, and it traces each step in this process through a series of forking paths. The basic structural unit in the plot is a numbered series of logical steps, and each number corresponds to a different "character" or voice: proposal, alternative, positive hypothesis, negative hypothesis, choice, conclusion.[28] These voices, rather than the employee himself, constitute the play's cast of characters. The number of steps in each unit and the order of the voices vary as the play progresses. The voiceless employee is trapped in the relentless bifurcations of the causal chains set in motion. He moves toward his goal only to find himself back at his starting point, forced to retrace his paths. He cannot control which way events will turn; it is others (other absent characters, but more strikingly the voices of the logical or causal sequence) who determine which of the two hypotheses will be true. The bureaucratic maze that the employee is forced to negotiate is reminiscent of Kafka's novels. Given the main character's powerlessness, the element of randomness implied by the story (will a particular person be in the office at a particular time, or not?) gives way to a sense of the inexorable. Circumstances conspire in such a way that the employee has very few chances of having his salary readjusted.[29]

In other Oulipian texts, explicit references to labyrinths take on metatextual significance. At the beginning of *La Disparition,* for example, Anton Voyl attempts to decipher a strange figure in his carpet (*D,* 19). This search for forms echoes the protagonist's fascination with ceiling patterns in *Un homme qui dort.* Voyl, however, is no deluded would-be Daedalus, for the lipogrammatic universe in which he is trapped does in fact constitute a labyrinth with a hidden secret. The conjunction of text and labyrinth becomes explicit in the novel's final chapter, where Swann characterizes the narrative to which he belongs as a circuitous labyrinth ("insinuant circuit labyrinthal") that is only partially illuminated by a weak guiding light ("fanal"), a "fil d'Ariana toujours rompu" (literally "an always-broken Ariana's thread") (*UHD,* 304). The lexical unorthodoxies of the passage ("labyrinthal" instead of "labyrinthique"; "Ariana" for "Ariane") draw our attention to both the labyrinth analogy and the lipogram. The broken Ariadne's thread is the novel's lipogrammatic discourse itself, which allows only one step at a time, since each of its words must be carefully chosen.

The constraint creates a labyrinthine space of maneuver—in this case an e-less universe. It also prescribes a goal—the creation of a novel within this universe—yet it does not determine which path must be taken through the maze: "Il y a un but, mais il n'y a aucun parcours" (You know what your goal is but you don't know of any path to that goal) (*UHD,* 304/*MA,* 277). The lipogrammatic constraint favors narrative discontinuity rather than continuity, hence the reference to the repeated breaking of Ariadne's thread. In this context, it is only writing that finally abolishes chance by fixing words on the page once and for all. The image of the labyrinth thus represents the writer's dilemma, his attempt to transform arbitrary paths into a necessary form. On the other hand, it also suggests the reader's ability to negotiate the fixed structure of the text in different ways.[30]

Similarly, in *"53 jours,"* references to labyrinths function as metatextual clues to the book's plot structure and to the challenges of the reading process. Among the texts Veyraud intends to read is "un truc de Rosenstiehl sur les labyrinthes" (a thing on labyrinths by Rosenstiehl) (*"53J,"* 15/*"53D,"* 4), while the opening paragraph of Serval's *La Crypte,* the text he is asked to decipher, includes the following words: "Des gardes l'escortèrent à travers le labyrinthe des couloirs, étincelants de propreté et de froideur métallique" (Guards escorted him through a labyrinth of sparkling clean, steely cold corridors) (*"53J,"* 37/*"53D,"* 22). As Jacques-Denis Bertharion notes, this labyrinth is a metaphor for the "inextricable complication" characteristic of all good detective fiction of the "enigma" model and prefigures the difficulties that Veyraud will face in his inquiry.[31]

La Vie mode d'emploi contains scattered references to labyrinths, as well as to rats and other rodents. The constraints include the element "rat, mouse" in the "animals" category, but the novel's allusions to these animals are not limited to chapters that are subject to this particular constraint. Although the rodents are not explicitly linked to the labyrinth references, Dominique Jullien has shown that they can be interpreted, via intertexts from Shakespeare and Kafka, as figures of the artist.[32] While *Un homme qui dort* ironically refers to the prowess of the laboratory rat, *La Vie mode d'emploi* presents us with several examples of remarkable rodent achievements: Polonius's domino playing; the acrobatic skills of another hamster, Ludovic; and the seventy-one white mice, offered as wedding gifts to Olivia Norvell/Rorschash and her first husband Jeremy Bishop, which are able to group themselves in the form of Olivia's name (*VME,* 46, 452).

As for labyrinths, one reference occurs in chapter 15: Smautf's room contains an engraving that represents "un jeune enfant recevant d'un vieux magister un livre de prix" (a child receiving a book as a prize from an old dominie) and has a title "apparemment sans rapport avec la scène représentée" (apparently unrelated to the represented scene): *Laborynthus* (*VME,* 83–84/*LUM,* 56). In a Perec novel, the expression "apparently unrelated" should raise our suspicions. If we look to the *Cahier des charges,* we learn that the title fulfills the constraint "contemporary music" by alluding to a 1965 vocal and chamber piece, *Laborinthus II,* by Luciano Berio. However, this explanation of the title does not eliminate its peculiarity in the context of the chapter, where the allusion is disguised by its transformation into a title but is apparently not motivated by the image it names. The arbitrariness of the initial constraint is thus transformed into an enigma in the final text. It is possible to suggest some directions of interpretation. First, the schoolboy is being offered a book, which suggests, as Ewa Pawlikowska notes, that the engraving refers to the labyrinthine structure of writing.[33] The spelling—*laborynthus*—points toward Berio's title but might also remind us of the association between labyrinth and *labor*atory in *Un homme qui dort.* If we look beyond Perec and Berio, we discover that this was the common medieval spelling of the word, which popular etymology derived from *labor* and *intus.*[34] Possible connections between title and image then appear: the prize rewards the schoolboy's inner labor, or an artistic work lies within the offered book.

This interpretation, itself rather labyrinthine, is typical of the kind of "reticulated reading" (to adopt Bernard Magné's term) encouraged by Perec's works.[35] By juxtaposing heterogeneous elements, the text initially suggests arbitrariness yet sets in motion an interpretative drift whose limits are never clearly marked. We can never be sure whether we have reached the center of the hermeneutic labyrinth or whether we have overinterpreted an accidental conjunction. This very problem is thematized in the detective narrative of *"53 jours,"* while it is enacted on another level by many of Perec's works, insofar as they leave us in doubt about the accidental or motivated nature of our readings.

Easier to analyze in thematic terms is the labyrinth that appears in Bartlebooth's final (and forever incomplete) jigsaw puzzle. The image represents "un petit port des Dardanelles près de l'embouchure de ce fleuve que les Anciens appelaient Maiandros, le Méandre" (a little port in the Dardanelles at the mouth of the river which the Ancient Greeks called Maiandros, the Meander) (*VME,* 574/*LUM,* 493). On the right of the picture are the ruins of an ancient city, recently excavated:

> C'est un entrecroisement de ruelles d'une étroitesse extrême, plan, à l'échelle, d'un labyrinthe exemplaire fait d'impasses, d'arrière-cours, de carrefours, de chemins de traverse, enserrant les vestiges d'une acropole vaste et somptueuse bordée de restes de colonnes, d'arcades effondrées, d'escaliers béants ouvrant sur des terrasses affaissées, comme si, au cœur de ce dédale presque déjà fossile, cette esplanade insoupçonnable avait été dissimulée exprès, à l'image de ces palais des contes orientaux où l'on mène la nuit un personnage qui, reconduit chez lui avant le jour, ne doit pas pouvoir retrouver la demeure magique où il finit par croire qu'il n'est allé qu'en rêve. (*VME,* 575)

> It is a crisscross of extremely narrow streets, a life-size model of an exemplary labyrinth made of blind alleys, backyards, crossroads, side streets, which girdle the remnants of a huge and sumptuous acropolis surrounded by the remnants of pillars, crumbling arcades, gaping stairways opening onto collapsed balconies, just as if, in the heart of this now almost fossilised maze, this unforeseeable vista had been purposely concealed, in the manner of those palaces in oriental tales whither mysterious agents convey by night a person who, brought back home before daybreak, can never find his way back to the magic dwelling which he ends up believing he visited only in a dream. (*LUM,* 494)

It is perhaps no coincidence that this labyrinth is situated near the mouth of the Maiandros; in Ovid, the winding paths of Daedalus's maze are explicitly compared to the flow of this river.[36] Nor is it accidental that precisely this jigsaw should mark Bartlebooth's failure and precipitate his death. In *"Le Grand Incendie de Londres"* (*"The Great Fire of London"*), Jacques Roubaud notes that Meander vainly strives to prevent its inevitable end in the ocean. He suggests that this moment of Perec's novel stands both for the triumph of death and for the failure of the project of constraint itself.[37] According to this view, the labyrinthine paths of constraint are an attempt to defer the inevitable arrival of death. Like the "man asleep," Bartlebooth needs to impose his will on existence, to say to himself, "C'est ainsi parce que je l'ai voulu ainsi, je l'ai voulu ainsi ou sinon je suis mort" (It is this way because I wanted it this way, I wanted it this way, otherwise I am dead) (*UHD*, 122/*MA*, 205).

The Art of the Jigsaw

In *La Vie mode d'emploi,* the jigsaw puzzle rather than the labyrinth is the predominant metatextual metaphor, although the two figures come together in the novel's final chapter. Like the labyrinth, the jigsaw involves a two-stage process: first, fabrication of the dilemma, then pursuit of the solution. In Perec's novel, both Winckler and Bartlebooth occupy ambiguous roles as inventors and interpreters—or, if we return to our labyrinth analogy, as scientist-architects or as the rats that are the object of the experiment. The initial conception of the puzzle project belongs to Bartlebooth. The enterprise is labyrinthine in many respects, since the character deliberately chooses to put obstacles in his own path, to create difficulties that he must then overcome. Chapter 26 contains a detailed account of his program: Bartlebooth decides to paint five hundred seascapes, have them cut up as jigsaw puzzles, then reconstitute them before dissolving the watercolors in order to return to his starting point: the blank page. This enterprise is defined first and foremost as a form of order imposed on the disorder of the world. Bartlebooth's whole life from this point on will be organized around "un projet unique dont la nécessité arbitraire n'aurait d'autre fin qu'elle-même" (a single project, [whose arbitrary necessity would have] no purpose outside its own completion) (*VME,* 152/*LUM,* 117; translation modified).

From the outset, this project hinges upon several paradoxes. First, it sets itself against the disorder of a world that it nonetheless aims to represent. Second, like the protagonists analyzed in Marina van Zuylen's study of monomania, Bartlebooth desires to "reorganize the world according to a long-lost model of wholeness" yet attempts to expel indeterminacy from his world by "turning the world as a whole into a fragment."[38] As Tiphaine Samoyault points out, Bartlebooth's procedure is reminiscent of the notion of the microcosm.[39] However, given that the whole is understood here to be irreducibly incoherent, it is unclear that the fragment can encapsulate its characteristic qualities. A further paradox is found in the notion of "arbitrary necessity" that provides the foundation and justification for Bartlebooth's project. The expression is puzzling, especially in light of Marina van

Zuylen's observation that monomaniacs wish to "keep the arbitrary out of their lives."[40] Yet Bartlebooth has recognized that this is, strictly speaking, impossible: in the absence of any overarching necessity that governs life, there can only be a chosen necessity, imposed by an act of will.

The three governing principles that Bartlebooth imposes upon his project are linked by the moral, logical, and aesthetic demand for absolute rigor. The first principle, moral in nature, specifies both the discreet, nonspectacular character and the existential scope of the enterprise, which will govern Bartlebooth's entire life. The third principle is the aesthetically motivated striving for pure gratuity: "Le projet se détruirait lui-même au fur et à mesure qu'il s'accomplirait; sa perfection serait circulaire" (The plan would destroy itself as it proceeded; its perfection would be circular) (*VME,* 153/*LUM,* 118). However, it is the second, described as a "logical" constraint, that seems to come closest to the Oulipian enterprise in general, and in particular to the mode of organization adopted by Perec for *La Vie mode d'emploi:* the enterprise will exclude any recourse to chance, and will make time and space function as abstract coordinates (*VME,* 153). The *Cahier des charges* of *La Vie mode d'emploi,* with its rules for the narrator's movements and its bi-squares that distribute a finite set of elements, achieves a similar abstraction of time and, in particular, space.

We have seen that Bartlebooth, despite formulating a project that excludes all recourse to chance, chooses the spaces he represents "plus ou moins au hasard" (more or less at random) according to his whims (*VME,* 80/*LUM,* 52). Furthermore, chance necessarily enters into the project through the arbitrariness of its parameters: the narrator notes ironically that it would have been better to paint 480 rather than 500 watercolors, in order to create a simpler timetable for their completion (*VME,* 462). The "arbitrary necessity" of Bartlebooth's project is also that of Perec's novel: why choose 420 elements and twenty-one bi-squares as a foundation for the constraint system? Why include two citations in every chapter, for example? Of course, the choices involved are never completely arbitrary; for Perec, as for Bartlebooth, they are partially motivated by a totalizing ambition (hence Bartlebooth's choice of a large number of ports and Perec's of a large number of basic elements) and by personal preference (for particular places or elements). Yet neither system of constraints can completely disguise its arbitrary origin. The acceptance of the arbitrary ultimately implies an acceptance of chance, even if chance is limited and controlled as far as possible. Chance is transformed into a rule, and the project creates its own internal logic.

If the parallel between Perec and Bartlebooth is indisputable, what are the implications of Bartlebooth's failure for our reading of Perec's novel? Unlike Jacques Roubaud, who emphasizes the triumph of death over Bartlebooth's project, Claude Burgelin sees the unexpected letter *W* as the victory of life, memory, and indeed chance over Bartlebooth's destructive and deadly obsession.[41] It is true that life's accidents—both those chance elements internal to the system and contingencies external to it—contribute to defeating Bartlebooth. As Perec himself points out in a 1981 interview, the novel's title can be read in terms of an opposition between life and the derisory plans for its "use" ("modes d'emploi") that individuals attempt to formulate for it (*EC* 2:173). Nevertheless, it is life that makes such projects possible and perhaps even necessary (few, if any, of Perec's characters are able to live without a project or a "game"). In this sense, the "mode d'emploi" inevitably affirms life even as it denies chance.

That said, Perec's project differs from Bartlebooth's in a fundamental sense: he does not apply an abstract system to the world in order to reduce it symbolically to a blank page, but uses constraints as building blocks for the creation of a fictional universe. While Bartlebooth's project is potentially a creative endeavor (it produces the microcosm of the jigsaws), it is ultimately nihilistic. It aims to transform and ultimately obliterate the real, denying both time and chance in the process. It is only thanks to the project's failure that the billionaire's life leaves traces. However, we should not forget that this failure is not due only to the intervention and victory of the aleatory and the precarious, but also, and perhaps primarily, to the success of another project and another will to power: that of the puzzle fabricator, Gaspard Winckler.[42] In important respects, Winckler's project is also a form of anti-chance.

The preamble to *La Vie mode d'emploi* offers a reflection on Winckler's particular skill, the art of making jigsaw puzzles. Significantly, the problem is framed in terms of necessity and chance: if most puzzles are machine-made and are cut by a press that is "réglée selon un dessin immuable" (set up once and for all), the narrator tells us, the result is a cutting pattern that is "aléatoire" (*VME,* 18/*LUM,* "Preamble," n.p.). In what sense can this mechanistic (i.e., strictly determined) cutting-out be deemed aleatory? The answer lies in the lack of relationship between the design of the cut and the subject of the image. The former remains purely arbitrary and abstract, without any relationship to what it fragments, and this unmotivated encounter between structure and material can therefore be attributed to chance. It is for similar reasons, as we have seen, that some critics have attacked the Oulipian approach to writing. Significantly, Perec's preamble refuses the results of the machine's rules in favor of the manual craft of the artisan, who in each individual case creates an adequate form in relation to the image.

The repetition of the passage on the "art of the puzzle" (with minor variations) later in the novel suggests that it should be read on two levels. In chapter 44, where it introduces the account of Gaspard Winckler's fabrication of jigsaws, its function is principally diegetic; as a "preamble" to the novel, on the other hand, it serves not only as an introduction to, but a "user's manual" for the text. Much critical ink has been spilled over this second reading. At first view, the parallels between jigsaw and text seem self-evident: both the rooms of the apartment building and the multiple stories of the novel correspond to the jigsaw pieces whose unity and meaning the reader must reconstitute.[43] In this context, the preamble promises the reader that this apparently chaotic, fragmentary novel does possess coherence, but one that must patiently be discovered and even reconstructed by the reader. The reference to the traps set by the jigsaw maker reinforces this guarantee: even if the reader initially sees in the novel only "éléments inertes, amorphes, pauvres de signification et d'information" (inert, formless elements containing little information or signifying power) rather than a meaningful whole, this semblance of insignificance is the result of a deliberate strategy by the author, an optical illusion created by the subtle nature of the text's structure. Furthermore, for the reader who knows of the *Cahier des charges,* this fitting together of parts to make a whole also functions on two other levels. As Bernard Magné notes, the initial elements of the cahier are the jigsaw pieces of each chapter, while *La Vie mode d'emploi* is also a piece that has its place in literature as a whole. However, Magné points out that the jigsaw not only stands for the creative operation but is also a metaphor for the eradication of all traces of this operation—all the more so since Bartlebooth has Morellet glue all the pieces together to reconstitute a seamless whole; the result is a self-referential aporia.[44]

The jigsaw puzzle has other limits as a metaphor for Perec's Oulipian approach, since (as we have seen) Perec's writing process did not involve simply "piecing together" the various elements of the *Cahier des charges.* These reservations notwithstanding, I believe that the preamble on the art of the puzzle sheds light on Perec's own Oulipian practice, warning against an overly mechanical conception of the constraint that would separate structure from material and therefore place the two in a relationship based only on chance. Gaspard Winckler's art of creating jigsaws involves an intense process of invention, beginning with careful study of the image that leads to a decision about the cut, followed by a second stage of the cutting itself, a work which necessitates "une technique délicate et lente, exigeant une habileté scrupuleuse, mais où n'entrait plus aucune invention" (a slow and dainty procedure demanding scrupulous care and craft but requiring no further inventiveness) (*VME,* 244/*LUM,* 194). Indeed, we have seen that the constraints of *La Vie mode d'emploi* do not function mechanically.

The figure of the puzzle is perhaps most intriguing in its implications for the relationship between writer and reader, although once again caution is important.[45] Cécile de Bary argues that Perec's novel is open in a way that the completed puzzle is not, and in a similar vein, Chris Andrews points out that to read Perec's work is not simply to reassemble a singular totality of meaning.[46] However, it is worth noting that the Winckler-Bartlebooth relationship does not so much imply a harmony between whole and part as it enacts a struggle between openness and closure, fragmentation and totality. The struggle between these two characters can be seen as a conflict between two forms of anti-chance. One form aims to reconstitute, then to destroy, a coherent whole, while the other attempts to prevent this process through the perfect prediction, and therefore control, of the other's actions. Of these two methods—on the one hand the expression of a will to both totality and nothingness (or even to totalitarianism, as Burgelin suggests)[47] and on the other hand an opposing will toward fragmentation (which nevertheless leaves traces)—it is difficult to decide which is the most disturbing.

In any case, it is Winckler's power of fragmentation that wins, as Bartlebooth, in his very struggle to reconstruct his jigsaws, gradually loses sight of the rules of his own game and is caught in a cycle of sterile repetition and ritual (*VME,* 163). Caught in a labyrinth with no Minotaur and no exits, Bartlebooth is at an impasse; the narrator tells us that the very essence of his passion is "une sorte de torpeur, de ressassement, d'abrutissement opaque à la recherche de quelque chose d'informe dont il n'arrivait qu'à marmonner les contours" (a sort of repetitious boredom, a veiled befuddlement in search of a shapeless something whose outlines he could barely manage to mumble in his mind) (*VME,* 403/*LUM,* 337).[48] The final chapter of *La Vie mode d'emploi* leaves us with an image of absence and incompletion—the gap between the X-shaped gap and the W of the final puzzle piece, the signature that enacts Winckler's revenge. This lack serves to reaffirm Winckler's control over meaning, a mastery founded on his ability to predict and exhaust all future possibilities. He thus realizes the ideal symmetry, posited in the preamble, between fabrication and reconstitution—and, by implication, between reading and writing:

> En dépit des apparences, [le puzzle] n'est pas un jeu solitaire: chaque geste que fait le poseur de puzzle, le faiseur de puzzle l'a fait avant lui; chaque pièce qu'il prend et reprend, qu'il examine, qu'il caresse, chaque tâtonnement, chaque intuition, chaque espoir, chaque découragement, ont été décidés, calculés, étudiés par l'autre. (*VME,* 20)

> Despite appearances, puzzling is not a solitary game: every move the puzzler makes, the puzzle maker has made before; every piece the puzzler picks up, and picks up again, and studies and strokes, every combination he tries, and tries a second time, every blunder and every insight, each hope and each discouragement have all been designed, calculated, and decided by the other.

Winckler succeeds in anticipating each of Bartlebooth's gestures and therefore in excluding chance from their game. How else could he have achieved his revenge, signing Bartlebooth's last jigsaw puzzle with his own initial, a form that has long been predictable (*VME,* 578)? Winckler's success presents us with the utopian notion of an ideal text, one whose every possibility has been predicted and intended by the author. Hiding his strategies behind apparent chance, he minimizes the possibility that Bartlebooth will make accidental discoveries. Chance therefore remains strictly under Winckler's control and is manipulated for the ends of his vengeance. In his control over Bartlebooth's actions, Winckler takes on a sinister resemblance to the Officials of W. In the development of this story, *La Vie mode d'emploi* presents us with a disconcerting image of authorial mastery.

Artists and Quests

Beyond the Bartlebooth-Winckler conflict, *La Vie mode d'emploi* contains many other "mirrors" of artistic creation that articulate the tension between chance and anti-chance in different ways. Valène's goal is in an important sense the opposite of Bartlebooth's, since the painter aims not to abolish but to create. In this respect, he seems closer to Perec; indeed, chapter 51 of *La Vie mode d'emploi* presents us with a list of the characters who will be included in Valène's painting, and it turns out that these are precisely the characters who appear in Perec's novel (*VME,* 281–86). Valène's ambition, like Bartlebooth's (and like Perec's) is to incorporate an amorphous whole—all the random elements of life—into a constraining grid, in Valène's case the space of the canvas divided into squares. Yet the disparity between the overabundance of material and the limits of the medium is so enormous that Valène's enterprise becomes absurd and ends in failure, in a practically blank canvas—or in what may be seen more positively as a virtual work (*VME,* 580). To an even greater extent than for Bartlebooth's project, Valène's ambition collapses, or rather is smothered, under the weight of its internal contradictions. The tension between chance and anti-chance, between the inextricable incoherence of the world and the order that attempts to contain and represent it, becomes in this case an irreducible opposition between the two terms.

If Gaspard Winckler is a figure of complete authorial control, chapter 51 of the novel presents us with a more complicated view of the artist's relationship to his audience. Valène plans to occupy a tiny place in his own painting, "comme si cela avait été fait comme ça, en passant, un peu par hasard" (as if it had been done just like that, in passing, a little accidentally). This self-portrait would then remain unnoticed until the day it is discovered by one means or another, or even "d'une manière tout à fait fortuite, comme lorsque, lisant un livre, on tombe sur des phrases que l'on a déjà lues ailleurs" (in a completely haphazard fashion, just as when reading a book you come across sentences you have read before somewhere else) (*VME,* 279/*LUM,* 226). Once again, chance seems to play almost no role in the creative process itself: there is little doubt that Valène fully intends to represent himself on the canvas. Yet the work of art creates an impression of spontaneity and indeed of randomness; the self-portrait is there "as if" by chance. Chance, which is only an appearance from the point of view of the creator, nevertheless plays an important role in the viewing or reading process. The artist cannot entirely govern the process of interpretation. The comparison between this chance revelation of the self-portrait and a reader's discovery of sentences already read before hints at Perec's own citational practice, at the quotations and allusions hidden in the body of *La Vie mode d'emploi.* The viewer/reader may uncover such textual secrets by following a method, but can also make these discoveries accidentally. Valène's hidden self-portrait also alludes to the autobiographical mark that Perec claims is present in almost all of his texts.[49] In such cases, it is not just the possibility of discovery, but its validity that is under question.

We find a parallel treatment of the problem of intertextuality in Perec's short story *Le Voyage d'hiver,* which deals precisely with a reader who happens upon expressions he has already read elsewhere. For the protagonist, Degraël, no particular method is necessary since the intertextual "borrowings" in Vernier's text jump out as he reads at random ("au seul hasard de la lecture" [*VH,* 18]). In this case, the similarities are too numerous to be dismissed as accidental. Perec's own incorporation of citations into *La Vie mode d'emploi* is less blatant; like Valène, he deliberately introduces the appearance of randomness to create the impression of spontaneity and simultaneously increases the degree of randomness in the work's reception by disguising his complex strategies. In this context, the comparison of Valène's self-portrait to "une signature pour initiés" (a signature to be read by initiates) (*VME,* 279/*LUM,* 226) aptly characterizes the ambiguity of Perec's own writing practice.

The other painter of Perec's novel, Hutting, is a composite figure whose history traces various avatars of the twentieth-century artist: he has an "art brut" phase, makes Rauschenberg-like combines, and holds "happenings" in his apartment (*VME,* 564) before pursuing a kind of formalism. These various approaches are close to each other in spirit, motivated by Hutting's two principal desires: financial gain and novelty. Hutting's formalist phase coincides with the time of the novel's narration, and is the result of his search for an original protocol, or a recipe ("recette" [*VME,* 337]). Once again, the character's self-imposed rules parallel the constraints that govern the writing of the novel, sometimes in very specific terms. For a reader who knows of the constraints, Hutting's "fog period"[50] is a reminder of the presence of disguised quotations in *La Vie mode d'emploi,* and the transformation of the original model in his "imaginary portraits" corresponds to the "hypographic" appearance of the Oulipo in the list of these paintings.[51]

Whatever the similarities between Hutting and Perec, however, the former's methods apparently lead to aesthetic failure, even if they are commercially successful. The narrator presents critics' enthusiasm for the "fog period" paintings ironically. Hutting himself is dissatisfied with his initial method of portraiture, which involves choosing the colors for the portrait on the basis of three pieces of information: the date and time of the painting's "birth," the phase of the moon at the moment of the painting's conception, and the asking price. Although he is charmed by the system's impersonality, the results are disconcerting: "Surtout Hutting vivait avec l'impression confuse et souvent désagréable d'utiliser sans génie une formule que, manifestement, quelqu'un d'autre avant lui avait su plier à ses propres exigences artistiques" (Above all Hutting had the confused and awkward feeling that he was using without any spark of genius a formula which someone else before him had obviously managed to bend to his own artistic requirements) (*VME,* 338/*LUM,* 279). This phrase contains an ironic intertextual reference: the "someone else" who knew how to adapt the formula to his needs is in fact none other than a character from Harry Mathews's *Conversions,* from whom Perec borrows Hutting's method.[52] In Mathews's novel, the painter Félix Namque[53] initially claims to be "averse to letting chance or taste decide" the key elements of his works. Yet the narrator soon discovers that this painter uses various ruses to manipulate the system and "to achieve and justify what he felt like doing."[54]

Perec's Hutting applies Namque's system with more rigidity than does his model.[55] Overly inflexible systems are condemned at various other points in *La Vie mode d'emploi,* for example, in the case of Bartlebooth's project, whose rigidity becomes an obstacle to its successful completion (*VME,* 462). Hutting's tendency to reuse his "recipes" also suggests a lack of formal invention; he imposes the same constraints—sometimes borrowed from others—to many different kinds of material.[56] The result is not a productive tension but rather a complete rupture between the material and the form (as with the mass-produced jigsaws dismissed in the novel's preamble). If Hutting's later "imaginary portraits" (which combine fact and fiction) are more successful, it is because he reintroduces a subjective element into his practice of constraint and shows greater aesthetic ambition in his hope of situating his work between fantasy and reality (*VME,* 340). The constraints now serve as a spur to imagination and creation rather than as a rigid, impersonal system.

Although *La Vie mode d'emploi* describes numerous other rule-governed methods adopted by various characters, a final example will serve to illustrate the ambiguity of constraint systems. Madame Marcia's strict schema for the transfer and exchange of her furniture between her apartment, cellar, store, and back shop limits the twelve possible permutations to four permitted directions of movement. These displacements are determined by two apparently contradictory factors: on the one hand, the choice of object can depend on the spontaneity of sudden inspirations, infatuations, caprices, or dislikes; on the other hand, a strict method determines the possibilities of movement (*VME,* 136–37). The detailed exposition is humorously amplified by two diagrams that imitate Greimas' semiotic squares. The gentle irony of this presentation is only partially directed at Madame Marcia herself; the description and the allusion to Greimas remind us of the structuralist effort to provide a formal explanation for various types of systems. Yet something is missing in the account of Madame Marcia's behavior: the model succeeds in defining the rules that govern her movements but does not give us the determining factors of these rules. We learn from the text that the motivation of each movement can vary. Not only is there mobility within the system—Madame Marcia has different paths open to her at each point, despite the various self-imposed prohibitions—but there are a set of factors that escape the structure entirely. Perec's text thus suggests a critique of the closed structuralist models that ignore temporality and indeterminacy.[57] The spatial, geometric model does not explain the dynamic impulses behind Madame Marcia's movements.

Chance and System

The labyrinth and the jigsaw puzzle are polyvalent figures in Perec's works, standing both for order and for inextricable complication. They point to the ways in which Oulipian constraints control chance, while generating complex systems that can give the appearance of disorder. The classical labyrinth tends to become rhizome-like, while the puzzle's fragments may obscure the whole. Perec's labyrinth builders and puzzle makers also dramatize the split in Oulipian writing. The Oulipian author is both rat and labyrinth maker, observer and observed, inside and outside, puzzle maker and puzzle solver; and the self-consciousness of Oulipian writing is inherent in the group's project. It is precisely the gap between the constraint and the text, between invention and actualization, that allows the transformation of chance into anti-chance. Nevertheless, Perec's works also caution against exaggerating this divide, which would result in a mechanical and aleatory relationship between form and content. If Perec's labyrinths and puzzles do incorporate chance, it is because they are dynamic rather than static models, and involve indeterminacy along with temporality.

Perec's Oulipian works generally thematize their own constraints; as well as referring to the specific constraint used to generate them, they deal in a more general sense with the aesthetics of constraint. This self-reflexivity corresponds to what Lucien Dällenbach, in his typology of the *mise en abyme* in narrative, calls the "mise en abyme of the code" and the "mise en abyme of the utterance."[58] The first instance has been extensively studied by Bernard Magné under the auspices of the "metatextual," in an approach that generally focuses on the microstructural level and searches for hidden references to the constraint.[59] In the second instance, the *mise en abyme* of the utterance, the text mirrors its relationship to its own author and reader. Dominique Jullien has pointed out that the proliferation of such mirrors in *La Vie mode d'emploi* creates problems of interpretation: Perec's novel simply contains too many "partial doubles" of the writer.[60] Indeed, Perec often appears to be playing a double game similar to the one in Gide's *Faux-Monnayeurs,* where the *mise en abyme* exists in simultaneous correspondence and discordance with the text that contains it.[61] The differences between Perec and Bartlebooth, for example, are just as instructive as the similarities. Bartlebooth's project concerns not a work of art but his entire life, and it is a program that ultimately implies a refusal of creation, the desire to efface all traces. Sydney Lévy argues that Perec and Bartlebooth are separated by two opposing conceptions of time: while Bartlebooth sees time as linear and reversible, Perec's novel constructs a multiple space-time of diverging and converging paths, forming a temporal labyrinth comparable to Borges's garden of forking paths.[62] In fact, the possibilities of both comparison and distinction between Perec and his monomaniacal characters seem almost endless.

Finally, the figures of the labyrinth and the jigsaw aptly characterize the reader's dilemma when confronted with Perec's texts. The Bartlebooth/Winckler story presents a strikingly perverse view of the writer-reader relationship: Winckler uses his puzzle-making art to multiply false relationships, to ensure that Bartlebooth's enterprise ends in failure. Faced with the pieces, Bartlebooth's undertaking is an attempt to reconstitute the total picture of meaning. But this is the process that Winckler deliberately tries to block. The very existence of this final meaning—of the total image—is called into question in the novel's final chapter. Winckler intensifies incoherence to the point of making final coherence impossible. Winckler's methods tend toward the same effects as chance (discontinuity and fragmentation) but improve upon it. That is, he substitutes a method for chance—"au lieu de laisser le hasard brouiller les pistes, il entend lui substituer la ruse, le piège, l'illusion" (instead of allowing chance to cover his tracks, [he] aims to replace it with cunning, trickery, and subterfuge) (*VME,* 18/*LUM,* "Preamble," n.p.)—not with the goal of creating order, but on the contrary, to accentuate the effects of fragmentation and thereby exacerbate the difficulty of reconstituting "l'espace organisé, cohérent, structuré, signifiant, du tableau" (the organised, coherent, structured, signifying space of the picture) (*VME,* 19/*LUM,* "Preamble," n.p). For Bartlebooth, it is then difficult to distinguish between the effects of constraint and the effects of chance.

For Perec's readers, the possibility of making the distinction between the random and the meaningful depends to some extent on knowledge of the constraints used by the author. Even if Perec often makes this information accessible, the readability of the constraint and the forms of mediation between book and reader vary.[63] As Bernard Magné points out, Perec's strategy becomes highly confusing in texts such as *Deux cent quarante-trois cartes postales en couleurs véritables,* where he complicates the combinatorial rules to the point that patterns are hard to detect: "There are too many recurrences for us to believe in a stochastic arrangement, but too many deviations for us to believe in an automatic system."[64] In Perec's narrative texts, in particular *La Disparition* and *La Vie mode d'emploi,* the proliferation of stories disguises the underlying principle of the constraint. The metatextual references offer some insights into the initial system. However, the emphasis on metatextuality as a doorway to meaning risks becoming circular in *La Disparition,* leading us to conclude that the metatextual level of meaning is the primary one. In *La Vie mode d'emploi,* Perec adopts a quite different strategy: the constraints are disclosed only outside the text, in what Genette would call the "paratext,"[65] and the novel's metatextual dimension in itself does not suffice to reveal them. To the extent that the constraints enter into the play of meanings, Perec seems to deny full participation in the interpretative process to his "uninitiated" readers.[66]

For this reason, Perec's strategy in hiding his constraints has given rise to critical comment and even accusations of "elitism."[67] The proliferation of *mises en abyme* and the use of hidden allusions have a similar effect; as Gaspard Winckler does for Bartlebooth, Perec pulls the interpretative ground out from under our feet by means of fragmentation and subterfuge. The enigmatic *Laborynthus* engraving is a case in point, since the constraints provide a degree of justification for an apparently arbitrary element. We find a similar example in chapter 8, where Winckler persuades Valène to accompany him to see what turns out to be a mediocre film, *Les Verts Pâturages* (*Green Pastures*): when asked why he wanted to see it, he replies, "Que c'était seulement à cause du titre, à cause de ce mot 'pâturage'" (It was only because of the title, because of that word "pastures") (*VME,* 54/ *LUM,* 30). The ironic significance of this statement is apparent only to someone who knows that "pasture" is one of the constraint elements for this chapter.[68] In both of these cases, something that seems to be accidental or arbitrary is in fact determined by a constraint. Perec does not provide a complete narrative motivation for these elements but emphasizes their arbitrary status. The multiple levels of interpretation set arbitrariness at one remove from the text, simultaneously foregrounding it and ironically undermining it.

These cases can be seen as illustrations of what Roubaud calls "chance that is exorcised because it is acknowledged"[69]—in other words as an example of Oulipian anti-chance. Anti-chance therefore comes perilously close to chance, and the distinction between them can depend on a secret. Just as the maze depicted in Bartlebooth's final puzzle is designed to hide the splendid acropolis at its center, the text often blocks our path to interpretation.[70] Within this labyrinth, the reader may make discoveries by chance or by having access to a map. Of course, the essential step is to realize that one is inside a labyrinth (in Borges's "The Garden of Forking Paths," for example, Ts'ui Pen's novel begins to be comprehensible only once it is identified as a labyrinth). The maze therefore does not deny meaning. Indeed, Clément Rosset views the modern fascination with the labyrinth as a refusal to confront meaning's absence, as "a temple of meaning, and a temple for the initiated."[71] Perec's concealment of his strategies seems to fit this account; it transforms chance into anti-chance, apparent chaos into meaning. At the same time, Perec's Oulipian texts do confront the possibility of meaninglessness, of chaos, of absolute chance. Perec's use of constraints points us to a more general problem, related to rule-following in general: the fact that, as Wittgenstein puts it, "there is no sharp distinction [. . .] between what you are inclined to call 'random' and what 'systematic.'"[72]

The self-referentiality of Perec's Oulipian works is therefore not simply an end in itself, nor is it merely a form of complicity with an elite readership. Rather, the metatextual dimension of these texts creates multiple levels of interpretation that enact key epistemological problems, and in particular the problem of distinguishing the meaningful from the random. In this context, neither the use of constraints nor the self-referential aspect of Perec's works necessarily constitutes a refusal of reference, a turning-in of the text upon itself. There is nevertheless a tension between constraints and the real; clearly, the obsessive characters who populate Perec's novels construct their systems as a refuge from the formlessness and randomness of everyday life.[73] How, then, do we account for Perec's own fascination with the everyday? It is to this problem that I turn in chapter 8, which brings together the thematic and formal elements of my argument in a reflection on chance and its representation.

La série des signes se multipliait dans la série des signes de signes, de signes répétés un nombre innombrable de fois, toujours égaux et toujours de quelque façon différent, parce qu'au signe fait exprès s'ajoutait le signe tombé là par hasard.

The series of signs multiplied itself into the series of signs of signs, of signs repeated an innumerable number of times, always the same and always in some way different, for to the sign made on purpose was added the sign fallen there by chance.

—Italo Calvino

8. Ordering the Infraordinary

Chance and the Real

In a 1967 talk at the University of Warwick in England, Perec declared that he had always wanted to be a realist writer.[1] In a 1978 article, he opted instead for the notion of the "sociological," distinguishing this aspect of his work from three others: the autobiographical, the ludic, and the novelistic ("NSC," 28). As Perec increasingly adopts Oulipian methods from the late 1960s onward, his preoccupation with the real seems to shift from the ideal of a committed literature that refuses chance, to an investigation of everyday life that in many ways acknowledges and incorporates chance. While his fascination with contingent "everydayness" may seem puzzling in the light of the Oulipian insistence on formal "anti-chance," I believe it is a mistake to separate the "realist" or "sociological" Perec—the recorder of the "infraordinary"—from the Oulipian, ludic Perec. Rather, the Oulipian constraint constitutes one response, among others, to the acute awareness of life's contingency.[2] Perec's negotiation of the chance/order relationship in his novels shapes his own particular form of realism, a skeptical version that hesitates between optimism and pessimism about the categories and classifications with which individuals shape and understand their existence.[3] Perec's realist accomplishment hinges on his incorporation of the infraordinary into the structure of his works. While ordinary events and objects are necessarily transformed, rendered significant by the process of representation, Perec's works also resist their own sense-making enterprise and question their mode of organizing the real.

For many writers of the nineteenth and twentieth centuries, the realist novel offered the ideal form for investigating the everyday. Ian Watt points out that the modern novel, with its "insistence on the time process" in its most minute details, allows a greater "closeness to the texture of daily experience" than had previously been available to literary representation.[4] For many critics, this attention to the everyday goes hand in hand with a heightened consciousness of contingency and chance, although framed by a totalizing perspective. Thus for Erich Auerbach, the "serious treatment of everyday life," exemplified by the nineteenth-century French novel, requires "the embedding of random persona and events in the general course of human history."[5] This structure of insertion breaks down, according to Auerbach, in the modernist narratives of the twentieth century. Proust, Woolf, and Joyce exploit the random occurrence in itself—a change in emphasis that coincides for Auerbach with a shift toward pessimism in literature.[6] More hostile to modernism, Georg Lukács asserts that true realism establishes a "hierarchy of significance" in the situations and characters presented, and that modernist works do not.[7]

If the novel is often perceived as formless, Ian Watt notes, it is arguably because its language plays a more largely referential function than in other literary genres; "the poverty of the novel's formal conventions would seem to be the price it must pay for its realism."[8] Yet despite the realist novel's resistance to the "elegant concentration" of, say, tragedy or the ode,[9] Watt emphasizes that the novel's realism is formal, in that it involves a set of typical narrative procedures—including details of the story, the actors involved, and the times and places of actions—that embody its "circumstantial view of life."[10] Yet this view, with its insistence on contingency and chance, may come into conflict with the demands of form; this is Flaubert's concern when he states that the novel should be more logical than the haphazardness of things. Henri Mitterand argues that the novel's construction creates an order of facts, situations, and characters that negates the disorder of real life.[11] However, the problem here is not simply the tension between the supposed formlessness of the real and the ideal of an autonomous aesthetic order. As both Erich Auerbach and Georg Lukács make clear, the ordering of events in the novel can be seen to embody a particular worldview. At stake here is the extent to which reality adheres to a given pattern or structure.[12]

In this context, chance has an ambiguous role, seeming to stand for both background disorder (Flaubert's "haphazardness of things") and the significant event. When Balzac describes chance as "the greatest novelist in the world," he refers to chance as a creator of stories, a point of emergence for narrative form. In fact, chance continues to play this role, albeit in intensified form, in the modernist novel that many critics—notably Auerbach and Lukács, once again—contrast with the realism of Balzac. The "epiphanies" experienced by Joyce's characters are triggered by chance encounters that transfigure commonplace objects.[13] The chance event plays an equally crucial role in Proust's *À la recherche du temps perdu* (*In Search of Lost Time*), where access to the past depends on the individual's fortuitous encounter with a particular sensation.[14] For Proust's narrator, the emphasis on chance indicates lack of control over access to the past, but precisely for this reason it guarantees the authenticity of memories.[15] The chance event is thus less a sign of universal contingency than an event that simultaneously emerges from this contingency and marks its transformation. It involves an element of ordinary reality that suddenly moves into the realm of the extraordinary through its impact on individual consciousness. It is characterized both by inherent insignificance, on one level, and by the significance of its consequences, on another.

For other twentieth-century authors equally preoccupied with chance, the novel form is seen as inadequate for capturing the essential nature of daily life. André Breton's concept of "objective chance" can be tied to his rejection of the novel and his preference for hybrid forms that juxtapose text and image, past and present, anecdote and philosophical meditation, in order to create uncanny conjunctions between causal chains. Chance events for Breton nevertheless reveal an underlying necessity that is revealed, as for Proust, by the construction of a narrative.[16] In both cases, the chance encounter triggers a process of association and construction that is also a form of self-exploration. Lacking the vast social scope of Proust's novel, surrealist prose texts instead adapt the motif of the Baudelairean flaneur to explore the subject's embedding in everyday reality. Although less hostile to the novel than Breton, Louis Aragon adopts a fluid and digressive form in *Le Paysan de Paris* (1926; *Paris Peasant*), in accordance with his sense of being the plaything "of the senses and of chance." As in so many texts, chance serves here a point of "passage" (to adopt one of the motifs of Aragon's text), providing the impetus for the construction of new myths.[17]

Thus, even when writers resist integrating chance events into the totalizing structure of the traditional novel, chance remains a paradoxical source of meaning. This is true even of texts that proclaim a doctrine of radical insignificance, such as Sartre's *Nausée* and Camus' writings on the absurd.[18]

The chance event indicates the site of a transformation, the precise point at which the insignificant takes on significance from a human point of view, while still remaining connected to its origin in contingency. Chance is thus related to the representation of the everyday not because it stands for the raw contingency of reality, but as a transitional point in the perception and construction of meaning in relation to the problem of contingency. The literary use of chance provides a key to understanding the various ways in which literary texts construct meaning from the raw materials of daily life.

If the realist novel has traditionally been considered a privileged locus for the representation of the everyday, it is surely because, as Michel Butor puts it in a powerful defense of the genre, a fundamental continuity links it to the "murmure des choses" (the murmur of things). At the same time, the novel also criticizes and transfigures reality. In so doing, argues Butor, the novel is capable of illuminating the internal process of its own emergence, of showing "comment il se produit au milieu de la réalité" (how it is produced in the midst of reality).[19] Nevertheless, it is significant that twentieth-century writers have so often found the conventions of the novel inadequate for the investigation of everyday life, and have actively explored other forms of writing that address this dimension of reality differently. The surrealists are a case in point, but are not alone: in twentieth-century France, concern with the quotidian is at the heart of Roland Barthes' semiological studies of contemporary culture (in *Mythologies* and *L'Empire des signes,* in particular), Henri Lefebvre's Marxist philosophy, the radical political writings of the situationists, and the sociology of Michel de Certeau. Less dogmatic or theoretical in his approach than many of these others, Perec is a significant figure in this intellectual tradition.[20] He uses both the novel and other forms in his quest to uncover hidden aspects of the ordinary—or what he terms the *infra-ordinaire* (infraordinary).

The term *infra-ordinaire* first appears in Perec's work in the 1970s. Perec's early writings on the novel insist instead on the notion of the "real" and argue for a form of literary realism that leaves little room for chance. Echoing Lukács's *Meaning of Contemporary Realism,* Perec argues in "Pour une littérature réaliste" (1962; "For a Realist Literature") that realism requires the selection of relevant details from the mass of inessential ones. If writers have the correct ethical and political perspective, he claims, they will be able to see the hierarchy and interconnectedness of various phenomena, to select the typical element from the immediate mass of perceptible reality (*L.G.,* 61–62).[21] In this context, any role accorded to chance indicates a failure of interpretation and representation. Perec's later writings on the infraordinary appear at first glance to attempt the precise opposite of the writer's early realist project, abandoning the organized form of the novel in order to record, in seemingly random order, the flow of nonhierarchized perceptions on the surface of consciousness. Derek Schilling therefore distinguishes between Perec's early insistence on the literary mastery of the real and the later texts that assign an autonomous value to everydayness; he argues that the author soon abandons his semi-Marxist critical vocabulary in favor of other terms "which suggest the impossibility of a totalization, indeed the futility of any philosophical approach."[22] Perec's literary works, and especially his writings on the infraordinary, certainly do call into question the possibility of establishing a hierarchy of significance within a totalizing framework. However, this is already the case in the first and perhaps the most traditionally realist of Perec's novels, *Les Choses.*

Les Choses: Objects as Signs

Dominated as it is by minute descriptions of spaces and objects, *Les Choses* has inevitably invited comparison with the work of such contemporaries as Alain Robbe-Grillet—who is nevertheless denounced, along with the whole New Novel, in Perec's "Ligne générale" texts. Jacques-Denis Bertharion suggests that Perec's writing is close to the New Novel in its insistence on language's fundamental inadequacy to represent the real, and in its display of its own codes.[23] Patrizia Molteni, on the other hand, insists on the difference between Perec and the attempt of the New Novelists to empty words of all meaning.[24] In a series of interviews given in 1965, Perec strives to differentiate *Les Choses* from Robbe-Grillet's work, distinguishing between Robbe-Grillet's neutral descriptions and his own efforts to saturate words with meanings and resonances (*EC* 1:50).[25] Adopting Roland Barthes' idea that Robbe-Grillet's language is entirely denotative, preoccupied with the surfaces of things,[26] Perec states that his own concern is to discover the values that surround and lie beneath things (*EC* 1:60).

Perec's "connotative," value-laden use of description is evident from the first chapter of *Les Choses,* as the hypothetical viewer observes Jérôme and Sylvie's imaginary apartment: "La première porte ouvrirait sur une chambre, au plancher recouvert d'une moquette claire. Un grand lit anglais en occuperait tout le fond" (The first door would open onto a bedroom, its floor covered with a light-colored fitted carpet. An English double bed would fill the whole rear part of it) (*C,* 11/*T,* 22–23). The conditional tense marks this interior as a yet nonexistent possibility; we surmise that it corresponds to Jérôme and Sylvie's shared fantasy. The largely static fictional space, suspended in the half-light of evening ("dans la pénombre"), nevertheless has points of mobility: the opening of the door, the implied movement of the gaze through the room, the sliding curtains. The enumeration of objects is organized around several spatial reference points, all defined in relation to the viewer's position: the door, the back of the room, the space to the right and left, the partially visible room glimpsed through the half-open door to the bathroom ("une porte entrouverte donnant sur une salle de bains"), the walls, the more distant foot of the bed ("plus loin, au pied du lit"). The accumulation of furnishings, coverings, and decorations suggests abundance; the prevalence of soft materials (wool, silk, carpet) and the choice of adjectives point to luxury, comfort ("d'épais peignoirs de bain"—thick bathrobes; "les doubles rideaux, gris, en lainage épais"—thick woolen double curtains, grey), and refined taste ("deux petites lampes alsaciennes"—two small wall lamps; a photograph of a bird that surprises by its "perfection un peu formelle"—slightly formal perfection) (*C,* 12–13/*T,* 23). The passage contains several leitmotifs that recur throughout the whole chapter: the adjectives *gris* and *épais* (grey, thick) and the presence of silk, wood, copper, and leather as Jérôme and Sylvie's materials of predilection. The old oak wardrobe ("vieille armoire de chêne") connotes solidity, tradition, and reserves of yet further possessions, while the well-used books, along with the magazines by the bedside, imply intellectual sophistication and curiosity. Many of the connotative values attached to this opening description may be historically specific, yet a reader unaware of the predominant fashions of 1960s France is still likely to grasp the significance of details such as the Englishness of the bed or the Scottishness of the bedspread.

Through the lives and imaginings of its two characters, *Les Choses* presents a critical picture of a particular social and historical environment. This approach is in many ways characteristic of the nineteenth-century tradition often termed "critical realism."[27] However, Perec's novel is unusual in the detailed attention it devotes to the objects of everyday reality. Even if this can be seen as a form of realism, Andrew Leak points out that the novel's starting point is "a certain mismatch between language and the real," since language is mediated and refracted by the discourses which characterize consumer society.[28] Jean Baudrillard argues in *Le Système des objets* (*The System of Objects*) that the consumerist relationship to objects is structured around difference and lack, since the object stands for the whole series of objects to which it belongs. Baudrillard defines consumerism as a systematic manipulation of objects that have been transformed into arbitrary signs, which only take on meaning in their abstract and systematic relationship to other object-signs.[29] *Les Choses* provides Baudrillard with the conclusion to his meditation on consumer society: citing the novel's opening, Baudrillard distinguishes between the object's symbolic value in a Balzacian description (where it stands for human relations) and its status as "pure sign" in the consumerist system investigated by Perec. In this universe, states Baudrillard, the consumption of objects no longer has anything to do with the reality principle: successive objects and their significations take over from the very project of living. Particularly convincing is the connection that Baudrillard establishes between this project and the protagonists' frustrated desire for totality.[30]

In *Les Choses,* the multiplication of signs ultimately undermines the hope of finding a unified, total vision of the world. At the precise moment when a utopian vision seems to be within the characters' grasp, the universe of signs and connotations threatens to collapse. In chapter 10, Jérôme and Sylvie are inspired by the sight of farmhouses in the French countryside and develop a vast, sumptuous, and progressively more fantastic daydream. The protagonists imagine appropriating the entire universe, which appears to them as "une complète image du monde, une organisation cohérente" (a total picture of the world, a coherent structure) (*C,* 114/*T,* 93). Yet this complete image soon dissolves into fragments, and unity is replaced by "une fragmentation crispée" (a brittle fragmentation) (*C,* 115/*T,* 93). The whole system of sign-objects destabilizes itself through its own inner power of proliferation, and Jérôme and Sylvie are confronted with nothingness. They flee for Tunisia soon after this episode, in a futile attempt to escape the system of values and desires in which they are trapped.

Common Things: Perec and the Infraordinary

Curiously, the protagonist of Perec's next novel, *Un homme qui dort,* aspires to precisely the kind of neutrality that Barthes associates with Robbe-Grillet's denotative language.[31] In his interactions with the world, this nameless character attempts to read without interpreting, to watch without establishing categories and hierarchies (*UHD,* 64, 69), and to transform himself into a passive observer of everyday life: "Tu ne sais rien des lois qui font se rassembler ces gens qui ne se connaissent pas, que tu ne connais pas, dans cette rue où tu viens pour la première fois de ta vie

[. . .]. Des milliers d'actions inutiles se rassemblent au même instant dans le champ trop étroit de ton regard presque neutre" (You know nothing of the laws which preside over the meeting of all these people, these people who do not know each other and whom you do not know, in this street that you are visiting for the first time in your life [. . .]. Thousands of futile actions come together in the same instant in the too-narrow field of your almost neutral vision) (*UHD*, 58/*MA*, 165). Absolute neutrality, however, proves to be unattainable, just as the description above inevitably involves judgment—of the actions observed as "futile," of the man's field of vision as "too narrow." It is even impossible for the protagonist truly to desire neutrality; the text betrays his anxiety about the lack of order in the apparently chaotic reality that he observes. In this respect, Perec's novel may be read as a commentary on the claims of Robbe-Grillet's New Novel. At the same time, it anticipates the central problem of perception that reemerges in the "infra-ordinaire" texts.

Perec's early novels, with their iterative temporality and emphasis on ordinary objects, are close to the rhythms of daily life; at the same time, as Michael Sheringham aptly puts it, they are "fables of disconnection" that expose their protagonists' failures either to engage with or to disengage from the everyday.[32] The Oulipian methods that Perec adopts in the late 1960s initially seem to take his work away from such preoccupations; in *La Disparition,* for instance, exuberant linguistic and narrative invention trumps realism. However, Perec's Oulipian texts often use very ordinary material as their starting point. Two humorous examples are "Deux cent quarante-trois cartes postales en couleurs véritables" ("Two Hundred and Forty-three Postcards in Real Color") and "81 fiches-cuisine à l'usage des débutants" ("81 Recipes for Beginners") both use combinations of an initial set of elements to produce a parody of a common everyday writing practice. More ambitious in scope, Perec's unfinished project "Lieux" (1969–75; "Places") employed a different kind of constraint, temporal and existential, in order to take an intimate look at the details of the Parisian landscape. The enterprise entailed visiting, in the course of a year, twelve places in Paris of particular personal significance; each place would be described once in situ and once from memory, and the operation would be repeated each year for twelve years. Texts such as "La Rue Vilin" ("The Rue Vilin")[33] and "Allées et venues rue de l'Assomption" ("Comings and Goings on the Rue de l'Assomption") belong to the "Lieux" project and were published in various journals and magazines after the project was abandoned in 1975. Other works based on the principle of in situ description include *Tentative d'épuisement d'un lieu parisien* (1975; *Endeavor to Exhaust a Parisian Place*) and the radio broadcast *Tentative de description de choses vues au carrefour Mabillon le 19 mai 1978* (*Endeavor to Describe Things Seen at the Mabillon Intersection on May 19, 1978*). The short text "Still Life/Style Leaf" (1981) foregrounds in spectacular manner the ambiguous intertwining of time and space that characterizes many of these descriptive writings.[34]

Soon after beginning the "Lieux" project, Perec found a new focus for his fascination with the everyday through his participation in the *Cause commune* journal.[35] Founded in 1971 by the sociologist Jean Duvignaud, with Paul Virilio and Perec among the principal collaborators, *Cause commune* announced a set of sociological, political, and anthropological goals, among them an "investigation of daily life at all its levels in its recesses and caverns that are generally disdained or repressed."[36] Metaphors of depth predominate in this editorial pronouncement: everyday life, far from being the visible surface of the real, possesses its own underground geography. Investigation of these hidden depths will both uncover and potentially threaten the foundations of social and cultural life. The idea of depth is also suggested by the term *infra-ordinaire,* coined by Virilio, used as the title for issue 5 of *Cause commune* (February 1973), and henceforth adopted by Perec to describe a whole range of descriptive writing projects. The *infraordinary* is first and foremost the opposite of the *extraordinary,* of that which immediately leaps to our attention. It does not entirely correspond to the *ordinary,* but rather, as the prefix suggests, to what lies hidden beneath the surface of ordinariness (*EC* 2:93).

As Michael Sheringham and Derek Schilling have shown, the anthropological and sociological claims of the *Cause commune* journal should be understood in the context of existing French discourses on everyday life. The latter had developed largely in response to the economic development and rapid modernization of the postwar years.[37] A key figure here is the Marxist philosopher Henri Lefebvre, whose *Critique de la vie quotidienne* (*Critique of Everyday Life*) was published in three volumes in 1947, 1961, and 1981. Inspired by the vision of human flourishing and the analysis of alienation found in early Marx, Lefebvre argues that any true critique of the conditions of everyday life has to begin with the rehabilitation of a reality that had previously been repressed and misunderstood by both literature and philosophy.[38] Lefebvre influenced Guy Debord and the situationist group, and remained close to them until a quarrel in 1963; from the late 1950s to the early '70s, the situationists attempted to demolish the boundary separating art from everyday life, with the goal of transforming reality.

Jean Duvignaud, the founder of *Cause commune,* had in the 1950s worked with Lefebvre on the leftist review *Arguments,* with which Perec was also briefly involved. Nevertheless, although Perec also met Lefebvre personally (and read Marcel Mauss on his recommendation), Roland Barthes' semiology probably had a more direct influence on his work than Lefebvre's brand of Marxism. Perec attended Barthes' seminars on rhetoric at the École pratique des hautes études, and the influence of *Mythologies* is evident in *Les Choses.*[39]

In his texts for *Cause commune,* Perec does not set out a particular ideological or philosophical program.[40] Rather, his investigations of the everyday subtly question the tenacity of perceptual habits and writing's ability to question and transform these habits. Perec's *Cause commune* writings are diverse in their focus and approaches. "Autoportrait: Les Gnocchis de l'automne" (issue 1, May 1972; "Self-Portrait: The Gnocchi of Autumn") has an important personal and psychological dimension, as does the text "Six rêves" (issue 2, June 1972; "Six Dreams"), a set of dream narratives later included in the collection *La Boutique obscure* (*The Obscure Shop*). The burlesque radio play "Fonctionnement du système nerveux dans la tête" (issue 3, October 1972; "Functioning of the Nervous System in the Head") juxtaposes neurophysiological discourse with a description of the Freudian primal scene. Considered as a whole, the texts usually associated with Perec's "infra-ordinaire" project were written for a variety of purposes and audiences. The representation of space is the focus of *Espèces d'espaces* (1974; *Species of Spaces*). The short texts published posthumously in the volume *L'Infra-ordinaire* (1989) comprise a rather eclectic mix, even if they have in common a fascination with the everyday; they include pieces written for *Cause commune,* but also magazine articles and short writings for various literary journals.[41]

Things are therefore much more complicated than Perec suggests when he divides his own work into sociological, autobiographical, ludic/Oulipian, and novelistic "fields" (*PC,* 10). Rather than remaining separate categories, these dimensions of Perec's work exist in complex interaction with one another, an interaction that is articulated differently in different works. *Je me souviens,* for example, is an autobiographical text that focuses on infraordinary memories while adopting the weak constraint of the list form. *La Vie mode d'emploi,* to which I will return shortly, is an Oulipian novel that incorporates numerous kinds of story as well as long lists of ordinary objects. The effort to disrupt habits of perception is common to the infraordinary texts and to Perec's Oulipian writings.

There are echoes here of the Russian formalists' view of artistic devices as a means of liberating our relation to objects from perceptual automatism.[42] As early as 1963, Perec argues that realist writers should use a mediating "grid" that distorts our immediate vision of reality. In an essay published in *Partisans,* Perec praises the indirect, fragmented mode of narration adopted by Robert Antelme to describe his experience in a concentration camp. It is by distancing the reader from the immediacy of the writer's experience that Antelme forces his reader to reach a real understanding of the situation (*L.G.,* 95). Unlike Perec's other early essays on realism, the piece on Antelme departs from the Lukácsian view that presupposes the existence of an initial mass of unselected, uninterpreted facts that the writer must then organize in order to construct a totalizing representation. Instead, Perec argues that we necessarily hierarchize experience *prior* to representing it. Our habitual hierarchies of significance rest on interpretative habits that must be questioned and indeed disrupted, if necessary by means of artifice, if we are to understand the true nature of experience.

This difficulty comes to the forefront once again in the short programmatic text "Approches de quoi?" ("Approaches to What?"), first published in the fifth issue of *Cause commune,* where Perec sets out the goals of his quest for the infraordinary. Rather than making pronouncements about the true nature of "les choses communes" (common things),[43] this text presents questions: "Ce qui se passe chaque jour et qui revient chaque jour, le banal, le quotidien, l'évident, le commun, l'ordinaire, l'infra-ordinaire, le bruit de fond, l'habituel, comment en rendre compte, comment l'interroger, comment le décrire?" (How should we take account of, question, describe what happens every day and recurs every day: the banal, the quotidian, the obvious, the common, the ordinary, the infraordinary, the background noise, the habitual?) ("AQ," 11/"AW," 206). Although this enumeration suggests an equivalence between the various terms, some of them imply frequency and regularity (the common, the everyday, the habitual), others bring in a negative value judgment (the notions of the banal and background noise both indicating insignificance), while yet others highlight the question of perception (the evident or obvious). Perec also uses the term "l'endotique" (the endotic) in opposition to the exotic ("AQ," 11), emphasizing the unfamiliarity of what is inside (*endo*), rather than the strangeness of the outside or the other.

The reference to the object of investigation as the interrogative "what?" in the title of Perec's text indicates that the object of study, the infraordinary, is not predefined. This object is, in fact, bound to flee the writer's grasp at every turn. Perec's repeated characterization of "infraordinary" reality as "background noise" ("AQ," 11/"AW," 206)[44] illuminates a key paradox. On the one hand, background noise is precisely that which is insignificant, which disrupts the path of communication without itself conveying any information. On the other hand, Perec's ambition is to give things significance, to "dig out" precious material that is then rescued from the domain of the infraordinary: "Comment parler de ces 'choses communes,' comment les traquer plutôt, comment les débusquer, les arracher à la gangue dans laquelle elles restent engluées, comment leur donner un sens, une langue: qu'elles parlent enfin de ce qui est, de ce que nous sommes" (How are we to speak of these 'common things', how to track them down rather, flush them out, wrest them from the dross in which they remain mired, how to give them a meaning, a tongue, to let them, finally, speak of what is, of what we are) ("AQ," 11/"AW," 206). Mixing metaphors of hunting ("traquer") and mining ("gangue"), Perec again indicates the elusive and hidden nature of his object. Once these "common things" are hunted down or brought to the surface, however, they are by definition no longer "infra" and will become simply ordinary, or perhaps even extraordinary. In other texts (such as *Tentative d'épuisement d'un lieu parisien*), metaphors of depth are replaced with metaphors of surface texture; thus Perec speaks of the fabric of the everyday and rents in this fabric. Yet the fundamental problem remains the same: once an aspect of the fabric comes to our attention, it becomes an exceptional element, a break in the normal texture of the everyday.

This paradox of the everyday is articulated in an intriguing text by Maurice Blanchot: the constitutive trait of the everyday is the fact that it goes unnoticed,[45] in other words, that it remains background noise. Inspired by the second volume of Lefebvre's *Critique de la vie quotidienne,* Blanchot argues that the everyday will always elude our efforts to grasp it through knowledge, since it belongs to a realm that is prior to all knowledge and all information (*L'Entretien infini,* 359–60). Perec is aware of this ambiguity at the heart of his project but is nevertheless not paralyzed by the impossibility of expressing the infraordinary in its pure insignificance and nothingness. He does not suggest, as Blanchot does, that we can only experience the everyday as a kind of radical nihilism.[46] Rather, Perec is fascinated by the mechanisms of perception and interpretation, by the ways in which the insignificant is drawn to our attention, by the shifting boundaries of our vision. The notion of chance plays a central role in this reflection on habit, attentiveness, and knowledge. To illustrate this point, I will consider an exemplary exercise in direct description, the short text *Tentative d'épuisement d'un lieu parisien,* published under the auspices of the *Cause commune* project in 1975.

Chance, Perception, Habit: *Tentative d'Épuisement d'un Lieu Parisien*

Returning to cafés in the Place Saint-Sulpice in Paris for three consecutive days (October 18–20, 1974), Perec attempted to write down not the objects that have already been noticed, photographed, described, and narrated by others (such as the church and the fountain) but rather what is left over, "ce que l'on ne note généralement pas, ce qui ne se remarque pas, ce qui n'a pas d'importance: ce qui se passe quand il ne se passe rien, sinon du temps, des gens, des voitures et des nuages" (*TE,* 12) (what is generally not noted, what is not noticed, that which has no importance: what happens when nothing happens, except the passing of time, people, cars, and clouds).[47] While it might initially seem that Perec sets out to passively and randomly record objects and events around him, without any particular order or hierarchy, his project in fact requires a method of training the gaze to notice things that might otherwise escape attention. He begins his first day's account with a preliminary categorization of visible things: letters of the alphabet and words ("KLM," "P" for "parking," "Hôtel Récamier"); conventional symbols (arrows, one-way street signs); numbers (86 on a bus, 6 for the sixth arrondissement); slogans; earth; stones; trees, cars, human beings (*TE,* 13–14). The list of groups is punctuated by a few individual elements: a piece of sky, a type of basset dog, a baguette, and a type of lettuce or endive in a basket (*TE,* 14).

This oscillation between the general and particular, between systematic (but arbitrarily organized) enumeration and random observations, occurs throughout the text. In the following passage, for example, Perec begins a list of bus routes, then interjects an advertising slogan before moving to the description of some aspects of the square and back to his original list:

> Trajectoires:
> Le 96 va à la gare Montparnasse
> Le 84 va à la porte de Champerret
> Le 70 va Place du Dr Hayem, Maison de l'O.R.T.F.
> Le 86 va à Saint-Germain-des-Prés

Exigez le Roquefort Société le vrai dans son ovale vert
Aucune eau ne jaillit de la fontaine. Des pigeons se sont posés sur le rebord d'une de ses vasques.
Sur le terre-plein, il y a des bancs, des bancs doubles avec un dosseret unique. Je peux, de ma place, en compter jusqu'à six. Quatre sont vides. Trois clochards aux gestes classiques (boire du rouge à la bouteille) sur le sixième.
Le 63 va à la Porte de la Muette
Le 86 va à Saint-Germain-des-Prés
Nettoyer c'est bien ne pas salir c'est mieux
Un car allemand
Une fourgonnette Brinks
Le 87 va au Champ-de-Mars
Le 84 va à la Porte Champerret (*TE,* 14–15)

Trajectories:
The 96 goes to Montparnasse station
The 84 goes to Porte de Champerret
The 70 goes to the Place du Dr Hayem, Maison de l'O.R.T.F.
The 86 goes to Saint-Germain-des-Prés
Demand the real Roquefort Société in its green oval
No water is gushing from the fountain. Some pigeons have settled on the edge of one of its basins.
On the central island, there are benches, double benches with a single back. From my seat, I can count up to six of them. Four are empty. Three tramps with typical gestures (drinking red wine from the bottle) on the sixth.
The 63 goes to Porte de la Muette
The 86 goes to Saint-Germain-des-Prés
Cleaning is fine not dirtying is better
A German coach
A Brinks van
The 87 goes to the Champ-de-Mars
The 84 goes to Porte Champerret

Perec's prose, with its more or less regular repetitions (the repeated passings of the 84 and 86 buses), its alternation of monotony and difference, aims to capture the rhythms of the everyday. The two slogans ("exigez le Roquefort

Société" and "nettoyer c'est bien ne pas salir c'est mieux") are not marked as quotations but placed on the same level as Perec's observations of the buses. This is not to say that no hierarchy or order is present in this text. Indeed, as Mikhail Bakhtin noted in 1924, and as Perec implicitly acknowledges, there is no such thing as a pure, nonhierarchical act of perception, and representation never deals with an absolutely disordered and fortuitous raw material; our usual view of reality is already a representation, although a hybrid and unstable one.[48] In *Tentative d'épuisement,* perception is in fact continuous with reflection and judgment: for example, the tramps' gestures are interpreted as typical; the fountain is associated with gushing water, even though the latter is absent. In investigating the everyday, Perec is not seeking to eliminate his own subjectivity in order to give an objective, neutral account of reality, as some critics have suggested.[49] Instead, he investigates his own mechanisms of perception, knowledge, and representation. As Michael Sheringham states, *Tentative* indicates "the sheer multiplicity of the channels with which we engage with the world" by making us aware of "the concrete presence of the experiencing subject."[50]

The description of the second day at Place Saint-Sulpice begins with a classification of the various microevents that Perec witnesses: discussions, modes of locomotion; ways of carrying; degrees of determination or motivation—"attendre, flâner, traîner, errer, aller, courir vers, se précipiter [. . .], chercher, musarder, hésiter, marcher d'un pas décidé" (*TE,* 18–19) (wait, roam, traipse, wander, move, run toward, dash [. . .], seek, dawdle, hesitate, walk at a decided pace). (This enumeration of verbs is clearly as much an exploration of language, and of its ways of representing, as of the real in itself.) At the same time, Perec is acutely aware of the extent to which his enterprise is determined—both made possible and limited—by chance:

> Un 70 passe
> (c'est seulement par hasard, de la place que j'occupe, que je peux voir passer, à l'autre bout, des 84)
> [. . .]
> Retour (aléatoire) d'individus déjà vus [. . .]
> [. . .]
> Il n'y a plus que deux vélomoteurs garés sur le trottoir devant le café: je n'ai pas vu le troisième partir (c'était un vélosolex) (*Limites évidentes d'une telle entreprise: même en me fixant comme seul but de regarder, je ne vois pas ce qui se passe à quelques mètres de moi: je ne remarque pas, par exemple, que des voitures se garent*). (*TE,* 20, 21, 25–26)

A 70 goes by
(it's only by chance, from where I am sitting, that I can see 84s going by at the other end)
[. . .]
(Unpredictable) return of individuals already seen [. . .]
[. . .]
There are now only two mopeds parked on the sidewalk in front of the café: I didn't see the third one leave (it was a Solex bike) (*Obvious limits of this kind of enterprise: even in appointing watching as my only goal, I don't see what is happening a few meters away from me: I don't notice, for example, that some cars are being parked*).

The references to chance and to the "aleatory" cover a complex set of factors: the conjunction between Perec's situation in the café and the actions of others, the unknowable motivations that determine individuals' movements, and Perec's own observational capacities. Of even greater concern to Perec than the physical constraints of his position in the café, or his inability to know the causes behind the events surrounding him, is his psychological tendency to notice some things and events rather than others:

> Quelle différence y a-t-il entre un conducteur qui se gare du premier coup et un autre ("90") qui n'y parvient qu'au bout de plusieurs minutes de laborieux efforts? Cela suscite l'éveil, l'ironie, la participation de l'assistance: ne pas voir les seules déchirures, mais le tissu (mais comment voir le tissu si ce sont seulement les déchirures qui le font apparaître: personne ne voit jamais passer les autobus, sauf s'il en attend un, ou s'il attend quelqu'un qui va en descendre, ou si la R.A.T.P. l'appointe pour les dénombrer...) (*TE*, 46)

> What difference is there between a driver who parks his car immediately and another ("90") who only manages it after several minutes of laborious effort? It provokes attention, sarcasm, the participation of the spectators: don't see only the tears in the fabric, but the fabric itself (but how can we see the fabric if only the tears make it apparent: no one ever sees buses passing, unless he is waiting for one, or waiting for someone who will get off one, or if the R.A.T.P. appoints him to count them...)

In both cases the event or microevent appears to be a rupture or tear ("déchirure") in the expected order of things, yet this rupture itself enters into an order of perception that prevents us from being attentive to the texture of the everyday.

In this context, the classifications of *Tentative d'épuisement* represent a form of resistance to habit, an attempt to see the fabric of things: "Projet d'une classification des parapluies selon leurs formes, leurs modes de fonctionnement, leurs couleurs, leurs matériaux..." (*TE,* 54) ("Project for a Classification of Umbrellas According to their Forms, Modes of Functioning, Colors, Materials..."). Perec's classifications are not rigid or systematic; they are constantly interrupted by other elements that seize Perec's attention, and which may be remarkable for their linguistic possibilities as much as for their visual or narrative qualities: "Passe un papa poussant poussette" (*TE,* 35) (A papa passes pushing a pushchair).[51] However provisional and tactical, the activity of classification nevertheless represents an effort to organize experience and resist chance. Hence Perec's predilection for recording the passing of buses:

> (pourquoi compter les autobus? sans doute parce qu'ils sont reconnaissables et réguliers: ils découpent le temps, ils rythment le bruit de fond; à la limite ils sont prévisibles.
>
> Le reste semble aléatoire, improbable, anarchique; les autobus passent parce qu'ils doivent passer, mais rien ne veut qu'une voiture fasse marche arrière, ou qu'un homme ait un sac marqué du grand "M" de Monoprix, ou qu'une voiture soit bleue ou vert pomme, ou qu'un consommateur commande un café plutôt qu'un demi...) (*TE,* 34)

> why count buses? doubtless because they are recognizable and regular: they cut up time, they regulate background noise; at the very least they are predictable.
>
> The rest seems random, improbable, anarchic; the buses pass because they must pass, but there is no reason for a car to reverse, or for a man to have a bag marked with the capital *M* of Monoprix, or for a car to be blue or apple-green, or for a customer to order a coffee rather than a beer...

Later, Perec comments ironically on his preference for the systematic and the predictable, suggesting that he has finally discovered his vocation: a controller for the RATP, the Paris transport authority (*TE,* 39).[52]

Perec's distinction between the predictable and the aleatory might be understood in terms of ignorance of causes. Evidently, he knows that buses run according to a schedule, while he does not know the causes behind the movement or color of a car, or another customer's choice of a particular drink. Since the buses form a group that behave in the same way, he can infer a general rule of causality; it is more difficult to discover the causal laws that govern individual cars and people. The administrative order of the RATP controls one aspect of the Parisian daily rhythm, but no overarching organizational project governs the whole set of events that Perec observes. In his discomfort with the apparently unmotivated and ungoverned aspects of reality, Perec admits to an impulse to ignore, or indeed repress, the unsystematic. This suggests that our impression of basic regularity in daily life may stem from our tendency to ignore the singularity of the event, of a particular place and time. Chance is the sudden mark made by this singularity on the surface of consciousness, as the apparently banal event suddenly becomes surprising or significant. Yet this point of emerging significance is in turn called into question by Perec's observations; the perception of chance as singularity and rupture may itself stem from habit, thus blocking our access to the fabric of the infraordinary.

The Event and the Everyday

Tentative d'épuisement d'un lieu parisien and Perec's other "infra-ordinaire" texts document description as a temporal process rather than a static "snapshot" of objects in space. Chance appears on two levels here. First, there is the randomness that characterizes the coexistence of objects in space, the presence of contiguity without logical connection. Second, there is the accidental nature of events. The two aspects are related, since our impression of the randomness of things lies in our inability to perceive a causal link between them. Furthermore, representation of space in language is necessarily temporalized in the act of writing. This temporality can be explicit, as in the "real time" description of the "infra-ordinaire" texts, which are therefore also narrations. In the fictional universe of *La Vie mode d'emploi,* the almost frozen time of narration (the instants preceding Bartlebooth's death) brings Perec close to traditional realist "scene-setting" description, yet the latter is given so much space that it almost takes over from narrative. The narrator nevertheless moves through this immobile space, and dramatizes the shift of vision in almost cinematographic terms: "Maintenant nous sommes dans la pièce que Gaspard Winckler appelait le salon" (Now we are in the room Gaspard Winckler called the lounge) (*VME,* 49/*LUM,* 25).

In its emphasis on the insignificant and disjointed character of all that occurs in the fictional apartment building, *La Vie mode d'emploi* is close to the ambition that animates Perec's infraordinary writings. Yet the novel contains not only fragments and echoes but also multiple, more or less complete stories, with beginnings, middles, ends, reversals and dénouements. The novel thus establishes a tension between the infraordinary and the extraordinary. It also reflects on this tension, perhaps most explicitly in chapter 28, where the painter Valène foresees the future of the building and its inhabitants. By anticipating or inventing these future or potential stories, he places himself in the position of the novelist himself:[53]

> Encore une fois alors se mettait à courir dans sa tête la triste ronde des déménageurs et des croque-morts, les agences et leurs clients, les plombiers, les électriciens, les peintres, les tapissiers, les carreleurs, les poseurs de moquettes: il se mettait à penser à la vie tranquille des choses, aux caisses de vaisselles, pleines de copeaux, aux cartons de livres, à la dure lumière des ampoules nues se balançant au bout de leur fil, à la lente mise en place des meubles et des objets, à la lente accoutumance du corps à l'espace, toute cette somme d'événements minuscules, inexistants, irracontables—choisir un pied de lampe, une reproduction, un bibelot, placer entre deux portes un haut miroir rectangulaire, disposer devant une fenêtre un jardin japonais, tendre d'un tissu à fleurs les rayons d'une armoire—tous ces gestes infimes en quoi se résumera toujours de la manière la plus fidèle la vie d'un appartement, et que viendront bouleverser, de temps à autre, imprévisibles et inéluctables, tragiques ou bénignes, éphémères ou définitives, les brusques cassures d'un quotidien sans histoire: un jour la petite Marquiseaux s'enfuira avec le jeune Réol, un jour Madame Orlowska décidera de repartir, sans raisons apparentes, sans raisons véritables; un jour Madame Altamont tirera un coup de revolver sur Monsieur Altamont et le sang se mettra à gicler sur les tomettes vernissées de leur salle à manger octogonale; un jour la police viendra arrêter Joseph Nieto et trouvera dans sa chambre, dissimulé dans une des boules de cuivre du grand lit Empire, le célèbre diamant dérobé jadis au prince Luigi Voudzoï. (*VME,* 165)

> Once again his head began to whirl with the sad round of removers and undertakers, property agents and their customers, plumbers, electricians, painters, decorators, tilers, and carpet-layers: he began to think of the tranquil life of things, of crockery chests full of wood shavings,

> of cartons of books, of the harsh light of bare bulbs swinging on their wires, of the slow installation of furniture and objects, of the slow adaptation of the body to space, that whole sum of minute, nonexistent, untellable events—choosing a lamp-stand, a reproduction, a knick-knack, placing a tall rectangular mirror between two doors, putting a Japanese garden in front of a window, lining cupboard shelves with a flower-printed fabric—all those infinitesimal gestures in which the life of a flat is always most faithfully encapsulated, and which will be upset from time to time by the sudden—unforeseen or ineluctable, tragic or benign, ephemeral or definitive—fractures of an ahistorical daily grind: one day the young Marquiseaux girl will run off with the Réol boy, one day Madame Orlowska will leave again for no apparent reason, for no real reason either; one day Madame Altamont will fire a revolver at Monsieur Altamont and the blood will spurt onto the glazed hexagonal tiles of their octagonal dining room: one day the police will come to arrest Joseph Nieto and will find hidden in one of the brass spheres of his large Empire bedstead in his bedroom the famous diamond stolen long ago from Prince Luigi Voudzoï. (*LUM,* 128)

Daily life, the "ahistorical daily grind," is contrasted here with the violence and unpredictability of the event; the minute gestures of those moving into or out of the building are opposed to the sudden breaks, the sudden fractures ("brusques cassures") which overturn the tranquil course of the days. The event rescues life from dullness, from the absence of story, from the minute, insignificant nonevents that nevertheless constitute the life of the apartment and that Valène, in order to be faithful to the real, must portray. Yet ultimately, the truth of daily life is untellable, for in attempting to articulate it we are already constituting events and constructing stories.

The "daily grind" might seem to be the domain of the aleatory, the disordered, the unstructured; in short, of what Michel de Certeau calls the "temps accidenté" (broken time) of everyday practices.[54] And yet a structure emerges from this unformed accumulation of gestures: the pattern of repetition, regularity, the "sad round." On the other hand, the extraordinary events that disrupt this pattern also seem to depend both on chance and on necessity: they are "imprévisibles et inéluctables"—if we translate literally, unforeseeable *and* ineluctable. Significantly, Perec uses the same pair of adjectives to characterize the possibility of the Athlete's death in *W ou le souvenir d'enfance* (*W,* 148).[55] These two words capture the essential nature of chance in Perec's works: the sudden but inevitable irruption of the unexpected. However, we need only look at the catalog of these "unpredictable" breaks in the continuity of daily life to notice that they fall into the category of novelistic stereotypes: elopements, murder, theft. The name Luigi Voudzoï belongs to a character in Raymond Queneau's *Pierrot mon ami* (1942; *My Friend Pierrot*), so we are firmly in the domain of the literary and even of the hyperliterary. While the novel's entertaining stories surprise the reader, they nevertheless conform to some of his or her expectations (including the expectation of surprise).

The tension between "background noise" and event, between the infraordinary and the extraordinary, is not a conflict between clearly defined opposites; rather, the two poles are constantly shifting in relation to each other. The insignificant and extraordinary incidents of the novel are situated on a continuum, and it is, precisely, chance that represents the point of contact between the two domains. The most banal daily gestures—Grifalconi reading a letter, Beyssandre noticing a newspaper article, Madame Echard eating some fish—can entail, "by chance," serious consequences (in these cases: the breakdown of the Grifalconi family, Beyssandre's destructive quest to acquire Bartlebooth's puzzles, Madame Echard's choking to death on a fishbone). The notion of chance concerns not so much the event in itself as this disproportion between the human significance of the cause and that of the effect. It is from this gap that the story emerges, as a sudden fracture in daily life.

The two primary temporal modes of *La Vie mode d'emploi* correspond to the two levels of infraordinary and extraordinary. While the latter belongs above all to the realm of plot—the novel's detective stories, adventure narratives and melodramas—the infraordinary level, although not atemporal, generally corresponds to the level of description. It is, in general, objects that have the task of encapsulating the life of the building. As Thomas Pavel points out, the reader's impression of "realism" hinges largely on the detailed enumerations of the objects found in the apartment building, while the stories often seem to belong to another realm entirely, to an autonomous repertoire assembled from various fictional genres.[56] Whereas my third chapter addressed the narrative pole of this tension, I turn here to Perec's inventorial representation of fictional space.

Perec's Lists

From Aristotle's discussion of the imitation of actions to Lessing's insistence on the temporal dimension of literature, Western reflection on literary mimesis has traditionally privileged narrative rather than spatial representation.[57] As Philippe Hamon points out, the descriptive has often been viewed as a random drifting that, in its uncontrollable freedom and potentially infinite continuation, threatens the cohesion of a literary work.[58] This perennial criticism of description, expressed in the seventeenth century by Boileau and in the twentieth century by Valéry, associates uncontrolled linguistic proliferation with redundancy and chance.[59] Nevertheless, description has come to be associated with modern realism precisely because of its incorporation of apparently random elements. Roland Barthes, for example, accounts for the presence of structurally superfluous details in literary texts (such as the reference to Mme Aubain's barometer in Flaubert's "Un Cœur simple") in terms of the "reality effect." Barthes argues that in realist literature, description is no longer founded on the traditional rhetorical criterion of the beautiful; rather, descriptive details resist meaning, expel the signified from the sign, and aim to create a direct collusion between the signifier and the referent. Such concrete details affirm, by connotation, that "we are the real."[60] However, Barthes' various uses of the denotation/connotation distinction signal the slipperiness of the term *realism.* Although Barthes asserts that reference in Flaubert is an illusion, he often suggests that Robbe-Grillet's works reveal the neutral, objective reality of things, stripped of the meanings we tend to attribute to them—thus echoing Robbe-Grillet's own proclamations of a new realism in the 1950s and '60s.[61] At stake in this debate is the whole question of the significance or insignificance of reality itself, as revealed or created by literary representation.

The inventorial form of description favored by Perec confronts us with the perception of randomness and superfluity in a particularly forceful way. As Jacques Roubaud puts it, Perec's texts are "consumed by lists."[62] It has been argued that Perec moves from the "connotative" descriptions of *Les Choses* to a more "denotative" use of language (and therefore closer to his earlier countermodel, Robbe-Grillet) in the inventories of *La Vie mode d'emploi.*[63] However, the distance between the two novels is not as extreme as this suggests. The difference between description and inventory is arguably one of degree rather than nature. The "list effect," according to Philippe Hamon, is characteristic of description in general, although the list or catalog is an extreme form that threatens the stability of the text's meaning. The list appears to us as a gratuitous or foreign element in the text, thus as intrinsically and extrinsically aleatory (its elements may be permuted, and the list may be substituted for other texts).[64] Perec's use of enumeration is a totalizing gesture, but the list is nevertheless a semiotic system that always points beyond itself and remains open. In "Notes concernant les objets qui sont sur ma table de travail" (1976; "Notes Concerning the Objects That Are on My Work-Table"), Perec observes that making a list is more complicated than it seems: "On oublie toujours quelque chose, on est tenté d'écrire etc., mais justement un inventaire, c'est quand on n'écrit pas etc." (You always forget something, you are tempted to write etc., but an inventory is when you don't write etc.).[65] Even in the most complete of Perec's lists, the "etc." remains implicit. Perec's enumerations rarely claim to be exhaustive; they are merely *attempts* at exhaustivity or at drawing up inventories ("tentatives d'épuisement" or "tentatives d'inventaire").

In the case of *Les Choses,* the seeds of the disorder and fragmentation unleashed in chapter 10 were already present at the text's beginning. More objects and more details could have been added to the novel's initial description, multiplying signs indefinitely. The fundamental arbitrariness of description is an ever-present threat to the system of values associated with objects. It is tempting to see this problem (following Baudrillard) as inherent to the consumerist experience criticized by this "sociological" novel. However, *Les Choses* inaugurates Perec's characteristic inventory style, and its lists hold a particular fascination. Although the openness of enumeration threatens the stability of the characters' worldview, it can also be seen in positive terms as an acknowledgment of the infinite multiplicity of the real. In "Notes concernant les objets qui sont sur ma table de travail," Perec complains that most contemporary writing (with a few exceptions, such as the work of Butor) has forgotten the art of enumeration exemplified by Rabelais or Jules Verne.[66] Of course, Perec himself is another exception to this rule. Reflecting in "Penser/Classer" on the "joys of enumeration," Perec identifies two contradictory tendencies: "la première est de TOUT recenser, la seconde d'oublier tout de même quelque chose" (the first is to list *everything,* the second is to forget something). On the one hand, classification is reassuring, creating points of reference that give our world meaning; on the other hand, it can be frightening: "Il y a dans l'idée que rien au monde n'est assez unique pour ne pas pouvoir entrer dans une liste, quelque chose d'exaltant et de terrifiant à la fois" (There is something at once uplifting and terrifying about the idea that nothing in the world is so unique that it can't be entered on a list) ("PC," 167/"TC," 194). This last idea is exemplified in *La Vie mode d'emploi* by James Sherwood's collection of unica—a unicum being an object of which only one copy exists (*VME,* 115). Valène's painting also attempts to assemble a collection of heterogeneous objects and stories; his failure to complete it is due in part to his inability to capture, in the closed pictorial space of the painting, what Philippe Hamon terms the "infinite etc." of description.[67]

La Vie mode d'emploi abounds with enumerations of various types: inventories, bibliographies, catalogues, indexes, even two separate lists that summarize some of the stories recounted in the novel (the "Compendium" of chapter 51 and an index at the end). Both the spatial inventories and nonspatial lists of Perec's novel have a vertical, paradigmatic status that can be contrasted with the syntagmatic "vectorization" of the narrative;[68] however, I will focus on those lists that organize the spatial dimension of Perec's fictional universe. The frozen tableaux of *La Vie mode d'emploi* resist the passage of time, and with it the impact of chance events on characters' lives. The apparently random proliferation of the inventory thus participates in an aspiration to temporal stability, which is set against the proliferation of stories. Given this double source of multiplicity, the "constraining linearity" of narration (Hamon) and the apparent freedom of the list do not form a simple dichotomy but coexist and interact in a complex fashion.

The lists that constitute the novel's system of constraints establish a paradigmatic model and a logic of narrative discontinuity that can be related to the paradoxical space-time of Perec's novel: the suspended time of narration is reanimated through the narrator's movement in space and through the proliferation of description. Perec structures his novel primarily through an organization of fictional space. The map of the building, superimposed onto the Latin bi-square of the constraints, subdivides the topography of the novel, and the narrator's gaze moves around in this segmented space, room by room, according to the knight's tour constraint. The building is constructed like a jigsaw puzzle. The space of the novel is further subdivided within each chapter, as the unity of the room is fragmented by the paratactic form of the inventory. The status of the jigsaw puzzle as a metaphor for the text then becomes increasingly problematic: can the list's heterogeneity be integrated into a superior order, with all its pieces reassembled? Or do these attempts at exhaustive description of fictional space become an uncontrollable proliferation?

In many cases, the assembling of various objects is motivated by their insertion into a narrative or thematic whole (for example, Hutting's eclectic art projects, Madame Marcia's antiques shop). Elsewhere, the reader is struck by the apparent randomness of the collection of objects. The most extreme case is that of the two "tentatives d'inventaire de quelques-unes des choses qui ont été trouvées dans les escaliers au fil des ans" (draft inventories of some of the things found on the stairs over the years) (in chapters 68 and 94: *VME,* 391–92; 544–47/*LUM,* 327–28; 465–67), in which Perec establishes only a minimum of continuity between the various constraint elements. Perec's lists are determined in part by his initial constraints. However, although these constraints—which themselves take the form of a list—function as a generative principle for the resulting text, they do not contain any ordering principle for the inventories of *La Vie mode d'emploi.* Rather, the initial elements are absorbed into an open form. If the *Cahier des charges* is in itself a closed, jigsaw puzzle–like system, *La Vie mode d'emploi* is theoretically an open one (although it is necessarily limited in its actualization). The novel's lists of miscellaneous objects strike us as potentially infinite.

In the case of the inventories of objects found in the staircase during the apartment building's history, the space-time of the fictional staircase defines a set whose members are theoretically finite. Yet in practice the list only attempts to be exhaustive. Furthermore, we do not know what principle governs the selection of these particular things over others. This inventory might be compared to a jigsaw puzzle that has some missing pieces but that could in theory, if not in practice, be completed. However, this metaphor implies that there is one single way of organizing the parts to make a whole. This is not the case: although there is a membership rule, at least for the total set of objects—an element is a member of the set if it has been found in the staircase—there appears to be no ordering rule for the series, nothing that justifies mentioning, in chapter 68, first some photos, then a radio, then a shoe. The grouping of the elements makes no distinction between temporal succession ("over the years") and spatial contiguity ("on the stairs"), nor does it seem to obey any other discernable thematic or formal principle. Yet it is precisely in this apparent disorder that the meaning of the list is to be found: the bewildering series signifies the disconnectedness and heterogeneity of things and their enigmatic survival once their connection to their function in human life—and their links with other objects—have disappeared.

By according a privileged place to the list, Perec's novel thus creates a powerful realist effect, imitating the chaotic multiplicity of the world. Yet it would be a mistake to characterize the lists of *La Vie mode d'emploi* as purely denotative, and their contents as wholly redundant and gratuitous in themselves. The enumerations of the inventory chapters present an extreme case of resistance to interpretation, yet they are profoundly linked to the themes of memory and absence.[69] The elements of other lists are even more easily analyzable in terms of the novel's narrative and thematic structure. The following passage, from the description of Madame de Beaumont's cellar, provides a good example:

> Vieux objets: lampe jadis de bureau avec un socle de cuivre et un abat-jour hémisphérique en opaline vert clair, largement ébréché, un restant de tisanière, des portemanteaux. Souvenirs rapportés de voyages ou de vacances: étoile de mer séchée, minuscules poupées habillées en couple serbe, petit vase décoré d'une vue d'Étretat; boîte à chaussures débordant de cartes postales, paquets de lettres d'amour serrées dans des élastiques aujourd'hui détendus, prospectus de pharmacie [. . .] (*VME,* 434)

> Old things: a lamp with a brass stand and a very chipped semicircular shade of pale-green opaline, formerly a desk lamp; the remains of a teapot; coat hangers. Souvenirs of voyages and holidays: a dried starfish, two tiny dolls dressed as a Serbian couple, a small vase decorated with a view of Etretat; then shoe-boxes brimful of postcards and love letters in elastic bands that have gone loose now; a pharmaceutical prospectus [. . .] (*LUM,* 365–66)

The inventory continues for three more pages. The cellars store the leftovers, debris, or traces of human life; they are spaces of both memory and forgetting. The reader may well struggle to interpret or to connect the objects that have been united in the fictional space of the building, the words that have been put together on the space of Perec's page. Yet the elements of this description are not grouped completely at random but are classified by type: first a group of old objects formerly used in the Beaumont apartment; next the holiday souvenirs; then the shoe boxes containing various documents. Later in the chapter, we find children's books with missing pages and old, yellowing photographs. These details are neither redundant nor unreadable; they become signs of loss, deliberate forgetting, melancholy, and death. They can be integrated into larger thematic networks; for example, the reference to the love letters echoes a passage in chapter 40 that describes the anecdotes that Anne and Béatrice Breidel invent on the subject of their grandmother's romantic entanglements (*VME,* 221–22).[70] The elements of the list can therefore have a narrative function and may also introduce narrative insertions within the description. The old photographs mentioned in chapter 76 thus become the pretext for recounting a few episodes from the life of the Breidel girls—a vacation at their uncle's home, Véronique Altamont's costume party (*VME,* 435). Another photograph reveals the rather surprising fact that Fernand de Beaumont was good friends with Bartlebooth, a character whom we know to be reclusive and solipsistic (*VME,* 426–27).

Classifications

Various principles of classification structure the novel's lists. In the case of descriptions of novelistic space, the order is often topographic. In chapter 18, for example, the narrator describes first the floor of the Rorschash's dining room, then the left-hand wall, then the back wall, then the right-hand wall (*VME,* 91–92). Other descriptions are organized around the characters present in the room, for example, the two salesmen on the fourth-floor landing in chapter 42 (*VME,* 231–32). The alphabetical order of the novel's indexes is an arbitrary but usefully neutral organizing principle.[71] Philippe Hamon argues that literary description is a metaclassification rather than a classification, bringing together diverse vocabularies and official forms of knowledge.[72] What is particularly striking in Perec's work is the extent to which he multiplies his references to various discourses of classification. Perec also reflects explicitly on the practical and philosophical problems raised by the attempt to classify. In *Espèces d'espaces,* for example, he mentions various possible ordering principles for his (ultimately unfinished) project of describing all the rooms in which he has slept: chronological, alphabetical, geographical, or thematic (*EE,* 47–48). Precisely because it is wholly arbitrary and conventional, alphabetical order is supremely functional and does not require justification.[73] Other types of order, however, entail implicit epistemological claims, and it is these orders that fascinate Perec.

Perec's own classifications establish a complex relationship between order and disorder. A particularly revealing example is found in chapter 33 of *La Vie mode d'emploi,* which juxtaposes two very different forms of list, corresponding to two different attitudes to space and things. First, the chapter enumerates the contents of the Altamonts' well-stocked cellar, which contains several categories of object, carefully classified. On the shelves of the left-hand wall are food products; on the back wall to the left are bottles of wine that are divided, "selon un ordre apparemment canonique" (in an apparently canonical order) (*VME,* 196/*LUM,* 154), into table wines, young wines, and vintage wines (which are in turn organized by region and date). Finally, at the far right of the cellar is "la zone des produits d'entretien, et des *divers*" (the maintenance, cleansing, and miscellaneous supplies section) (*VME*, 197/*LUM*, 155). The Altamonts have carefully filled and organized this space in order to have "une place pour chaque chose et chaque chose à sa place" (a place for every thing, and every thing in its place) (*VME*, 195/*LUM*, 153).

Appearing immediately after this inventory, the description of the Gratiolets' cellar presents a striking contrast:

> Des générations ont empilé là des rebuts que personne n'a jamais rangés ni triés. [. . .]
>
> L'œil, s'habituant petit à petit à l'obscurité, finirait par reconnaître sous leur fine couche de poussière grise des restes épars provenant de tous les Gratiolet: le châssis et les montants d'un lit bateau, des skis d'hickory ayant depuis longtemps perdu toute leur élasticité [. . .] une vieille machine Underwood, de la célèbre série des Quatre Millions qui, à cause de son tabulateur automatique passa en son temps pour un des objets les plus perfectionnés jamais conçus, sur laquelle François Gratiolet se mit à dactylographier ses quittances quand il décida qu'il lui fallait moderniser sa comptabilité. (*VME*, 197–98)

> Here generations have heaped up rubbish unsorted and unordered by anyone [. . .]
>
> The eye, slowly becoming accustomed to the dark, could end up making out beneath the layer of fine grey dust heteroclite remains coming from each of the Gratiolets: the base and posts of an Empire bed, hickorywood skis having lost their spring long ago, a pith helmet that was of purest white once upon a time, tennis racquets held in heavy trapezoidal presses, an old Underwood typewriter of the celebrated Four Million model, which was held to be, in its time, and owing to its automatic tabulator, one of the most sophisticated objects ever made, and on which François Gratiolet began to type his invoices when he decided he had to modernise his accounting systems. (*LUM*, 155)

The first half of the chapter produces in the reader what Perec elsewhere calls "un vertige taxonomique" (*PC*, 162). At the same time, the excessive accumulation of provisions and the mode of their organization in space are implicitly mocked. Of course the Altamonts' claim to exhaustivity can only be illusory: something can always be added to the supply (for example, they only stock three types of sugar: lumps, granulated, and castor). Their classificatory system also has its limits, which is why at the end of the description we find the list of "miscellaneous supplies"—in other words, objects that do not have a place in a specific category (*VME*, 197).[74]

The second list, the description of the Gratiolets' cellar, presents us with an unorganized accumulation of discarded objects. However, these things are far from meaningless from a narrative and thematic point of view, for they allow us to reconstitute certain elements of the Gratiolets' family history. The elements of the list are not gratuitous, nor are they neutral of human value; even these leftover fragments are signs of life. The cellar's state of abandonment and the almost total absence of organization are themselves indications of the tragic dimension of the Gratiolets' saga, just as the obsessive ultra-organization of the Altamonts' cellar is part of a generally unsympathetic portrait of that family.[75] Of these two ways of using space, these two types of list, the Altamonts' order is perhaps more disconcerting than the Gratiolets' disorder. The two apparent extremes are nevertheless relative, since we are confronted with neither absolute chance nor absolute order. The Gratiolets' jumble is not a wholly random collection of objects, and the Altamonts' efforts at order do not eliminate arbitrariness.

The Altamonts' classificatory activity presents us with the epistemological crux of the problem of classification. It aims to create, within the space of the cellar, a continuity that is normally absent among objects. In fact, it believes it is restoring this continuity, returning each thing to its proper place, in other words, reconstituting an order that is considered to be natural. It is just that this order is not normally situated anywhere in the world. Although the Altamonts' system is applied only to provisions, not to the whole of nature, this type of classification recalls Michel Foucault's characterization of natural history in the classical era. According to Foucault, the attempt to establish order in nature and to discover its general categories rests on the assumption that nature must be continuous but that over time this continuity has been disrupted by chance. The classificatory effort is necessary precisely because real geographical space presents us with beings and things tangled up with one another, in a random and disordered manner when compared to the table of taxonomies.[76] The movement of time is viewed as something external to the true order (the "gradation of beings"), which it disperses and entangles at random.[77] The reorganization of space is an attempt to repair the damage done by time and chance.

We find a more explicit point of connection between Foucault, Perec, and the problem of classification in Perec's short text "Penser/Classer" (1982; "Think/Classify"). Perec refers to the Borges passage that supposedly inspired Foucault's *Les Mots et les choses:* the account of a "Chinese encyclopedia" that classifies animals under such categories as "those drawn with a very fine camel's hair brush," "etc.," and "those that have just broken the flower vase."[78] Perec points out that classifications as startling as Borges's can easily be produced by making selections from official administrative texts ("PC," 165). It is significant that another passage in "Penser/Classer," under the heading "Utopie" (Utopia), directly echoes the description of the Altamonts' cellar: "Derrière toute utopie, il y a toujours un grand dessin taxinomique: une place pour chaque chose et chaque chose à sa place" (Behind every utopia there is always some great taxonomic design: a place for each thing and each thing in its place). But utopias are depressing, states Perec, "parce qu'elles ne laissent pas de place au hasard, à la différence, aux 'divers'" (because they leave no room for chance, for difference, for the 'miscellaneous'" ("PC," 155/"TC," 186).

Classification, for the obsessive Altamonts of *La Vie mode d'emploi,* is a means of struggling against disorder. It is not surprising that the anxious protagonist of *Un homme qui dort* also develops a classificatory obsession, an indication of his desire to control the images that surround and oppress him (*UHD,* 31). What is at stake in his attempt to organize a simple pack of cards is nothing less than the ordering of the world; and in fact he soon imagines methods for classifying roads, neighborhoods, and buildings (*UHD,* 59). In more sinister fashion, the fictional dystopia of *W ou le souvenir d'enfance* is based on a strict classification of people according to their function (*W,* 103). The Athletes themselves are categorized by village, team, and skill, and participate in events that determine their ranking (*W,* 117). Ultimately, ordered classification turns into a scene of generalized carnage—the will to produce order is no longer distinguishable from the will to destroy.

The World as Jigsaw

The Altamonts of *La Vie mode d'emploi,* by attempting to put each thing in its place, try to re-establish an order that has supposedly been disrupted by the course of events. The disorder that exists in the world is seen as the result of chance, the latter being identified with the passage of time itself. The world is essentially treated as a jigsaw puzzle whose pieces have been scattered.[79] Once again, Perec makes this association explicit in "Penser/Classer," titling one of his sections "Le Monde comme puzzle" ("The World as Puzzle"):

> Tellement tentant de vouloir distribuer le monde entier selon un code unique; une loi universelle régirait l'ensemble des phénomènes; deux hémisphères, cinq continents, masculin et féminin, animal et végétal, singulier pluriel, droite gauche, quatre saisons, cinq sens, six voyelles, sept jours, douze mois, vingt-six lettres.
>
> Malheureusement ça ne marche pas, ça n'a même jamais commencé à marcher, ça ne marchera jamais.
>
> N'empêche que l'on continuera encore longtemps à catégoriser tel ou tel animal selon qu'il a un nombre impair de doigts ou des cornes creuses. ("PC," 155)

> So very tempting to want to distribute the entire world in terms of a single code. A universal law would then regulate phenomena as a whole: two hemispheres, five continents, masculine and feminine, animal and vegetable, singular plural, right left, four seasons, five senses, six vowels, seven days, twelve months, twenty-six letters.
>
> Unfortunately, this doesn't work, has never even begun to work, will never work.
>
> Which won't stop us continuing for a long time to come to categorize this animal or that according to whether it has an odd number of toes or hollow horns. ("TC," 186)

The analogy between classifications, cartography, and puzzles indicates a parallel with Bartlebooth's project: Bartlebooth aims precisely to reduce the world to a set of jigsaws, that is, to a continuous surface that can be cut up and pieced back together.[80] He allows time and chance to scatter the pieces, but only so that he can subsequently restore order and thereby abolish chance. Epistemologically, however, there is no reason to privilege the Altamonts' cellar or Bartlebooth's jigsaw as taxonomic sites for mapping our knowledge of the world. To adopt Foucault's terms, nothing guarantees the unity of the "marvelous and smooth space" that nevertheless permits words and things to be held together in categories. As Foucault observes, in the modern age there emerges the suspicion—exemplified by Borges's Chinese encyclopedia—that there is a worse kind of disorder than incongruous grouping: "Ce serait le désordre qui fait scintiller les fragments d'un grand nombre d'ordres possibles dans la dimension, sans loi ni géométrie, de l'hétéroclite" (It would be the disorder that reveals the glittering fragments of a large number of possible orders in the dimension, without law or geometry, of the heterogeneous).[81]

This glimpse of multiple orders is the real disorder that lies behind Perec's classifications and metaclassifications, and that is explicitly allegorized in one episode of *La Vie mode d'emploi.* One of Gaspard Winckler's projects, after he has fabricated Bartlebooth's jigsaws, is an attempt at classification: he tries to organize the hotel labels sent to him by Smautf, Bartlebooth's servant. Chronological and geographical solutions do not satisfy him; he would like to find a more subtle form of organization. However, the enterprise is ruined by the idea of chance:

> Ce qu'il aurait voulu c'est que chaque étiquette soit reliée à la suivante, mais chaque fois pour une raison différente; par exemple, elles pourraient posséder un détail commun, une montagne ou un volcan, une baie illuminée [. . .], ou bien une relation fondée, non sur une ressemblance, mais sur une opposition, ou sur une association fragile, presque arbitraire: un minuscule village au bord d'un lac italien suivi par les gratte-ciel de Manhattan, des skieurs succédant à des nageurs [. . .]. Ce n'est pas seulement difficile, ajoutait Winckler, c'est surtout inutile: en laissant les étiquettes en vrac et en choisissant deux au hasard, on peut être sûr qu'elles auront toujours au moins trois points communs. (*VME,* 56)

> What he would have liked would be to link each label to the next, but each time in respect of something else: for example, they could have some detail in common, a mountain or a volcano, an illuminated bay [. . .], or a relationship based not on similarity but on opposition or a fragile, almost arbitrary association: a minute village by an Italian lake, followed by the skyscrapers of Manhattan, skiers followed by swimmers [. . .] It's not just hard, Winckler added, above all it's useless: if you leave the labels unsorted and take two at random, you can be sure they'll have at least three things in common. (*LUM,* 31–32)

Having put away his labels, Winckler undertakes no further projects before his death, as if the uselessness of classification implied the futility of all human endeavor.

The labels in question come from Bartlebooth's journeys, and Winckler's attempt at classification mirrors Bartlebooth's jigsaw project: both aim to dominate part of the world by reconstituting its image from fragments. Winckler, who can cut up paintings into puzzles and who thereby triumphs over Bartlebooth, finds himself powerless when he attempts in turn to assemble a different sort of jigsaw, by reassembling fragments (linking each label to another). The problem is not that this linking is impossible, but on the contrary, that it is too easy to find possible associations. The fact that by choosing two labels "au hasard" he can discover links between them suggests that all order may result from a similar retrospective projection, while having its origin in chance. The problem opens up a dizzying and unbearable alternative. On the one hand, what appears meaningful may in fact be due to chance; on the other hand, perhaps nothing is chance, and everything is determined by a hidden order. The fact that it seems impossible to choose between these alternatives helps to explain the reversibility of binary oppositions in which chance is one of the terms.

Perec's own classifications—whether of cars, umbrellas, reading habits, or eyeglasses[82]—might seem to be symptomatic of a "utopian" obsession with producing order and excluding chance. However, Perec's texts also undermine the notion of classification, suggesting that no ordering principle can ever completely account for the real—or rather, that too many organizing principles can be found or invented, none of which can be privileged. Perec's lists thus suggest the existence of a disorder more radical than the disorder of incompletion. As Perec claims in "Notes brèves sur l'art et la manière de ranger ses livres" (published in the same year as *La Vie mode d'emploi,* 1978; "Brief Notes on the Art and Manner of Arranging One's Books"):

> Nous oscillons sans cesse entre l'illusion de l'achevé et le vertige de l'insaisissable. Au nom de l'achevé, nous voulons croire qu'un ordre unique existe qui nous permettrait d'accéder d'emblée au savoir; au nom de l'insaisissable, nous voulons penser que l'ordre et le désordre sont deux mêmes mots désignant le hasard.
>
> We oscillate between the illusion of perfection and the vertigo of the unattainable. In the name of completeness, we would like to believe that a unique order exists that would enable us to accede to knowledge all in one go; in the name of the unattainable, we would like to think that order and disorder are in fact the same word, denoting pure chance.[83]

However, Perec goes on to suggest that even this hesitation between two views of the chance/order relationship may rest on a false alternative: "Il se peut aussi que les deux soient des leurres, des trompe-l'œil destinés à dissimuler l'usure des livres et des systèmes" (It's possible also that both are decoys, illusions meant to disguise the erosion of both books and systems).[84] This statement of epistemological skepticism illuminates the significance of Perec's literary forms. Perec's works, both in their unstable classifications and the "arbitrary necessity" of their constraints, convey a hesitation to accept either that all is order or that all is chance.[85]

Order and Constraint

What survives, in the face of this uncertainty, is the possibility of finding happiness in a purely personal version of classification that does not claim to establish a universal order. This choice of classification as play is represented in *La Vie mode d'emploi* by a twelve-year-old boy, Rémi Plassaert, who organizes his collection of promotional blotters "selon des critères qui n'appartiennent qu'à lui" (using criteria known only to himself) (*VME*, 247/*LUM*, 196). The blotters refer metonymically to ink, pointing to Perec's own writing practice. Other characters also invent their own classificatory criteria. Bartlebooth, Winckler, Valène, Hutting, and others select and reassemble pieces, recompose categories and units on the basis of fragments. This is how they fabricate their own "user's manuals" for life, by superimposing an arbitrary grid on a world which is perhaps, after all, composed of nothing but chance. If these characters often fail, it may be because they try to make absolute claims for their own systems, or because these systems are not sufficiently open to the randomness of the world. Unlike Rémi Plassaert, they do not know how to play.

The gap in Bartlebooth's final puzzle is generally interpreted in terms of lack or loss. In leaving Bartlebooth's puzzle incomplete, however, Perec carries out the positive gesture of opening a closed space. Furthermore, the final piece of Bartlebooth's puzzle is not really missing but has the incorrect form. We are confronted with incongruity rather than lack, with an element that does not fit into a particular system of representation. Winckler has managed to disrupt the apparently stable system constructed by Bartlebooth. Of his own classifications, Perec says in "Penser/Classer" that they do not last: "À peine ai-je fini de mettre de l'ordre que cet ordre est déjà caduc" (Hardly have I finished putting things into an order before that order is obsolete) ("PC," 163/"TC," 192). While he admits to sometimes being overcome by an organizational frenzy, this never reaches a conclusion. Similar provisional organizations appear in his writings—in his "infra-ordinaire" texts, where they operate both as an ordering principle and as a tool for training the gaze to notice what normally goes unnoticed, and in the enumerations of *La Vie mode d'emploi*.[86]

The subsections of "Penser/Classer" are arranged not alphabetically but following the order in which the letters of the alphabet appear in the seventh story of the French translation of Italo Calvino's novel *If on a Winter's Night a Traveler* ("PC," 176). This preference for an idiosyncratic constraint over an equally arbitrary convention is a typical Oulipian gesture. Oulipian constraints are not necessarily classificatory, but we recall that the constraint system of *La Vie mode d'emploi* begins by categorizing different narrative and descriptive functions. Classification and constraint have similar functions as preliminary ordering activities, and the author's treatment of classification may therefore shed light on the constraint's relationship to literary realism. Like classification, the notion of constraint takes on an existential and epistemological meaning that places it at the heart of Perec's worldview, whether in the arbitrariness that destroys the Athletes of *W,* the compulsive rule making practiced by the protagonist of *Un homme qui dort,* or the evil fate that condemns the characters of *La Disparition.* Perec, unlike many of his characters, discovers creative, questioning, and playful forms of constraint and classification.

Life, as presented in Perec's works, both allows the endless production and proliferation of arbitrary modes of use ("modes d'emploi") and enters into a struggle with these attempts to impose order upon it. Understood in this context, the anti-chance of Oulipian constraints is only apparently at odds with Perec's fascination with the randomness of the infraordinary: constraints both incorporate and resist disorder, while acknowledging that all order may be founded on chance—or vice versa. Perec's constraints convert this epistemological problem into an interpretative one, since they often create the impression of randomness—for example, in the inclusion of a particular constraint element in a particular chapter—while in fact they represent a staging of chance, a self-conscious and ironic use of the arbitrary. But Perec's constraints are also fundamentally creative in their relationship to the real and to writing. Like the provisional classifications of the infraordinary, which make no claims to absolute validity as order but point the way to new modes of perception, constraints dislocate conventional ways of writing in order to discover new potentialities for representation, new ways of capturing the real.

Conclusion

In its combination of bold experimentation, theoretical modesty, and appeal to the reader's participation, the Oulipo adopts a uniquely intriguing approach to writing. Its provocative playfulness also confronts readers with fundamental problems of artistic and narrative form. The contemporary fascination with the aleatory is not alien to the group; rather, the Oulipo's self-designation as "anti-chance"—the source of so much critical confusion—is best understood in terms of a response and challenge to chance. The creativity of Oulipian constraints depends precisely on their capacity to produce the accidental and the unexpected, while at the same time controlling and directing this chance element into particular channels.

What is striking in Georges Perec's work is his ability to harness Oulipian anti-chance to his exploration of the place of chance in reality and human experience. The conjunction of chance and constraints is especially effective in his Oulipian narratives, in particular *La Disparition* and *La Vie mode d'emploi.* Perec exploits the tension between narrative organization and the logic of constraints as a means of investigating the dilemma of chance. In particular, the combinatorial constraints of *La Vie mode d'emploi* allow Perec to combine the impression of systematic, rule-governed distribution with the appearance of disorder, discontinuity, and unpredictability. This tension corresponds to the thematic friction at the heart of the novel between the infraordinary and the extraordinary, between the contingencies of life and the search for order represented by the characters' various projects.

Inherently unstable, the notion of chance both gestures toward the absence of meaning and bridges the gap between insignificance and significance. It brings together the ideas of the mechanical and the intentional, and represents precisely the point at which the inherently meaningless becomes meaningful, in terms of its human consequences. It has a special place in the literature and thought of an era fraught with metaphysical ambivalence and epistemological skepticism. As Perec emphasizes in his "infraordinary" writings, chance is at the heart of our perceptions and organizations of reality but never occupies a stable position within these systems. Perec's constraints have a similarly ambiguous status, since they represent a hesitation between order and disorder. The organizations they produce are only ever provisional, arbitrary, and indeed playful—the rules of an artificial game rather than the rules of nature or of a natural art. Constraints do not eliminate chance in favor of authorial control; rather, they displace and problematize both chance and intention. In their arbitrariness, they suggest a loss of faith in any absolute order, and yet an unwillingness to accept the world as pure chaos. For Perec's vision is not wholly dysphoric: life still provides the means to invent multiple "modes d'emploi," kinds of use that range from the most humble pastime to the creation of works of art.

Constraints are only one of the means by which Perec dramatizes the problem of chance. As a theme, chance is not entirely absent from the deterministic universe of *Les Choses,* where it is tied to the characters' hopes of sudden fortune. However, chance first takes center stage in *Un homme qui dort,* where the protagonist is confronted with the existential and ethical problem of ordering his life, and uses both random and rule-governed behavior in his attempt to escape history. This reflection on chance is inseparable from Perec's use of narrative forms. *W ou le souvenir d'enfance,* although not an Oulipian text in the strict sense, exploits narrative discontinuity as a strategy for questioning our retrospective constructions of causal sequences. In the fictional section of the book, chance serves as a principle of unjust distribution that is then, paradoxically, systematized as a form of rule. If the precept that "chance is also part of the rule" takes its most extreme form here (as rules and chance become virtually indistinguishable), it may also be applied to Perec's fictional universes as a whole and to the functioning of his constraints. Perec's anxiety about the destructive aspects of chance has as its positive counterpart a continual effort to explore its creative possibilities.

The preoccupation with chance is a point of continuity in Perec's writing practice, which at first glance seems scattered among various commitments and projects: sociological, realist, autobiographical, and experimental. While chance is perhaps a disruption of the order of things, it might more accurately be considered a sign of our constant struggle to wrest order and meaning from chaos. The "metatextual" aspect of Perec's texts plays an essential part in the self-conscious staging of both chance and rules, which suggests on the one hand that chance may conceal a hidden order, and on the other hand that all order may ultimately be founded on chance. From the reader's point of view, the interpretative uncertainties of deciphering Perec's constraints enact the epistemological dilemmas that confront our readings of the world.

Perec's treatment of chance has an important place in the history of literature. In particular, it opens up new possibilities for the novel—a genre that has long been caught between the effort to represent contingency and the creation of internal structure and laws. Perec's constraints are significant, in this context, because their logic is itself a form of negotiation with chance. Perec acknowledges chance as an irreducible presence in experience, yet does not abandon or simplify the importance of order both as a human need and as a principle of writing. His work expresses a philosophical and aesthetic irresolution between order and disorder, significance and insignificance. Caught in the labyrinth of Perec's text and wary of the author's ruses, the reader participates in the play of these tensions through the uncertainties of the interpretative process itself, while always hoping to find the exit—by design or by chance.

Notes

Introduction

The chapter epigraph is from Balzac, "Avant-propos" (1842), in *La Comédie humaine* 1:11.

1. Cicero, *De Natura Deorum,* bk. 2, sec. 37. I am indebted to Larry Norman for bringing this example to my attention.

2. William Paley's *Natural Theology* of 1802 contains perhaps the most famous modern version of the argument from design: if a watch were found lying on the ground, Paley asserts, it would be absurd to conclude that it was not the result of purposeful design. However, with Darwin's theory of evolution came an alternative explanation for complexity in nature; natural selection plays the role of a "blind watchmaker," to adopt Richard Dawkins's expression (Dawkins, *The Blind Watchmaker,* 4–6). Although Dawkins is at pains to show that evolution is not random (in the sense of unpredictable and chaotic), the simultaneous absence and illusion of design does arguably constitute a form of chance.

3. See Hacking, *The Taming of Chance.*

4. Baudelaire, "Le peintre de la vie moderne" (1863), *Écrits sur l'art,* 518.

5. Perec, "Entretien avec Gabriel Simony" (June 1981), in *Entretiens et conférences* 2:214.

6. For some passing comments on the problem of chance in Perec, see Burgelin, *Georges Perec,* 176 and Bertharion, *Poétique de Georges Perec,* 107–8. In *The Poetics of Experiment,* Warren Motte defends Perec against the charge that his work is "aleatory" or "gratuitous" (133). Jean-François Chassay's *Le Jeu des coïncidences dans "La Vie mode d'emploi"* does not focus specifically on chance, but rather explores the conjunctions between contemporary scientific ideas and Perec's themes. Sabine Hillen's article "Mode d'emploi du hasard" is more directly concerned with chance, relating it to everyday incidents in *La Vie mode d'emploi.* However, Hillen does not investigate Perec's use of constraints or consider the place of chance in his work as a whole.

7. *Oxford English Dictionary,* 2nd ed., s.v. "chance."

8. *Grand Robert de la langue française.* 2nd ed., s.v. "hasard."

9. See Long, *Hellenistic Philosophy,* 164 and Nicole Hecquet-Noti, "*Fortuna* dans le monde latin: chance ou hasard?" in Foehr-Janssens and Métry, *La Fortune: thèmes, représentations, discours,* 15, 25.

10. Lucretius, *De Rerum Natura,* bk. 2, lines 1057–59.

11. Ibid., bk. 2, lines 216–93.

12. Aristotle, *Physics,* trans. W. Charlton, bks. 1–2, 197a 20–23, 32–35, 12–23.

13. Ibid., 197b 18–32.

14. Ibid., 197b 1–10. While other English translators render *to automaton* as "spontaneity," W. Charlton translates it as "the automatic" and *tuché* as "luck." However, he notes that the former term refers to chance in general (*Physics,* 105, note on chaps. 4–6). The Hellenistic and medieval association of the goddesses Tuché and Fortuna justifies following Henri Carteron's French translation in using "chance" (*hasard*) for *to automaton* and "fortune" for *tuché* (Aristote, *Physique,* 1–4, ed. Carteron).

15. Aristotle, *Physics,* 196b 32–197a 5.

16. Barreau, "Le concept du hasard," 212.

17. Aristotle, *Physics,* 198a 1–8.

18. On ancient Greek notions of chance see Saïd, "Part, contrainte ou hasard? Les mots du destin chez Homère."

19. Augustine, *City of God,* bk. 5, chap. 1 and bk. 7, chap. 3. In the *Retractations,* Augustine regrets having used the term *fortune* at all in his earlier books, stating that "men have a very bad habit of saying 'Fortune willed this' when they should say 'God willed this'" (bk. 1, chap. 1, sec. 2).

20. Boethius, *Consolation of Philosophy* (A.D. 524), bk. 4, prose 5, 5–7, and bk. 5, prose 1.18–19. For a recent discussion of Boethius's argument see Emmanuelle Métry, "*Fortuna* et *Philosophia:* Une alliance inattendue: Quelques remarques sur le rôle de la Fortune dans la *Consolation de Philosophie* de Boèce," in Foehr-Janssens and Métry, *La Fortune,* 59–70. For a general overview of Fortune's role in medieval literature see Patch, "The Tradition of the Goddess Fortuna" and "Fortuna in Old French Literature."

21. See Descartes, *Meditations,* no. 4, sec., 55; Spinoza, *Ethics,* pt. 1, prop. 36, appendix.

22. Hume, *An Enquiry Concerning Human Understanding* (1739–40), sec. 6.1. See also the "Discours préliminaire des éditeurs" and the article "Fatalité," in the *Encyclopédie* (1751–80), 1:xiv and 6:422–25.

23. Laplace, *Essai philosophique sur les probabilités,* 32–33.

24. The uncertainty principle of quantum theory states that we can never know precisely both the position and momentum of any particular fundamental particle. At the quantum level, physical assertions can concern only observational probabilities rather than definite measurements. See Gribbin, *In Search of Schrödinger's Cat,* 157. Chaos theory is concerned with deterministic systems that behave in complex, unpredictable ways, often due to sensitive dependence on initial conditions (Edward Lorenz's "butterfly effect"). See Ruelle, *Hasard et chaos,* 127, 89.

25. See Monod, *Le Hasard et la nécessité,* and Atlan, *Entre le cristal et la fumée.*

26. In *La Nouvelle Alliance: Métamorphose de la science,* Ilya Prigogine and Isabelle Stengers claim that science's "new alliance" rescues us from Laplace's depthless world and restores a universe where randomness, irreversibility, and microscopic indeterminacy are the rule (20, 90).

27. See, for example, Thom, "Halte au hasard, silence au bruit." For an over-

view of the various arguments in this debate, see the articles collected in Pomian, *La Querelle du déterminisme.*

28. Cournot, *Matérialisme, vitalisme, rationalisme,* 175–76. We find the same example in Spinoza, who uses it to argue that final causes are figments of the imagination (*Ethics,* pt. 1, app. to prop. 36), but it may be traced back as far as Aristotle: "The stone did not fall for the purpose of hitting someone; it fell, then, as an automatic outcome, in that it might have fallen through someone's agency and for hitting" (*Physics,* 197b 30–32).

29. Poincaré, "Le hasard," in *L'Analyse et la recherche,* 138–39.

30. Bergson, *Les Deux Sources de la morale et de la religion,* 154–55.

31. Bergson, *L'Évolution créatrice,* 254.

32. Ibid., 255.

33. Bergson, *Les Deux Sources,* 155.

34. Two examples, one a continental and the other an analytic philosopher, are Clément Rosset and Richard Rorty. In *Logique du pire* (1971), Rosset identifies a tradition of "tragic philosophy" founded on the idea of an original chance that precedes the dichotomies of order and disorder, necessity and contingency. According to Rosset, the idea of chance is properly speaking an "anti-concept," which indicates the fundamental nothingness of the universe. In a similar vein, Rorty argues in *Contingency, Irony, and Solidarity* (1989) for the desirability of a "postmetaphysical" culture in which "we try to get to the point where we no longer worship anything, where we treat nothing as a quasi-divinity, where we treat everything—our language, our conscience, our community—as a product of time and chance" (22).

35. The notions of chance and contingency both rest on the absence of certainty in future events. Aristotle discusses the problem of future contingents in *On Interpretation:* since some statements about the future are not necessarily true—it is not necessary that tomorrow's sea-battle take place—such statements are neither true nor false (Aristotle, *On Interpretation,* 18 a 34–19 a 39). However, this account of contingency makes room for the operation of free will, whereas I argue that the concept of chance signals the limits of agency. Various forms of mind-body dualism have allowed certain philosophers (Descartes, Kant, Bergson) to preserve a space for human free will in a universe of scientific necessity. Whether the discoveries of twentieth-century science make room for a materialist account of free will is a matter for debate, especially since it is not clear that human freedom is implied by indeterminism on the level of particles. For a discussion of this problem, see Popper, *Objective Knowledge,* 226–32.

36. Clément Rosset associates "tragic philosophy" with the idea of chance in *Logique du pire* (see introduction, note 34). In *The Fragility of Goodness,* Martha Nussbaum examines "the aspiration to rational self-sufficiency in Greek ethical thought: the aspiration to make the goodness of a good human life safe from luck through the controlling power of reason" (3). At the same time, according to Nuss-

baum, Greek tragic poetry reveals "the vulnerability of human lives to fortune, the mutability of our circumstances and our passions, the existence of conflicts among our commitments" (13).

37. According to Eric Charles White, *kairos* in the rhetorical sense is "a passing instant when an opening appears which must be driven through with force if success is to be achieved" (*Kaironomia,* 13). As Frank Kermode points out in *The Sense of an Ending, kairos* in its theological sense is "the season, a point in time filled with significance, charged with a meaning derived from its relation to the end." Unlike *chronos,* which is "passing time" or "waiting time," *kairos* is essentially a narrative conception of time (47). While I will use the word *kairos* primarily in its rhetorical sense, the very notion of the "right moment" seems to imply the other sense of *kairos,* the idea of time as fundamentally narrative and meaningful in nature.

38. "Vous voyez, lecteur, que je suis en beau chemin, et qu'il ne tiendrait qu'à moi de vous faire attendre un an, deux ans, trois ans le récit des amours de Jacques, en le séparant de son maître et en leur faisant courir à chacun tous les hasards qu'il me plairait. [. . .] Qu'il est facile de faire des contes!" (You see, Reader, I'm into my stride and I have it entirely in my power to make you wait a year, two years, three years, to hear the story of Jacques' love affairs, by separating him from his Master and making the both of them undergo all the perils I please. [. . .] How easy it is to make up stories!). Diderot, *Jacques le fataliste,* in *Œuvres,* 476; *Jacques the Fatalist,* trans. Coward, 4.

39. In *Circumstances: Chance and the Literary Text,* David F. Bell studies chance phenomena in the context of the nineteenth-century French realist novel, in particular Stendhal and Balzac. For a more general survey of the theme of chance in modern literature, see Erich Köhler's *Der literarische Zufall, das Mögliche und die Notwendigkeit.* Both Bell and Köhler focus on the problem of human agency, contrasting the positive potentiality of chance with the Laplacian determinism that leaves no room for human free will.

40. Balzac, "Avant-propos" (1842), *La Comédie humaine* 1:11.

41. Gérard Genette comments on these "pseudo-determinations" in "Vraisemblance et motivation," *Figures II,* 82–84.

42. Flaubert, Letter to René de Maricourt, *Correspondance* 3:587.

43. Mitterand, *L'Illusion réaliste,* 1.

44. See Auerbach, *Mimesis,* 491; Lukács, *The Meaning of Contemporary Realism,* 34.

45. Proust, *À la recherche du temps perdu* 1:43–44.

46. Breton, *L'Amour fou,* in *Œuvres complètes* 2:691.

47. Sarraute, *L'Ère du soupçon.*

48. See Barthes, *Le Degré zéro de l'écriture,* in *Œuvres complètes* 1:190. According to Barthes, narrative embodies the logical fallacy known as *post hoc ergo propter hoc,* conflating temporal succession and necessity.

49. "Le temps devient humain dans la mesure où il est articulé de manière

narrative; en retour le récit est significatif dans la mesure où il dessine les traits de l'expérience temporelle" (Time becomes human time to the extent that it is organized after the manner of a narrative; narrative, in turn, is meaningful to the extent that it portrays the features of temporal experience). Ricoeur, *Temps et récit* 1:17; *Time and Narrative,* trans. McLaughlin and Pellauer, 1:3. See also Kermode, *The Sense of an Ending,* 35.

50. Baudelaire, "Salon de 1846," in *Écrits sur l'art,* 155–56. Baudelaire is responding here to those who attribute Delacroix's greatness to the "god of chance."

51. Mallarmé, "Crise de vers," in *Œuvres complètes* 2:208.

52. Ibid., 2:213.

53. Plato's dialogue presents two opposing points of view of language (conceived of here as a nomenclature): Cratylus believes that each thing possesses a natural and correct name; Hermogenes claims that names are determined by convention (Plato, *Cratylus,* in *Dialogues,* 383–84). Significantly, Cratylus argues that names must resemble things because "representation by likeness [. . .] is infinitely better than representation by any chance sign" (434).

54. Milner, "Hasard et langage," 44.

55. Saussure, *Cours de linguistique générale,* 104.

56. Ibid., 127. Others, including Roman Jakobson, refuse to accept Saussure's view of language change as unsystematic (Cercle Linguistique de Prague, "Les thèses de 1929," 8).

57. Mallarmé insists that poetry would not exist were it not for the "perversity" of ordinary language. According to Milner, neither would linguistics: it is the underlying chance dimension of language that allows the articulation of rules (Milner, "Hasard et langage," 46).

58. Mallarmé, "Crise de vers," in *Œuvres complétes* 2:213.

59. Tzara advises cutting up a newspaper article, shaking up the words in a bag, and then drawing them out at random. Tzara, "Pour faire une poème dadaïste" (1920), in *Sept Manifestes Dada,* 64.

60. Pataphysics is defined in Jarry's *Gestes et opinions du Docteur Faustroll* (1898) as "the science of imaginary solutions," and as a science not of the general but of the particular, the exceptional, and the accidental (*Œuvres complètes* 1:669). Established in 1948 (forty years after Jarry's death), the "Collège de 'Pataphysique" included among its members Eugène Ionesco, Jacques Prévert, and Boris Vian, and by 1960, three members of the future Oulipo: Raymond Queneau, Latis, and Noël Arnaud (see Braffort, "Oulipo et 'Pataphysique," 57). Dossier 17 of the *Cahiers du Collège de 'Pataphysique* (December 22, 1961) contains a presentation of some of the Oulipo's first constraints.

61. See Oulipo, *La Littérature potentielle,* 7; Queneau, "La Littérature potentielle," in *Bâtons, chiffres et lettres,* 322.

62. Arnaud, "Twenty questions for Noël Arnaud," 302.

63. Oulipo, *Atlas de littérature potentielle,* 431.

64. Critics sometimes argue that the Oulipo's poetics is a form of neoclassicism (see Lapprand, *Poétique de l'Oulipo,* 154; Burgelin, "Quelques remarques sur le sujet oulipien en guise de préface," in Bénabou, *Un art simple et tout d'exécution,* 12). However, while neoclassicism claims that its rules have normative value, the Oulipo tends to emphasize the arbitrary nature of the constraint. See Marcel Bénabou, "La Règle et la contrainte," 101–6.

65. See Michelle Grangaud's transformation of Du Bellay sonnets into haikus in "D'une petite haie, si possible belle, aux regrets" (*La Bibliothèque oulipienne* 6:75–111), and Jacques Roubaud's use of the tanka in the poetry collections *Mono no aware* and *Trente et un au cube.*

66. Arnaud, "Twenty questions," 300.

67. Bens, *OuLiPo 1960–63,* 136.

68. Robin, *Le Deuil de l'origine,* 235.

69. Barthes, "Introduction à l'analyse structurale des récits" (1966), in *Œuvres complètes* 2:841.

70. Bellos, *Georges Perec,* 363. The PALF procedure, otherwise known as "littérature sémo-définitionnelle" (LSD), consists in substituting for each "signifying" word its definition, or rather one of its definitions, in a dictionary and then repeating this operation a number of times. Bénabou and Perec claimed they could eventually transform, through successive stages, any phrase in the French language into any other.

71. Perec, "Queneau et après" (1980), in *Entretiens et conférences* 2:149.

72. See, for example, Jacques Jouet's account of his arrival in the group shortly after Perec's death (Oulipo, *Moments oulipiens,* 84).

73. The manuscripts reveal supplementary constraints that govern the order of the poem sequence. See Mireille Ribière, "Alphabets déchiffré."

74. A "beau présent" is a poem that uses only the letters of the addressee's name, whereas in a "belle absente," "each line of the poem includes all the letters of the alphabet except for the letter appearing in the dedicated name at the position corresponding to that of the line" (Mathews and Brotchie, *Oulipo Compendium,* 56).

Chapter 1

The chapter epigraph is from Nietzsche, *The Gay Science,* 258.

1. Joyce, *Ulysses,* 42.
2. Benjamin, "Theses on the Philosophy of History," in *Illuminations,* 257–58.
3. Judt, *Past Imperfect,* 1.
4. Ibid., 244.
5. Sartre, *Critique de la raison dialectique,* 36, 72.
6. Ibid., 78.
7. See Judt, *Marxism and the French Left,* 188.

8. Founded in 1956 by Edgar Morin, Henri Lefebvre, and Jean Duvignaud, the *Arguments* group also involved François Fejto, Roland Barthes, Kostas Axelos, and Pierre Fougeyrollas. Duvignaud had been Perec's philosophy teacher at the Collège Geoffroy-Saint-Hilaire in Étampes (Duvignaud, *Perec ou la cicatrice,* 27; Judt, *Marxism and the French Left,* 189).

9. See Bellos, *Georges Perec,* 205–8. Eisenstein's *General Line* (*Staroye i novoye,* 1929), also known by the title *The Old and the New,* deals with a peasant woman's struggle to promote collective action and the sharing of resources in a poor rural community. (Not accidentally, the making of the film coincided with the implementation of Stalin's policy of collectivization of farms.)

10. In *Marxism and the French Left,* Tony Judt offers harsh criticism of the various postwar maneuverings of Sartre, Leiris, Merleau-Ponty, and others in relation to official PCF dogma.

11. Bénabou, "Présentation," *Cahiers Georges Perec* 3 (1989): 8. Bénabou identifies Lukács as the group's dominant intellectual influence.

12. Bellos, *Georges Perec,* 275.

13. These articles are now included in Perec, *L.G.:Une aventure des années soixante.* All translations of this text are my own.

14. A glance at Roland Barthes's articles from this period shows that the "reactionary" nature of the New Novel was a point of debate in leftist circles. In an article published in *Clarté* in 1961, Roland Barthes initially defends Robbe-Grillet's texts by asserting that all literature is necessarily "ontologically" reactionary, because representation involves the construction of essences. Barthes nevertheless goes on to criticize as "ideologically" reactionary Robbe-Grillet's decision to collaborate with Alain Resnais on the film *L'Année dernière à Marienbad,* since the film constructs a universe and a story (Barthes, "Témoignage sur Robbe-Grillet," in *Œuvres complètes* 1:1117).

15. Lukács's *Meaning of Contemporary Realism* appeared in French translation in 1960, under the title *La Signification présente du réalisme critique* (Gallimard).

16. "While traditional realism transforms the positive and negative elements of bourgeois life into 'typical' situations and reveals them for what they are, modernism exalts bourgeois life's very baseness and emptiness with its aesthetic devices" (Lukács, *The Meaning of Contemporary Realism,* 68).

17. "In socialist society the individual will enjoy greater freedom to choose a place for himself in society than under capitalism ('freedom' being understood here, of course, as conscious acceptance of historical necessity—a necessity which subsumes much that is apparently arbitrary)" (ibid., 112).

18. Judt, *Marxism and the French Left,* 174.

19. In defense of Perec, it is worth noting that Antelme's text itself emphasizes the problem of moral survival. See chapter 2, notes 25 and 26.

20. Sartre, "La République du silence," in *Situations III,* 11–13.

21. David Bellos has pointed out that this envoi (beginning "le moyen fait par-

tie de la vérité, aussi bien que le résultat"—the means is as much part of the truth as the result) is in fact not taken directly from Marx but is "an overlay of linguistic transformations." Perec found it translated from Russian into French in Eisenstein's *Réflexions d'un cinéaste,* while Eisenstein was quoting the Russian translation of Marx's German (Bellos, "'Le Moyen fait partie de la vérité . . .' The Languages of Georges Perec's *Les Choses,*" 326–28).

22. For a detailed account of this reception see Schilling, *Mémoires du quotidien,* 71–75. One notable example of a sociological reading of *Les Choses* can be found in the conclusion to Jean Baudrillard's 1968 book on consumer culture, *Le Système des objets,* 278–81.

23. *Les Choses* contains direct borrowings from *L'Éducation sentimentale,* for example the nostalgic episode at the end of the novel, initiated by Jérôme's question "Te souviens-tu?" (Do you remember?) (*Les Choses,* 156; see also Perec, "Emprunts à Flaubert"). Perec also strives to adopt the "passionate coldness" characteristic of Flaubert's style (Perec, *Entretiens et conférences* 1:48). Both authors emphasize the gap that separates the individual's life from the dramatic developments of history; in this respect, the Algerian War plays the same role in *Les Choses* as the 1848 Revolution does in *L'Éducation sentimentale.*

24. Mathews, "Georges Perec," in *The Case of the Persevering Maltese,* 272.

25. The epigraph, taken from the English text of Malcolm Lowry's *Under the Volcano,* begins: "Incalculable are the benefits civilization has brought us," but ends with the suggestion that this "new life [. . .] still remains closed to the thirsty lips of the people who follow in their griping and bestial tasks" (Perec, *Les Choses,* 7). While the reference to progress can be read as ironic, a further layer of irony is added, as David Bellos has noted, by the original context of the passage. In Lowry's novel, this is "a simulated word-for-word translation," in an odd hybrid English, of a political speech in Mexican Spanish (Bellos, "'Le Moyen fait partie de la vérité . . .'," 326).

26. Camus, *Le Mythe de Sisyphe,* 164.

27. Beckett's *L'Innommable* ends with the sequence: "Il faut continuer, je ne peux pas continuer, je vais continuer" (213) (I must go on, I can't go on, I will go on).

28. Sartre, *La Nausée,* 180–92.

29. Pedersen, *Perec ou les textes croisés.*

30. Proust, *À la recherche du temps perdu,* 1:5. In its original context, near the beginning of "Combray," Proust's phrase suggests the infinite potentialities of memory rather than a will to power. However, once invoked by Perec's title and read in relation to the themes of *Un homme qui dort,* it takes on an altered meaning and, as Claude Burgelin points out, expresses the protagonist's dream of mastery (Burgelin, *Georges Perec,* 62).

31. As John Pedersen points out, the reconnection with the world occurs through the intermediary of texts, since a montage of quotations (from Melville, Joyce, and Kafka, among others) constitutes the work's final pages. He reads this

as a metatextual commentary on Perec's own evolution—the move away from the effort to master history and toward the construction of an image of the world based on intertextuality ("Histoires *per* excellence," 137). However, we should note that intertextual allusions are all construed negatively in *Un homme qui dort;* it is unclear what image they can construct.

32. Dana, *Fictions pour mémoire,* 129.

33. Perec, *La Clôture,* no. 5.

34. Rosset, *Le Réel,* 13.

35. Paul Valéry sees this powerlessness in the face of infinite combinations as the essence of the notion of chance: "L'homme à appelé *Hasard* la cause de toutes les surprises, la divinité sans visage qui préside à tous les espoirs insensés, à toutes les craintes sans mesure, qui déjoue les calculs les plus soigneux, qui change les imprudences en décisions heureuses, les plus grands hommes en jouets, les dés et les monnaies en oracles; qui fait les batailles comparables à des *parties*" (Mankind has called *Chance* the cause of all surprises, the faceless divinity which presides over all senseless hopes, over all measureless fears, which foils the most careful calculations, which changes reckless acts into happy decisions, the greatest men into puppets, dice and coins into oracles; which makes battles comparable to *games*). Valéry, *Cahiers* 1:1305.

36. I use *tactics* here in the sense defined by Michel de Certeau: unlike strategy, which is a calculation of power relationships that becomes possible when an autonomous subject can be isolated from an environment, tactics is a calculation that cannot rely upon this autonomous space, nor on a boundary that makes the other visible as a distinct whole (Certeau, *L'Invention du quotidien* 1:20–21).

Chapter 2

The chapter epigraph is from Montaigne, *Essais,* bk. 3, essay 8, p. 148 ; trans. Frame, 713.

1. To avoid any confusion between these sections, I will maintain the roman/italics distinction of the original in my quotations of *W.* In Perec's book, both texts are interrupted by the ellipses ("points de suspension") that follow chapter 11. This point marks a shift in both narratives: in the fictional text, Gaspard Winckler's first-person narration gives way to the third-person description of the island of W; in the autobiographical text, the division follows Perec's account of his separation from his mother and his departure for the unoccupied zone.

2. The break in the middle of the adventure story leaves the young Gaspard Winckler's fate uncertain, as the quest ends in a shipwreck but the child's body is not recovered. The older Gaspard's personal experiences on the island of W are not recounted, although we know that his quest for his namesake led him there (Perec, *W,* 13).

3. Aristotle defines the notion of "justice in distribution" as a justice which must accord with some kind of worth (*Nicomachean Ethics,* 1131a–b). It is distinct from "justice in rectification," which looks only at differences in the degree of harm inflicted, and treats the people involved as equals (1131b–1132b).

4. Caillois, *Les Jeux et les hommes,* 154.

5. Ibid., 306–7.

6. For Caillois, the principles of *agon* and *alea* are not purely ludic but express particular values. They also develop alongside each other in a particular historical context, where their association both reflects and resists social and economic developments (ibid., 223). Here, Caillois' initial insistence on the division between the play sphere and "real life" (7) begins to break down.

7. Camus, *L'Étranger,* 154–55; *The Stranger,* trans. Ward, 111.

8. Deleuze and Guattari, *Kafka: Pour une littérature mineure,* 90. The subject of *The Trial* is precisely the confrontation between the individual and an implacable but arbitrary law. Joanna Spiro, in her article "The Testimony of Fantasy in Georges Perec's *W ou le souvenir d'enfance,*" compares *W* to Kafka's "In the Penal Colony."

9. Plato, *Republic,* 460a.

10. Perec, *W,* 187; Plato, *Republic,* 468c, 413, 460c.

11. Plato, *Republic,* 389, 459.

12. Anne Roche points out that the W universe can also be associated with the utopias imagined in the eighteenth century by Sade, Marivaux, and Rousseau (Roche, "Souvenir d'enfance," 28).

13. Mouillard-Fraisse, "Cherchez Angus. *W:* Une réécriture multiple"; Bouchot, "L'Intertextualité vernienne dans *W ou le souvenir d'enfance.*"

14. In an interview with Alain Hervé in 1978, Perec responds to a mention of Borges's text: "Oui, oui, sur le hasard devenu nécessité ou la nécessité déguisée en hasard. Le hasard sanctionné devient nécessité et, en fait, est manipulé par les maîtres du jeu" (*Entretiens et conférences* 1:280) (Yes, yes, on chance become necessity or necessity disguised as chance. Sanctioned chance becomes necessity and is, in fact, manipulated by the masters of the game). Even if the interview in question focuses on *La Vie mode d'emploi,* the relevance of this comment to *W ou le souvenir d'enfance* is clear. Perec mentions Borges as a source of inspiration on numerous other occasions (*Entretiens et conférences,* 1:49, 144, 280; 2:77, 78, 306; "Histoire du lipogramme," 74; *Penser/Classer,* 164). *La Disparition* paraphrases part of Borges's story "The Zahir," adopting the title word to refer to the missing letter (Perec, *La Disparition,* 134–35). Borges is also one of the sources of "preprogrammed" quotations in *La Vie mode d'emploi* (the Borges stories listed in the *Cahier des charges* are "Tlon, Uqbar, Orbis Tertius," "The Garden of Forking Paths," "The Circular Ruins," "Death and the Compass," and texts from *A Universal History of Infamy*).

15. Borges, "The Lottery in Babylon," in *Collected Fictions,* 103.

16. Ibid.

17. Ibid., 104.

18. Ibid.

19. Arendt, *Eichmann in Jerusalem,* 11–12.

20. Simone de Beauvoir's preface to Steiner's book begins by citing the question "Pourquoi les Juifs se sont-ils laissé mener à l'abattoir comme des moutons?" (Why did the Jews allow themselves to be led to the abattoir like sheep?) before arguing that the story of the Treblinka uprising allowed Steiner to recover his pride (Steiner, *Treblinka,* 5, 6).

21. Moyn, *A Holocaust Controversy,* 4–5, 143–45, 39; Rousso, *Le Syndrôme de Vichy,* 189–90.

22. Moyn, *A Holocaust Controversy,* 11.

23. *Les Dieux du stade* is the French title used for Leni Riefenstahl's film of the 1936 Berlin Olympics, *Olympia: Fest der Völker, Fest der Schönheit.* In a conversation with Eugen Helmle in 1975, Perec refers to this film as "une des premières images qui pour moi rassemble le monde nazi et le monde du sport" (*Entretiens et conférences* 1:193) (one of the first images which brings together for me the Nazi world and the world of sport). The association between concentration camps and sport also appears in one of Perec's dream narratives, "Camp de concentration sous la neige ou Sports d'hiver au camp" (*La Boutique obscure,* no. 46, January 1971) ("Concentration Camp in the Snow or Winter Sports in the Camp").

24. Rousset, *L'Univers concentrationnaire,* 105.

25. "Plus on est contesté en tant qu'homme par le SS, plus on a de chances d'être confirmé comme tel. Le véritable risque que l'on court, c'est celui de se mettre à haïr le copain d'envie, d'être trahi par la concupiscence, d'abandonner les autres." (The more our condition as men is contested by the SS, the more likely our chances of being confirmed as such. The real risk we run is that of starting to hate another guy out of envy, of being betrayed by our longings, of abandoning others.) Antelme, *L'Espèce humaine,* 101; *The Human Race,* trans. Haight and Mahler, 96.

26. Although Perec does not refer directly to Primo Levi, the latter also emphasizes the importance of "moral survival" in an environment where "all are enemies or rivals," and where the threat to human conscience and personality is even greater than the threat to life (Levi, *Survival in Auschwitz,* 40, 42, 55).

27. In general, Perec's points of reference are concentration camp accounts by French political deportees (Robert Antelme in the "Ligne générale" articles, David Rousset in *W*), not those by Jewish Holocaust survivors. Many critics are disturbed by this, pointing out that Perec blurs the boundaries between forced labor camps and extermination camps. See, for example, Molkou and Robin, "De l'arbre à l'herbier: L'histoire pulvérisée," 92. Dan Stone even states that "what we are faced with in Perec's lionization of Antelme is a Holocaust without Jews" ("Perec's Antelme," 170). However, the universalizing tendency that we find in Perec is typical of the initial responses to the Holocaust, such as Alain Resnais' 1955 film *Nuit et brouillard* (*Night and Fog*). Samuel Moyn points out that the distinc-

tion between concentration and extermination camps gradually came to receive emphasis only after the *Treblinka* affair of 1966 (Moyn, *A Holocaust Controversy,* 158). However, if Perec's essay on Antelme does avoid the question of Jewish victims, this is clearly not the case in *W.* Besides, whatever the shortcomings of Perec's universalism, it is not clear that all forms of generalization and analogy based on specific historical events should automatically be condemned.

28. Montfrans, *Georges Perec: La contrainte du réel,* 225. The totalitarian ruler, according to Arendt, "is confronted with a dual task which at first appears contradictory to the point of absurdity: he must establish the fictitious world of the movement as a tangible working reality of everyday life, and he must, on the other hand, prevent this new world from developing a new stability; for a stabilization of its laws and institutions would surely liquidate the movement itself and with it the hope for eventual world conquest" (Arendt, *The Origins of Totalitarianism,* 391).

29. Hartje, "*W* et l'histoire," 53–66. Jacques Lecarme argues that Perec treats as a "faute originelle" the childhood passion for sport which, while the author was between the ages of nine and fourteen, found expression in the drawings of athletes that later became the starting point for *W* (Lecarme, "La Page des sports," 41).

30. Perec comments on these connections between sporting venues and violence in a 1979 interview (*Entretiens et conférences* 2:60). Robert Misrahi reads *W* as an interpretation and condemnation of the Munich Olympics attack (Misrahi, "*W,* un roman réflexif," 86).

31. Borges, "The Lottery in Babylon," in *Collected Fictions,* 106.

32. Anne Roche rightly emphasizes the complexity of the W fiction, and suggests that it can be read as a metaphor of the potential inhumanity of all society (Roche, "'*W ou le souvenir d'enfance,*'" 145).

33. Viegnes, "L'Imaginaire des jeux de hasard dans la littérature européenne," 225.

34. In an earlier, unpublished version of the novel, "La Grande Aventure," Jérôme and Sylvie plan a burglary but fail to carry it out (see Bellos, *Georges Perec,* 294).

35. Lefebvre, *Critique de la vie quotidienne* 1:131.

36. Moscovici, "Le Hasard du sens commun," 15.

37. The reference to roulette in this chapter is not "preprogrammed" by the novel's *Cahier des charges,* but the constraints do contain the category "games and toys." Games of chance appear in the form of the constraint "dés, osselets" (dice, jacks). We find three games which combine chance and skill: cards, dominos, and backgammon. The list also includes, as one element, "Go, chess, checkers." It could be said of this trio that "le hasard y est exclu, sauf dans les mécanismes psychologiques des joueurs" (Lusson, Perec, and Roubaud, *Petit Traité invitant à la découverte de l'art subtil du go,* 21–22) (chance is excluded, except in the psychological mechanisms of the players). The remaining games in the list are more solitary games of skill: solitaire, crossword puzzles, and the jigsaw puzzle (*Cahier des charges,* "tableau général des listes").

38. Sylvie Rosienski-Pellerin compares these solitary games to the narrative strategy of *Un homme qui dort:* despite appearances, pinball does not establish a dialogue with the player; despite the use of the second person, the reader cannot enter into dialogue with the text (*Perecgrinations ludiques,* 181).

39. Nietzsche, *On the Genealogy of Morals,* 97.

40. As Caillois points out, the person who cheats does not in fact destroy the game: "The one who ruins [games] is the naysayer who denounces the absurdity of the rules, their purely conventional nature, and who refuses to play because the game has no meaning." Caillois, *Les Jeux et les hommes,* 38.

41. Dangy-Scaillierez, *L'Énigme criminelle dans les romans de Georges Perec,* 222.

42. Huizinga, *Homo ludens,* 52, 198. Huizinga tends to insist on the importance of contest, yet also seems to see chance as an essential element in the definition of play. For example, he claims that the play mood has little scope in such games as chess, checkers, and backgammon, where "chance is at a minimum" (198). Caillois reproaches Huizinga for excluding chance (*Les Jeux et les hommes,* 34), but he himself establishes a hierarchy of play principles in which the "passive" *alea* (chance) and *ilinx* (vertigo, dizziness) are morally subordinate to the active, creative values of *mimicry* and *agon* (326). Jean Duvignaud, who disapproves of Huizinga's and Caillois' obsession with rules, blames the spirit of positivism and market economics for repressing the idea of chance in contemporary thought, and identifies his own idea of "play" with "free play without rules" (Duvignaud, *Le Jeu du jeu,* 14–15). From an Oulipian standpoint, however, Duvignaud's idea that freedom comes from the absence of rules might seem naive.

43. Freud, *Beyond the Pleasure Principle,* 10–11; Huizinga, *Homo ludens,* 198.

44. Moscovici, "Le Hasard du sens commun," 12.

45. Jean-François Chassay sees François de Dinteville's explanation as a reference to positivist attitudes, given that Laurelle's death is due "entirely to chance" (Chassay, *Le Jeu des coïncidences,* 97). However, the problem with the causal explanation for Laurelle's death, as I see it, is not that the chance nature of the event makes it essentially inexplicable, but that the (perfectly valid) explanation is, in itself, of no interest whatsoever. We expect causes to be equal to their effects.

46. *Le Grand Robert de la langue française* (1992) gives four definitions for *fatalité:* "caractère de ce qui est fatal" (the character of what is fatal); "force naturelle ou surnaturelle par laquelle, selon certaines doctrines, tout ce qui arrive est déterminé d'avance d'une manière inévitable" (natural or supernatural force by which, according to certain doctrines, all that happens is determined in advance in an inevitable manner); "nécessité, détermination"; "suite de coïncidences inexpliquées qui semblent manifester une finalité supérieure et inconnue et, plus spécialement, série persistante de malheurs" (sequence of unexplained coincidences which seem to manifest a higher and unknown finality and, more specifically, a persistent series of misfortunes). Flaubert's *Dictionnaire des idées reçues* (*Dictionary of Received Ideas*) glosses *fatalité* as a "mot exclusivement romantique" (*Bouvard et Pécuchet,*

351) (an exclusively romantic word). *Fatalité* appears as a cliché in Perec's play *La Poche Parmentier:* "Moi je suis une jeune fille pure. La fatalité seule m'a accablée" (Perec, *Théâtre I,* 105) (I am a pure young girl. Fate alone overpowered me).

47. Bergson, *Les Deux Sources,* 154–55.

48. Popper, *Objective Knowledge,* 206–55; *The Open Universe,* 18–27.

49. The word *sort,* in this case, signifies a treatment reserved for a particular person or social class (Robert, s.v. "sort," def.1).

50. According to Jewish medieval legends, a man made of earth could be animated by writing the word *emet* (truth) on his forehead, but destroyed by erasing the first letter of the word (*aleph*), to leave the word *met* (dead). The most famous version of the legend is the story of Rabbi Loew of Prague, who created a golem to serve him but was forced to restore it to dust when it began to endanger people's lives (Scholem, *Kabbalah,* 353–54). The golem legend became a favorite literary subject in nineteenth-century German literature, and later in modern Hebrew and Jewish literature.

51. Diderot, *Œuvres,* 483.

Chapter 3

The chapter epigraph is from Camus, *L'Étranger,* 135; *The Stranger,* trans. Ward, 95.

1. The "Compendium," as Perec baptizes it (*Entretiens et conférences* 2:98), is ostensibly an enumeration of all the characters that Valène intends to include in his painting, but it is also a summary of stories already told or to be told in future chapters of Perec's novel. The list obeys strict constraints: each line contains sixty typographical characters (including spaces and apostrophes), and the lines are presented in eighteen groups of ten (with the exception of the last group, which contains nine lines). In turn, the groups are divided into three sections of six groups each. Less apparent is the constraint that inscribes the letters of the word *âme* (soul) in a right-to-left, top-to-bottom diagonal, one letter for each section.

2. In *Espèces d'espaces,* Perec muses on the function of doors: "La porte casse l'espace, le scinde, interdit l'osmose, impose le cloisonnement: d'un côté, il y a moi et mon chez-moi, le privé, le domestique [. . .], de l'autre côté, il y a les autres, le monde, le public, le politique" (The door breaks space in two, splits it, prevents osmosis, imposes a partition. On one side, me and *my place,* the private, the domestic [. . .]; on the other side, other people, the world, the public, politics) (*Espèces d'espaces,* 73; *Species of Spacies,* trans. Sturrock, 37).

3. "'The king died and then the queen died' is a story. 'The king died, and then the queen died of grief' is a plot. The time-sequence is preserved, but the sense of causality overshadows it." Forster claims that a story requires only curiosity of its reader, and is only worthy of "a gaping audience of cave-men" who can be kept awake by "And then— and then— " (Forster, *Aspects of the Novel,* 60).

4. Barthes, "Introduction à l'analyse structurale des récits," in *Œuvres complètes* 2:840–41.

5. Genette, "Vraisemblance et motivation," in *Figures II,* 94.

6. Ibid., 97.

7. Hamon, "Un discours contraint," in Genette and Todorov, *Littérature et réalité,* 136.

8. Flaubert criticizes René de Maricourt's novel *La Veuve* because the female protagonist's actions are not sufficiently justified; events are not inevitably derived from characters (Flaubert, *Correspondance,* 3:587).

9. Camus, *L'Étranger,* 125, 135, 141.

10. "Un homme, c'est toujours un conteur d'histoires, il vit entouré de ses histoires et des histoires d'autrui, il voit tout ce qui lui arrive à travers elles; et il cherche à vivre sa vie comme s'il la racontait" (Sartre, *La Nausée,* 64) (A man is always a storyteller, he lives surrounded by his own stories and the stories of others, he sees everything that happens to him through them; and he attempts to live his life as if he were narrating it).

11. Ibid., 64–65.

12. Barthes, *Le Degré zéro de l'écriture,* in *Œuvres complètes* 1:190; "Introduction à l'analyse structurale des récits," in *Œuvres complètes* 2:841.

13. "Je propose [. . .] de nommer *histoire* le signifié ou contenu narratif [. . .], *récit* proprement dit le signifiant, énoncé, discours ou texte narratif lui-même, et *narration* l'acte narratif producteur et, par extension, l'ensemble de la situation réelle ou fictive dans laquelle il prend place" (Genette, "Discours du récit," in *Figures III,* 72) (I propose to call *story* the signified or narrative content, *narrative* strictly speaking the signifier, utterance, discourse, or narrative text itself, and *narration* the productive narrative act and, by extension, the whole of the real or fictive situation in which it is placed).

14. Nelson, *Causality and Narrative in French Fiction from Zola to Robbe-Grillet,* 94–95.

15. Genette, "Vraisemblance et motivation," *Figures II,* 84.

16. Tiphaine Samoyault contrasts the closed structure of the collector's world, in Perec's works, with the open world of the flaneur or the archeologist, and sees both forms as modes of a "melancholy apprehension of the world" (Samoyault, "Le Collectionneur," 94). Madame Marcia's chaotic approach to collecting makes her an exception, and allows her to live in a world that is at once open and closed—a way, perhaps, of escaping melancholy.

17. I disagree with Sabine Hillen's assertion that the word *hasard* is not often explicit in Perec's works (Hillen, "Mode d'emploi du hasard," 71). In *La Vie mode d'emploi* alone, I counted twenty-nine occurrences of the word *hasard;* this is without including the very frequent occurrences of other, semantically related words (*coïncidence, aléatoire,* etc.), which just as explicitly conjure up the notion of chance. *La Disparition* contains more than fifty references to chance.

18. Aristotle, *Poetics,* 1452a. As Paul Ricoeur argues, Aristotle presents us with a structural model that can to some extent be detached from its initial tragic context and applied to narrative organization in general (Ricoeur, *Temps et récit* 1:56).

19. Reggiani, "Amours et naufrages," 34.

20. The *Poetics* emphasizes the importance of this element of the story—the passage from ignorance to knowledge which is accompanied, ideally, by a *peripeteia* (1452a). Terence Cave has shown that Aristotle concentrates on cases of obscured identity; similarly, in Renaissance commentary on Aristotle, recognition is recognition of persons. The term has nevertheless drifted away from this origin in more recent critical practice (see Cave, *Recognitions,* 34–35, 63, 221). Although recognition of persons does occur in *La Vie mode d'emploi,* I use the term *anagnorisis* in a more general sense, to mean recognition of any state of affairs.

21. Ricoeur, *Temps et récit* 1:74; *Time and Narrative,* trans. McLaughlin and Pellauer, 1:44.

22. Cave, *Recognitions,* 2.

23. Ibid., 9, 3.

24. Ibid., 368.

25. These encounters are partially "preprogrammed," since the constraint "receive a letter" is one of the elements of the "[plot] mainspring" list in the *Cahier des charges,* and "read or write" appears in the "activity" category.

26. We never discover, for example, who is the father of Célia Crespi's child (*La Vie mode d'emploi,* 497), or the name of the old woman who owned a dog named Dodéca (164, 200). In this, we share Valène's ignorance.

27. Hillen, "Mode d'emploi du hasard," 70–71.

28. Ibid., 71.

29. Reggiani, "Amours et naufrages," 42.

30. More specifically, Zola's *Pot-Bouille* can be seen as one of Perec's literary models, since it also has a Parisian apartment building as its setting (see Jullien, "Portrait de l'artiste en mille morceaux," 394–96).

31. "Wherever Greek adventure-time appears in the subsequent development of the European novel, initiative is handed over to chance, which controls meetings and failures to meet—either as an impersonal, anonymous force in the novel or as fate, as divine foresight, as romantic 'villains' or romantic 'secret benefactors.'" Bakhtin, "Forms of Time and on the Chronotope in the Novel," in *The Dialogic Imagination,* 95.

32. Motte, *The Poetics of Experiment,* 130. Perec refers to these works in his 1967 talk on "Écriture et mass-media," emphasizing their playful use of discontinuous narrative (Perec, *Entretiens et conférences* 1:103).

33. According to Daniel Couégnas, narrative prolixity is one of the characteristic traits of the paraliterary model (*Introduction à la paralittérature,* 145–46). Paraliterary works are dominated by narrative and by the hermeneutic code, with effects of suspense playing an essential role (150); their characters are only superfi-

cially realistic (182). Many of the stories and characters of *La Vie mode d'emploi* fit this account. Other aspects of Perec's writing, however—its parodic elements, its self-consciousness, and the role of description—distance it from the paraliterary model as defined by Couégnas (*Introduction à la paralittérature,* 182).

34. Pavel, *La Pensée du roman,* 395.

35. Perec, *La Poche Parmentier,* in *Théâtre I,* 105.

36. Mozart's *Don Giovanni* features in the plot of *La Disparition:* Douglas Haig dies during a performance of the opera, in which he is singing the role of the Commandant (105–6). Ali Magoudi argues that this episode, by leaving Don Giovanni triumphant over Donna Anna's father, reverses the dialectic of the tragedy and leaves parricide triumphant (Magoudi, *La Lettre fantôme,* 82–83).

37. Mathews, "That Ephemeral Thing," in *The Case of the Persevering Maltese,* 293.

38. Clément Rosset, who associates necessity and chance, also argues that the comic and the tragic are "in some ways the two complementary aspects of a single human reality grasped in the intuition of necessity." Rosset, *Le Monde et ses remèdes,* 23.

39. Duquesne, *"Les Choses" de Georges Perec,* 40–41, 82.

40. Ibid., 109. This is perhaps even truer of *Les Choses* than of *L'Éducation sentimentale,* for the latter does have moments of dramatic tension and turning points (Frédéric's recognition of Sénécal, for example).

41. Béhar, *Georges Perec: Écrire pour ne pas dire,* 34.

42. Pedersen, "Histoires *per* excellence," 136.

43. "Récit rétrospectif en prose qu'une personne réelle fait de sa propre existence, lorsqu'elle met l'accent sur sa vie individuelle, en particulier sur l'histoire de sa personnalité" (Lejeune, *Le Pacte autobiographique,* 14) (Retrospective narrative in prose that an actual person makes of his or her own experience, with an emphasis on his or her individual life, in particular the history of his or her personality).

44. Roubaud, *La Boucle,* 163.

45. Lejeune, *La Mémoire et l'oblique,* 65.

46. Magné, "L'autobiotexte perecquien," 6.

47. Bem, "La Mémoire, l'écriture et l'impossible à dire," 38.

48. Perec claims, in an interview with Jean-Marie Le Sidaner, that *Je me souviens* is a project of collective autobiography (*Entretiens et conférences* 2:95). However, Jacques-Denis Bertharion has shown that numerous references to Perec's personal memories are also encrypted in the text (Bertharion, "*Je me souviens:* un cryptogramme autobiographique," 81).

49. Perec, *Je me souviens,* back cover.

50. Noting Perec's mistrust of memory, Claude Burgelin goes so far as to call him the "anti-Proust" (*Les Parties de dominos chez Monsieur Lefèvre,* 73).

51. Philippe Lejeune argues that *W* is a fragmented autobiography ("Une autobiographie sous contrainte," 19).

52. Magné, "Les Sutures dans *W ou le souvenir d'enfance.*"

53. In a conference paper on "Écriture et mass-media" (1967), Perec describes *Melmoth the Wanderer* as an important model of discontinuous narrative (*Entretiens et conférences* 1:103).

54. As Marc Angenot points out, between 1822 and 1825 Balzac wrote such works as the "gothic" novel *Clotilde de Lusignan,* and the "noir" novels *Le Vicaire des Ardennes* and *Le Centenaire* (Angenot, *Le Roman populaire,* 44).

55. Tryphiodorus is in fact the name of a real person—a fifth-century writer who produced a lipogrammatic version of the *Odyssey,* in each book of which one particular letter of the alphabet did not appear (Curtius, *European Literature and the Latin Middle Ages,* 283).

Chapter 4

The chapter epigraph is from Perec, *La Disparition,* 75; *A Void,* trans. Adair, 59.

1. The same expression occurs in Perec's short monovocalic text "What a man": "Passant par là, pas par hasard" (in Oulipo, *Atlas de littérature potentielle,* 215) (passing by, not by chance).

2. Genette, "Discours du récit," *Figures III,* 245.

3. This episode is generated by Raymond Roussel's phrase "Les lettres ['signes typographiques'] du blanc ['craie'] sur les bandes ['bordures'] du vieux billard" (The white letters on the cushions of the old billiard table) which along with its homophonic counterpart "Les lettres ['missives'] du blanc ['homme blanc'] sur les bandes ['hordes guerrières'] du vieux pillard" (The letters of the white man about the hordes of the old plunderer) provided the beginning and ending concepts for the story "Parmi les noirs" (Roussel, *Comment j'ai écrit certains de mes livres,* 11).

4. The reference to a "tapis aux motifs [. . .] confus" (a carpet with scrambled motifs) is one of the novel's several intertextual references to Henry James's "The Figure in the Carpet," in which the figure stands for the "exquisite scheme" that the writer Vereker claims is at work in all his books and that the narrator, a critic, struggles in vain to identify. At one point in James's story, the three characters who are seeking to uncover the secret are compared to "the grim gamblers at Monte Carlo"; eventually, an "extraordinary chain of accidents" keeps the narrator in the dark (James, *Selected Tales,* 290, 299, 312). In *La Disparition,* Voyl attempts to decipher the mysterious patterns in his rug (19–20), which recall both James's figure and Borges's "Aleph," a point in space that contains all other points.

5. Motte, "Eradications," 35. See also Motte, "Jeux mortels," 49.

6. Roubaud, "Hypothèses génétiques concernant la perecquation de la forme roman," 10.

7. Genette, "Vraisemblance et motivation," in *Figures II,* 94.

8. See, for example, Motte, "Jeux mortels."

9. Brooks, *Reading for the Plot,* 22.

10. Rosset, *Le Principe de cruauté,* 30.

11. Rosset, *Le Réel,* 14.

12. The elision of the article before the aspirated *h* of *hasard,* which occurs a few times in *La Disparition,* introduces wordplay between *le hasard* and *Lazare*—Lazarus, the man raised from the dead in the New Testament, but whose French name obviously could not appear in *La Disparition.* This supports the reading that chance is never fully abolished in Perec's works, but always resurfaces. It is also worth noting that the Resistance deportee Jean Cayrol used the adjective *lazaréen* (Lazarean) to evoke the experience of the concentration-camp survivor, but also more generally the nature of the world that emerged from this human catastrophe. Cayrol also argued for a "Lazarean art" born directly of the concentration-camp experience (Cayrol, *Lazare parmi nous,* 1950).

13. Todorov, "Typologie du roman policier," in *Poétique de la prose,* 55.

14. Ibid., 57.

15. François Le Lionnais explores the different possible combinations of roles, motivations, and actions in "Les structures du roman policier: Qui est le coupable?" (Oulipo, *La Littérature potentielle,* 62–65); Paul Fournel and Jacques Roubaud's "L'Hôtel de Sens" uses combinations of letters, read in different directions, to generate narrative elements that produce and then solve a mystery (*La Bibliothèque oulipienne* 1, no. 10); and in "Une chambre close," Jacques Jouet writes a story in which the murderer is a constraint, the sestina (*La Bibliothèque oulipienne* 6, no. 78). In 1973, Le Lionnais inaugurated the Ouvroir de littérature policière potentielle (Workshop for Potential Detective Literature), or Oulipopo, a group that is independent of the Oulipo but includes some of the same members and that began by "dissecting many known or possible combinations concerning situation and character in the mystery story" (Mathews and Brotchie, *Oulipo Compendium,* 253).

16. Ewert, "'A Thousand Other Mysteries,'" 182, 186.

17. Perec, *Les Revenentes,* in *Romans et récits,* 639; *The Exeter Text,* trans. Monk, 113.

18. Hillen, "Mode d'emploi du hasard," 64.

19. Brooks, *Reading for the Plot,* 269.

20. Poe, *Tales of Mystery and Imagination,* 473. As Raymond Queneau points out in his afterword to an edition of Poe's stories, Dupin's confidence is in fact misplaced since he propounds an unscientific theory of coincidence, suggesting that past dice throws will affect the outcome of future ones (Queneau, "Poe et l' 'Analyse,'" in *Bords,* 77).

21. Merivale and Sweeney, "The Game's Afoot," in *Detecting Texts,* 1.

22. Borges, "Death and the Compass," in *Collected Fictions,* 147–57.

23. Jullien, "Fiat lux," 147.

24. Ewert, "'A Thousand Other Mysteries,'"182.

25. The narrator of part 1 (the text designated *53 jours*) remains anonymous until a late point in the text, when the name Veyraud is mentioned once (*"53 jours,"* 113).

26. The sentence is a version of Stendhal's definition of the novel.

27. When discussing this novel I follow Perec's designation for each of the texts: *"53 jours"* is the title of Perec's novel as a whole; *53 jours,* without quotation marks, is the text within the text that constitutes the first part of the novel (the fiction narrated by Veyraud and, on the primary diegetic level, read by Salini). On yet another level, *La Crypte* is the text read and summarized by Veyraud in *53 jours,* and written by the Robert Serval who is a character in *53 jours.*

28. Sirvent, "Reader-Investigators in the Post-*Nouveau Roman,*" in Merivale and Sweeney, eds., *Detecting Texts,* 173.

29. Dangy-Scaillierez, *L'Énigme criminelle,* 136.

30. Todorov, "Typologie du roman policier," 57. In *Looking Awry,* Slavoj Žižek follows Lacan in comparing the "eccentric," unengaged position of the detective to that of the psychoanalyst, who avoids being caught up in the symbolic network (60).

31. The name Léon Salini is an anagram of *Le Lionnais,* an allusion that pays homage to the founder of the Ouvroir de littérature potentielle and the Ouvroir de littérature policière potentielle. Salini is also the name of the detective in *La Vie mode d'emploi* who uncovers the cause of the Chaumont-Porcien murders with the help of chance events, such as the discovery of a story in a newspaper (Perec, *La Vie mode d'emploi,* 180).

32. Dangy-Scaillierez, *L'Énigme criminelle,* 138.

33. In *The Psychopathology of Everyday Life,* Freud distinguishes his own point of view—his belief that there is nothing accidental in psychic life—from that of superstitious and paranoid people, who on the contrary refuse to accept the existence of *external* chance. The paranoid person interprets others' actions and gestures in relation to his or her own mental life, whereas the superstitious person attributes a hidden meaning to the accidental events of the world. Both therefore see causal relationships in cases where there is really only simultaneity or coincidence (*The Psychopathology of Everyday Life,* 325–30).

34. Among the numerous hidden allusions to *La Chartreuse de Parme* in Perec's novel we find the name of the African town, Grianta (the name of the del Dongo château in *La Chartreuse*), a character named Fly (an English translation of Mosca), a song titled "Il pleut sur le lac de Côme" (*"53J,"* 16) ("It Is Raining on the Como Lake"), and a pun on "as de sa khâgne" (the ace of his class) and "Ascagne," a character in Stendhal's novel (*"53J,"* 36).

35. Magné, "Le Puzzle mode d'emploi," in *Perecollages,* 35–36.

36. "Il nous arrive parfois de découvrir qu'une structure que nous avions crue parfaitement inédite, avait déjà été découverte ou inventée dans le passé, parfois même dans un passé lointain. Nous nous faisons un devoir de reconnaître un tel

état de choses en qualifiant les textes en cause de 'plagiats par anticipation.'" (Le Lionnais, "Le Second Manifeste," in Oulipo, *La Littérature potentielle,* 23) (We sometimes happen to discover that a structure we believed to be completely new had already been discovered or invented in the past, sometimes even in a distant past. We make it our duty to recognize such a state of things by characterizing the texts in question as 'plagiary by anticipation.'")

37. This name, like that of Percival Bartlebooth in *La Vie mode d'emploi,* alludes to the legend of the Holy Grail and thus emphasizes the theme of the quest.

38. Žižek, *Looking Awry,* 53.

39. Sirvent, "Reader-Investigators in the Post-*Nouveau Roman,*" 173.

40. Bénabou, "Faux et usage du faux chez Perec," 34.

41. Magné, "'*53 jours*' pour lecteurs chevronnés," 188.

42. Dangy-Scaillierez, *L'Énigme criminelle,* 105.

43. See Jullien, "Fiat lux," 126–27.

44. Chambers, *Loiterature,* 25.

45. Motte, *The Poetics of Experiment,* 135–36.

46. Mathews, "That Ephemeral Thing," in *The Case of the Persevering Maltese,* 294.

47. Roubaud, "Hypothèses génétiques concernant la perecquation de la forme roman," 23.

48. Céline, *Voyage au bout de la nuit,* 7.

Chapter 5

Elements of this chapter appeared in Alison James, "Automatism, Arbitrariness, and the Oulipian Author," *French Forum* 31, no. 2 (University of Nebraska Press, 2006): 111–25. The chapter epigraph is from Mallarmé, "Igitur," in *Œuvres complètes* 1:841.

1. Vincent Kaufmann argues that the emphasis on collective practice does make the Oulipo an avant-garde group (*Poétique des groupes littéraires,* 48–49).

2. Roubaud, *La Bibliothèque de Warburg,* 242.

3. Le Lionnais, "La LiPo (le premier Manifeste)," *Cahiers du Collège de 'Pataphysique,* dossier 17 (1961); repr. in Oulipo, *La Littérature potentielle,* 17.

4. Le Lionnais, "Le Second Manifeste," in Oulipo, *La Littérature potentielle,* 19.

5. First presented by Jean Lescure (Lescure, "La Méthode S+7"), the method has since been taken up by other members of the Oulipo.

6. See Perec and Bénabou, "Presbytère et prolétaires: Le dossier PALF," in *Cahiers Georges Perec* 3.

7. Noël Arnaud, for example, states that there is no such thing as Oulipian literature, only potential literature (preface to Jacques Bens, *OuLiPo,* 11).

8. Le Tellier, *Esthétique de l'Oulipo,* 9.

9. Oulipo, *Atlas de littérature potentielle,* 431.

10. Quoted in Bens, *OuLiPo,* 136.

11. "Twenty Questions for Noël Arnaud," interview with Warren F. Motte Jr., 300.

12. Mathews and Brotchie, *Oulipo Compendium,* 123.

13. Hervé Le Tellier, *Esthétique de l'Oulipo,* 62.

14. Roubaud, "La Mathématique dans la méthode de Raymond Queneau," 56; Bens and Fournel, Interview, 55; Marcel Bénabou, "Quarante siècles de l'Oulipo," 21.

15. Perloff, *Radical Artifice: Writing Poetry in the Age of Media,* 139.

16. Perloff, "The Oulipo Factor: The Procedural Poetics of Christian Bök and Caroline Bergvall."

17. The classic example, which gave its name to the game, is "Le cadavre—exquis—boira—le vin—nouveau" (the exquisite corpse will drink the new wine). For more examples see Garrigues, *Les Jeux surréalistes,* 69–70.

18. Genette, *Palimpsestes,* 56.

19. Arnaud, "Gérard Genette et l'Oulipo," in Oulipo, *La Bibliothèque oulipienne* 5:15; Roubaud, *Poésie, etcetera: Ménage,* 209–10.

20. Meschonnic, *Politique du rythme, politique du sujet,* 180.

21. Jenny, *La Parole singulière,* 161.

22. Bertharion, *Poétique de Georges Perec,* 108; Motte, *The Poetics of Experiment,* 133.

23. Mathews and Brotchie, *Oulipo Compendium,* 41.

24. Breton's manifesto contains instructions on how to write an automatic text (Breton, *Œuvres complètes* 1:331–32). Of course, automatic writing does not define the whole of the surrealists' production. Furthermore, surrealist works manifest a gap between theory and practice: Pierre-Marc de Biasi notes that the manuscripts of Breton and Soupault's *Champs magnétiques* show crossings-out and corrections, "which, by their very existence, put an end to one of the great myths of modern literature" (*La Génétique des textes,* 74).

25. "I believe in external (real) chance, it is true, but not in internal (psychical) accidental events." Freud, *The Psychopathology of Everyday Life,* 329.

26. Breton, "Manifeste du surréalisme" (1924), in *Œuvres complètes* 1:328.

27. Breton, *L'Amour fou,* in *Œuvres complètes* 2:691. Although Breton claims to develop his definition of chance from Engels and Freud, Freud insists on preserving the distance between internal finality and external causality, carefully distinguishing the psychoanalytic attitude from the paranoid or superstitious tendency to conflate the external world and psychic states.

28. Breton, *Œuvres complètes* 2:755.

29. Calvino, "Philosophy and Literature," in *The Uses of Literature,* 47.

30. Queneau, "Qu'est-ce que l'art?" (1938), in *Le Voyage en Grèce,* 94.

31. "Il m'a été insupportable de laisser au hasard le soin de fixer le nombre des chapitres de ces romans" (It was unbearable for me to leave to chance the business of deciding the number of chapters in these novels) (Queneau, "Technique du roman," 29; "Technique of the Novel," trans. Campbell-Sposito, 28).

32. Quoted in Bens, *OuLiPo,* 35.

33. Perec, interview with Kaye Mortley (1981), in *Entretiens et conférences* 2:247.

34. Bens and Fournel, 55–56.

35. "Parce que la forme est contraignante, l'idée jaillit plus intense" (Baudelaire, *Correspondance* 1:676) (Because the form is constraining, the idea shines forth more intensely).

36. Valéry, "Cours de Poétique," December 10, 1937, in *Introduction à la poétique,* 26.

37. Claudel, "Réflexions et propositions sur le vers français," in *Positions et propositions,* 21.

38. "Ce qui est ou paraît du hasard chez les uns—est attribué au génie chez les autres. Les premiers sont de beaucoup les plus nombreux" (Valéry, *Cahiers* 2:1044) (What is or appears to be chance in some—is attributed to genius in others. The first are by far the most numerous). In his poetics lecture of December 10, 1937, Valéry also comments that strict formal rules often incite the poet to "inventions auxquelles une entière liberté ne l'aurait jamais conduit" (*Introduction à la poétique,* 25) (inventions to which a complete freedom would never have led him).

39. Some critics claim otherwise: see Lapprand, *Poétique de l'Oulipo,* 154; Burgelin, "Quelques remarques sur le sujet oulipien en guise de préface," in Bénabou et al., *Un art simple et tout d'exécution,* 12. Of all the members of the Oulipo, it is perhaps Queneau (whose exploration of spoken "neo-French" nevertheless takes the written language very far from classical norms) who shows the most affinity for French classicism. Some of Queneau's formal choices reflect this tendency; each section of his first novel *Le Chiendent,* for example, obeys the three unities of French classical tragedy (Queneau, "Technique du roman," in *Bâtons, chiffres et lettres,* 30).

40. Jouet, "With (and Without) Constraints," 5.

41. Zumthor, *Le Masque et la lumière,* 16.

42. Curtius, *European Literature,* 282.

43. Bénabou, "La Règle et la contrainte," 101.

44. Queneau, *Entretiens avec Georges Charbonnier,* 152.

45. See Hughes, *The Shock of the New,* 334–35 and 344–46.

46. Winter, "À propos de l'Oulipo et de quelques contraintes musico-textuelles," 186.

47. Boulez, *Par volonté et par hasard,* 70.

48. Xenakis, "La Crise de la musique sérielle," in *Kéleütha,* 39–43.

49. Griffiths, *Modern Music and After,* 26.

50. Ibid., 25.

51. Lutz, "Stochastiche Texte," 8–9. As well as developing mathematically inspired semiotic theories, Max Bense's group explored the use of new technologies (such as random number generators) in writing.

52. Within the broader category of "open" works, Eco defines "works in movement" as works that "characteristically consist of unplanned or physically incomplete structural units." Eco, *The Open Work,* 12.

53. Mallarmé's extant notes toward this work were published posthumously in 1957 by Jacques Scherer (*Le "Livre" de Mallarmé*).

54. *The Oxford Dictionary of Music* defines *aleatory music* as "music that cannot be predicted before performance or music which was composed through chance procedures (statistical or computerized)."

55. Queneau, "Littérature potentielle," in *Bâtons, chiffres et lettres,* 322. See also Bénabou, "Quarante siècles de l'Oulipo," 21.

56. Oulipo, "Oulipo et informatique," in *Atlas de littérature potentielle,* 297–331.

57. See Neefs, "La Profondeur spéculaire," 112.

58. Philippe Drogoz, who was Perec's collaborator on a number of other musical projects (he composed the music for Bernard Queysanne's film of *Un homme qui dort* and worked with Perec on an opera project, *L'Art effaré*), comments on the title's pun and notes that the piece was composed during the era of aleatory music; he adds that he does not know whether the composition of the score itself was based on chance ("Georges Perec et la musique," 277).

59. This opposition is proposed by Colin Symes, in "Writing by Numbers: OuLiPo and the Creativity of Constraints," 90–91.

60. See also Queneau's *Un conte à votre façon,* a narrative in which the reader is asked to choose the order of the paragraphs (Oulipo, *La Littérature potentielle,* 273–76).

61. Quoted in Bens, *OuLiPo,* 136.

62. Bens, "Queneau oulipien," in Oulipo, *Atlas de littérature potentielle,* 25.

63. See Thomas, *La Langue la poésie,* 183–84; and Reggiani, *Rhétoriques de la contrainte,* 71.

64. Mathews, "Translation and the Oulipo: The Case of the Persevering Maltese," in *The Case of the Persevering Maltese,* 81.

65. Boulez and Cage, *Correspondance,* 181–82.

66. Boulez, "Alea," (1957), in *Points de repère,* 44, 46.

67. Nyman, *Experimental Music,* 49 and 4. Nyman's distinction echoes elements of Peter Bürger's distinction between "modernist" works and the productions of the "historical avant-garde," although the terminology is different (Nyman's "experimental" corresponds to Bürger's "avant-garde," and Nyman's "avant-garde" to Bürger's modernist aestheticism). For Bürger, the avant-gardes of the early twentieth century aim to negate the institution of art in bourgeois society (including

the modernist doctrine of aesthetic autonomy) and to integrate art into the praxis of life (*Theory of the Avant-Garde,* passim).

68. Reggiani, *Rhétoriques de la contrainte,* 149, 178, 206. Similarly, Jan Baetens and Bernardo Schiavetta (the editors of the journal *Formules*) criticize the Oulipo for its contradictory goals. Baetens and Schiavetta, "Écrivains encore un effort . . . pour être absolument modernes," 18.

69. Eco, *The Open Work,* 19–20. Commenting on the tension between form and chance in abstract painting, Roland Barthes makes the similar point that the artist's creative work consists in creating meaning through form. While art may try to incorporate the perception of the world's randomness, it must necessarily establish "un certain contre-hasard" (a certain counterchance) that distinguishes the work from the randomness of the world. Barthes, "Art, forme, hasard," in *Œuvres complètes* 2:562.

70. Cage, *Silence,* 10.

71. Griffiths, *Modern Music and After,* 25–28.

72. "La parole poétique tend à remotiver les signes" (Kerbrat-Orecchioni, *La Connotation,* 35) (Poetic speech tends to remotivate signs).

73. Barthes, "Proust et les noms," in *Œuvres complètes* 4:76.

74. Genette, "Avatars du cratylisme," *Poétique* 11 (1972): 394.

75. Leiris glosses words by dislocating the signifier, playing on homophonies or anagrams, for example: "SOLEIL—seul œil" (sun—only eye) or "TRAVAILLER—t'avilir et te lier" (to work—to debase and bind yourself). Leiris, *Glossaire j'y serre mes gloses,* in *Mots sans mémoire,* 109, 112.

76. Motte, "L'Oulipo: Pour une littérature non-jourdanienne," 178.

77. Jouet, "With (and Without) Constraints," 6.

78. Bénabou, "Bris de mots," in *La Bibliothèque oulipienne* 3:59. A *surdéfinition* is composed of two definitions of which one refers to the signified, the other to the signifier; for example, the word *angle* is defined as "obtus parfois en Angleterre" (54) (sometimes obtuse in England).

79. Mallarmé, "Crise de vers," in *Œuvres complètes* 2:213.

80. Queneau, "La Redondance chez Phane Armé," in Oulipo, *La Littérature potentielle,* 181–85.

81. In *Comment j'ai écrit certains de mes livres,* Roussel describes the evolution of his "procédé très spécial" (very special procedure) which, in its original form, consisted in interpreting the words of a particular phrase in two different senses, and using these two meanings to generate a narrative element. Thus the expression "palmier à restauration" generated the ideas both of a restaurant where a type of pastry (*palmier*) is served, and of the palm tree (*palmier*) which commemorates the reestablishment of a dynasty on the throne—two elements used in the novel *Impressions d'Afrique* (14). Later, says Roussel, he generated images through the phonic dislocation of phrases; thus a line from a popular song, "J'ai du bon tabac

dans ma tabatière" (I have good tobacco in my snuff box), became "jade tube onde aubade en mat a basse tierce" (jade tube wave serenade in dullness has low third) (20). See also chapter 4, note 4 above.

82. Foucault, *Raymond Roussel,* 54–55.

83. Leiris, *Biffures,* 45.

84. Ritte, *Sprachspiel der Moderne,* 48–49.

85. Perec summarizes Borges's "A Defense of the Kabbalah" (1932), which was published in *Selected Non-Fictions,* 85.

86. Reggiani, *Rhétoriques de la contrainte,* 68.

87. Queneau, "Technique du roman," in *Bâtons, chiffres et lettres,* 33; "Technique of the Novel," trans. Campbell-Sposito, 30.

88. Bourbaki, *Éléments de Mathématique,* bk. 1, chap. 4, p. 65, note 1.

89. "[W]hen [speeches] have been once written down they are tumbled about anywhere among those who may or may not understand them, and do not know to whom they should reply, to whom not: and, if they are maltreated or abused, they have no parent to protect them, and they cannot protect or defend themselves" (Plato, *Phaedrus,* 275).

90. Barthes, "La Mort de l'auteur" (1968), in *Œuvres complètes* 3:40.

91. Derrida argues in *De la grammatologie* that the traditional opposition between a fully present, originary act of speech that does not need interpretation, and an artificial, exterior writing cut off from its origin, is grounded in metaphysical and indeed theological assumptions (18–30).

92. Calvino, "Cybernetics and Ghosts" (1967), in *The Uses of Literature,* 21.

93. Compagnon, *Le Démon de la théorie,* 78.

94. I borrow my terminology here from Michel de Certeau, who considers reading as a tactic, a means of working against the imposed system of the text through a process that he compares to poaching. Certeau, *L'Invention du quotidien* 1:24.

95. See, for example, Magné, "Les Cahiers des charges de Georges Perec," 72; Raynaud, "Du double jeu," 92.

96. Oulipo, "S+7, le retour," in *La Bibliothèque oulipienne* 4:36.

97. Ibid., 47. François Caradec, "Le Souvenir de Jean Queval," in *La Bibliothèque oulipienne,* vol. 4 © Le Castor Astral and François Caradec, 1997.

98. Jouet, "L'Éclipse," in *La Bibliothèque oulipienne* 2:202. Although the name suggests that the second version obscures the first, the effect of the "eclipse" in fact depends upon both parts of the text being present and read together.

99. Oulipo, "S+7, le retour," in *La Bibliothèque oulipienne* 4:52.

100. Reggiani, *Rhétoriques de la contrainte,* 110.

101. Marcel Bénabou's aphorisms, which are generated by computer on the basis of several basic syntactic formulas and a given lexicon, follow a similar procedure. "Un aphorisme peut en cacher un autre," in *La Bibliothèque oulipienne* 1:251–69.

102. Mathews, *Selected Declarations of Dependence,* 18.

103. Roubaud, "La Mathématique dans la méthode de Raymond Queneau," 57.

104. Ibid., 57.

105. Boulez, "Éventuellement . . ." (1952), in *Points de repère,* 288.

106. Aragon, *Je n'ai jamais appris à écrire ou les incipit,* 43–44.

107. Roubaud, "La Mathématique dans la méthode de Raymond Queneau," 58.

Chapter 6

Elements of this chapter appeared in Alison James, "Pour un modèle diagrammatique de la contrainte: L'écriture oulipienne de Georges Perec," *Théorie, littérature, enseignement* 22 (Presses Universitaires de Vincennes, 2004): 55–81. The chapter epigraph is from Valéry, *Cahiers* 2:990.

1. Perec, *Beaux Présents belles absentes,* 11.

2. Bernard Magné claims to detect another constraint at work in this line: the latter contains eleven words and forty-three letters, and these figures have an important autobiographical significance in Perec's works as a commemoration of the date of his mother's deportation (February 11, 1943). Therefore, argues Magné, the allusions to "chance" and "vague prose" are all the more ironic ("Georges Perec oulibiographe," 54–55). Of course, despite the overwhelming evidence that these numbers are indeed recurring motifs in Perec's works (see Magné, "L'Autobiotexte perecquien," 5–42), it is tempting to see the number of letters in a particular line as purely accidental. In a similar reading, Wilfred Mazzorato and Serge Rousséguier claim that the word *hasard* appears eleven times in *W ou le souvenir d'enfance,* a fact that inscribes the presence of an "autobiographeme" and makes this usage ironic ("Intervention du dix-sept," 100n). However, I counted twelve occurrences of the word . . .

3. Lapprand interprets the reference as wholly ironic, since Perec's text is far from the dice throw of zanzibar (*Poétique de l'Oulipo,* 79).

4. In *Espèces d'espaces* and "Quatre figures pour *La Vie mode d'emploi*" (in *Atlas de littérature potentielle,* 387–95). Perec explains his use of the ten-by-ten orthogonal Greco-Latin bi-square, the knight's tour move, and the list of forty-two elements per chapter.

5. In response to an attempt by Jean Ricardou to "improve" a passage from *La Disparition* by removing redundancies and repetitions, Bernard Magné rightly emphasizes the important place of repetition, accumulation, saturation, and variation in Perec's novel (Ricardou, "La Contrainte corollaire"; Magné, "Le RAPT de *La Disparition,*" 207).

6. On the expression "l'hasard" in *La Disparition,* see chapter 4, note 12.

7. As Jacques Roubaud puts it: "La contrainte y est à la fois principe de l'écriture du texte, son mécanisme de développement, en même temps que son sens" ("La

Mathématique dans la méthode de Raymond Queneau," 55) (Constraint is here at once the principle of the text's writing, its mechanism of development, and simultaneously its meaning).

8. Parayre, "Lire *La Disparition* de Georges Perec," 165.

9. Developing this analogy, Vincent Bouchot argues that Perec aims for a total mastery of language, a wholly necessary text ("De la musique dans l'œuvre de Georges Perec," 115). Jacques-Denis Bertharion draws a very different conclusion, arguing that it may be illegitimate to look for lexical or thematic recurrences in texts that abandon the syntactic and lexical structure, and hence the space of meaning and discourse, to an arbitrary combinatoric rule (*Poétique de Georges Perec,* 83 and 92). While my reading differs from that of both critics, the possibility of these two opposing descriptions highlights the central ambiguity of Oulipian anti-chance.

10. The French text of the table is printed from Georges Perec, *Alphabets* © Éditions Galilée, 1976, with permission.

11. Mallarmé, *Œuvres complètes* 1:37.

12. We find numerous other references to Mallarmé in Perec, particularly to the poem "Un coup de dés jamais n'abolira le hasard": "nul discours jamais n'abolira l'hasard" (*La Disparition,* 50) (literally: no discourse will ever abolish chance); "le verbe enivré [. . .] lu n'abolira le hasard" ("Palindrome," 103) (the intoxicated word, when read, will not abolish chance). *La Vie mode d'emploi* implicitly alludes to the "Sonnet on X" via two key words ("bibelot" [trinket] is among the forty-two initial categories in the initial table of lists, and this constraint is actualized as "onyx" in chapter 16).

13. Bernard Magné, "L'Autobiotexte perecquien," 23.

14. As Claude Burgelin points out, the resulting poetry often seems closer to algebra than to music (*Georges Perec,* 87).

15. According to the Robert dictionary, the word *trublion,* adapted from the Latin *trublium* (plate or bowl), was coined by the writer Anatole France to designate the duc d'Orléans, nicknamed "Gamelle" (a soldier's mess kit), who led a royalist plot during the Dreyfus affair. The word now means "troublemaker" or "agitator."

16. Magné indicates a use of the word that relates "ours" (bear) and "règles" (rules), and he points out that Perec and Bénabou's PALF procedure made use of precisely such semantic manipulations. He also relates the word *ours* to Perec's childhood, emphasizing the possible bilingual wordplay on the word *oursons* (bear cubs, but also "our sons") in *W ou le souvenir d'enfance* ("Quelques considérations sur les poèmes hétérogrammatiques de Georges Perec," 78–83). "Ulcérations," a text from 1974 which uses a similar constraint to that of *Alphabets,* supports this reading: Perec speaks of "Art OuLiTien: ours, calcul et raison" ("OuLiTian Art: Bear [Rules?], Calculation, and Reason") (10).

17. The existence of a ten-by-ten Greco-Latin bi-square was in fact only estab-

lished in 1960. It was the Oulipo's Claude Berge, a mathematician, who first suggested to the group the possibility of using it in a novel, and discussed the idea with Perec and Roubaud. See Berge, "Pour une analyse potentielle de la littérature combinatoire"; Perec, "Quatre figures pour *La Vie mode d'emploi,*" 386.

18. The end-words of a quenina's lines change position with each stanza according to a circular permutation, which needs as many stanzas to complete its circle as there are lines in the stanza (see Oulipo, "N-ines, autrement dit quenines," *La Bibliothèque oulipienne* 5:57–95). Perec's version is only a *pseudo*-quenina because the circular permutation does not function for the number 10, but nevertheless allows Perec to vary the basic model of the bi-square (see Magné, "Cinquième figure pour *La Vie mode d'emploi,*" 173–77).

19. Hartje, Magné, and Neefs, preface to Perec, *Cahier des charges,* 25–26.

20. In *The Anxiety of Influence,* Harold Bloom adopts the notion of the clinamen as a metaphor for poetic "misprision" (44–45). The philosopher of science Michel Serres also insists on the importance of the clinamen, using it to refer to the production of pockets of microturbulence within the general movement of things (*La Naissance de la physique dans le texte de Lucrèce,* 97). For more details see Warren Motte "Clinamen redux."

21. Jarry, *Gestes et opinions du Docteur Faustroll, pataphysicien,* in *Œuvres complètes* 1:714.

22. Mathews and Brotchie, *Oulipo Compendium,* 126.

23. In "Prose et anticombinatoire," for example, Calvino argues that the use of computers can liberate the artist from combinatoric exploration, thus allowing him or her to concentrate on the clinamen, which, alone, can make of the text a true work of art (Oulipo, *Atlas de littérature potentielle,* 331). While Calvino's use of the term suggests the emergence of the unexpected from within the functioning system (as an opportunity to be recognized and exploited by the author), Perec more clearly refers to *transgressions* of the system (Perec, *Entretiens et conférences* 2:165, 202).

24. "J'ai passé autant de temps à tricher qu'à respecter les règles, ce qui ne me gêne pas du tout" (I spent just as much time cheating as obeying the rules, and that doesn't bother me at all). Perec, interview with Claudette Oriol-Boyer (1981), in *Entretiens et conférences* 2:165.

25. In an interview with Ewa Pawlikowska in 1981, for example, Perec affirms that "il faut—et c'est important—détruire le système des contraintes" (you must—and it is important—destroy the system of constraints) and also cites Paul Klee's formula: "Le génie, c'est l'erreur dans le système" (Genius is the error in the system). Perec, *Entretiens et conférences* 2:202.

26. Bernard Magné suggests that the clinamen prevents the text from becoming too "programmatic" or "mechanical," allowing meaning to emerge ("Le Puzzle mode d'emploi," 46; "Textus ex machina," 226; "Écriture et déconstruction," 237). Jean-François Chassay echoes this argument, claiming that the clinamen prevents

the game from stagnating (*Le Jeu des coïncidences,* 53). Warren Motte suggests that the clinamen, this "swerve" in Oulipian theory, might represent "the final victory of the aleatory over the motivated" (introduction to *Oulipo: A Primer of Potential Literature,* 19–20). He also argues that Perec came to see the clinamen as the "real locus of poetic creativity" ("Clinamen redux," 274). David Bellos asserts that the clinamen introduces a "randomizing effect" ("Literary Quotations," 188). Peter Schulman reiterates this judgment: "Despite his adherence to formal constraint, Perec emphasizes that what really makes a work of art a masterpiece is the unpredictable, the imperfect, the unbalanced" (*Sunday of Fiction,* 99). What I would like to question here is not the importance of the unpredictable and the unbalanced, but rather the binary opposition between chance and constraint implied by these accounts of the clinamen.

27. Reggiani, *Rhétoriques de la contrainte,* 68–69.

28. Ibid., 72.

29. Ibid., 9 and 478.

30. Bernard Magné identifies a vast "isotopie du manque" (isotopy of lack) in Perec's works ("Le Puzzle mode d'emploi," 51).

31. Lévy, "Emergence in Georges Perec," 36–55.

32. Neefs, "Des lieux, des pages, des œuvres," 37.

33. "Genetic" work, based on extant manuscripts of *La Vie mode d'emploi,* has been carried out by Hans Hartje (*Georges Perec écrivant*), and by Danielle Constantin ("'Ne rien nier. Énoncer.'").

34. The French text of the table is printed from Georges Perec, *La Vie mode d'emploi* © Hachette, 1978, with permission. The English translation of the table is reprinted from *Life A User's Manual by Georges Perec,* translated from the French by David Bellos. Reprinted by permission of David R. Godine, Publisher, Inc. Translation copyright © 1987 by David Bellos.

35. Perec, *Cahier des charges,* "Tableau général des listes" and chapter 16; *La Vie mode d'emploi, 86/Life A User's Manual,* 58.

36. Thomas Mann, *La Montagne magique* [*Der Zauberberg*], 351–52.

37. Presenting the knight's tour constraint in "Quatre figures pour *La Vie mode d'emploi,*" Perec states: "Il aurait été fastidieux de décrire l'immeuble étage par étage et appartement par appartement. Mais la succession des chapitres ne pouvait pas pour autant être laissée au seul hasard" (389) (It would have been tedious to describe the building floor by floor and apartment by apartment. But the succession of chapters could not, for all that, be left to chance alone).

38. Constantin, "'Ne rien nier. Énoncer,'" 276.

39. Quoted in Philippe Lejeune, *La Mémoire et l'oblique: Georges Perec autobiographe,* 206. Perec's letter to Chakravarti is dated June 10, 1969, and requests a twelve-by-twelve Latin square for use in the *Lieux* project (to determine which of the twelve places he would visit each month). However, his reference to the "aléa-

toire déterminé" (determined randomness) seems even more valid in the case of his later work on *La Vie mode d'emploi,* where the permutational operations are more complicated.

40. Cécile de Bary, for example, argues that the reader's knowledge of the combinatory system destabilizes thematic interpretation, since authorial intention inevitably gives way to a degree of randomness, in the form of an external mechanism which prevents perfect authorial mastery of a signifying system ("Contre une littérature réaliste?" 74–75).

41. Valéry, *Cahiers* 2:990.

42. The phrase is Bernard Magné's ("Saint Jérôme mode d'emploi," 99).

43. Motte, *The Poetics of Experiment,* 34.

44. See, for example, Motte, *The Poetics of Experiment,* chapter on "Formal Constraint"; Prigent, *Ceux qui merdRent,* 145; Lévy, "Oulipian Messages," 156; Andrews, "Constraint and Convention: The Formalism of the Oulipo," 223–32.

45. In particular, Deleuze and Guattari's concept of "minor literature," presented in *Kafka: pour une littérature mineure,* invokes a set of constraints—in this case political and linguistic ones, since minor literature is written from a marginalized position. In an interview with Antoine Dulaure and Claire Parnet (1985), Deleuze makes a more general argument for the role of constraint: "Si l'on n'a pas un ensemble d'impossibilités, on n'aura pas cette ligne de fuite, cette sortie qui constitue la création, cette puissance du faux qui constitue la vérité" (Deleuze, *Pourparlers,* 182–83) (If you do not have a set of impossibilities, you will not have that line of flight, that exit which constitutes creation, that power of the false which constitutes truth).

46. Foucault, *Surveiller et punir,* 239; *Discipline and Punish,* trans. Sheridan, 205. The term appears only once; Foucault generally uses the term "schéma" or "dispositif" (schema or mechanism) more or less interchangeably to describe the functioning of power. For example, he contrasts disciplinary schemas (whose image is the plague-stricken town, or later, the Panopticon) with schemas of exclusion (whose image is leprosy); or he discusses the "dispositif panoptique" (the panoptic mechanism) the disciplinary figure par excellence (*Surveiller et punir,* 241; *Discipline and Punish,* trans. Sheridan, 206).

47. Deleuze, "Écrivain non, un nouveau cartographe," in *Foucault,* 41. The definition of Panopticism in terms of function is already explicit in Foucault: "Le dispositif panoptique n'est pas simplement une charnière, un échangeur entre un mécanisme de pouvoir et une fonction; c'est une manière de faire fonctionner des relations de pouvoir dans une fonction, et une fonction par ces relations de pouvoir" (The panoptic mechanism is not simply a hinge, a point of exchange between a mechanism of power and a function; it is a way of making power relations function in a function, and of making a function function through these power relations) (*Surveiller et punir,* 241; *Discipline and Punish,* trans. Sheridan,

206–7). However, by emphasizing the role of the diagram as dynamic and mobile, Deleuze focuses on the *becoming* of history, the driving forces behind historical change, rather than the archeology of forms.

48. Deleuze, *Foucault,* 43.

49. Deleuze and Guattari, *Mille Plateaux,* 115; A *Thousand Plateaus,* trans. Massumi, 91.

50. Deleuze and Guattari, *Mille Plateaux,* 176.

51. Ibid., 178 and 182.

52. Deleuze, "Entretien sur *Mille Plateaux*" (1989), in *Pourparlers,* 50.

53. Ibid., 51.

54. "[T]he [involuntary] marks are made, and you survey the thing like you would a sort of graph. And you see within this graph the possibilities of all types of fact being planted" (Bacon and Sylvester, *Interviews with Francis Bacon,* 56).

55. Deleuze, *Francis Bacon: Logique de la sensation,* 95; *Francis Bacon,* trans. Smith, 83.

56. Deleuze, *Francis Bacon,* 94; *Francis Bacon,* trans. Smith, 82.

57. Deleuze, *Francis Bacon,* 93–95; *Francis Bacon,* trans. Smith, 82–83.

58. Deleuze, *Francis Bacon,* 103; *Francis Bacon,* trans. Smith, 89.

59. Yves Abrioux traces Deleuze's uses of the term *diagramme* in Sasso and Villani, *Le Vocabulaire de Gilles Deleuze,* s.v. "diagramme," 109.

60. For a more detailed version of this reflection on the Deleuzian diagram as a model of the Oulipian constraint, see my article "Pour un modèle diagrammatique de la contrainte: L'Écriture oulipienne de Georges Perec."

61. Mathews, "Translation and the Oulipo," in *The Case of the Persevering Maltese,* 81.

62. Deleuze is not the only writer to argue that the artistic work integrates diverse elements that are initially destratified and heterogeneous. The Russian semiotician Yuri Lotman argues that the artistic text is composed from a series of functionally heterogeneous elements, juxtaposing different units of signs, languages and structures which, even if they constitute a common structure on a particular level, create a degree of unpredictability that guarantees a high level of information (Lotman, *La Structure du texte artistique,* 383). Lotman extends a principle from information theory to literature: the less probable the message, the greater its information. For Lotman, every text's structure is based on a permanent struggle between the heterogeneity of its constitutive elements, on the one hand, and the tendency toward unification and dissimulation of these elements (387). Lotman also bases his argument on the notion of a "compositional principle" (382), an idea that owes much to the work of the Russian formalist critics. Yuri Tynianov, for example, insists on the heterogeneity of the artistic material, and the dynamic nature of the constructive principle that organizes this material. "La Notion de construction" (1924), in Todorov, *Théorie de la littérature,* 114–15.

63. In his radio interviews with Georges Charbonnier, Queneau insists that

the role of mathematical constraints in his works is limited to that of scaffolding (*Entretiens avec Georges Charbonnier,* 53–54), and that the Oulipo does not wish to transform the way in which people read (150). However, it seems to me that Oulipian constraints necessarily have an effect on the reading process.

Chapter 7

The chapter epigraph is from Borges, afterword to "The Maker," in *Collected Fictions,* 327.

1. Doob, *The Idea of the Labyrinth from Classical Antiquity Through the Middle Ages,* 1.

2. The epigraph to *Portrait* is line 188 of book 8 of Ovid's *Metamorphoses,* which describes Daedalus's ingenuity in finding an escape from Crete: "Et ignotas animum dimittit in artes" (He turned his mind toward unknown arts). For references to the "fabulous artificer," see Joyce, *Portrait of the Artist,* 143; *Ulysses,* 270.

3. "The Garden of Forking Paths" contains the story of Ts'ui Pen, "who was governor of Yunan province and who renounced all temporal power in order to write a novel containing more characters than the Hung Lu Meng and construct a labyrinth in which all men would lose their way" (Borges, *Collected Fictions,* 122). It emerges that Ts'ui Pen's apparently impenetrable novel and his labyrinth are one and the same (124): the novel's subject is the problem of time, understood as "an infinite series of times, a growing, dizzying web of divergent, convergent and parallel times" (127).

4. Eco, "Postscript," in *The Name of the Rose,* 525–26.

5. Robbe-Grillet, "Sur quelques notions périmées" (1957), in *Pour un nouveau roman,* 31–32.

6. Perec expresses disapproval of Robbe-Grillet (and of the whole *Nouveau Roman*) in the "Ligne générale" texts. He also mentions his dislike of the author in interviews (*Entretiens et conférences* 1:15), and in "J'aime, je n'aime pas" (*L'Arc* 76: 38–39). The cinema-loving characters Jérôme and Sylvie in *Les Choses* prefer American westerns, thrillers, and comedies to Robbe-Grillet's *L'Année dernière à Marienbad* (*Les Choses,* 60).

7. A crack in the dresser, for example, leads the soldier's gaze to the painting that will generate another level of the narrative (Robbe-Grillet, *Dans le labyrinthe,* 8).

8. Lance Olsen aptly characterizes Robbe-Grillet's mode of writing as a form of "fantastic autism" (Olsen, "Diagnosing Fantastic Autism: Kafka, Borges, Robbe-Grillet," 36).

9. This phrase appears in the report from an early Oulipo meeting (April 17, 1961) but is not attributed to any one member in particular (Bens, *OuLiPo,* 43). It has since been mentioned on numerous other occasions; for example, in the 2001 Oulipo dossier of the *Magazine littéraire* (20) and in Jacques Roubaud's 1991 pre-

sentation of the Oulipo (in both *Poésie, etcetera: Ménage,* 209–10 and *La Bibliothèque de Warburg,* 226).

10. Apollodorus, *Library,* vol. 1, sec. 12.

11. "Welcome, O life, I go to encounter for the millionth time the reality of experience and to forge in the smithy of my soul the uncreated conscience of my race" (Joyce, *Portrait,* 213).

12. Kafka, *Ein Landarzt und andere Prosa,* 21; *Der Process,* 229–31. The closing paragraphs of *Un homme qui dort* also allude to and reject the endings of other works, including Kafka's *Trial,* Melville's *Moby-Dick,* and Saint-Exupéry's *Vol de nuit* (*Un homme qui dort,* 137–39). In a letter that probably dates from 1963, Perec discusses the problem of literary endings. Comparing, among other examples, the ending of *Portrait of the Artist* with that of *Ulysses,* he notes that the former belongs to the category of "fins épiques [. . .] qui débouchent sur la conquête du monde" (epic endings that lead to the conquest of the world), while the latter has a more nuanced ending, leaving us in doubt as to the characters' fates (Perec, "Lettre à Denise Getzler," 63).

13. Sartre's Roquentin, for example, experiences his discovery of freedom as a loss of hope: "Je suis libre: il ne me reste plus aucune raison de vivre, toutes celles que j'ai essayées ont lâché et je ne peux plus en imaginer d'autres" (Sartre, *La Nausée,* 221) (I am free: I no longer have any reason for living; all those that I tried have given way and I can no longer imagine any others).

14. The protagonist is also fascinated by the scar that marks the upper lip in "le portrait incroyablement énergique d'un homme de la Renaissance" (*Un homme qui dort,* 93)—a portrait whose energy is a negative reflection of the protagonist's lethargy. We know from Perec's other texts that the Renaissance painting is Antonello da Messina's *Condottiere.* Perec's first (unpublished) novel, "Le Condottiere," told the story of a forger who did not succeed in fabricating a copy of the portrait in question (see Perec, *W,* 146; and Bellos, *Georges Perec,* 225–30). In *W ou le souvenir d'enfance,* Perec mentions the significance he attributes to a scar on his own upper lip, which became for him a mark of identity and permanence.

15. The philosopher Pius Servien, faced with the impossibility of defining chance in mathematical terms, argues that the word refers to a mode of choice that takes place without aesthetic or any other preferential criteria (Servien, *Hasard et probabilités,* 61 and 65–66). As Clément Rosset points out, however, choosing something at random ("au hasard") is strictly speaking impossible, for all actions are determined in some way: "On peut certes faire tout ce qu'on veut, on ne pourra jamais pour autant faire *n'importe quoi*" (Rosset, *Le Réel,* 12) (We can undoubtedly do as we like, but we can never, for all that, do *anything whatsoever*).

16. Walter Benjamin draws a parallel between the flaneur and the gambler; the former devotes himself to the "phantasmagorias of space," the latter to the "phantasmagorias of time" ("Paris, the Capital of the Nineteenth Century," *Selected Writings,* 42). However, there is also a temporal dimension to the flaneur's fascination

with the city, which implies movement and the possibility of the event; as David Bell points out, the flaneur who wanders the streets of Paris "is the very embodiment of the potential for chance encounters" (Bell, *Circumstances,* 118).

17. Bell, *Circumstances,* 121.

18. Bellos, *Georges Perec,* 360.

19. This sentence from *Oedipus Rex* (which, in its original context, refers to the discovery of Oedipus's guilt) appears in the same French translation as an epigraph to Robbe-Grillet's *Les Gommes* (*The Erasers*) (7). Robbe-Grillet, rather than Sophocles, may therefore have been Perec's source.

20. Burgelin, *Les Parties de dominos chez Monsieur Lefèvre,* 110.

21. Perec, *Je suis né,* 73.

22. See Marcel Detienne and Jean-Pierre Vernant, *Les Ruses de l'intelligence: La mètis des Grecs.* As Michael Sheringham notes, "mètis" designates "the form of guile or rusing which allows a weaker party to overcome a stronger by exploiting gaps and blind spots in the systems of power" (Sheringham, "Attending to the Everyday," 191).

23. Jacques-Denis Bertharion, for example, sees Perec's Oulipian writing strategies as a protective wall against reality and against the trauma of his own past (Bertharion, *Poétique de Georges Perec,* 46 and 63). Christian Prigent presents a similar view (*Ceux qui merdRent,* 145).

24. As Warren Motte points out, there is a fundamental contradiction in *La Disparition* between the creative and fatal functions of the letter (Motte, "Embellir les letters," 115).

25. Bold, "Labyrinths of Invention from the New Novel to Oulipo," 545. Bold contrasts the tradition of literary *inventio* with the anti-rhetorical and anti-inventive currents that have come to dominate literature (partly due to Cartesianism), and which cast invention as scandalous. The Oulipo, he argues, is "first and last a project of literary invention" (550), and the Oulipian labyrinth is a model of inventive self-discovery (551).

26. Ovid, *Metamorphoses,* bk. 8, lines 166–68.

27. Bens, *OuLiPo,* 43.

28. Perec, *Théâtre I,* 10.

29. One of the stories of *La Vie mode d'emploi* takes up the plot of *L'Augmentation;* after the Réols have spent more than eleven thousand francs on decorating their bedroom, various circumstances conspire against Maurice Réol to prevent his obtaining a raise from the vast company for which he works. In this case, in accordance with the narrative logic of *La Vie mode d'emploi,* a solution appears in the form of an unexpected reversal of fate: Réol is unexpectedly promoted just in time to avert financial disaster (Perec, *La Vie mode d'emploi,* 572).

30. Michel de Certeau's characterization of reading is relevant here: "In effect, to read is to travel within an imposed system, that of the text, similar to the constructed order of a city or a supermarket." Certeau, *L'Invention du quotidien,* 1:285.

31. Bertharion, *Poétique de Georges Perec,* 173.

32. Jullien, "Le Cas Polonius." Most striking are the allusions that link rodents to *Hamlet:* Olivia Rorschash owns a domino-playing hamster named Polonius (Perec, *La Vie mode d'emploi,* 466); one of the paintings that hangs in the Marquiseaux's salon is entitled *Un Rat derrière la tenture* (*A Rat Behind the Arras*) (*La Vie mode d'emploi,* 35/*Life A User's Manual,* 15), echoing Hamlet's words upon killing Polonius; the title *La Souricière* (*The Mousetrap*), attributed to a detective novel in chapter 19 of *La Vie mode d'emploi* (97), is a disguised allusion both to the play-within-the-play in *Hamlet* and to Agatha Christie's *Mousetrap.* Dominique Jullien shows that the intertextual links to Shakespeare and Kafka articulate the autobiographical themes of loss, memory, mourning, and family ties.

33. Pawlikowska, "La Colle bleue de Gaspard Winckler," 86.

34. Doob, *The Idea of the Labyrinth,* 97.

35. Magné, "Pour une lecture réticulée."

36. Ovid, *Metamorphoses,* bk. 8, lines 162–66.

37. Roubaud, *"Le Grand Incendie de Londres,"* 332.

38. Van Zuylen, *Monomania,* 5 and 134. In this book about "the obsessive strategies people use to keep the arbitrary out of their lives" (1), van Zuylen considers Pierre Janet's patients, Flaubert's obsession with style, Charles Nodier's "romantic monomania," as well as works by Baudelaire, George Eliot, Thomas Mann, Elias Canetti, Nina Bouraoui, and Sophie Calle. Although Perec does not figure in this study, many of his characters would serve as perfect illustrations of van Zuylen's argument.

39. Samoyault, "Romans-mondes," 542.

40. Van Zuylen, *Monomania,* 1.

41. "C'est du côté de l'aléatoire, du précaire, qu'est la vie" (Life is on the side of the random and the precarious). Similarly, Hugues Corriveau claims that Bartlebooth dies of the realization that despite his system, chance is never abolished. Burgelin, *Georges Perec,* 220; Corriveau, "Georges Perec ou le système de la déception," 146.

42. Sydney Lévy suggests that Winckler's vengeance is in fact unnecessary, for chance would have been sufficient to demolish Bartlebooth's project ("Le Temps mode d'emploi," 114). According to the narrator, however, the various effects of chance—the illogical character of the chosen number and the various contingencies involved in travel—are merely "minor flaws" in the project; Bartlebooth's failure is due principally to his general incapacity to face up to Winckler's efforts and to meet his goal of reconstituting and destroying the jigsaw puzzles (Perec, *La Vie mode d'emploi,* 461–62).

43. As Claude Burgelin has pointed out, the building is sometimes presented as labyrinthine as well as jigsaw-like (Burgelin, *Georges Perec,* 185). For example, in chapter 74, Valène imagines a complicated labyrinth of pipes, paths, and stairways hidden below the visible part of the building (Perec, *La Vie mode d'emploi,* 428).

44. Magné, "Le Puzzle mode d'emploi," 37 and 55–57.

45. David Bellos suggests that Winckler's vengeance is an affirmation that "it is the manipulator of signs who is the master, and not signs that master the manipulator" (Bellos, "Perec et Saussure," 95).

46. De Bary, "Il faut encore une fois partir de l'image du puzzle"; Andrews, "Puzzles and Lists," 789. Similarly, Bernard Magné points out that there is no simple symmetry between the writing and reading processes ("Le Puzzle mode d'emploi," 41–42).

47. Burgelin, *Les Parties de dominos chez Monsieur Lefèvre,* 192.

48. This description echoes Perec's account of his psychoanalysis in "Les Lieux d'une ruse," a text that foregrounds the figure of the labyrinth, but also evokes the jigsaw as a metaphor for Perec's search for meaning: "Lorsque j'essayais de parler [. . .] tout de suite j'avais l'impression d'être en train de recommencer le même puzzle [. . .]" (Whenever I tried to speak [. . .] I suddenly had the impression that I was starting on the same puzzle all over again [. . .]) (Perec, *Penser/Classer,* 69; "The Scene of a Stratagem," *Species of Spaces,* trans. Sturrock, 167).

49. As Bernard Magné points out, the readability of these biographical motifs (which Magné calls "autobiographemes") remains uncertain and aleatory ("L'autobiotexte perecquien," 10).

50. Hutting produces copies of famous paintings, such as the Mona Lisa, and paints fog effects on top of them (Perec, *La Vie mode d'emploi,* 64). This method is reminiscent of Marcel Duchamp's defacement of the Mona Lisa but seems to be motivated by commercial ambition rather than Dadaist aggression.

51. The descriptions of the paintings conceal names of Oulipo members. Perec reveals the secrets of this list in "Quatre figures pour *La Vie mode d'emploi*" (in Oulipo, *Atlas de littérature potentielle,* 394–95).

52. Mathews, *The Conversions,* in *The Sinking of the Odradek Stadium and Other Novels,* 338.

53. Mathews's novel revolves around wordplay and riddles, so it is no surprise that this proper name hides an allusion to a plainchant melody used in vocal compositions. The offertory "Felix namque es, sacra virgo Maria" was prescribed in medieval Masses of the Virgin and was frequently part of English organ settings in the sixteenth century (Caldwell, "Felix namque," *Grove Music Online*).

54. Mathews, *The Conversions,* 125 and 127.

55. Christelle Reggiani argues that Hutting's imaginary portraits represent a condemnation of Namque's laxity in the use of constraints (Reggiani, *Rhétoriques de la contrainte,* 392). However, Perec's narrator explicitly mentions the excessive rigidity of Hutting's approach.

56. In this respect, Hutting is very different from Perec, who claims that he never wants to reuse a formula and system elaborated in a previous book (Perec, "Notes sur ce que je cherche," in *Penser/Classer,* 9).

57. Critics of formalist criticism and structuralism have often emphasized the

inadequacy of its static, atemporal models (see, for example, Derrida, "Force et signification," 11; Brooks, *Reading for the Plot,* 36). While the Oulipo generally distances itself from structuralism (see Le Lionnais, "La Lipo," in Oulipo, *La Littérature potentielle,* 19; Jacques Roubaud, "La Mathématique dans la méthode de Raymond Queneau," 242), Perec was certainly familiar with structuralist criticism, having attended Roland Barthes' seminars at the École pratique des hautes études (Bellos, *Georges Perec,* 287).

58. Dällenbach, *Le Récit spéculaire,* 62.

59. See, for example, Magné's two articles on "Le Métatextuel" in *Texte en main* (5 and 6), as well as "Le Puzzle mode d'emploi" and "Le Métatextuel perecquien revisité." Dällenbach also introduces the word *métatextuel* (as an adjective) to characterize the "mise en abyme of the code" (*Le Récit spéculaire,* 128).

60. Jullien, "Portrait de l'artiste en mille morceaux," 403.

61. Dällenbach, *Le Récit spéculaire,* 49. Claude Burgelin argues that *La Vie mode d'emploi* incorporates its own negation or derision (Burgelin, *Georges Perec,* 220).

62. Lévy, "Le Temps mode d'emploi," 104.

63. Claude Burgelin notes that "Perec a laissé constamment entrouverte la porte de son ouvroir" (Burgelin, *Georges Perec,* 83) (Perec left the door of his workshop constantly ajar).

64. Magné, "Construire l'anodin," 46.

65. Genette, *Palimpsestes,* 9.

66. As Bernard Magné observes, Perec's metatextual clues often enlighten only those who do not need them (Magné, "Les Cahiers des charges de Georges Perec," 72). Perec's use of implicit quotations is particularly problematic since their often significant thematic implications are deliberately hidden from the reader (Magné, "Quelques problèmes de l'énonciation en régime fictionnel," 76).

67. See Peeters, "Échafaudages," 184; Lorente, "Quelles lunettes pour le lecteur?" 39.

68. I am indebted to Bernard Magné for bringing this example to my attention.

69. Roubaud, "La Mathématique dans la méthode de Raymond Queneau," 57.

70. Significantly, this description of a concealed palace itself conceals a modified quotation from Proust's *Albertine disparue:* "Comme ces palais des contes orientaux où l'on mène la nuit un personnage qui ramené avant le jour chez lui, ne doit pas pouvoir retrouver la demeure magique où il finit par croire qu'il n'est allé qu'en rêve" (Proust, *À la recherche du temps perdu* 4:229–30) (Like those palaces in oriental tales whither mysterious agents convey by night a person who, brought back home before daybreak, can never find his way back to the magic dwelling which he ends by believing that he visited only in a dream).

71. Rosset, *Le Réel,* 18.

72. Wittgenstein, *Philosophical Investigations,* sec. 143, p. 48.

73. This fits Marina van Zuylen's account of monomania as a flight from "the confusion of everyday life" (*Monomania,* 6).

Chapter 8

The chapter epigraph is from Italo Calvino's *Cosmicomics,* quoted by Perec in *Espèces d'espaces,* 158; *Species of Spaces,* trans. Sturrock, 80.

1. Perec, "Pouvoirs et limites du romancier français contemporain" (May 5, 1967), in Ribière, *Parcours Perec,* 32.

2. With the notable exception of Manet van Montfrans, critics are generally unwilling to acknowledge Perec's realist project, yet are more than happy to discuss the autobiographical aspects of his work. Jacques-Denis Bertharion, for example, collapses the first category into the second, claiming that Perec's early insistence on realism in the "Ligne générale" texts is nothing but "an indirect characterization of Perec's autobiographical desire" (*Poétique de Georges Perec,* 18).

3. In this respect, I disagree with other accounts that limit the "realist" aspect of Perec's writings to his formal encrypting of autobiographical elements (Bernard Magné's "autobiographeme") or which, at the other extreme, claim that the author's confidence in the cognitive and referential function of language is unproblematic (Montfrans, *Georges Perec,* 388).

4. Watt, *Rise of the Novel,* 22

5. Auerbach, *Mimesis,* 491.

6. The chance moment may nevertheless represent a glimmer of hope in an often grim universe. Auerbach says of Woolf's *To the Lighthouse,* despite his comments on the modern novel's "atmosphere of universal gloom": "It is precisely the random moment which is comparatively independent of the controversial and unstable orders over which men fight and despair; it passes unaffected by them, as daily life" (*Mimesis,* 552).

7. Lukács, *The Meaning of Contemporary Realism,* 551–52.

8. Watt, *Rise of the Novel,* 30, 13. Édouard, the novelist character in Gide's *Les Faux-Monnayeurs,* makes the inverse argument: perhaps it is the novel's "lawless" nature that leads it to cling fearfully to reality (Gide, *Les Faux-Monnayeurs,* 182).

9. Watt, *The Rise of the Novel,* 30.

10. Ibid., 32.

11. Mitterand, *L'Illusion réaliste,* 1.

12. Christopher Prendergast argues that both Auerbach and Lukács, in their commitment to the notion of "totality," take for granted "the principle which allows for the unproblematic passage from microcosm to macrocosm, the criteria by which the writer decides, and which enable the reader to accept, that one set of selections and combinations is representative, where another is merely random or arbitrary" (Prendergast, *Order of Mimesis,* 25–26).

13. The epiphany is mentioned in *Ulysses* but explained fully only in the posthumously published *Stephen Hero:* a "trivial incident" observed in the streets of Dublin leads Stephen Daedalus to formulate his theory of epiphanies, whereby "[t]he soul of the commonest object [. . .] seems to us radiant" (Joyce, *Stephen Hero,* 211, 213).

14. Proust, *À la recherche du temps perdu* 1:43–44.

15. Ibid., 4:457.

16. The expression "objective chance" first appears in *Les Vases communicants* (1932), where Breton characterizes it as a form of manifestation of necessity (*Œuvres complètes* 2:168).

17. Aragon, *Le Paysan de Paris,* 11–13 and 15–16.

18. In Sartre's *La Nausée,* Roquentin and Anny discover that there are no events, no adventures, and no privileged moments (*La Nausée,* 64 and 212). Yet Roquentin's flashes of nausea are nothing less than metaphysical epiphanies. Furthermore, it is a chance event—the overhearing of a jazz song—that leads Roquentin to experience a revelation of the power of art at the novel's end. While this apparently Proustian ending is equivocal, the fact remains that chance here does not stand for absolute insignificance. In Albert Camus' reflection on the absurd, chance is the sole source of certainty and thus of comfort: "Je peux tout réfuter dans ce monde qui m'entoure, me heurte ou me transporte, sauf ce chaos, ce hasard roi et cette divine équivalence qui naît de l'anarchie" (Camus, *Le Mythe de Sisyphe,* 73) (I can refute everything in this world that surrounds me, offends, or elates me, except for this chaos, this sovereign chance, and this divine equivalence that is born of anarchy).

19. Butor, "Le Roman et la poésie," in *Répertoire* 2:25–26.

20. On these French discourses on the everyday, see Michael Sheringham's *Everyday Life: Theories and Practices from Surrealism to the Present,* and Derek Schilling's *Mémoires du quotidien,* chapter on "La Pensée du quotidien."

21. This assertion by Perec takes up Lukács's distinction between naturalism, which dispenses with the selective principle, and true realism, which establishes "a 'hierarchy of significance' in the situations and characters presented" (Lukács, *The Meaning of Contemporary Realism,* 34). Formalism, on the other hand, is unaware of this distinction and rejects both naturalism and realism in order to focus on technique alone.

22. Schilling, *Mémoires du quotidien,* 53.

23. Bertharion, *Poétique de Georges Perec,* 115 and 125.

24. Molteni, "Faussaire et réaliste: le premier Gaspard de Georges Perec," 63.

25. Whether Robbe-Grillet's writing is truly neutral is of course highly questionable; Robbe-Grillet himself nevertheless presents it this way in the 1956 essay "Une Voie pour le roman futur" ("A Path for the Future Novel"), where he claims that the New Novel confronts us with fragments of raw reality (*Pour un nouveau roman,* 19).

26. In *Le Degré zéro de l'écriture,* Barthes argues that Camus' *L'Étranger* heralds a new solution to the modern problem of writing by adopting a destylized language that is neutral, innocent, and transparent (*Œuvres complètes* 1:217). In the articles he devotes to Robbe-Grillet and to the "Nouveau Roman" between 1954 and 1962, he claims that Robbe-Grillet's objects, freed of adjectives and meanings, are nothing more than "an optical resistance" ("Littérature objective," in *Œuvres complètes* 2:294): this writing is "a literature of pure report" ("Nouveaux problèmes du réalisme," in *Œuvres complètes* 1:658), and the author himself is "the writer of pure verbal vision" ("Témoignage sur Robbe-Grillet," in *Œuvres complètes* 1:1117).

27. "The serious treatment of everyday reality, the rise of more extensive and socially inferior human groups to the position of subject matter for problematic-existential representation, on the one hand; on the other, the embedding of random persona and events in the general course of contemporary history, the fluid historical background—these, we believe, are the foundations of modern realism" (Auerbach, *Mimesis,* 491).

28. Leak, "Phago-Citations," 59.

29. Baudrillard, *Le Système des objets,* 130, 277.

30. Ibid., 278 and 282–83.

31. Andrew Leak argues that the character's project is a precise counterpart of the "deconditioning of the reader with regard to the essentialist state of the bourgeois novel," which Barthes saw as Robbe-Grillet's aim in *Le Voyeur* (Leak, "Phago-Citations," 70). However, as Leak points out, this is the character's project, not Perec's (72).

32. Sheringham, *Everyday Life,* 256.

33. Perec, "La Rue Vilin," in *L'Infra-ordinaire,* 15–31.

34. Perec's enumeration of the objects on his desk apparently includes the text that we are reading, thus suggesting a potentially infinite recursion (and repetition of the same); yet as the text repeats itself we notice changes that indicate the passage of time: for example, the Casio calculator on the desk displays a different figure (and, read backward, a different word: 315308/BOESIE; 35079/GLOSE); the alarm clock first shows the time 10:18 A.M., but later displays 12:50 P.M. (*L'Infra-ordinaire,* 108, 114).

35. Michael Sheringham convincingly argues that participation in *Cause commune* contributed to a shift in Perec's attitude to the "reality texts" of the *Lieux* project, which he came to read in a new, nonautobiographical way (*Everyday Life,* 259).

36. Blanchard et al., "Introduction," *Cause commune* 1:1.

37. Schilling, *Mémoires du quotidien,* 19; Sheringham, *Everyday Life,* 5.

38. Lefebvre, *Critique de la vie quotidienne,* 1: 140. Lefebvre is particularly scathing in his account of surrealism, which claims to be interested in the real but only displaces it in order to discover another, imaginary world (123).

39. See Bellos, *Georges Perec,* 287; Schilling, *Mémoires du quotidien,* 21.

40. Among Perec's *Cause commune* writings, "L'Orange est proche," a discussion of the relationship between capitalism and violence, is unusual in its political stridence. However, this text does not focus on descriptions of everyday reality, instead taking as its starting point Perec's reaction to Stanley Kubrick's film *A Clockwork Orange* (*Cause commune* 3, October 1972). While Jacques-Denis Bertharion and Michael Sheringham have emphasized the affinity between Perec's "infra-ordinaire" writings and the Marxist project of Henri Lefebvre's *Critique de la vie quotidienne* (Bertharion, "Des *Lieux* aux non-lieux"; Sheringham, "Attending to the Everyday"), Gilbert Adair insists on the political and sociological neutrality of Perec's descriptions of everyday life ("The Eleventh Day," 99). However, I agree with Derek Schilling that Perec's proximity to the social sciences creates significant "field effects" that allow literature to harness new textual possibilities (Schilling, *Mémoires du quotidien,* 23).

41. These writings are: "Approches de quoi?" originally published in *Cause commune* 5; "La Rue Vilin," part of the *Lieux* project first published in *L'Humanité* in 1977; "Deux cent quarante-trois cartes postales en couleurs véritables"; two articles written for Air France's in-flight magazine ("Tout autour de Beaubourg" and "Promenades dans Londres"); another magazine article on offices ("Le Saint des Saints"), published in *Vogue Hommes* in September 1981; "Tentative d'inventaire des aliments liquides et solides que j'ai ingurgités au cours de l'année mil neuf cent soixante-quatorze," published in *Action poétique* in 1976; and "Still Life/Style Leaf" (*Le Fou parle,* 1981).

42. Shklovsky (Chklovski), "L'art comme procédé," 84.

43. Given the *Cause commune* group's concern with investigating the everyday, the journal's title can be read as a pun: *cause/choses commune*[s] (common cause/common things).

44. See also Perec, *Entretiens et conférences* 2:94.

45. Blanchot, "La parole ordinaire," in *L'Entretien infini,* 361.

46. Ibid., 365.

47. All translations of Perec's *Tentative d'épuisement d'un lieu parisien* are my own.

48. Bakhtin (Bakhtine), "Le Problème du contenu, du matériau et de la forme dans l'œuvre littéraire" (1924), in *Esthétique et théorie du roman,* 41–42.

49. Thus Catherine Kerbrat-Orecchioni, in an otherwise perceptive analysis of the various markers of subjectivity in Perec's text (selection and hierarchization of material, interpretative and affective statements, causal hypotheses, modal expressions, style), argues that Perec inevitably fails in his project of objective description. She rightly notes that the gaze and language necessarily act as filters between the referent and signifier (Kerbrat-Orecchioni, *L'Énonciation,* 147–62). However, as Michael Sheringham points out, Perec's goal is "to make the everyday visible, not as an objective reality but as something in which we participate" (Sheringham, *Everyday Life,* 168)—and in this he surely succeeds.

50. Sheringham, *Everyday Life,* 268–69.

51. Michael Sheringham argues that Perec attributes no particular value to these categorizations, but uses them as heuristic devices: "Such classifications are contingent products of the process of attention itself, as it oscillates, like a pupil dilating and contracting, between a passive 'attention flottante' and a more active interrogation of experience" ("Attending to the Everyday," 198). Nevertheless, I believe that the problem of classification is central to Perec's work and to his never abandoned totalizing ambition.

52. The preoccupation with buses can also be read as a homage to Raymond Queneau's *Exercices de style,* a text that combines an "infraordinary" theme (a minor quarrel in a bus) with stylistic experimentation.

53. Although Perec states in more than one interview that Valène is the narrator (*Entretiens et conférences* 1:239 and 270), Valène is always referred to in the third person. However, he often determines the narrative point of view (its *focalisation,* to adopt Genette's terminology). Furthermore, there are moments when the narration seems to refer to its object as if the latter were, in fact, not the apartment building but Valène's painting of the building. Danielle Constantin notes that Valène did play the role of narrator in early versions of the manuscript (Constantin, "'Ne rien nier. Énoncer,'" 292).

54. Certeau, *L'Invention du quotidien* 1:338.

55. This echo is possibly a deliberate, albeit hidden allusion to *W ou le souvenir d'enfance,* in accordance with one of the novel's intertextual constraints.

56. Pavel, *La Pensée du roman,* 395.

57. Aristotle, *Poetics* 1449b–1450a; Lessing, *Laokoon,* in *Lessings Werke,* 632.

58. Hamon, *Du descriptif,* 17.

59. As Philippe Hamon notes, for Valéry both narrative and description fall into the category of the aleatory and informal, and only poetry is an art of constraint and form (Hamon, *Du descriptif,* 18n). From this point of view, formal anti-chance appears incompatible with the genre of the novel.

60. Barthes, "L'Effet de réel," in *Œuvres complètes* 3:30, 32.

61. In "Les Choses signifient-elles quelque chose?" (1962), Barthes argues that Robbe-Grillet's purely denotative language is nonrealist (*Œuvres complètes* 2:46). Barthes nevertheless describes Robbe-Grillet's enterprise as a new form of realism in "Nouveaux Problèmes du réalisme" (1956) and "Le Point sur Robbe-Grillet?" (1962) (Barthes, *Œuvres complètes* 1:656–59 and 2:452–59).

62. Roubaud, "Notes sur la poétique des listes," 201.

63. Focusing on *La Vie mode d'emploi,* Claude Burgelin compares Flaubertian description, where the object functions as a kind of clue, to the Perecquian inventory which aims to be neutral, a "denotation as lacking in connotation as possible" ("Perec lecteur de Flaubert," 139–40). While this account contradicts Barthes' account of the "reality effect" in Flaubert, it in effect transfers this account from nineteenth-century "realist" description (now accepted as connotative) to Perec.

This shift should itself make us wary of applying a sharp denotation/connotation distinction to different types of description; the effects of description are relative.

64. Hamon, *Du descriptif,* 13.

65. Perec, "Notes concernant les objets qui sont sur ma table de travail," in *Penser/Classer,* 21–22; "Notes Concerning the Objects That Are on My Work-Table," in *Species of Spaces,* trans. Sturrock, 142.

66. Perec, "Notes concernant les objets," 22

67. Hamon, *Du descriptif,* 17.

68. For Philippe Hamon the merits of the descriptive reside precisely in its ability to counteract narrative, resisting the "constraining linearity" of the text, the "oriented dynamism" of the narrative (*Du descriptif,* 5). Of course, enumeration does not necessarily exclude the telling of a story. However, as Tiphaine Samoyault observes, Perec's enumerations and inventories are usually not directly related to the narrative itself (Samoyault, "Romans-mondes," 540). Although chapter 51 does contain a list of the stories recounted and to be recounted in the novel, it constitutes a cross section of the novel's fictional material rather than a chronological survey.

69. Jacques Roubaud emphasizes the relationship between the art of the list and the arts of memory ("Notes sur la poétique des listes," 206). This is one of Roubaud's own aesthetic preoccupations, as evidenced in such works as the list-poem *Kyrielle* (2003).

70. A manuscript note in the *Cahier des charges* supports this interpretation of chapter 76, stating that Madame de Beaumont hates memories and has hidden away her love letters in the cellar (Perec, *Cahier des charges,* chap. 76). In the final text, the psychological significance of the objects remains implicit.

71. As Perec notes in "Penser/Classer": "L'ordre alphabétique est arbitraire, inexpressif, donc neutre" (The order of the alphabet is arbitrary, inexpressive, and therefore neutral) (*Penser/Classer,* 160; "Think/Classify," in *Species of Spaces,* trans. Sturrock, 190).

72. Hamon, *Du descriptif,* 56, 60.

73. For a discussion of alphabetical order and the problem of knowledge, see Roger Shattuck, "The Alphabet and the Junkyard." After contrasting Bouvard and Pécuchet's inability to "fit the pieces of the world's puzzle together" in Flaubert's novel (33), with the Leibnizian faith in the world's unity held by Diderot and his fellow *encyclopédistes* (34), Shattuck links the modernist aesthetics of the fragment with the preference for the (arbitrary, illogical) alphabet as an ordering principle (39).

74. The category of the "miscellaneous" is defined by the predominant taxonomic system but also threatens that system, representing the class of things that defy classification. Perec's interest in the infraordinary entails an investigation of the category of the "divers."

75. As Pierre Bourdieu points out, we classify ourselves by our acts of classifi-

cation, as well as by the types of products we consume and the lifestyles we adopt (*La Distinction,* 216, 561). The Altamonts' distinctions between basic and luxury foods, and between different types of wines, indicate that they belong to a certain social class (and to the hyperconsciousness of this belonging). The Gratiolets' cellar, on the other hand, reveals the family's fall from prosperity to its current humble position.

76. Foucault, *Les Mots et les choses,* 160–61.

77. Ibid., 163.

78. Borges, *Selected Non-Fictions,* 231; Foucault, *Les Mots et les choses,* 7.

79. Gilbert Adair notes the connection between the "infra-ordinaire" project and the idea of the world as puzzle ("The Eleventh Day," 106). We should add to this point the observation that the puzzle metaphor suggests not only a collection of discrete things, but also an order according to which these things are connected. It is here that the real difficulty begins.

80. In "Je me souviens de Malet & Isaac" (1979), Perec copies out remembered fragments from his school history textbooks, in a parody of the way in which these books transformed events, ideas, and people into pieces of a jigsaw (Perec, *Penser/Classer,* 74).

81. Foucault, *Les Mots et les choses,* 9.

82. Perec, *Tentative d'épuisement;* "Lire: Esquisse socio-physiologique," in *Penser/Classer,* 109–28; "Considérations sur les lunettes," in *Penser/Classer,* 133–50.

83. Perec, "Notes brèves sur l'art et la manière de ranger ses livres," in *Penser/Classer,* 42; "Brief Notes on the Art and Manner of Arranging One's Books," in *Species of Spaces,* trans. Sturrock, 151.

84. Perec, "Notes brèves," 42; "Brief Notes," 151.

85. Jean-François Chassay rightly states that Perec, like other contemporary writers, refuses to believe in the perfect coherence of the world (*Le Jeu des coïncidences,* 20). However, Perec's works do not simply tell us that everything is random and absurd, but rather leave this question in suspense, weaving together chance and necessity, order and disorder.

86. This approach can be associated with a text that Perec praises in "Penser/Classer": the "Pillow Book" of the eleventh-century Japanese writer Sei Shônagon. Sei Shônagon lists her observations under such headings as "Hateful Things" (*Pillow Book,* 44), "Presumptuous Things" (170), "Things That Fall from the Sky" (210), or "Pleasing Things" (216). According to Perec, these are not really classifications but simple enumerations that can always be reworked and regrouped (Perec, *Penser/Classer,* 165).

Works Cited

Adair, Gilbert. "The Eleventh Day: Perec and the Infra-Ordinary." *Review of Contemporary Fiction* 13 (Spring 1993): 98–108.

Andrews, Chris. "Constraint and Convention: The Formalism of the Oulipo." *Neophilologus* 87 (2003): 223–32.

———. "Puzzles and Lists: Georges Perec's *Un homme qui dort.*" *Modern Language Notes* 111, no. 4 (1996): 775–96.

Angenot, Marc. *Le Roman populaire: Recherches en paralittérature.* Montreal: Presses de l'Université du Québec, 1975.

Antelme, Robert. *L'Espèce humaine.* Paris: Gallimard, 1978. Translated by Jeffrey Haight and Annie Mahler as *The Human Race* (Marlboro, Vt.: Marlboro, 1957).

Apollodorus. *The Library.* Translated by Sir James George Frazer. 2 vols. Cambridge, Mass.: Harvard University Press, 1921.

Aragon, Louis. *Je n'ai jamais appris à écrire ou les incipit.* Paris: Skira, 1969.

———. *Le Paysan de Paris.* Paris: Gallimard, 1926. Reprint, Folio, 1998.

Arendt, Hannah. *Eichmann in Jerusalem: A Report on the Banality of Evil.* 1962. Reprinted with an introduction by Amos Elon. New York: Penguin Books, 2006.

———. *The Origins of Totalitarianism.* 1951. New York: Harcourt, 1976.

Aristotle. *Nicomachean Ethics.* Translated and edited by Terence Irwin. 2nd ed. Indianapolis: Hackett, 1999.

———. *On Interpretation.* Translated by E. M. Edghill. In *The Basic Works of Aristotle,* edited by Richard McKeon, 38–61. New York: Random House, 1941.

———. *Physics.* Books I–II. Translated by W. Charlton. Oxford: Clarendon, 1970.

——— [Aristote]. *Physique* I–IV. Translated and edited by Henri Carteron. Paris: Les Belles Lettres, 1966.

———. *Poetics.* Translated and edited by James Hutton. Preface by Gordon M. Kirkwood. New York: W. W. Norton, 1982.

Arnaud, Noël. "Gérard Genette et l'Oulipo." In Oulipo, *La Bibliothèque oulipienne* 5:7–22.

———. "Twenty Questions for Noël Arnaud." Interview by Warren F. Motte. *Studies in Twentieth-Century Literature* 10, no. 2 (Spring 1986): 289–306.

Atlan, Henri. *Entre le cristal et la fumée: Essai sur l'organisation du vivant.* Paris: Éditions du Seuil, 1979.

Auerbach, Erich. *Mimesis. The Representation of Reality in Western Literature.* 1946. Translated by Willard R. Trask. Princeton, N.J.: Princeton University Press, 1953.

Augustine. *City of God.* A.D. 426. Translated by Henry Bettenson. Harmondsworth: Penguin Books, 1984.

———. *The Retractations.* Translated by Mary Inez Bogan. Washington, D.C.: Catholic University of America Press, 1968.

Bacon, Francis, and David Sylvester. *Interviews with Francis Bacon.* London: Thames and Hudson, 1975.

Baetens, Jan, and Bernardo Schiavetta. "Écrivains encore un effort . . . pour être absolument modernes." *Formules* 1 (1997–98): 9–24.

Bakhtin, Mikhail M. *The Dialogic Imagination: Four Essays.* Edited by Michael Holquist. Translated by Caryl Emerson and Michael Holquist. Austin: University of Texas Press, 1981.

——— [Bakhtine, Mikhaïl]. *Esthétique et théorie du roman.* 1975. Translated by Daria Olivier. Preface by Michel Aucouturier. Paris: Gallimard, 1978.

Balzac, Honoré de. *La Comédie humaine.* Edited by Pierre-Georges Castex. Vol 1. Paris: Gallimard, 1976.

Barreau, Hervé. "Le Concept du hasard." In Noël, *Le Hasard aujourd'hui,* 209–19.

Barthes, Roland. *Œuvres complètes.* Edited by Éric Marty. 5 vols. Paris: Éditions du Seuil, 2002.

Baudelaire, Charles. *Correspondance.* Edited by Claude Pichois. Vol. 1. Paris: Gallimard, 1973.

———. *Écrits sur l'art.* Paris: Le Livre de Poche, 1992.

Baudrillard, Jean. *Le Système des objets.* Paris: Gallimard, 1968.

Beckett, Samuel. *L'Innommable.* Paris: Éditions de Minuit, 1953.

Béhar, Stella. *Georges Perec: Écrire pour ne pas dire.* New York: Peter Lang, 1995.

Bell, David F. *Circumstances: Chance and the Literary Text.* Lincoln: University of Nebraska Press, 1993.

Bellos, David. *Georges Perec: A Life in Words.* Boston: David R. Godine, 1993.

———. "Literary Quotations in Georges Perec's *La Vie mode d'emploi.*" *French Studies* 41, no. 2 (April 1987): 181–94.

———. "'Le Moyen fait partie de la vérité . . .' The Languages of Georges Perec's *Les Choses.*" *Journal of the Institute of Romance Studies* 1 (1992): 325–31.

———. "Perec et Saussure: À propos de *La Vie mode d'emploi.*" In Ribière, *Parcours Perec,* 91–96.

Bem, Jeanne. "La Mémoire, l'écriture et l'impossible à dire: Robert Antelme, Patrick Modiano, Georges Perec." *Colloquium Helveticum* 27 (1998): 25–41.

Bénabou, Marcel. "Bris de mots." In Oulipo, *La Bibliothèque oulipienne* 3:49–84.

———. "Faux et usage du faux chez Perec." *Le Cabinet d'amateur* 3 (Spring 1994): 25–36.

———. "Quarante siècles de l'Oulipo." *Magazine littéraire* 398 (May 2001): 20–26.

———. "La Règle et la contrainte." *Pratiques* 39 (December 1983): 101–6.

———. "Un aphorisme peut en cacher un autre." In Oulipo, *La Bibliothèque oulipienne* 1:251–69.

Bénabou, Marcel, Jacques Jouet, Harry Mathews, and Jacques Roubaud. *Un art simple et tout d'exécution: Cinq leçons de l'Oulipo; cinq leçons sur l'Oulipo.* Paris: Circé, 2001.

Benjamin, Walter. *Illuminations.* Edited by Hannah Arendt. Translated by Harry Zohn. New York: Schocken Books, 1968.

———. "Paris, the Capital of the Nineteenth Century." 1935. In *Selected Writings,* translated by Edmund Jephrott, Howard Eiland, et al., edited by Howard Eiland and Michael W. Jennings, 3:32–49. Cambridge, Mass.: Belknap, 2002.

Bens, Jacques. *OuLiPo 1960–63.* Paris: Christian Bourgois, 1980.

———. "Queneau oulipien." In Oulipo, *Atlas de littérature potentielle,* 22–33. Originally published as "Littérature potentielle." *L'Arc* 28 (1966): 43–51.

Bens, Jacques, and Paul Fournel. Interview. *Action poétique* 85 (1981): 48–64.

Berge, Claude. "Pour une analyse potentielle de la littérature combinatoire." In Oulipo, *La Littérature potentielle,* 43–57.

Bergson, Henri. *Les Deux Sources de la morale et de la religion.* 1932. Paris: Quadrige/Presses Universitaires de France, 1982.

———. *L'Évolution créatrice.* Paris: Félix Alcan, 1907.

Bertharion, Jacques-Denis. "Des *Lieux* aux non-lieux: De la rue Vilin à Ellis Island." *Le Cabinet d'amateur* 5 (June 1997): 51–72.

———. "*Je me souviens:* Un cryptogramme autobiographique." *Le Cabinet d'amateur* 2 (Autumn 1993): 73–84.

———. *Poétique de Georges Perec: "Une trace, une marque ou quelques signes."* Saint-Genouph: Librairie A.-G. Nizet, 1998.

Biasi, Pierre-Marc de. *La Génétique des textes.* Paris: Nathan, 2000.

Blanchard, Albert, Christine Brunet, Alain Bourdin, Christine Brunet, Jean Duvignaud, Pascal Lainé, Françoise Maillet, Georges Perec, and Paul Virilio. Introduction. *Cause commune* 1. Paris: Denoël/Gontier, May 1972.

Blanchot, Maurice. *L'Entretien infini.* Paris: Gallimard, 1969.

Bloom, Harold. *The Anxiety of Influence: A Theory of Poetry.* 2nd ed. New York: Oxford University Press, 1997.

Boethius. *Consolation of Philosophy.* A.D. 524. Translated with an introduction and notes by Joel C. Relihan. Indianapolis: Hackett, 2001.

Bold, Stephen C. "Labyrinths of Invention from the New Novel to Oulipo." *Neophilologus* 82 (1998): 543–57.

Borges, Jorge Luis. *Collected Fictions.* Translated by Andrew Hurley. London: Penguin Books, 1998.

———. *Selected Non-Fictions.* Edited by Eliot Weinberger. Translated by Esther Allen, Suzanne Jill Levine, and Eliot Weinberger. London: Penguin Putnam, 1999.

Bouchot, Vincent. "De la musique dans l'œuvre de Georges Perec: Fréquentations, thèmes, structures." *Cahiers Georges Perec* 4 (1990): 97–120.

———. "L'Intertextualité vernienne dans *W ou le souvenir d'enfance.*" In Magné, *Georges Perec: Écrire/Transformer,* 111–20.

Boulez, Pierre. *Par volonté et par hasard, entretiens avec Célestin Deliège.* Paris: Éditions du Seuil, 1975.

———. *Points de repère.* Edited by Jean-Jacques Nattiez and Sophie Galaise. Introduction by Jean-Jacques Nattiez. Musical examples identified by Robert Piencikowski. Vol. 1. Paris: Christian Bourgois, 1995.

Boulez, Pierre, and John Cage. *Correspondance.* Edited by Françoise Davoine, Jean-Jacques Nattiez, Hans Oesch, and Robert Piencikowski. Translated from English and French adaptation by Gaétan Martel. Paris: Christian Bourgois, 1991.

Bourbaki, Nicolas. *Éléments de mathématique.* 1939. Vol 1, *Théorie des ensembles.* Paris: Hermann, 1970.

Bourdieu, Pierre. *La Distinction: Critique sociale du jugement.* Paris: Éditions de Minuit, 1979.

Braffort, Paul. "Oulipo et 'Pataphysique." *Magazine littéraire* 338 (June 2000): 57–59.

Breton, André. *Œuvres complètes.* Edited by Marguerite Bonnet. 3 vols. Paris: Gallimard, 1988–99.

Brooks, Peter. *Reading for the Plot: Design and Intention in Narrative.* New York: Alfred A. Knopf, 1984.

Burgelin, Claude. *Georges Perec.* Paris: Éditions du Seuil, 1988.

———. *Les Parties de dominos chez Monsieur Lefèvre: Perec avec Freud, Perec contre Freud.* Paris: Circé, 1996.

———. "Perec lecteur de Flaubert." *La Revue des lettres modernes.* Série Flaubert 1:135–71. Paris: Minard, 1984.

———. "Quelques remarques sur le sujet oulipien en guise de préface." In Bénabou et al., *Un art simple et tout d'exécution,* 9–20.

Bürger, Peter. *Theory of the Avant-Garde.* Translated by Michael Shaw. Foreword by Jochen Schulte-Sasse. Minneapolis: University of Minnesota Press, 1984.

Butor, Michel. *Répertoire* 2. Paris: Éditions de Minuit, 1964.

Cage, John. *Silence.* 1961. Cambridge, Mass.: MIT Press, 1966.

Caillois, Roger. *Les Jeux et les hommes: Le masque et le vertige.* Paris: Gallimard, 1958.

Caldwell, John. "Felix namque." *Grove Music Online.* Edited by L. Macy. http://www.grovemusic.com (accessed March 5, 2005).

Calvino, Italo. "Prose et anticombinatoire." In Oulipo, *Atlas de littérature potentielle,* 319–31.

———. *The Uses of Literature.* Translated by Patrick Creagh. New York: Harcourt Brace, 1986.

Camus, Albert. *L'Étranger.* 1942. New York: Random House, Pantheon Books, 1963. Translated by Matthew Ward as *The Stranger* (New York: Vintage, 1989).

———. *Le Mythe de Sisyphe: Essai sur l'absurde.* 1942. Paris: Gallimard, 1956.

Cave, Terence. *Recognitions.* Oxford: Oxford University Press, 1990.

Cayrol, Jean. *Lazare parmi nous.* Paris: Éditions du Seuil, 1950.

Céline, Louis-Ferdinand. *Voyage au bout de la nuit.* Paris: Gallimard, 1952. Reprint, collection Folio, 1996.

Cercle Linguistique de Prague. "Les Thèses de 1929." *Travaux du Cercle Linguistique de Prague,* 7–29. Nendeln, Liechtenstein: Kraus, 1968.

Certeau, Michel de. *L'Invention du quotidien.* Vol. 1, *Arts de faire.* Paris: 10/18, 1980.

Chambers, Ross. *Loiterature.* Lincoln: University of Nebraska Press, 1999.

Chassay, Jean-François. *Le Jeu des coïncidences dans "La Vie mode d'emploi" de Georges Perec.* Ville LaSalle, Quebec: Hurtubise HMH, 1992.

Cicero. *De Natura Deorum, Academica.* With an English translation by H. Rackham. London: William Heinemann, 1933.

Claudel, Paul. *Positions et propositions.* 10th ed. Paris: Gallimard, 1928.

Compagnon, Antoine. *Le Démon de la théorie: Littérature et sens commun.* Paris: Éditions du Seuil, 1998.

Constantin, Danielle. "'Ne rien nier. Énoncer': La mise en place des instances énonciatives et narratives dans les premiers temps de la rédaction de *La Vie mode d'emploi* de Georges Perec." *Texte* 27/28 (2000): 267–95.

Corriveau, Hugues. "Georges Perec ou le système de la déception." In Magné, *Georges Perec: Écrire/Transformer,* 134–48.

Couégnas, Daniel. *Introduction à la paralittérature.* Paris: Éditions du Seuil, 1992.

Cournot, Antoine Augustin. *Matérialisme, vitalisme, rationalisme: Étude sur l'emploi des données de la science en philosophie.* 1875. In *Œuvres complètes.* Edited by Claire Salomon-Bayet. Vol. 5. Paris: J. Vrin, 1979.

Curtius, Ernst Robert. *European Literature and the Latin Middle Ages.* 1953. Translated by Willard R. Trask. Princeton, N.J.: Princeton University Press, 1990.

Dällenbach, Lucien. *Le Récit spéculaire: Essai sur la mise en abyme.* Paris: Éditions du Seuil, 1977.

Dana, Catherine. *Fictions pour mémoire: Camus, Perec et l'écriture de la Shoah.* Paris: L'Harmattan, 1998.

Dangy-Scaillierez, Isabelle. *L'Énigme criminelle dans les romans de Georges Perec.* Paris: Éditions Champion, 2002.

Dawkins, Richard. *The Blind Watchmaker: Why the Evidence of Evolution Reveals a Universe Without Design.* New York: W. W. Norton, 1987.

De Bary, Cécile. "Contre une littérature réaliste?" *Formules* 6 (2002): 69–84.

———. "Il faut encore une fois partir de l'image du puzzle." In Joly, *L'Œuvre de Georges Perec: Réception et mythisation,* 79–93.

Deleuze, Gilles. *Foucault.* Paris: Éditions de Minuit, 1986.

———. *Francis Bacon: Logique de la sensation.* 1981. Reprint, Paris: Éditions du Seuil, 2002. Translated by Daniel W. Smith as *Francis Bacon: The Logic of Sensation* (Minneapolis: University of Minnesota Press, 2003).

———. *Pourparlers, 1972–90.* Paris: Éditions de Minuit, 1990.

Deleuze, Gilles, and Félix Guattari. *Kafka: Pour une littérature mineure.* Paris: Éditions de Minuit, 1975.

———. *Mille Plateaux.* Paris: Éditions de Minuit, 1980. Translated by Brian Massumi as *A Thousand Plateaus* (Minneapolis: University of Minnesota Press, 1987).

Derrida, Jacques. *De la grammatologie.* Paris: Éditions de Minuit, 1967.

———. "Force et signification." In *L'Écriture et la différence,* 9–49. Paris: Éditions du Seuil, 1967. Originally published in *Critique* 193–94 (June–July 1963).

Descartes, René. *Discourse on Method and Meditations on First Philosophy.* Translated by Donald A. Cress. 4th ed. Indianapolis: Hackett, 1998.

Detienne, Marcel, and Jean-Pierre Vernant. *Les Ruses de l'intelligence: La mètis des Grecs.* Paris: Flammarion, 1974.

Diderot, Denis. *Jacques le fataliste.* In *Œuvres.* Edited by André Billy. Paris: Gallimard, 1951. Translated by David Coward as *Jacques the Fatalist* (Oxford: Oxford University Press, 1999).

Didier, Béatrice, and Jacques Neefs, eds. *Penser, classer, écrire: De Pascal à Perec.* Paris: Presses Universitaires de Vincennes, 1990.

Doob, Penelope Reed. *The Idea of the Labyrinth from Classical Antiquity Through the Middle Ages.* Ithaca, N.Y.: Cornell University Press, 1990.

Drogoz, Philippe. "Georges Perec et la musique: Questions à Philippe Drogoz." *Cahiers Georges Perec* 1 (1985): 267–77.

Duquesne, Dominique. *"Les Choses" de Georges Perec.* Paris: Bertrand-Lacoste, 2001.

Duvignaud, Jean. *Le Jeu du jeu.* Paris: Balland, 1980.

———. *Perec ou la cicatrice.* Paris: Actes Sud, 1993.

Eco, Umberto. *The Name of the Rose.* 1980. Translated by William Weaver. Postscript by the author. New York: Harcourt, 1983.

———. *The Open Work.* 1962. Translated by Anna Cancogni. Cambridge, Mass.: Harvard University Press, 1989.

Encyclopédie, Dictionnaire raisonné des sciences, des arts et des métiers. Chicago: ARTFL Project, University of Chicago, 2001. http://www.lib.uchicago.edu/efts/ARTFL/projects/encyc/ (accessed January 6, 2008).

Ewert, Jeanne C. "'A Thousand Other Mysteries': Metaphysical Detection, Ontological Quests." In Merivale and Sweeney, *Detecting Texts,* 179–98.

Flaubert, Gustave. *Bouvard et Pécuchet.* Paris: Garnier-Flammarion, 1966.

———. *Correspondance.* Edited by Jean Bruneau. Vol. 3. Paris: Gallimard, 1991.

Foehr-Janssens, Yasmina, and Emmanuelle Métry, eds. *La Fortune: Thèmes, représentations, discours.* Geneva: Droz, 2003.

Forster, E. M. *Aspects of the Novel.* 1927. London: Hodder and Stoughton, 1974.

Foucault, Michel. *Les Mots et les choses.* Paris: Gallimard, 1966.

———. *Raymond Roussel.* Paris: Gallimard, 1963.

———. *Surveiller et punir: Naissance de la prison.* Paris: Gallimard, 1975. Translated by Alan Sheridan as *Discipline and Punish: The Birth of the Prison,* 2nd ed. (New York: Vintage, 1997).

Freud, Sigmund. *Beyond the Pleasure Principle.* Translated and edited by James Strachey. New York: W.W. Norton, 1961.

———. *The Psychopathology of Everyday Life.* Translated and edited by James Strachey. New York: W.W. Norton, 1965.

Garrigues, Emmanuel, ed. *Les Jeux surréalistes: Mars 1921–septembre 1962.* Archives du surréalisme 5. Paris: Gallimard, 1995.

Genette, Gérard. "Avatars du cratylisme." *Poétique* 11 (1972): 367–94.

———. *Figures II.* Paris: Éditions du Seuil, 1969.

———. *Figures III.* Paris: Éditions du Seuil, 1972.

———. *Palimpsestes: La littérature au second degré.* Paris: Éditions du Seuil, 1982.

Genette, Gérard, and Tzvetan Todorov, eds. *Littérature et réalité.* Paris: Éditions du Seuil, 1982.

Gide, André. *Les Faux-Monnayeurs.* Paris: Gallimard, 1925. Reprint, collection Folio, 1977.

Gribbin, John. *In Search of Schrödinger's Cat: Quantum Physics and Reality.* New York: Bantam Books, 1984.

Griffiths, Paul. *Modern Music and After: Directions Since 1945.* New York: Oxford University Press, 1995.

Hacking, Ian. *The Taming of Chance.* Cambridge: Cambridge University Press, 1990.

Hamon, Philippe. *Du descriptif.* Paris: Hachette, 1993.

Hartje, Hans. *Georges Perec écrivant.* Villeneuve d'Ascq: Presses Universitaires du Septentrion, 1995.

———. "*W* et l'histoire d'une enfance en France." In Jørgensen and Sestoft, *Georges Perec et l'histoire,* 53–66.

Hillen, Sabine. "Mode d'emploi du hasard: Sur Georges Perec." In *Écrire l'insignifiant: Dix études sur le fait divers dans le roman contemporain,* edited by Paul Pelckmans and Bruno Tritsmans, 63–75. Amsterdam and Atlanta, Ga.: Rodopi, 2000.

Hughes, Robert. *The Shock of the New.* 6th ed. New York: Alfred A. Knopf, 1998.

Huizinga, Johan. *Homo Ludens: A Study of the Play Element in Culture.* 1950. Boston: Beacon, 1966.

Hume, David. *An Enquiry Concerning Human Understanding.* 1739–40. Edited by Tom L. Beauchamp. Oxford/New York: Oxford University Press, 1999.

James, Alison. "Automatism, Arbitrariness, and the Oulipian Author." *French Forum* 31, no. 2 (Spring 2006): 111–25.

———. "Pour un modèle diagrammatique de la contrainte: L'écriture oulipienne de Georges Perec." *Théorie, littérature, enseignement* 22 (2004): 55–81.

James, Henry. *Selected Tales.* New York: Penguin Classics, 2001.

Jarry, Alfred. *Œuvres complètes.* Edited by Michel Arrivé. Vol. 1. Paris: Gallimard, 1972.

Jenny, Laurent. *La Parole singulière.* Paris: Belin, 1990.

Joly, Jean-Luc, ed. *L'Œuvre de Georges Perec: Réception et mythisation, Actes du colloque de Rabat (1–3 novembre 2000).* Rabat: Publications de la Faculté des Lettres et des Sciences Humaines, Université Mohammed-V, 2002.

Jørgensen, Steen Bille, and Carsten Sestoft, eds. *Georges Perec et l'histoire: Actes du colloque international, Université de Copenhague, du 30 avril au 1er mai 1998.* Copenhagen: Museum Tusculanum, 2000.

Jouet, Jacques. "With (and Without) Constraints." Translated by Roxanne Lapidus. *SubStance* 30, no. 3 (2001): 4–16.

Joyce, James. *A Portrait of the Artist as a Young Man.* 1914. Edited by Jeri Johnson. Oxford: Oxford University Press, 2000.

———. *Stephen Hero.* New York: New Directions Books, 1963.

———. *Ulysses.* London: Penguin, 1992.

Judt, Tony. *Marxism and the French Left: Studies in Labour and Politics in France, 1930–81.* Oxford: Clarendon, 1986.

———. *Past Imperfect: French Intellectuals, 1944–56.* Berkeley/Los Angeles/Oxford: University of California Press, 1992.

Jullien, Dominique. "Le Cas Polonius." *Le Cabinet d'amateur* 5 (June 1997): 73–85.

———. "Fiat lux." *Revue des sciences humaines* 235 (October–December 1994): 125–51.

———. "Portrait de l'artiste en mille morceaux: les avatars du roman d'artiste dans *La Vie mode d'emploi.*" *Romanic Review* 83, no. 3 (May 1992): 389–404.

Kafka, Franz. *Ein Landarzt und andere Prosa.* Stuttgart: Reklam, 1995.

———. *Der Process.* Frankfurt: Fischer Taschenbuch, 1993.

———. *Das Urteil und andere Prosa.* Stuttgart: Reklam, 1995.

Kaufmann, Vincent. *Poétique des groupes littéraires (Avant-gardes 1920–1970).* Paris: Presses Universitaires de France, 1997.

Kavanagh, Thomas, ed. *Chance, Culture and the Literary Text.* Ann Arbor: Michigan Romance Studies, 1994.

Kerbrat-Orecchioni, Catherine. *La Connotation.* Lyon: Presses Universitaires de Lyon, 1977.

———. *L'Énonciation: De la subjectivité dans le langage.* 4th ed. Paris: Armand Colin, 1999.

Kermode, Frank. *The Sense of an Ending: Studies in the Theory of Fiction.* New York: Oxford University Press, 1967.

Köhler, Erich. *Der literarische Zufall, das Mögliche und die Notwendigkeit.* Munich: Wilhelm Fink, 1973.

Kuon, Peter, ed. *Oulipo-Poétiques: Actes du colloque de Salzburg, 23–25 avril 1997.* Études littéraires françaises 69. Tübingen: Gunter Narr, 1999.

Laplace, Pierre-Simon. *Essai philosophique sur les probabilités.* 5th ed., 1825. Reprinted with a preface by René Thom and afterword by Bernard Bru. Paris: Christian Bourgois, 1986.

Lapprand, Marc. *Poétique de l'Oulipo.* Amsterdam: Rodopi, 1998.

Leak, Andrew. "Phago-Citations: Barthes, Perec and the Transformation of Literature." *Review of Contemporary Fiction* 13 (Spring 1993): 57–75.

Lecarme, Jacques. "La Page des sports." *Magazine littéraire* 316 (December 1993): 40–42.

Lefebvre, Henri. *Critique de la vie quotidienne.* 2nd ed. 2 vols. Paris: L'Arche Éditeur, 1958–61.

Leiris, Michel. *Biffures* (*La Règle du jeu 1*). 1948. Paris: Gallimard, 1975.

———. *Mots sans mémoire.* Paris: Gallimard, 1969.

Lejeune, Philippe. *La Mémoire et l'oblique: Georges Perec autobiographe.* Paris: P.O.L., 1991.

———. *Le Pacte autobiographique.* 1976. Paris: Éditions du Seuil, 1996.

———. "Une autobiographie sous contrainte." *Magazine littéraire* 316 (December 1993): 18–21.

Le Lionnais, François. "Le Second Manifeste." In Oulipo, *La Littérature potentielle,* 19–23.

Lescure, Jean. "La Méthode S+7." In Oulipo, *La Littérature potentielle,* 139–44.

Lessing, Gotthold Ephraim. *Lessings Werke.* Salzburg: Bergland-Buch, 1953.

Le Tellier, Hervé. *Esthétique de l'Oulipo.* Bordeaux: Le Castor Astral, 2006.

Levi, Primo. *Survival in Auschwitz: The Nazi Assault on Humanity.* 1958. Translated by Stuart Woolf. New York: Touchstone, 1996.

Lévy, Sydney. "Emergence in Georges Perec." *Yale French Studies* 105 (2004): 36–55.

———. "Oulipian Messages." *Studies in Twentieth Century Literature* 12, no. 2 (Spring 1998): 149–61.

———. "Le Temps mode d'emploi." *Littérature* 109 (1998): 98–115.

Long, A. A. *Hellenistic Philosophy: Stoics, Epicureans, Sceptics.* London: Duckworth, 1974.

Lorente, Catherine. "Quelles lunettes pour le lecteur?" *Le Cabinet d'amateur* 7–8 (1998): 31–39.

Lotman, Yuri. *La Structure du texte artistique.* Translated by Anne Fournier, Bernard Kreise, Ève Mallaret, and Joëlle Yong. Edited by Henri Meschonnic. Paris: Gallimard, 1973.

Lucretius. *De Rerum Natura.* Translated by W. H. D. Rouse. Edited and revised by Martin Ferguson Smith. Cambridge, Mass.: Harvard University Press, 1975.

Lukács, György. *The Meaning of Contemporary Realism.* 1955. Translated by John Mander and Necke Mander. London: Merlin, 1972.

Lusson, Pierre, Georges Perec, and Jacques Roubaud. *Petit Traité invitant à la découverte de l'art subtil du go.* Paris: Christian Bourgois, 1969.
Lutz, Theo. "Stochastiche Texte." *Augenblick* 4, no. 1 (1959): 3–9.
Magné, Bernard. "L'Autobiotexte perecquien." *Le Cabinet d'amateur* 5 (June 1997): 5–42.
———. "Les Cahiers des charges de Georges Perec." *Magazine littéraire* 316 (December 1993): 69–74.
———. "'*53 jours*' pour lecteurs chevronnés." In Magné, *Georges Perec: Écrire/Transformer,* 185–201.
———. "Cinquième figure pour *La Vie mode d'emploi.*" *Cahiers Georges Perec* 1 (1985): 173–77.
———. "Construire l'anodin: Les 'Deux cent quarante-trois cartes postales en couleurs véritables.'" *Le Cabinet d'amateur* 1 (Spring 1993): 29–55.
———. "Écriture et déconstruction dans les textes de Georges Perec." In Magné, *Perecollages,* 231–38.
———, ed. *Georges Perec: Écrire/Transformer. Études littéraires* 23, nos. 1–2 (Summer–Autumn 1990).
———. "Georges Perec oulibiographe." In Kuon, *Oulipo-Poétiques,* 41–61.
———. "Le Métatextuel." *Texte en main* 5 (Spring 1986): 83–90.
———. "Le Métatextuel (2)." *Texte en main* 6 (Winter 1986): 67–69.
———. "Le Métatextuel perecquien revisité." *Le Cabinet d'amateur* (July 2002). http://www.cabinetperec.org/articles/magne/magne-article.html (accessed January 6, 2008).
———. *Perecollages 1981–88.* Toulouse: Presses Universitaires du Mirail-Toulouse, 1989.
———. "Pour une lecture réticulée." *Cahiers Georges Perec* 4 (1990): 143–79.
———. "Le Puzzle mode d'emploi: Petite propédeutique pour une lecture métatextuelle de *La Vie mode d'emploi.*" *TEXTE* 1 (1982): 71–96. Reprinted in Magné, *Perecollages,* 33–60.
———. "Quelques considérations sur les poèmes hétérogrammatiques de Georges Perec." *Cahiers Georges Perec* 5 (1992): 27–85.
———. "Quelques problèmes de l'énonciation en régime fictionnel: L'exemple de *La Vie mode d'emploi.*" In Magné, *Perecollages,* 61–98.
———. "Le RAPT de *La Disparition.*" *Formules* 5 (2001): 202–19.
———. "Saint Jérôme mode d'emploi." *Cahiers Georges Perec* 6 (1996): 91–112.
———. "Les Sutures dans *W ou le souvenir d'enfance.*" *Cahiers Georges Perec* 2 (1988): 39–55.
———. "Textus ex machina (de la contrainte considérée comme machine à écrire dans quelques textes de Georges Perec)." In Magné, *Perecollages,* 219–29.
Magoudi, Ali. *La Lettre fantôme.* Paris: Éditions de Minuit, 1996.
Mallarmé, Stéphane. *Œuvres complètes.* Edited by Bertrand Marchal. 2 vols. Paris: Gallimard, 1998–2003.

Mann, Thomas. *La Montagne magique* [*Der Zauberberg*]. Translated by Maurice Betz. Paris: Fayard, 1982.

Mathews, Harry. *The Case of the Persevering Maltese: Collected Essays.* Normal, Ill.: Dalkey Archive, 2003.

———. *Selected Declarations of Dependence.* Los Angeles: Sun & Moon Press, 1996.

———. *The Sinking of the Odradek Stadium and Other Novels.* New York: Harper and Row, 1975.

Mathews, Harry, and Alastair Brotchie, eds. *Oulipo Compendium.* London: Atlas, 1998.

Mazzorato, Wilfrid, and Serge Raysséguier. "L'Intervention du dix-sept." *Le Cabinet d'amateur* 4 (1995): 97–103.

Merivale, Patricia, and Susan Elizabeth Sweeney, eds. *Detecting Texts: The Metaphysical Detective Story from Poe to Postmodernism.* Philadelphia: University of Pennsylvania Press, 1999.

———. "The Game's Afoot: On the Trail of the Metaphysical Detective Story." In Merivale and Sweeney, *Detecting Texts,* 1–24.

Meschonnic, Henri. *Politique du rythme, politique du sujet.* Lagrasse: Verdier, 1995.

Milner, Jean-Claude. "Hasard et langage." In Noël, *Le Hasard aujourd'hui,* 43–53.

Misrahi, Robert. "*W,* un roman réflexif." *L'Arc* 76 (1979): 81–86.

Mitterand, Henri. *L'Illusion réaliste.* Paris: Presses Universitaires de France, 1994.

Molkou, Elizabeth, and Régine Robin. "De l'arbre à l'herbier: L'histoire pulvérisée." In Jørgensen and Sestoft, *Georges Perec et l'histoire,* 87–104.

Molteni, Patrizia. "Faussaire et réaliste: Le premier Gaspard de Georges Perec." *Cahiers Georges Perec* 6 (1996): 56–78.

Monod, Jacques. *Le Hasard et la nécessité: Essai sur la philosophie naturelle de la biologie moderne.* Paris: Éditions du Seuil, 1970.

Montaigne. *Essais.* Vol. 3. Paris: Garnier Flammarion, 1979. Translated by Donald Frame in *The Complete Essays of Montaigne* (Stanford, Calif.: Stanford University Press, 1965).

Montfrans, Manet van. *Georges Perec: La contrainte du réel.* Amsterdam and Atlanta, Ga.: Rodopi, 1999.

Moscovici, Serge. "Le Hasard du sens commun." In Noël, *Le Hasard aujourd'hui,* 11–23.

Motte, Warren F., Jr. "Clinamen redux." *Comparative Literature Studies* 23, no. 4 (Winter 1986): 263–81.

———. "Embellir les lettres." *Cahiers Georges Perec* 1 (1985): 110–24.

———. "Eradications." *Romance Notes* 29, no. 1 (Fall 1988): 29–37.

———. "Jeux mortels." In Magné, *Georges Perec: Écrire/Transformer,* 43–52.

———. "L'Oulipo: Pour une littérature non-jourdanienne." *Romance Quarterly* 33, no. 2 (May 1986): 169–80.

———, ed. and trans. *Oulipo: A Primer of Potential Literature.* Lincoln and London: University of Nebraska Press, 1986.

———. *The Poetics of Experiment: A Study of the Work of Georges Perec.* Lexington, Ky.: French Forum, 1984.

Mouillard-Fraisse, Geneviève. "Cherchez Angus: *W:* Une réécriture multiple." *Cahiers Georges Perec* 2 (1988): 85–96.

Moyn, Samuel. *A Holocaust Controversy: The Treblinka Affair in Postwar France.* Waltham, Mass.: Brandeis University Press, 2005.

Neefs, Jacques. "Des lieux, des pages, des œuvres." *Magazine littéraire* 316 (December 1993): 35–37.

———. "La Profondeur spéculaire." *Littérature* 125 (March 2002): 111–26.

Nelson, Roy Jay. *Causality and Narrative in French Fiction from Zola to Robbe-Grillet.* Columbus: Ohio State University Press, 1990.

Nietzsche, Friedrich. *The Gay Science.* 1887. Edited and translated by Walter Kaufmann. New York: Vintage Books, 1974.

———. *The Genealogy of Morals* and *Ecce Homo.* 1887–89. Edited and translated by Walter Kaufmann. New York: Vintage Books, 1989.

Noël, Émile, ed. *Le Hasard aujourd'hui.* Paris: Éditions du Seuil, 1991.

Nussbaum, Martha C. *The Fragility of Goodness: Luck and Ethics in Greek Tragedy and Philosophy.* Cambridge: Cambridge University Press, 1986.

Nyman, Michael. *Experimental Music: Cage and Beyond.* 2nd ed. Cambridge: Cambridge University Press, 1999.

Olsen, Lance. "Diagnosing Fantastic Autism: Kafka, Borges, Robbe-Grillet." *Modern Language Studies* 16, no. 3 (Summer 1986): 35–43.

Oulipo. *Atlas de littérature potentielle.* 1981. Paris: Gallimard, 1988.

———. *La Bibliothèque oulipienne.* Vol. 1. Paris: Éditions Ramsay, 1987.

———. *La Bibliothèque oulipienne.* Vol. 2. Paris: Éditions Ramsay, 1987. Reprint, Paris: Seghers, 1990.

———. *La Bibliothèque oulipienne.* Vol. 3. Paris: Seghers, 1990.

———. *La Bibliothèque oulipienne.* Vol. 4. Bordeaux: Le Castor Astral, 1997.

———. *La Bibliothèque oulipienne.* Vol. 5. Bordeaux: Le Castor Astral, 2000.

———. *La Bibliothèque oulipienne.* Vol . 6. Bordeaux: Le Castor Astral, 2003.

———. *La Littérature potentielle (Créations, Re-créations, Récréations).* Paris: Gallimard, 1973.

———. *Moments oulipiens.* Bordeaux: Le Castor Astral, 2004.

Ovid. *Metamorphoses.* Edited by William S. Anderson. Norman: University of Oklahoma Press, 1972.

Oxford Dictionary of Music. Revised edition by Michael Kennedy. Oxford: Oxford University Press, 1994.

Parayre, Marc. "Lire *La Disparition* de Georges Perec." Ph.D. diss., Université de Toulouse-Le-Mirail, 1992.

Patch, Howard Rollin. "Fortuna in Old French Literature." *Smith College Studies in Modern Languages* 4, no. 4 (July 1923).

———. "The Tradition of the Goddess Fortuna in Medieval Philosophy and Literature." *Smith College Studies in Modern Languages* 3, no. 4 (July 1922).

Pavel, Thomas. *La Pensée du roman.* Paris: Gallimard, 2003.

Pawlikowska, Ewa. "La Colle bleue de Gaspard Winckler." *Littératures* 7 (1983): 79–86.

Pedersen, John. "Histoires *per* excellence . . . Une lecture d'*Un Homme qui dort.*" In Jørgensen and Sestoft, *Georges Perec et l'histoire,* 129–42.

———. *Perec ou les textes croisés. Revue romane,* supp. no. 29. Copenhagen: Munksgaards, 1985.

Peeters, Benoît. "Échafaudages." *Cahiers Georges Perec* 1 (1985): 178–91.

Perec, Georges. "Allées et venues rue de l'Assomption." *L'Arc* 76 (1979): 28–34.

———. *Alphabets: Cent soixante-seize onzains hétérogrammatiques.* Paris: Galilée, 1976.

———. "Approches de quoi?" In *L'Infra-ordinaire,* 9–13. Translated by John Sturrock as "Approaches to What?" in *Species of Spaces and Other Pieces,* 205–7 (London: Penguin Books, 1997).

———. *Beaux Présents belles absentes.* Paris: Éditions du Seuil, 1994.

———. *La Boutique obscure: 124 rêves.* Afterword by Roger Bastide. Paris: Denoël-Gonthier, 1973.

———. *Un cabinet d'amateur: Histoire d'un tableau.* Paris: Balland, 1979. Reprint, Paris: Éditions du Seuil, 1994. Translated by Ian Monk as *A Gallery Portrait,* in *Three by Perec* (London: Harvill, 1996).

———. *Cahier des charges de "La Vie mode d'emploi."* Edited by Hans Hartje, Bernard Magné, and Jacques Neefs. Paris: CNRS Éditions and Zulma, 1993.

———. "La Chose." *Magazine littéraire* 316 (December 1993): 55–64.

———. *Les Choses: Une histoire des années soixante.* Paris: Julliard, 1965. Reprint, Paris: Pocket, 1990. Translated by David Bellos as *Things: A Story of the Sixties* (Boston: David R. Godine, 1990).

———. *"53 jours."* Text established by Harry Mathews and Jacques Roubaud. Paris: P.O.L., 1989. Reprint, collection Folio no. 2547. Paris: Gallimard, 1994. Translated by David Bellos as *"53 Days"* (Boston: David R. Godine, 2000).

———. *La Clôture et autres poèmes.* Paris: Hachette/P.O.L., 1980.

———. *La Disparition.* Paris: Denoël, 1969. Reprint, collection L'Imaginaire no. 215. Paris: Gallimard, 1999. Translated by Gilbert Adair as *A Void* (London: Harvill, 1994).

———. "Emprunts à Flaubert." *L'Arc* 79 (1980): 49–50.

———. *Entretiens et conférences.* Edited by Dominique Bertelli and Mireille Ribière. 2 vols. Paris: Joseph K., 2003.

———. *Espèces d'espaces.* Paris: Galilée, 1974. Translated by John Sturrock as *Spe-*

cies of Spaces, in *Species of Spaces and Other Pieces* (London: Penguin Books, 1997).
———. "Histoire du lipogramme." In Oulipo, *La Littérature potentielle*, 77–93.
———. *Un homme qui dort.* Paris: Denoël, 1967. Reprint, collection Folio 2197. Paris: Gallimard, 1999. Translated by Andrew Leak as *A Man Asleep* (Boston: David R. Godine, 1990).
———. *L'Infra-ordinaire.* Paris: Éditions du Seuil, 1989.
———. "J'aime, je n'aime pas." *L'Arc* 76 (1979): 38–39.
———. *Je me souviens.* Paris: Hachette, 1978. Reprint, Paris: Hachette/Littératures, 1998.
———. *Je suis né.* Paris: Éditions du Seuil, 1990.
———. "Lettre à Denise Getzler." Ca. 1963. *Littératures* 7 (1983): 60–67.
———. *L.G.: Une aventure des années soixante.* 1959–63. Paris: Éditions du Seuil, 1992.
———. "Les Lieux d'une ruse." In *Penser/Classer*, 59–72. Paris: Hachette, 1985. Reprint, Paris: Hachette/Littératures, 2000. Translated by John Sturrock as "The Scene of a Stratagem," in *Species of Spaces and Other Pieces*, 161–69 (London: Penguin Books, 1997).
———. "L'Orange est proche." *Cause commune* 3 (1972): 1–2.
———. "Palindrome." In Oulipo, *La Littérature potentielle*, 101–6.
———. "Penser/Classer." In *Penser/Classer*, 151–77. Paris: Hachette, 1985. Reprint, Paris, Hachette/Littératures, 2000. Translated by John Sturrock as "Think/Classify," in *Species of Spaces and Other Pieces*, 184–201 (London: Penguin Books, 1997).
———. *Penser/Classer.* Paris: Hachette, 1985. Reprint, Paris: Hachette/Littératures, 2000.
———. "Un peu plus de quatre mille poèmes en prose pour Fabrizio Clerici." *Action poétique* 85 (1981): 65–72.
———. "Pouvoirs et limites du romancier français contemporain." Lecture at Warwick University, U.K., May 5, 1967. In Ribière, *Parcours Perec*, 31–40.
———. "Quatre figures pour *La Vie mode d'emploi*." *L'Arc* 76 (1979). Reprinted in Oulipo, *Atlas de littérature potentielle*, 387–95.
———. *Quel petit vélo à guidon chromé au fond de la cour?* Paris: Denoël, 1966. Translated by Ian Monk as *Which Moped with Chrome-Plated Handlebars at the Back of the Yard?* in *Three by Perec* (London: Harvill, 1996).
———. *Les Revenentes.* Paris: Julliard, 1972. Reprinted in *Romans et récits*, 563–639. Translated by Ian Monk as *The Exeter Text: Jewels, Secrets, Sex*, in *Three by Perec* (London: Harvill, 1996).
———. *Romans et récits.* Edited by Bernard Magné. Paris: Le Livre de Poche, 2002.
———. "Souvenir d'un voyage à Thouars." *Cahiers Georges Perec* 1 (1985): 301–6.
———. *Tentative d'épuisement d'un lieu parisien.* Paris: 10/18, 1975. Reprint, Paris: Christian Bourgois, 2000.

———. *Théâtre I.* Paris: Hachette/P.O.L., 1981. Reprint, Paris: Hachette/Littératures, 2001.

———. "Ulcérations." 1974. In Oulipo, *La Bibliothèque oulipienne* 1:1–15.

———. *La Vie mode d'emploi.* Paris: Hachette/P.O.L., 1978. Reprint, Paris: Le Livre de Poche, 1998. Translated by David Bellos as *Life A User's Manual* (London: Harvill, 1996).

———. *Le Voyage d'hiver.* Paris: Éditions du Seuil, 1993. Translated by John Sturrock as *The Winter Journey* (London: Syrens, 1995). *Le Voyage d'hiver* was first published in 1983 in *Magazine littéraire.*

———. *W ou le souvenir d'enfance.* Paris: Denoël, 1975. Reprint, collection L'Imaginaire no. 293. Paris: Gallimard, 1993. Translated by David Bellos as *W, or the Memory of Childhood* (London: Harvill, 1988).

Perec, Georges, and Marcel Bénabou. "Presbytère et prolétaires: Le dossier PALF." *Cahiers Georges Perec* 3 (1989).

Perec, Georges, and Robert Bober. *Récits d'Ellis Island: Histoires d'errance et d'espoir.* Paris: P.O.L., 1994. Translated by Harry Mathews as *Ellis Island* (New York: New Press, 1995).

Perec, Georges, and Jacques Poli. *Peintures entomologiques 1978–79.* Paris: Galerie Adrien Maeght, 1979.

Perec, Georges, and Cuchi White. *L'œil ébloui.* Paris: Chêne/Hachette, 1981.

Perloff, Marjorie. "The Oulipo Factor: The Procedural Poetics of Christian Bök and Caroline Bergvall." *Jacket* 23 (August 2003). http://jacketmagazine.com/23/perlof-oulip.html (accessed January 6, 2008).

———. *Radical Artifice: Writing Poetry in the Age of Media.* Chicago: University of Chicago Press, 1991.

Plato. *The Dialogues.* Translated by B. Jowett. 4 vols. New York: Random House, 1937.

Poe, Edgar Allan. *Tales of Mystery and Imagination.* London: Everyman, 1993.

Poincaré, Henri. "Le Hasard." *Revue du mois* 3 (1907). Reprinted in *L'Analyse et la recherche.* Edited by Girolamo Ramunni. Paris: Hermann, 1991.

Pomian, Krzysztof, ed. *La Querelle du déterminisme.* Paris: Gallimard, 1990.

Popper, Karl R. *Objective Knowledge: An Evolutionary Approach.* Oxford: Oxford University Press, 1972.

———. *The Open Universe: An Argument for Indeterminism.* 1982. London and New York: Routledge, 1992.

Prendergast, Christopher. *The Order of Mimesis: Balzac, Stendhal, Nerval, Flaubert.* Cambridge: Cambridge University Press, 1986.

Prigent, Christian. *Ceux qui merdRent* (*Essai*). Paris: P.O.L., 1991.

Prigogine, Ilya, and Isabelle Stengers. *La Nouvelle Alliance: Métamorphose de la science.* Paris: Gallimard, 1979.

Proust, Marcel. *À la recherche du temps perdu.* Edited by Jean-Yves Tadié. 4 vols. Paris: Gallimard, 1987–89.

Queneau, Raymond. *Bâtons, chiffres et lettres.* Paris: Gallimard, 1965.

———. *Bords: Mathématiciens, précurseurs, encyclopédistes.* 1963. Paris: Hermann, 1978.

———. *Cent mille milliards de poèmes.* Paris: Gallimard, 1961.

———. *Le Chiendent.* Paris: Gallimard, 1933.

———. *Entretiens avec Georges Charbonnier.* Paris: Gallimard, 1962.

———. "Qu'est-ce que l'art?" In *Le Voyage en Grèce,* 89–96. Paris: Gallimard, 1973.

———. "Technique du roman." In *Bâtons, chiffres et lettres,* 27–33. Translated by Mary Campbell-Sposito as "Technique of the Novel" (*Review of Contemporary Fiction* 17, no. 3 [September 1997]: 27–30).

Raynaud, Jean-Michel. "Du double jeu." *Cahiers Georges Perec* 1 (1985): 83–95.

Reggiani, Christelle. "Amours et naufrages: Contrainte et romanesque dans *La Vie mode d'emploi.*" *Formules* 6 (2002): 32–44.

———. *Rhétoriques de la contrainte: Georges Perec—l'Oulipo.* Saint-Pierre-du-Mont: Éditions InterUniversitaires, 1999.

Ribière, Mireille. "Alphabets déchiffré." *Cahiers Georges Perec* 5 (1992): 87–150.

———, ed. *Parcours Perec: Colloque de Londres (Mars 1988).* Lyon: Presses Universitaires de Lyon, 1990.

Ricardou, Jean. "La Contrainte corollaire." *Formules* 3 (1999): 183–97.

Ricoeur, Paul. *Temps et récit.* Vol. 1, *L'Intrigue et le récit historique.* Paris: Éditions du Seuil, 1983. Translated by Kathleen McLaughlin and David Pellauer as *Time and Narrative* (Chicago: University of Chicago Press, 1984).

Ritte, Jürgen. *Das Sprachspiel der Moderne: Eine Studie zur Literaturästhetik Georges Perecs.* Cologne: Janus, 1992.

Robbe-Grillet, Alain. *Dans le labyrinthe.* 1959. Edited by David Meakin. Oxford: Blackwell, 1983.

———. *Les Gommes.* 1953. Followed by *Clefs pour "Les Gommes,"* by Bruce Morrissette. Paris: 10/18, 1964.

———. *Pour un nouveau roman.* Paris: Éditions de Minuit, 1963.

Robin, Régine. *Le Deuil de l'origine: Une langue en trop, la langue en moins.* Saint-Denis: Presses Universitaires de Vincennes, 1993.

Roche, Anne. "Souvenir d'enfance." *Magazine littéraire* 193 (March 1983): 27–29.

———. *"W ou le souvenir d'enfance" de Georges Perec.* Paris: Gallimard, 1997.

Rorty, Richard. *Contingency, Irony, and Solidarity.* 1989. New York: Cambridge University Press, 1999.

Rosienski-Pellerin, Sylvie. *Perecgrinations ludiques: Étude de quelques mécanismes du jeu dans l'œuvre romanesque de Georges Perec.* Toronto: Éditions du Gref, 1995.

Rosset, Clément. *Logique du pire.* Paris: Presses Universitaires de France, 1971.

———. *Le Monde et ses remèdes.* Paris: Presses Universitaires de France, 2000.

———. *Le Principe de cruauté.* Paris: Éditions de Minuit, 1988.

———. *Le Réel: Traité de l'idiotie.* Paris: Éditions de Minuit, 1977.

Roubaud, Jacques. *La Bibliothèque de Warburg.* Paris: Éditions du Seuil, 2002.

———. *La Boucle.* Paris: Éditions du Seuil, 1993.

———. *"Le Grand Incendie de Londres": Récit, avec incises et bifurcations.* Paris: Éditions du Seuil, 1989.

———. "Hypothèses génétiques concernant la perecquation de la forme roman." *Le Cabinet d'amateur* 4 (1995): 9–23.

———. *Kyrielle.* Paris: Nous, 2003.

———. "La Mathématique dans la méthode de Raymond Queneau." In Oulipo, *Atlas de littérature potentielle,* 42–72. Originally published in *Critique* 359 (1977).

———. *Mono no aware, le sentiment des choses: Cent quarante-trois poèmes empruntés au japonais.* Paris: Gallimard, 1970.

———. "Notes sur la poétique des listes chez Georges Perec." In Didier and Neefs, *Penser, classer, écrire,* 201–8.

———. *Poésie, etcetera: Ménage.* Paris: Stock, 1995.

———. *Trente et un au cube.* Paris: Gallimard, 1973.

Roussel, Raymond. *Comment j'ai écrit certains de mes livres.* Paris: Jean-Jacques Pauvert, 1963.

Rousset, David. *L'Univers concentrationnaire.* Paris: Éditions de Minuit, 1965.

Rousso, Henry. *Le Syndrôme de Vichy: De 1944 à nos jours.* 2nd ed. Paris: Éditions du Seuil, 1987–90.

Ruelle, David. *Hasard et chaos.* Paris: Odile Jacob, 1991.

Saïd, Suzanne. "Part, contrainte ou hasard? Les mots du destin chez Homère." *Nouvelle Revue de psychanalyse* 30 (Autumn 1984): 39–54.

Samoyault, Tiphaine. "Le Collectionneur." *Le Cabinet d'amateur* 6 (December 1997): 83–100.

———. "Romans-mondes: Les formes de la totalisation romanesque au vingtième siècle." 3 vols. Ph.D. diss., University of Paris 8, 1996.

Sarraute, Nathalie. *L'Ère du soupçon.* Paris: Gallimard, 1956.

Sartre, Jean-Paul. *Critique de la raison dialectique.* 1960. Vol. 1. Paris: Gallimard, 1985.

———. *La Nausée.* 1938. Paris: Gallimard, 1988.

———. "Qu'est-ce que la littérature?" *Situations II.* Paris: Gallimard, 1948.

———. *Situations III.* Paris: Gallimard, 1949.

Sasso, Robert, and Arnaud Villani, eds. *Le Vocabulaire de Gilles Deleuze. Les Cahiers de Noesis,* no. 3. Paris: Vrin, 2003.

Saussure, Ferdinand de. *Cours de linguistique générale.* Paris: Payot, 1968.

Scherer, Jacques, ed. *Le "Livre" de Mallarmé.* 2nd ed. Paris: Gallimard, 1977.

Schilling, Derek. *Mémoires du quotidien: Les lieux de Perec.* Lille: Presses Universitaires du Septentrion, 2006.

Scholem, Gershom. *Kabbalah.* New York: Quadrangle/New York Times Book Co., 1974.

Schulman, Peter. *The Sunday of Fiction: The Modern French Eccentric.* West Lafayette, Ind.: Purdue University Press, 2003.

Sei Shônagon. *The Pillow Book of Sei Shônagon.* Translated and edited by Ivan Morris. New York: Columbia University Press, 1991.

Serres, Michel. *La Naissance de la physique dans le texte de Lucrèce: Fleuves et turbulences.* Paris: Éditions de Minuit, 1977.

Servien, Pius. *Hasard et probabilités.* Paris: Presses Universitaires de France, 1949.

Shattuck, Roger. "The Alphabet and the Junkyard." In *The Innocent Eye: On Modern Literature and the Arts,* 32–39. Boston: MFA Publications, 2003.

Sheringham, Michael. "Attending to the Everyday: Blanchot, Lefebvre, Certeau, Perec." *French Studies* 54, no. 2 (2000): 187–99.

———. *Everyday Life: Theories and Practices from Surrealism to the Present.* New York: Oxford University Press, 2006.

Shklovsky, Viktor [Chklovski, Victor]. "L'Art comme procédé." 1917. In Todorov, *Théorie de la littérature,* 76–97. Originally published as "O teorii prozy." Moscow, 1925.

Sirvent, Michel. "Reader-Investigators in the Post-*Nouveau Roman:* Lahougue, Peeters, and Perec." In Merivale and Sweeney, *Detecting Texts,* 157–78.

Spinoza, Baruch. *The Ethics and Selected Letters.* Translated by Samuel Shirley. Edited by Seymour Feldman. Indianapolis: Hackett, 1982.

Spiro, Joanna. "The Testimony of Fantasy in Georges Perec's *W ou le souvenir d'enfance.*" *Yale Journal of Criticism* 14, no. 1 (2001): 115–54.

Steiner, Jean-François. *Treblinka.* Preface by Simone de Beauvoir. Paris: Fayard, 1966.

Stone, Dan. "Perec's Antelme." *French Cultural Studies* 10, no. 2 (June 1999): 161–72.

Symes, Colin. "Writing by Numbers: OuLiPo and the Creativity of Constraints." *Mosaic* 32, no. 3 (September 1999): 87–107.

Thom, René. "Halte au hasard, silence au bruit." In Pomian, *La Querelle du déterminisme,* 61–78. Originally published in *Le Débat* 3 (1980): 119–32.

Thomas, Jean-Jacques. *La Langue la poésie: Essais sur la poésie française contemporaine.* Lille: Presses Universitaires de Lille, 1989.

Todorov, Tzvetan. *Poétique de la prose.* Paris: Éditions du Seuil, 1971.

———, ed. *Théorie de la littérature: Textes des formalistes russes.* Preface by Roman Jakobson. Paris: Éditions du Seuil, 1965.

Tynianov, Yuri. "La Notion de construction." In Todorov, *Théorie de la littérature,* 114–19. Originally published as *Problema stixotvornogo jazyka.* Leningrad, 1924.

Tzara, Tristan. *Sept Manifestes Dada.* Paris: Pauvert, 1963.

Valéry, Paul. *Cahiers.* Edited by Judith Robinson. Vols. 1 and 2. Paris: Gallimard, 1973–74.

———. *Introduction à la poétique.* Paris: Gallimard, 1938.

Van Zuylen, Marina. *Monomania: The Flight from Everyday Life in Literature and Art.* Ithaca, N.Y., and London: Cornell University Press, 2005.

Viegnes, Michel. "L'Imaginaire des jeux de hasard dans la littérature européenne." In Kavanagh, *Chance, Culture and the Literary Text,* 225–41.

Watt, Ian. *The Rise of the Novel: Studies in Defoe, Richardson and Fielding.* 1957. 2nd ed. Berkeley and Los Angeles: University of California Press, 2001.

White, Eric Charles. *Kaironomia: On the Will-to-Invent.* Ithaca, N.Y., and London: Cornell University Press, 1987.

Winter, Suzanne. "À propos de l'Oulipo et de quelques contraintes musico-textuelles." In Kuon, *Oulipo-Poétiques,* 173–92.

Wittgenstein, Ludwig. *Philosophical Investigations.* 1953. Translated by G. E. M. Anscombe. 3rd ed. Oxford: Blackwell, 2001.

Xenakis, Iannis. *Kéleütha: Écrits.* Edited by Alain Galliari. Preface by Benoît Gibson. Paris: L'Arche, 1994.

Žižek, Slavoj. *Looking Awry: An Introduction to Jacques Lacan Through Popular Culture.* Cambridge, Mass.: MIT Press, 1991.

Zumthor, Paul, ed. *Le Masque et la lumière: La poétique des grands rhétoriqueurs.* Paris: Éditions du Seuil, 1978.

Index

About the Author

Alison James is an assistant professor of French literature at the University of Chicago.

Avant-Garde & Modernism Studies

Avant-Garde & Modernism Collection